OPENING DOORS TO DIVERSITY IN LEADERSHIP

OPENING DOORS

TO DIVERSITY

IN LEADERSHIP

BOBBY SIU

UNIVERSITY OF TORONTO PRESS
Toronto Buffalo London

Rotman-UTP Publishing
An imprint of University of Toronto Press
Toronto Buffalo London
utorontopress.com

© University of Toronto Press 2021

Library and Archives Canada Cataloguing in Publication

Title: Opening doors to diversity in leadership / Bobby Siu.
Names: Siu, Bobby, 1948– author.
Description: Includes bibliographical references and index.
Identifiers: Canadiana (print) 20200394444 | Canadiana (ebook) 20200394533 |
    ISBN 9781487500870 (cloth) | ISBN 9781487511982 (EPUB) | ISBN
    9781487511975 (PDF)
Subjects: LCSH: Leadership. | LCSH: Diversity in the workplace.
Classification: LCC HD57.7.S58 2021 | DDC 658.4/092–dc23

ISBN 978-1-4875-0087-0 (cloth)   ISBN 978-1-4875-1198-2 (EPUB)
                                    ISBN 978-1-4875-1197-5 (PDF)

We acknowledge the financial support of the Government of Canada, the
Canada Council for the Arts, and the Ontario Arts Council, an agency of the
Government of Ontario, for our publishing activities.

 Canada Council   Conseil des Arts
for the Arts   du Canada

 ONTARIO ARTS COUNCIL
CONSEIL DES ARTS DE L'ONTARIO
an Ontario government agency
un organisme du gouvernement de l'Ontario

Funded by the   Financé par le  Canadä
Government   gouvernement
of Canada   du Canada

To my wife, Stephanie, my son, Nicholas, and my daughter, Bernadette, with love, gratitude, and hope

Contents

Appendices I, II, and III are all available on the book's University of Toronto Press webpage: https://utorontopress.com/us/opening-doors-to-diversity-in -leadership-2.

Figures

Tables

OPENING DOORS TO DIVERSITY IN LEADERSHIP

Introduction – A Changing World

This book is about current leadership and its inertia in the midst of a changing world. The backdrop is our corporate leaders' commitment to effecting changes in their leadership circles and the workforces they lead. This book focuses on the linkages between the relative absence of diversity in leadership, the mindsets of leaders, the human resources mechanisms they put in place to maintain the status quo, and the corporate culture.

In this book, the term *leaders* refers to boards of directors and senior executive teams in the private sector. In Canada, the United States, and Europe, many business leaders are white, non-Indigenous, able-bodied males. Current leadership barely reflects the changing labour force and remains homogenous even in times of global change.

Some large corporations in Western countries have embraced the fashionable terms "diversity" and "inclusiveness," which lends them a good reputation. Yet their leaders have made little actual effort to diversify their ranks. The world around them is changing, yet most corporate leaders continue to perpetuate their homogeneity.

This chapter begins with a big-picture overview of contemporary trends necessitating organizational change. Diversity both in the workforce and in leadership will meet current challenges and add value to businesses. As substantiated by evidence later in the book, the business sector in Canada shows diversity gaps. This chapter summarizes several approaches – psychological, organizational, and cultural – for analysing these gaps and provides options for change as well as practical solutions for businesses to increase diversity in their leadership.

Social Changes

For effective leadership and to align human resources with business strategies, we must first examine five macro-level changes that are affecting Canada, the United States, and the European countries: globalization, aging populations, declining growth, international migration, and the emerging labour force. These changes are beyond the control of one leader or one company. They pose numerous human resources challenges but simultaneously provide opportunities to the business sector. In reviewing these challenges, one may ask the following questions:

- Can today's business leaders resist these macroscopic trends and maintain their homogeneity and their relatively monolithic approach to running their businesses?
- Are business leaders ready to harness the rise in international migration to address the challenges they face?
- Is this the time for business leaders to rethink how they do business and modernize their workforces and leadership?
- In light of these structural changes, does being diverse and inclusive in leadership offer a business edge?

Let us look closer at these changes and the challenges they pose for business leaders.

Globalization

Globalization demands new and diverse leadership.

Globalization changes how businesses are run in a multitude of ways. Of particular relevance are the following factors: the increasing flow of labour, technology, and capital into the world economy; emerging markets; global competition; job market changes; and the internationalization of decision-making (Beach 2008, 205). These new forces require new leadership that can utilize these changes to organizations' benefit (Juniper 2014, 18).

In a globalized business world, national boundaries become less relevant. Countries become more interconnected as international agreements determine the flows of exports and imports, capital flows, and the money supply. People (talents), capital (investments), technology (transfers), and work (outsourcing) move across borders rapidly. Business decisions that were once predominantly local now depend increasingly on a deep understanding of the world and ever-changing global forces. Business is now more competitive than ever before, and this means that business leaders must have sufficient knowledge of the world to network internationally; they must also be alert to emerging global perspectives and directions as well as innovative in steering their workforces and technology.

Diverse peoples and nations are now converging as communication and transportation technologies rapidly evolve. As a result of this, and the cross-fertilization of cultures and ideas, different ways of conducting business are sprouting all over the world and competing for dominance in many industry sectors. Organizations that once focused on traditional extraction (of natural things), manufacturing (of goods), and provision (of services) are under great pressure to change their strategies and operations and to innovate so as not to go extinct. Leaders are under growing pressure to become more flexible, adaptable, and open to diverse approaches to running their organizations. Those who have limited imagination and who surround themselves with people who look, think, and behave like them may have a hard time navigating business and social territories that are foreign to them.

Aging Population

The population in the developed world is getting older. In 1950, only 8% of the world's people were older than sixty; by 2050, the figure will likely be 21%. Also by 2050, for the first time in human history, the number of older people in the world will exceed the number of younger ones, and these older people are expected to account for one third of the world population (United Nations 2001, xxvii–xxxi).

In line with this global trend, Canada's population is getting older. By 2061, 24 to 28% of Canadians will be sixty-five or older, compared to 8% in 1960 (Statistics Canada 2011f). This trend is common among member countries of the Organisation for Economic Co-operation and Development (OECD). Among those countries, Canada is in the middle of the pack: its population is younger (median age 38.9) than that of Germany (42.0) and Japan (42.8) but older than that of the United States (35.9) (Beach 2008, 197–9). This suggests that countries that are more open to immigration (such as Canada and the United States) have slowed their aging trends, while those that are less open to immigration (such as Germany and Japan) have not.

An aging population means an older labour force. This is happening throughout the world, especially in the more developed countries (United Nations 2001, xxvii–xxxi). In 2011, people over fifty-five accounted for 18.7% of Canadian workers; in 2006, the figure had been only 15.5% (Statistics Canada 2015b). Contrary to expectations, some people over sixty-five in Canada, the United Kingdom, and the United States are not retiring and indeed have been returning to the labour force since 1997. This has actually made the workforces a little older in these countries (Beach 2008, 199–207). Those who lead aging workforces may have to develop new ways to lead. They will also need to find ways to replenish and rejuvenate their workforces. Older workers are valuable and worth retaining because of their institutional memories and experiences.

An aging workforce also means that more employees will become disabled over time. The Canadian Survey on Disability (CSD) found in 2012 that 4.4% of Canadians between fifteen and twenty-four reported a disability, 6.5% of those between twenty-five and forty-four, and 16.1% of those between forty-five and sixty-four. For those between sixty-five and seventy-four, the proportion reached 26.3%, and for those over seventy-five, 42.5%. It is clear that as the workforce gets older, more workers will likely report disabilities (Statistics Canada 2015a). An increasingly disabled workforce may require that leaders find new ways to address issues of work design and productivity. Otherwise, persons with disabilities may find it increasingly difficult to find work, and those who do may be unable to utilize their talents fully and thus be less likely to be promoted to leadership roles.

A business organization that does not have a strategy for recruiting, retaining, and promoting older workers and persons with disabilities may find itself passing up a growing talent pool. And when it does hire these workers, it may not place them in the leadership pipeline. Indeed, it may be forgetting that older people and the disabled are themselves consumers of different goods and services. Leaders who exclude these people from leadership roles may be displaying a blind spot.

Decline in Growth

It has been noted that the labour force, productivity, and the economy are all facing declining growth.

The aging population is having some negative impacts on the labour force. One of these is the decline in labour force growth. Canada's National Household Survey of 2011 found that close to 18 million people (age fifteen and over) were in the labour force and that most of them (92%) were employed. But the employment rate had actually dropped, from 62.6% in 2006 to 60.9% in 2011. In other words, a smaller proportion of the population was employed, reflecting a broader trend toward slowing labour force growth (Statistics Canada, 2015b). In Canada, the retirement of baby boomers (who were born during the twenty-five years following the Second World War) launched a downward trend in labour force growth that will not end until 2031. The participation rate in the labour force is expected to decline from 67% in 2010 to 58% in 2031. The latter percentage will be the lowest since the late 1970s.

An aging population also results in slower productivity growth. As the proportion of older workers increases, a workforce becomes less flexible and less adaptable to technical and organizational change. Adjustment costs for these older workers are higher, for they tend to be less educated, less technically agile, and less willing to adapt. Growth in skills also slows, along with productivity (Hellerstein, Neumark, and Troske 1999). Employment and Social Development Canada and the Policy Research Directorate predicted that the rate of skill growth would slow as a result of the aging population (Skills Research Initiative 2008, 1). And this has been accompanied by a decline in the productivity growth rate, from 2.9% (1961–79) to 1.6% (1980–99) and 0.7% (2000–8) (Roy-Cesar 2011, 2–3). Furthermore, Canada's Parliamentary Budget Officer has projected that Canadian economic growth will be around 1.8% over the next few decades, in sharp contrast to the 2.6% growth the country experienced between 1977 and 2011 (Beltrame 2014).

Declining growth in labour force, productivity, and the economy will require new ways of thinking about growth, as well as new business strategies for attracting and retaining business and industrial talent. Leaders will need to develop new human resources strategies, tap into traditionally overlooked labour pools (such as Indigenous peoples, persons with disabilities, racialized minorities, and women), and re-examine the leadership arena when preparing succession.

International Migration

Global migration is growing. In 2000, there were 175 million international migrants; by 2013, 232 million. Annual migration rates grew from 1.2% to 2.3% between 1990–2000 and 2000–10. More migrants have been going to developed countries. North America had the largest gain in absolute numbers of international migrants (25 million) between 1990 and 2013. It also has the fastest growth rate per year (2.8%) among all regions (United Nations 2013).

In the second half of the twentieth century, Canada liberalized its immigration policy so as to open the door for immigrants from developing countries. Citizenship and Immigration Canada set immigration goals each year, and these have been increasing since the 1980s. In 2012, the number of immigrants (including refugees) approved for landing was 281,984 (CanadaVisa 2012). Immigration has been the key source of population growth for Canada, accounting for two thirds of its population increase (Statistics Canada 2012a). It has also helped slow the declining labour force growth rate, which had fallen from 18% in 1971–6 to 4% in 1991–6.

Prior to the 1970s, most immigrants were from Europe. A review of the share of racialized minorities among immigrants in recent decades confirms that, proportionately speaking, more and more immigrants to Canada are coming from non-European countries: 12.4% before 1971, 53.0% in the 1970s, 67.4% in the 1980s, 74.8% in the 1990s, 76.7% between 2001 and 2006, and 78.0% between 2006 and 2011. By 2011, most racialized minorities in Canada (65.1%) were born outside of Canada (Statistics Canada 2013a; Siu 2011a, 12).

In 2006 about 5,068,100 Canadians identified as racialized minorities (16.2% of the total population). Five years later, in 2011, around 6,264,800 identified as such (19.1%) – almost one in five people in Canada (Statistics Canada 2013e). Because of this influx of immigrants, Canada now has the highest population growth rate among G7 countries (Maher and Luongo 2019). By 2031, Canada is expected to be home to between 11.4 and 14.4 million racialized minority people, accounting for 29% to 32% of the population (Malenfant, Lebel, and Martel 2012). The South Asian, Chinese, Filipino, and black populations are expected to double between 2006 and 2031. And the Arab and West Asian populations could more than triple during the same period (Statistics Canada 2010c).

The United States and Canada, as well as many European countries, are undergoing rapid changes in their populations, workforces, and consumer markets. The growing number of immigrants, especially those of racialized minority backgrounds, has implications for Canada's labour force. Businesses will have to rethink how they are run, how they will develop and leverage their human resources, and how succession to leadership will be managed.

Emerging Labour Force

Younger Educated Racialized Minorities

As a group, racialized minorities in Canada are younger than the population as a whole. In 2011 their median age was 33.4, compared to 40.1 for the overall population. Besides being younger, they are better educated than other Canadians: 43% of working-age Canadians have a post-secondary degree, while 58% of their racialized minority immigrant counterparts have one (Samuel and Basavarajappa 2006, 246; Jedwab 2008, 1–17).

Given Canada's aging population, declining labour force, and slower-growing economy, the presence of younger racialized minorities in Canada is an advantage: in 2017, for every 100 older racialized minorities (aged fifty-five to sixty-four) ready to retire, 142 younger racialized minorities (aged fifteen to twenty-four) were ready to join the labour force to replace them. In contrast, for every 100 older persons (aged fifty-five to sixty-four) in the rest of the population ready to retire, only 75 younger ones (aged fifteen to twenty-four) were ready to enter the labour force to replace them. The labour force growth rate of racialized minorities was expected to be four times higher than that of the total labour force between 2001 and 2017 (Samuel and Basavarajappa 2006, 247–8; Statistics Canada 2013c; Antunes 2004; Baklid et al. 2005).

As racialized minorities replenish aging segments in the labour force, their share in the labour force will increase (Curry and Torobin 2011). This replenishing of the aging labour force is confirmed by the National Center for Public Policy and Higher Education (2005) in the United States. Between 1980 and 2020, the white working-age population was expected to decline from 82% to 63%, but the racialized minority population to double from 18% to 37% and the Hispanic/Latino segment to almost triple from 6% to 17%. Thus, increasingly, in both the United States and Canada, labour forces are shifting from whites to racialized minorities as the latter replenish the declining white labour force.

However, the current influx of immigrants will not on its own be able to replenish the labour force sufficiently (Roy-Cesar 2011, 1; Beltrame 2014). This poses an additional challenge for businesses, for they will have to find additional pools of talent to address the declining labour force, productivity, and economic growth rates. More importantly, business leaders will have to find ways to retain these new employees, lest they exit through a revolving door. In other words, strategies and tactics for recruiting, hiring, retaining, and promoting employees will need to be rethought in order to adapt to changing demographics.

Younger Educated Women

Women comprise an increasing share of Canada's labour force (Canadian HR Reporter 2014a, 4). In 1976, only 37% of employed Canadians were women; that figure had grown to 48% by 2011. This increase came about because more men left the employment market and more women joined it (Statistics Canada 2011e). In addition, Canadian women are more educated now. Between 1990 and 2009, the proportion of women with a bachelor's or postgraduate degree more than doubled, to 28%. By that same year, a lower proportion of men had a university degree compared to women. In 1990, the figures had shown the opposite (Statistics Canada 2011f). These findings suggest that women will play a key role in resolving the problem of the declining labour force and reduced productivity growth.

Among women, there are two subgroups – Indigenous women and racialized minority women – that are growing and are readily available to work. They are younger and represent the emerging labour force. Indigenous women are only 4% of Canada's female population, but as a group they grew much faster than the overall female population between 2001 and 2006. During those five years, the population of Indigenous women grew by 20%, the total female population by only 6%. The Indigenous female population is also younger than the non-Indigenous female population. In 2006, the median age for Indigenous women was 27.7 and that of non-Indigenous women was 40.0. Forty-six per cent of Indigenous women were younger than twenty-four (Statistics Canada 2011f). Their post-secondary educational level (51%) is lower than that of non-Indigenous women (65%), but the younger Indigenous women have higher level of post-secondary education than the older (Statistics Canada 2016b).

Racialized minority women in Canada are younger as a group than the overall female population. In 2006, 47.7% of racialized minority women were between twenty-five and fifty-four; 43.4% of non-racialized minority women were in that same age group. The median age of racialized minority women was 33.3 and that of non-racialized minority women was 41.5 (Chui and Maheux 2011, 14–15).

In addition, racialized minority women were relatively well-educated. In 2006, 26.3% of them had a university degree or a certificate, compared to 16.6% of white women (Statistics Canada 2015d). When only women between twenty-five to fifty-four were considered, the proportion of racialized minority women (35%) with a university degree or a certificate was even higher than that of white women (23%) (Chui and Maheux 2011, 18–19). Incidentally, immigrant women (a significant portion of whom are of racialized minority backgrounds) also possess higher educational levels than their Canadian-born counterparts (Maher and Luongo 2019).

In these times of change, one of the best things business leaders can do is harness the talents of these two emerging labour pools – women and racialized minorities. Doing so can help them respond to the issues arising from an aging population, a shrinking labour force, economic growth decline, and globalization and international migration; it will also enrich their workforces and make their businesses more representative, profitable, innovative, productive, sustainable, and competitive. It is the last of these to which we turn in the following section.

A Business Case for Diversity

This book contends that the business sector must acknowledge that the structural changes listed above have implications for leadership and for the ways businesses conduct themselves in human resources development. Unless they acknowledge this, it will be difficult for them to start diversifying the business workforce and leadership circles.

This book also maintains that diversity in leadership *and* in the workforce works to the advantage of businesses. This position aligns well with the results of many research studies such as those by Robinson, Pfeffer, and Buccigrossi (2003), Cukier (2007), Mattis (2010), Bilimoria (2010), Selby (2010), and Catalyst (2013), among others. Research findings, while still inconclusive, increasingly point to the likelihood of positive business results when diversity in leadership and the workforce is substantial and sustained.

Randall Stephenson, chairman and chief executive officer of AT&T, summarized his view on the relationship between diversity and business quite succinctly:

> Diversity and inclusion are powerful success drivers, making us a better company and a much stronger competitor. When you attract and retain the best people and seek out diverse backgrounds and experiences, you set yourself up for continued success. That's why we've always embraced diversity at AT&T – from our Board to our executives to our retail and service employees to our suppliers. It's a core part of who we are. (DiversityInc 2016a)

The business case for diversity is gaining more traction, according to McKinsey's 2010 global survey of executives. However, although 72% of company respondents believed there is a connection between diverse leadership and financial success, only 28% said that gender diversity was a top-ten priority for their senior leadership. Many corporations do not see the need to make changes in their leadership though they do see the value of changing their ways of doing business. Even so, they do not see a linkage between diversity in leadership and doing business differently in a changing world. For them, homogeneity in business ideas and strategies has nothing to do with homogeneity in leadership.

So far, this chapter has placed the issue of diversity in leadership in a changing global context – one of closer connectedness among countries, aging populations, an emerging new labour force, declining productivity and growth, and international migration. While diversity in leadership and the workforce is not a panacea for all issues arising from the changes the world is undergoing, it *can* provide fresh, creative, and diverse perspectives in terms of developing business strategies, forging better connections to different cultures, finding better ways of doing things, and fostering more sustainable and inclusive environments for working together and relating to communities and markets.

Next, we outline the business case for diversity based on Canadian, American, and international data as well as evidence provided by leading diversity practitioners. Overall, diversity could bring to businesses at least six advantages:

- Diverse perspectives and business competitiveness
- Innovation and expanded markets
- Talent retention and replenishment
- Economic and corporate growth
- Productivity
- Profitability

Note that these advantages often reinforce one another, achieving multiplier effects.

Diverse Perspectives and Business Competitiveness

As noted earlier, globalization strengthens connectedness among countries and necessitates new ways to run a business. In this global environment, the traditional model – that is, relying heavily on a small group of white, able-bodied male executives to make business decisions – may no longer be competitive or relevant. Such decision-makers are homogeneous in their national, ethnic, and linguistic backgrounds, think more or less in tandem, and very likely represent a narrow spectrum of ideas rooted in a pre-globalization world. Their decisions may not meet the challenges of the modern age. Leighton (2010, 259) has argued that only through a cross-fertilization of multiple perspectives from diverse groups and cultures can corporate issues be examined in a more fruitful and visionary manner. When board directors or senior executives come from more diverse backgrounds, they bring different perspectives to the table and are better positioned to formulate creative ideas and find fresh solutions.

Similarly, women can provide fresh perspectives on products and markets, both domestic and global. They also strengthen business advantages by contributing "a perspective different from those of male directors," "dealing more effectively with diversity in product and labour markets," providing "new ideas and approaches in business deliberations" as well as "more critical thinking and innovation," and "adding fresh views on strategic issues to augment the traditional men's 'cozy club' decision making that permeates most corporate boardrooms" (Mattis 2010, 52–4; Bilimoria 2010, 27, 30).

Diversity in leadership offers other advantages as well. Homogeneous groups tend to think alike (as in "groupthink"). They seldom notice their own assumptions and blind spots, let alone challenge them. In a globalizing business environment in which changes are constant and rapid, fresh or alternative views flourish only when board directors or senior executives are diverse in their backgrounds, perspectives, competencies, and experiences. It would be a mistake for a traditional cadre of white, able-bodied men to make major business decisions on foreign countries or new markets, domestic or international, without a thorough understanding of the economies, politics, cultures, and lifestyles of the new markets or foreign countries (Leighton 2010, 250).

After surveying 520 businesses and interviewing senior executives globally, Ernst and Young concluded that boards of directors, management teams, and workforces need to be more culturally diverse in order to meet the challenges of international markets. According to that study, the single most important element in being a successful player in a globalized environment is a mental transformation that will allow one to recognize and understand cultural diversity (Ernst and Young, n.d.). Steve Howe, US chairman and managing partner and American managing partner at Ernst and Young (EY), declared, "At EY [Ernst and Young], diversity drives our fundamental purpose to help build a better working world. Our teams leverage and learn from all the diverse perspectives at the table, creating an inclusive environment where people feel free to be themselves, are more engaged, and can deliver innovative, exceptional service to our clients" (DiversityInc 2016a).

As James Turley, chairman and CEO of Ernst and Young, observed, "the leading companies of tomorrow are already realizing the benefit of multicultural teams – teams that bring diversity of thought and culture" (Ernst and Young n.d.). David Garofalo, president and CEO of GoldCorp, remarked that "diversity is at the core of GoldCorp's success. We value our people and strive to represent the communities in which we operate. We recognize the benefits of different perspectives on our Board of Directors" (Canadian Board Diversity Council 2016, 16). This is because traditional ideas and practices are not applicable in a world in which customers and employees are from different cultures. Diversity in leadership, management, and workforces enables a better comprehension of customers and diverse markets. Businesses that are homogeneous in board and executive composition do not have the broad spectrum of analytical minds to understand the markets and to challenge conventional ways of doing things (Grillo 2014). This insight highlights the importance of greater inclusion of diverse group members in leadership circles.

Innovation and Markets

Innovation requires that conventional ways of seeing and doing things be dismantled and that fresh ways of running a business, creating better products, and providing better services all be introduced. This usually happens when people's perspectives based on various life experiences are allowed to cross-fertilize in an environment that is conducive to new ideas. Collins (2011) argued that diversity-driven innovation makes business more successful in a global market. Hill (2014), using her experience with creating new technological applications through her diverse team, confirmed that diversity is key to innovation.

A management team with a diverse composition can do much to generate more innovation revenue. The Boston Consulting Group surveyed more than 1,700 companies in various industries in eight countries. Its finding: companies with management teams with above-average diversity posted innovation revenues 19% higher than those with below-average diversity (Scarborough 2019). In this vein, Bhardwaj (2016) argued that "greater diversity promotes better governance, which in turn promotes more innovation." It follows that the level of innovation depends on the composition of board directors. A diverse board is likely to bring different perspectives and is more prepared for the changing world market. Bilimoria (2010, 29–30) notes that the first female director of Nike Corporation urged the board and management to develop sports shoes specifically for women. The result: one third of Nike's revenues eventually came from product lines aimed at women. James Preston, former CEO of Avon Products Inc., noted that "60% of all purchases in this country are made by women, [so] having women on the board just makes good business sense" (Sweetman 1996, 13).

Commenting on the role that diversity plays in business competitiveness, Antonio Perez, chairman and CEO of Eastman Kodak Company, said:

> The U.S. represents only five percent of the world's population. We will fail if we do not understand what the other 95 percent needs, wants to buy, and how to engage with them. Diverse teams deliberate better and make better choices; so having a diverse organization leads to better decisions. The board has to understand that diversity within the management team is fundamental for the return on investment, or it will miss opportunities we don't understand or don't even see. (Spence 2009)

Semple (2015) confirmed the value of diversity, using as an example how his QoC Health's development of a successful technology platform on post-surgical recovery. His diverse team members, having brought with them various occupational and industrial backgrounds, were able to "think several steps ahead" and designed a product well accepted by clients with different backgrounds.

After reviewing the returns on equity and margins on earnings of 180 publicly traded companies in France, Germany, the United Kingdom, and the United States between 2008 and 2010, Barta, Kleiner, and Neumann (2012) of the McKinsey Co. observed that the greater the diversity (women and foreign nationals) on boards and management teams, the greater the financial returns for companies. Similar findings were reported in 2011 by a *Forbes* survey of 321 executives of international corporations with $500 million or more in annual revenues. It found that 85% agreed or strongly agreed that a diverse workforce drives innovation in products, services, and business processes and creates a competitive edge (Tencer 2011).

Workforce and board diversity must reflect the communities that businesses serve. Lisa Lisson, president of FedEx Express Canada, noted:

> Diversity doesn't just help the bottom line, it drives it. The formula is simple – a diverse and inclusive workforce and board makes a company successful. To be competitive in today's business environment, it is critical that your organization reflects the very communities where you do business. Embracing diversity and inclusion in our everyday practices has enabled FedEx to connect people with possibilities across Canada and around the world. (Canadian Board Diversity Council 2016, 15)

Talent Retention and Replenishment

Leadership and human resources management are closely related. Almost all corporate board directors have worked as CEOs or senior executives. In some corporations, some of these executives rose through the ranks from front-line worker to a leadership position. Clearly, the existence of diversity in leadership implies that an effort was made to incorporate diversity as a guiding principle in human resources management. This is the only way that internal feeder pools for leadership can be developed.

There is a positive correlation between the proportion of women on a company's board and the proportion of women among the same company's senior executives (Brown, Brown, and Anastasopoulos 2002, 10). This correlation suggests that there may be openness to recruiting or promoting women to senior executive ranks when the board is already open to diversity, or that board diversity exerts some pressure on CEOs to open doors for women (or members of minority groups) to enter the ranks of executives. A diversified leadership circle is more receptive to recruiting racialized minorities and women, young Indigenous peoples, and older workers and persons with disabilities, be it to the organization or even to its own ranks.

Leaders with diverse backgrounds are likely to strategize how best to build diversity in the workforce so that employees acquire the knowledge and skills to conduct business in sync with changing economies and markets. These leaders look at the world with fresh perspectives and are more prepared to try something new in business, including in human resources. The drive to create a pipeline for senior executives from diverse backgrounds will likely be stronger when leadership is diverse rather than homogeneous.

Diversity is valuable in leadership as well as in the workforce. Older employees and persons with disabilities are assets to corporations. Older employees have accumulated institutional memory regarding corporate systems and practices and are valuable when it comes to transferring their knowledge and skills to new employees. Persons with disabilities can perform just as well as other employees, provided that they are extended appropriate accommodation and that managers have confidence in them. Executives with disabilities have a much better understanding of how best to work with employees with disabilities and other diverse groups because they have learned first-hand how best to treat employees with respect and dignity. They also see the value of flexibility in work styles and of alternative ways to provide services and design products. Overall, persons with disabilities are also loyal employees. According to a Statistics Canada's 2001 survey, 90% of persons with disabilities did as well at their jobs as those who are abled, or even better, and 86% were rated average or better in attendance; also, their retention rate was 72% higher. Having them in both leadership and the workforce is valuable.

Studies on the employment situation of racialized minorities in Canada (Galabuzi and Block 2013), African American women (O'Day and Foley 2008), Indigenous women (Canadian Labour Congress 2008, 2–5), and persons with disabilities in Canada (Canada 2014a, Table 7) suggest that their talents have been seriously underutilized in that past. Employers lose out badly when they overlook these people and do not hire them. So having a group of diverse leaders who understand the value of diversity will take advantage of the changing demographics and economies; it will also utilize the talents offered by Indigenous peoples, persons with disabilities, racialized minorities, and women.

Economic and Corporate Growth

Diversity has played a major role in lifting economic growth and corporate performance. That is the conclusion of most studies on the contribution of women. Regarding economic growth, the McKinsey Global Institute (2015) has estimated that when gender parity is reached in the workforce, global output will likely increase by more than one quarter; that amounts to $12 trillion more in global growth (Bouw 2019).

One of McKinsey and Company's research findings about gender parity in Canadian companies is that it has the potential to add $150 billion in increased economic activity – that is, a 0.6% increase in annual GDP growth (McGee and Sutton 2019). Citing McKinsey and Company's data, Kerby and Burns (2012) noted that women's increased share of the workforce from 37% to 47% over the past forty years in the United States accounted for about one quarter of that country's gross domestic product (GDP).

Regarding corporate growth, studies showed women's positive contribution. Companies with more women on their boards outperform their competitors "with 142% higher return in sales, 66% higher return on invested capital and 53% higher return on equity." And among European companies, when there is a higher proportion of women in senior management teams, there is stronger stock market performance (Almond 2013). The Hackett Group found that companies that are good at talent management increase their earnings by spending 27% less than their competitors (Vaccaro 2016). Dizikes (2014) reviewed the revenue data of one professional services firm with more than sixty offices worldwide between 1995 and 2002 and found that gender parity in an office could increase revenue by 41% over that of all-male or all-female offices.

Regarding corporate growth, positive connections have been found between gender parity on boards and executive teams and strong performance in environmental, social, and governance matters, including sustainability, human rights, and employee relations. It has been demonstrated that gender diversity leads to stronger employee benefits and performance incentives and a higher degree of transparency. Vancity Investment Management Ltd. reported working with Dollarama Inc. in committing to gender diversity and appointing a woman to its board. It also noted that one fund – IA Clarington Inhance Canadian SRI Class – includes companies that have women on 30% of their board seats. This fund has higher yields than those in TSX-listed companies, which have about 15% gender parity on an average (Foley 2019).

Productivity

Slowing productivity growth has negative impacts on businesses. Diverse groups offer a pool of qualified candidates with a good mix of knowledge, skills, and experiences. They are likely to add to the collective resources in the workplace and thereby enhance opportunities for higher productivity (Beach 2008, 210–13; Dizikes 2014). Productivity is not easy to measure, but a few studies seem to suggest that racialized minorities contribute to it. It has been estimated that more gender parity in financial institutions would increase their revenues by 3.5% and increase their productivity by 0.7% (McGee and Sutton 2019).

Citing lost productivity resulting from underutilization of racialized minorities in the workplace as well as the hidden costs of hiring and training new employees arising from these groups' job dissatisfaction and resultant higher turnover, Settles, Buchanan, and Yap (2010, 16) argued that racial discrimination impedes workplace productivity.

Profitability

Past studies on the relationship between female representation in leadership positions and profitability consistently showed positive correlations (Erhardt, Werbel, and Shrader 2003; Carter et al. 2007). After dividing Fortune 500 companies into quartiles according to the presence of women board directors and examining their returns in 2001–4, Catalyst's researchers found that the top-quartile companies outperformed those in the bottom quartile by 53% in return on equity, by 42% in return on sales, and by 66% in return on invested capital (Joy et al. 2007). Other Catalyst studies of women board directors all showed similar results (Catalyst 1993, 1997; Mattis 2010, 52).

Among the Fortune 500 companies, those with the highest percentage of female executives significantly outperformed the median ones in their respective industries (Orser 2000; Brady and McLean 2002, 3). Companies with greater diversity in their workforces are 33% more likely to lead their industrial peers in profits (Maher and Luongo 2019). Adler (2001, 2) reported that the top 25 of Fortune 500 companies with "a strong record of promoting women into executive positions" are 18% higher in return on assets and 69% higher in returns in investment than the Fortune 500's median companies in their industries. A McKinsey study found that companies with gender-diverse executive teams were 21% more likely to make above-average profits than those with less diverse teams (Bouw 2019). A research study by the Canadian Imperial Bank of Commerce found that, since 2009, S&P/TSX Composite

Index companies with more female board directors have outperformed than those with fewer female directors. The shares of the top one-third of these companies had a compound annual growth rate of 9.1%, the bottom one-third only 4.4% (Bouw 2019).

Few studies have been conducted on racial diversity and profitability. Using the 1996–7 National Organizations Survey data on business organizations in the United States, Herring (2009) showed that racial diversity is associated with increased sales revenues, more customers, greater market share, and greater relative profits; gender diversity showed a similar association (except regarding the indicator of market share).

Internationally, the same pattern of diversity and profits emerges. For example, the Boston Consulting Group's survey of more than 1,700 companies across a broad range of industries in eight different countries found that diverse management teams can bring more revenue than those without much diversity (Scarborough 2019). Other studies showed the same correlation (Slater, Welgand, and Zwirlein 2008; Campbell and Minguez-Vera 2008; McKinsey 2013).

Diverse Groups

So far I have situated the business sector in the broader context of economic and demographic changes and shown the value of diverse leadership. The next question is: Which diverse groups are to be highlighted for discussion in this book? All diverse groups are worthy of research and analysis. However, this book highlights only four: Indigenous peoples, persons with disabilities, racialized minorities, and women. Hereafter, the term *diverse groups* refers to these four groups. These diverse groups are described as follows:

- In Canada, *Indigenous peoples* include First Nations, Métis, and Inuit. Although they are racialized minorities, they are viewed as a separate group because of their historical and political importance.
- *Persons with disabilities* are those who have physical, mental, intellectual, or sensory impairments.
- *Racialized minorities* (also known as "racial minorities" or "visible minorities"; the federal Employment Equity Act coined this latter term, which was later adopted by Statistics Canada) include people who are not Caucasian and whose skin is not white. According to Statistics Canada, they include South Asians, Chinese, blacks, Filipinos, Latin Americans, Arabs, Southeast Asians, West Asians, Koreans, and Japanese. For the purposes of this book, this group does not include Indigenous peoples.

- Statistics Canada uses the term *women* to cover females, both adults and children.

The selection of these four groups for this book is based on a combination of factors: availability of leadership and labour force data and qualitative information about them; availability of studies of their employment and leadership experiences extensive public acknowledgment of their need for focus from the government, business, and community sectors; and the increasing international and jurisdictional actions of these groups. Most importantly, these four groups account for around two thirds of the population in Canada and in many other Western countries. The issue of intersectionality of gender, race, ability, and indigeneity is of topical importance. The literature in this field generally acknowledges the double or triple jeopardies experienced and testified by people with intersectional identities. However, there is limited statistical data available about them, and there have been few systematic research studies about their employment and presence at the leadership level, which renders data benchmarking, comparison, and generalization difficult. For these reasons, this issue will not be discussed in depth in this book. LGBTQs are not included in the analysis of this book mainly because the statistics about them regarding workplaces and a broad range of occupational groups are very limited, and are therefore unable to be used for comparison or cross-references. In addition, Statistics Canada does not have adequate employment data on LGBTQs or their data in terms of board participation.

Diverse groups have consistently been underutilized in the workplace. With the exception of women, they have a greater chance than their counterparts of being unemployed or not in the labour force. Here, "not in the labour force" includes people who are unemployed and who are not looking for work (i.e., "discouraged individuals"). In other words, they have dropped out of the labour force.

- In 2006, Indigenous peoples' unemployment rates (14.8%) were consistently higher than for non-Indigenous peoples (6.3%), and those rates rose more steeply during economic downturns (Statistics Canada 2010b, 2011a, 2011b, 2011c, 2011d, 2011e, 2011f; Siu 2011b). These data suggest that they are most likely underrepresented in many occupational groups; most importantly, they are underrepresented in the feeder pools for leadership positions.
- That same year, persons with disabilities in Canada had a high rate of not being in the labour force (49.3%) among those who were not in the labour force; the rate of their able-bodied counterparts was only 19.8%.

Their unemployment rates (10.4%) were higher than those of able-bodied persons (6.8%). These data suggest that they are very underrepresented in many occupational groups. More importantly, as we will note in chapters 6 and 8, they are also underrepresented in the feeder pools for middle and senior management positions.

- Similarly, the unemployment rates for racialized minorities are higher than those of white people (Statistics Canada 2013e), and if racialized minorities are immigrants, especially recent immigrants, their unemployment rates are even higher (Statistics Canada 2008g). They also experience difficulties in getting promotions or being trained or developed as leaders.
- The disadvantages women face in the labour force relate not to getting hired, as their unemployment rate is lower than that of men. Rather, their problems relate to the kinds of jobs in which they are employed – part-time, contract, and shift work, lower-wage jobs, and odd jobs, all of which are often viewed as precarious – and in the marginalization and the poor treatment they encounter. Also, the proportion of women holding multiple jobs has increased since 1987, as permanent full-time jobs are much harder to obtain (Status of Women Canada 2015; Statistics Canada 2005b). Women also experience difficulties in getting promotions or developmental opportunities for leadership positions; in addition, they face work-related problems such as pay inequity, stereotypical roles, harassment, and discrimination.

These research findings suggest that these four diverse groups have been highly unemployed, outside the labour force, or marginalized (by holding precarious jobs with lower pay) relative to their mainstream counterparts. Furthermore, because of their persistently employment-disadvantaged years, they are not adequately represented in positions that are likely to be considered for promotion to executive positions. And as this book will explore, without executive experience, they are also unlikely to be qualified or considered to be board directors in the private sector.

What Does This Book Offer?

So far we have discussed the broader economic and demographic forces that are changing the world and how diversity in human resources can provide value to the economy and businesses. This is the context in which this book is founded. Over the past few decades, businesses have found ways to make their workforces more diverse and inclusive. Making changes at the leadership level is much harder, and we still do not have a good representation of diverse groups in leadership positions.

Diversity in leadership is not yet common in Canada. This book will analyse the issue, posing two core questions:

- Why is diversity in leadership uncommon?
- What can be done about it?

The answers to these will provide an analysis of the status quo of leadership in Canada as well as a road map to achieving greater diversity among leaders. Michelle Scarborough (2019), managing partner of BDC Capital's Strategic Investment and Women in Technology Venture Fund, has noted that while leaders and managers may not have the knowledge and skills to bring diversity to the workplace, they do not lack willingness to tackle the issue. This book is an attempt to offer insights and solutions that will help readers make organizational changes that will foster greater diversity in leadership.

Analytical Approaches and Options for Change

This book begins by presenting statistical data indicating the underrepresentation of diverse groups in leadership positions – as board directors and senior executives. To understand why this is so, this book adopts three analytical approaches: psychological, organizational, and cultural.

Psychological Approach

The psychological approach takes the position that the *concept* of leadership is the starting point in understanding current diversity in leadership and how, by reimagining that concept, one may begin to make leadership more diverse. Why is the concept of leadership placed at the forefront for analysis? The short answer is that it has seldom been singled out for examination, which makes it high time to dissect it critically. Despite years of studying leadership, this concept is far from clear. Leadership is a complex and multifaceted concept, besides being a highly subjective one. As Stogdill (1974, 7) noted some time ago, "there are as many definitions of leadership as there are persons who have attempted to define the concept." As a concept, leadership is so subjective that it prompted Fairholm (2004, 579) to say that "leadership is like beauty. You know it when you see it."

If subjectivity is characteristic of the concept of leadership, it makes sense to uncover the key attributes of leaders (subjectively speaking), how current mainstream leaders themselves define "leadership," what the perspectives of diverse groups are on leadership, and how they behave as leaders. This will be our first step toward finding out why leadership is so homogeneous. Then there are issues related to the mindsets of leaders. Mindsets, including stereotypes and prejudice, are conscious or unconscious mechanisms that demarcate people's boundaries and elicit emotions (Stephan and Stephan 2000, 27–8; Li 2008, 21–33; Haddock, Zanna, and Esses 1994, 83–4).

Organizational Approach

The organizational approach focuses on the practices of human resources that drive exclusion at the leadership level. This book views people as entering leadership through various "pipelines," which extend throughout an organization (Sengupta 2012). The functions of human resources, such as recruitment, selection, performance management, promotion, development, and succession planning, play a crucial role in selecting, training, and developing candidates for leadership (Brown, Brown, and Anastasopoulos 2002, 10; Yarnall 2011). It is therefore essential to examine these practices carefully and determine how they hinder or enhance the chances of diverse groups to become leaders.

Unlike the psychological approach, this one assumes that human resources systems and processes, policies and guidelines, and procedures and programs may *seem* to shape the experiences of diverse groups in the workplace impartially even as they create adverse impacts on them. This approach cannot be utilized independently of the psychological approach because there are *people* behind every system, process, policy, guideline, procedure, and program in any human resources department. People can have unconscious biases in their perceptions and attitudes and in the ways they conceptualize leadership. Through them, organizational mechanisms are operationalized and have lives of their own.

Cultural Approach

Corporate cultures attach a broad range of social meanings to human behaviours, which may be crystallized in vision and value statements, workplace vocabularies, symbols, policies, procedures, norms, and daily activities. Like the concepts of leadership, these cultural traits are abstract, subjective, and difficult to pinpoint (Marshall 1995, 310; Selby 2010, 248–9).

The cultural approach considers what leaders and managers have or have not said or done that creates social messages for employees. These messages may take the form of institutional norms for getting things done, who gets promoted and who is fired, and how leaders and managers conduct

Figure 1.1. Analytical approaches and options for change

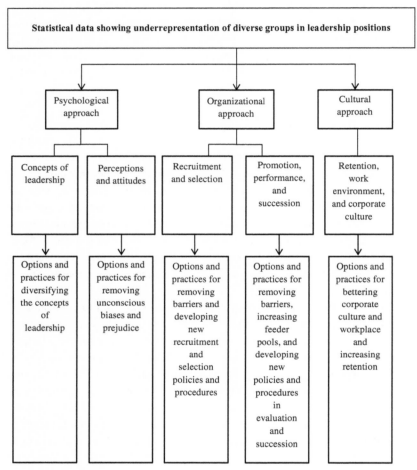

themselves. An understanding of corporate culture offers us insight into how human resources development and planning is managed and how groups feel and think about it. Thus a cultural approach goes hand-in-hand with the psychological and organizational approaches.

Options for Change
This book takes the position that these factors often affect how leaders determine the potential of leadership candidates, how employees decide whether they will stay in or quit their jobs, and how organizational pipelines carry

people into leadership. Psychological, organizational, and cultural factors keep leadership homogeneity intact; and when these are intertwined and reinforce one another, they result in a "glass ceiling" at the leadership level or even levels below for diverse groups.

This book will discuss the value of workforce data collection and analysis (chapter 2), identify biases in the concepts of leadership (chapter 3), discuss the damaging effects of stereotypes and prejudice (chapter 4), and expose the hidden barriers embedded in human resources practices (chapters 5 and 6) and in non-inclusive corporate cultures (chapter 7). Each chapter will present options for change as well as practices that have proven to be effective in enhancing the possibility of diverse groups to attain leadership positions. These options can help the business sector develop more encompassing and inclusive concepts of leadership, by indicating how leaders and employees view and feel about diverse groups, how human resources could operate, and how work culture could be adjusted so as to be better suited for diversity and inclusiveness.

These options have been called "best practices," because some organizations have tried them and thereby achieved diversity and inclusiveness at the leadership level and throughout their organizations. Some of these options have been discussed among human resources professionals and in media and publications but have not been fully adopted, although they are recognized by diversity and inclusiveness experts as effective and desirable.

The term "best practices" must be used cautiously, for it creates the impression that they are universally applicable to every organization. These practices have their limitations because each organization has its own values, norms, practices, and cultures. "Best practices" fulfil their objectives only in combination with other factors for success within the organization.

The Plan of the Book

It is against this backdrop of macro-level global changes that we will explore two core questions: Why are diverse groups underrepresented at the leadership level? And what can be done about it? The book will present data showing the extent of representation of diverse groups in leadership and will then zero in on why diverse groups are relatively absent from leadership, utilizing psychological, organizational, and cultural perspectives. The remainder of the book presents solutions and tactics for diversifying leadership effectively. Emphasizing the interlocking relationships between our thoughts and actions, *Opening Doors to Diversity in Leadership* stresses the importance of organizational review and self-reflection; the pivotal role of removing uncon-scious biases from the workplace; and how to identify the systemic biases embedded in many aspects of human resources management practices.

- Chapter 1 ("Introduction: A Changing World") places diversity in leader-ship in a global context and in that of Canada's economy and demograph-ics. It presents a strong business case for fostering diversity in leadership and the workforce. Diverse groups are emerging labour forces that have the potential to boost growth. The chapter defines the four diverse groups that will be the focus of the book.
- Chapter 2 ("Diversity Gaps in Leadership") provides data that show the extent to which diverse groups are underrepresented in leadership posi-tions in Canada. It also offers suggestions for improving data collection and analysis for the purpose of opening doors to diversity.
- Chapter 3 ("Concepts of Leadership") examines contemporary main-stream concepts of leadership as they relate to characteristics, styles, competencies, and cultural contributions. These contemporary main-stream concepts of leadership and those of diverse groups are an integral part of the broader literature on leadership. However, the emphases of the contemporary mainstream concepts are different from those of diverse groups. The chapter discusses the implications of these concepts on the composition of current leadership and puts forward various options for change.
- Chapter 4 ("Perceptions and Attitudes") reviews stereotypes and uncon-scious biases toward diverse groups and how they can act as "psychologi-cal filters" among mainstream leaders. This chapter discusses how these perceptions and attitudes impact the performance of diverse groups and their social interactions as well as the roles they play in perpetuating the exclusion of diverse groups from leadership positions.
- Chapter 5 ("Moving In – Recruitment and Selection") examines seem-ingly impartial recruitment and selection methods for leadership appointments and identifies their adverse impacts on diverse groups. It then discusses how perceptions and attitudes toward diverse groups affect leaders' decisions. This chapter discusses options for change in how leadership is defined and how recruiting and selection can be modified.
- Chapter 6 ("Moving Up – Promotion, Performance, and Succession") identifies biases in performance management and succession manage-ment and shows how perceptions and attitudes may strengthen their negative impacts on diverse groups. Options for change in these human resources functions are provided.

- Chapter 7 ("Moving Out – Retention, Work Environment, and Corporate Culture") examines how some workplaces, corporate culture, management practices, and human behaviours harm the psychology and social relations of diverse groups, their place in pipelines to leadership, and/or their workplace retention. Options for change in the workplace environment and culture are presented.
- Chapter 8 ("Diversity, Business, and Government") summarizes the major themes of the book – psychology, organizational and cultural factors, and how these interlock. It further discusses the change strategies based on the integration of these factors, the primacy of psychological changes, leadership commitment and accountability, and the roles of legislation and public education. The book concludes that the private and public sectors must collaborate in consultation with diverse groups to make diversity in leadership happen.

chapter two

Diversity Gaps in Leadership

As mentioned, this book defines leadership positions as those occupied by board directors and senior executives. Together, these are the power centres of a corporation, and there is a distinct relationship between them, as illustrated in Branson's (2007, 129) analogy of corporate governance as a solar system: "The board of directors is the sun and the highest ranked corporate officers, such as the chief executive officer (CEO), are the first circle of planets around that sun." The board directors determine who will sit on the board and choose CEOs and (in some cases) senior executives (Conger, Finegold, and Lawler III 1998; Burke 2010b, 181). CEOs report to the board of directors and are also members of that board. They act as a conduit between the board of directors and executives; they also hire executives and recommend future board directors.

Some scholars question whether board directors and senior executives should be lumped together under the umbrella of "leadership," distinguishing between "leaders," who provide vision, give direction, and energize people, and "managers," who follow directions, put them into action, and get things done (Zaleznik 2004; Mills 2005). Such distinctions may be useful for conceptual clarity but they have less application in the real world. In the real world, CEOs and senior executives take directions from boards of directors and manage the organization through middle managers. They also develop corporate and program policies and procedures and motivate staff members. They act as leaders and managers simultaneously, as defined by Zaleznik and Mills.

Using two analytical methods – composition and flow data analyses – this chapter examines the extent to which the four diverse groups are represented in leadership positions in Canada, beginning with the board directors, followed by senior executives. Snapshot comparisons (using composition data) are made between the representation rates of these diverse groups in the private sector and those in society at large. I discuss how various research studies utilize data from different industrial sectors and benchmarks, thus generating different pictures of diverse groups in leadership positions, and how this can lead to confusion. I clarify that this book uses labour market availability data for benchmarking purposes. Using the flow data method, I track new appointments of racialized minorities and women to estimate their rates of progress in leadership positions. The chapter ends with useful organizational practices for monitoring and analysing the progress of diversity.

In this book, for composition data, I used the labour market availability data from 2011 (made available in 2014) as a benchmark, comparing it with the data on diverse groups in the federally regulated sectors. The more recent labour market availability data of 2016 were not available at the time of the data analysis for this book. These Canadian national data sets, especially for gender data, are relatively large and show a high degree of stability through time. Significant fluctuation in data patterns is not expected, except for racial data in large census metropolitan areas in Canada. Meanwhile, flow data on women and racialized minorities derived from the *Globe and Mail*'s leadership appointments (2013) provide a preliminary insight into the extent to which diverse group members are entering leadership positions. One would expect some degree of fluctuation in these appointments; thus the findings that emerge may have limited value for generalization. Even so, they provide a snapshot for the year 2013.

Board of Directors

Historical data provide a longitudinal perspective on progress in gender parity with regard to board directorship. They show that white, non-Indigenous, able-bodied men have dominated both boards of directors and senior executives in Canada but that female representation has been growing slowly. Burke (2010a, 98) noted that "directors were almost exclusively white males until the 1970s." Leighton (2010, 251) found that on the boards of directors of Canada's 300 largest corporations, only 6% of members were women. Burke (2010a, 98), using data from the *Report on Business* Top 1000 Canadian companies, found the same – in 1996, of the 5,252 external corporate directors, only 6% were women. Catalyst's 2004 study produced a higher percentage: at the top-ranked 500 corporations in Canada, women constituted 14.4% of board directors. In 2014, Catalyst Canada's survey of women on the corporate boards of S&P/TSX60 companies showed better gender parity (20.8%) (Catalyst 2015).

The Canadian Board Diversity Council (2015; 2016; 2018) has been monitoring the progress of diverse groups sitting on corporate boards since 2001. Using annual surveys of *Financial Post* 500 companies, that organization notes:

- The representation rates of women on the boards of directors of these companies have been increasing, from 10.9% (2001) to 21.6% (2016) to 37% (2018).
- However, representation of Indigenous peoples has been uneven, increasing from 0.8% (2010) to 1.3% (2015), then dropping to 0.6% (2016), before rising slightly to 0.8% (2018).
- As for racialized minorities, their representation rates are uneven as well, regressing from 5.3% (2010) to 2.0% (2014), then jumping to 7.3% (2015), dropping to 4.5% (2016), and rising to 5.9% (2018).
- Representation rates of persons with disabilities have been also been uneven, regressing from 2.9% (2010) to 1.3% (2015), then to 1.8% (2016), then dropping to 0.8% (2018).

Given the short time frame for the data on Indigenous peoples, persons with disabilities, and racialized minorities, it is not clear whether all of this constitutes a trend. The sample size is too small – that is, there are too few people in these groups for us to confirm one.

The Diversity Institute (2020, 14–16) did a comprehensive study of board directors across multiple sectors in eight cities in Canada – Toronto, Montreal, Calgary, Vancouver, Halifax, Hamilton, London, and Ottawa – and noted that when all board directors of the "corporate sector" in these eight cities were combined, women made up 25.3% of board directors and racialized minorities 4.5%. These percentages are smaller than those presented by the Canadian Board Diversity Council's research results of 2018.

The variations in the representation rates of diverse groups on boards cited in the above studies are due largely to methodological issues, especially those related to scope and type of companies that are under research. For example, the Canadian Board Diversity Council uses *Financial Post* 500 companies for its annual surveys, whereas Osler, Hoskin & Harcourt uses sixty TSX 60-listed companies for its annual surveys, and the Diversity Institute has its own customized pools of companies. In 2019, women held over 18% of all board seats among all companies in Canada that disclosed their numbers. That figure rose to 30% when only S&P/TSX 60 companies were surveyed (MacDougall et al. 2019, 3). So one must be cautious when interpreting and comparing these statistics when the pools of companies and their board directors vary.

These rates tell only half the story. They are more meaningful when they are compared with the Canadian labour market availability data, which show the proportion of people who are qualified and experienced as senior managers and are available for such jobs in Canada. This data set has been selected as a benchmark here because it is the one the federal government uses when comparing the representation of diverse groups among employees with those in the broader labour force in communities. The qualifications and experiences also correspond to those outlined in job postings for board directors and senior executives in the *Globe and Mail* in 2013, which was the sample used in this study.

Labour market availability data are not the only benchmark that can be used when determining the representation rates of diverse groups in the workforce and in leadership positions; data on population or on working-age population (i.e., fifteen to sixty-five) may also be used. The latter two data sets have not been used in this book because they do not consider the qualifications and work experiences required for board directors and senior executives.

It is not meaningful to analyse the data from the Canadian Board Diversity Council's surveys on diversity on the boards of directors in terms of either annual progress or extent of representation for a few diverse groups. For Indigenous peoples, racialized minorities, and persons with disabilities, the comparison of any years since the council started collecting data would pose problems in data interpretation because of the small samples of these diverse groups and the council's research methodology. Any small increases in numbers for these three groups are bound to affect their representation rates in a significant manner. That said, given that the sample for women is much larger, year-by-year comparisons regarding the status of women in leadership positions or their representation with external benchmarks will be more meaningful.

The differences between the workforce data and labour market availability data are termed "diversity gaps." When the data are expressed in negative terms, this means the diverse groups are underrepresented among board directors. Given that the size of diverse groups and their benchmarks are different, the determination of the magnitude of each diversity gap is based on the division of each diversity gap by the respective labour market availability rate of each diverse group (i.e., the benchmark). This "magnitude" (expressed as a percentage) shows the utilization rate of each diverse group in leadership positions. The closer the utilization rate of a diverse group is to 100%, the more equitably that diverse group has been utilized and represented in leadership positions. Therefore, when the utilization rate of a diverse group is in the negative (i.e., below the 100% mark), the diverse group is considered to be underutilized and underrepresented. The larger the negative utilization rate (i.e., underutilization), the greater the distance the diverse group has to

Table 2.1. Diversity gaps and utilization rates of board directors, Canada, 2015

	Board directors			
	Representation 2015* (%)	Benchmark 2011** (%)	Diversity gaps (%)	Utilization rate of diverse group (%)****
Indigenous peoples	1.3	2.9	−1.6	**44.82**
Persons with disabilities***	1.3	4.3	−3.0	**30.23**
Racialized minorities	7.3	10.1	−2.8	**72.27**
Women	19.5	27.4	−7.9	**71.16**

*Data on board directors are based on *Financial Post* 500 boards of directors (Canadian Board Diversity Council 2015, 4, 9).

**Benchmark – National labour market availability rates of "senior managers" in Canada are based on the 2011 National Household Survey (Canada 2016a, Appendix A, Table B).

***Benchmark data on persons with disabilities are based on the 2012 Canadian Survey on Disability (Canada 2015, Appendix A, Table B).

****Utilization rate is calculated by dividing the representation rate by the benchmark of each diverse group. Any percentage under 100% is negative, which means that the diversity gap is negative and the diverse group is underutilized and underrepresented. Bolded values denote underrepresentation.

go to be equitably represented. When the utilization rate of a diverse group is in the positive (i.e., above the 100% mark), the diverse group is considered to be overutilized and overrepresented.

To make our analysis more robust, the "20% rule" has been used to determine how confident we are about the importance of the diversity gaps. When the utilization rate is 20% or more, be it positive (+120% to infinity) or negative (−80% to 0%), we have the confidence to say that the data are accurate and that the diversity gap is important enough that actions should be taken to address the issue of inequitable representation.

It is clear from the comparison of these two data sets that all four diverse groups have negative diversity gaps at the leadership level and that their negative utilization rates are higher than 20%. The actual magnitude implies the severity of underrepresentation. Persons with disabilities have the lowest utilization rate (30.23%), followed by Indigenous peoples (44.82%), women (71.16%), and racialized minorities (72.26%). The data show that persons with disabilities and Indigenous peoples have a much longer way to go than women and racialized minorities in reaching full representation (100%) among board directors.

A survey of the Toronto Stock Exchange (TSX) 60 companies by the Canadian Board Diversity Council in cooperation with the Conference Board of Canada in 2015 confirmed the general pattern of the underrepresentation of diverse groups. However, there are variations in diversity representation. The 2019 report by Osler, Hoskin & Harcourt LLP noted that women held 18% of board seats among 726 companies – a percentage even lower than what was found in the *Financial Post* 500 data cited above. And according to the Canadian Board Diversity Council's 2018 survey results, racialized minorities constituted 6% of board members among TSX 60 companies. On the basis of a calculation of TSX/S&P 60 companies conducted by Raymond Chan (Telus Corp. director, former CEO of Baytex Energy Corp.) in 2019, the proportion of racialized minorities among board directors amounted to 4%. Both these percentages (6% and 4%) are lower than the 7.3% tabulation based on the data for the *Financial Post* 500 mentioned above. As for persons with disabilities, they have "virtually no representation" on boards (Dobby 2019; Milstead 2019).

As confirmed by the data compiled by the Canadian Board Diversity Council, these statistics on diversity representation rose and fell over time and varied by their data sources and research methodologies. Notwithstanding the variations, the pattern is clear: diverse groups are still underrepresented as board members.

Appointments of new board directors may also shed light on progress in ensuring board diversity. The announcements of new appointments to corporate boards of directors published in the *Globe and Mail* were reviewed for this book. Using the "other identification" method (i.e., physical features identified by other persons and not by the diverse group members themselves), all forty-five announcements of board appointments placed in the newspaper in 2013 were reviewed on the basis of the physical appearance of the persons in the photographs. The results suggested that forty-four (97.8%) of the persons in the pictures that accompanied these announcements were white, and one (2.2%) was a racialized minority member.

Using the national labour market availability rate of 10.1% for racialized minorities in the "senior managers" occupational group (2011) as a benchmark (Canada 2015, Appendix A, Table B), racialized minorities are underrepresented. New appointments are one way to replenish departing board directors or enlarge the current corporate boards. If the appointment rate of racialized minorities (2.2%) does not approximate that of the labour market availability rate (10.1%), and if the appointment rate is consistently below that of labour market availability in future years, it is likely that the share of seats on boards held by racialized minorities will be further reduced and their representation rates will drop further.

Again, based on the announcements of board directors in the *Globe and Mail*, this study reviewed new appointments of women to corporate boards for the entire year of 2013. Of the forty-five appointees, thirty (or 66.7%) were

Table 2.2. Diversity gaps and utilization rates of new racialized minority board directors appointed, Canada, 2013

	Board directors			
	Representation 2013* (%)	Benchmark 2011** (%)	Diversity gap (in % points)	Utilization rate of diverse group (%)***
Racialized minorities	2.2	10.1	-7.9	**21.78**

*Data on new board directors appointed are based on a review of appointment announcements in the *Globe and Mail* for the entire year of 2013.

**Benchmark – National labour market availability rates of "senior managers" in Canada are based on the 2011 National Household Survey (Canada 2015, Appendix A, Table B).

***Utilization rate is calculated by dividing the representation rate by the benchmark of the diverse group (racialized minorities in this case). Any percentage under 100% is negative, which means that the diversity gap is negative and that racial minorities are underutilized in their share of appointments.

Bolded values denote underrepresentation.

Table 2.3. Diversity gaps and utilization rates of new female board directors appointed, Canada, 2013

	Board directors			
	Representation 2013* (%)	Benchmark 2011** (%)	Diversity gap (in % points)	Utilization rate of diverse group (%)***
Women	33.3	27.4	+5.9	121.53

*Data on new board directors appointed are based on a review of appointment announcements in the *Globe and Mail* for the entire year of 2013.

**Benchmark – National labour market availability rates of "senior managers" in Canada are based on the 2011 National Household Survey (Canada 2015, Appendix A, Table B).

***Utilization rate is calculated by dividing the representation rate by the benchmark of the diverse group (women in this case). Any percentage above 100% is positive, which means that the diversity gap is positive and women are overutilized in their share of appointments.

men and fifteen (33.3%) were women. Of the fifteen women appointed to boards, fourteen (or 93.33%) were white and one (or 6.67%) was a racialized minority member.

The 33.3% is above the national labour market availability rate of 27.4% for women (2011) (Canada 2015, Appendix A, Table B). In terms of new appointees to boards of directors, the diversity gap in 2013 was 5.9 percentage points in favour of women. If this rate of appointment of women continues, corporate boards will have a higher representation rate for women because they are being appointed in excess of their benchmark (or the national labour force availability).

Senior Executives

Since 1986, the federal government has been collecting data on the representation of the four diverse groups in senior management positions in the federally regulated private sector and Crown corporations. The federally regulated private sector is composed largely of banking, communication, and transportation companies with 100 or more employees. There were 507 companies in the data set, and together they have 738,053 employees, representing 4.1% of the Canadian workforce (Canada 2016b). While the numbers of companies and employees are not large, the data set is valuable because its collection is systematic and offers a profile of the representation of the four diverse groups that is worthy of analysis.

In this section, we need to determine whether there are "diversity gaps." A comparison of the shares of diverse groups among senior executives with their labour market availability showed that all four groups have negative diversity gaps, which means they are underrepresented in senior management positions: Indigenous peoples by –2.1%, persons with disabilities by –1.7%, racialized minorities by –2.8%, and women by –2.6%. Diversity gaps also indicate the utilization and representation of diverse groups – the larger the diversity gaps in negative term, the lower the utilization and representation of diverse groups. The results of the comparison showed that Indigenous peoples have the lowest utilization rate (27.58%), persons with disabilities have a higher rate (60.46%), racialized minorities have even higher one (80.19%), and women have the highest utilization rate (90.51%).

There are variations in female representation across industries (Canadian Board Diversity Council 2018). A study of more than 900 Canadian technology companies by #movethedial, PwC Canada, and MaRS Discovery District in 2017 found that women constituted 5% of CEOs and 13% of executives. These figures are further confirmed by the largest study done on the status of women in corporations in North America, conducted by LeanIn.org and McKinsey & Co. in 2018 (Kovitz 2019).

The author's review of the *Globe and Mail*'s announcements of appointees to executive positions in 2013 showed that, of the 135 executives appointed in the private sector and announced in the newspaper that year, 127 (or 94.1%) were white executives and 8 (or 5.9%) were racialized minority

Table 2.4. Diversity gaps and utilization rates of senior executives, Canada, 2014

	Senior executives			
	Representation 2014* (%)	Benchmark 2011** (%)	Diversity gaps (in % points)	Utilization rate of diverse group (%)****
Indigenous peoples	0.8	2.9	−2.1	**27.58**
Persons with disabilities***	2.0	4.3	−1.7	**60.46**
Racialized minorities	8.1	10.1	−2.0	**80.19**
Women	24.8	27.4	−2.6	**90.51**

*Data on "senior managers" in the federally regulated private sector (Canada 2016c, Appendix A, Table B)
**Benchmark – National labour market availability rates of "senior managers" in Canada are based on the 2011's National Household Survey (Canada 2015, Appendix A, Table B; Canada 2016a, Appendix A, Table B).
***Benchmark data of persons with disabilities are based on the 2012 Canadian Survey on Disability (Canada 2015, Appendix A, Table B; Canada 2016a, Appendix A, Table B).
****Utilization rate is calculated by dividing the representation rate by the benchmark of each diverse group. Any percentage under 100% is negative. Negative percentages denote the underutilization of the diverse group. A negative diversity gap is always found when there is an underutilization of a diverse group.
Bolded values denote underrepresentation.

Table 2.5. Diversity gaps and utilization rates of new racialized minority senior executives appointed, Canada, 2013

	Senior executives			
	Representation 2013* (%)	Benchmark 2011** (%)	Diversity gap (in % points)	Utilization rate of diverse group (%)***
Racialized minorities	5.9	10.1	−4.2	**58.4**

*Data on new board directors appointed are based on a review of appointment announcements in the *Globe and Mail* in 2013.
**Benchmark – National labour market availability rates of senior managers in Canada are based on the 2011 National Household Survey (Canada 2015, Appendix A, Table B).
***Utilization rate is calculated by dividing the representation rate by the benchmark of the diverse group (racialized minorities in this case). Any percentage in the utilization rate under 100% is negative, as the diversity gap is negative.
Bolded values denote underrepresentation.

executives. Among the eight racialized minority executives in the study, none were women.

When the proportion of racialized minority executives (5.9%) hired by the private sector in 2013 is compared with the benchmark of 10.1%, we find that the diversity gap is 4.2% points in magnitude. If the rate continues to fall

Table 2.6. Diversity gaps of new female senior executives appointed, Canada, 2014

	Senior executives			
	Representation 2014* (%)	Benchmark 2011** (%)	Diversity gap (in % points)	Utilization rate of diverse group (%)***
Women	26.7%	27.4	−0.7	**97.44**

*Data on new board directors appointed based on a review of appointment announcements in *Globe and Mail* in 2013.
**Benchmark – National labour market availability rates of senior managers in Canada are based on the 2011 National Household Survey (Canada 2015, Appendix A, Table B).
***Utilization rate is calculated by dividing the representation rate by the benchmark of the diverse group (women in this case). As the diversity gap associated with the utilization rate is negative, the utilization rate is also negative.
Bolded values denote underrepresentation.

below the benchmark in the next few years, it is likely that the representation rate of racialized minorities in senior executive positions will soon be even lower in Canada.

This author's study of the *Globe and Mail*'s announcements of appointees to executive positions in the private sector in 2013 found that, of the 135 appointees, 99 (or 73.3%) were men and 36 (26.7%) were women. All of the 36 women appointed to corporate boards (100%) were white.

The 26.7% representation rate for women in this study is just below the national labour market availability rate of 27.4% for women (2011) (Canada 2015, Appendix A, Table B). For new appointees to executive positions, the diversity gap in 2013 was 0.7 percentage points not in favour of women. The magnitude of the diversity gap was −0.7%. is in the negative term. If this appointment rate (26.7%) continues, there will be a slight underrepresentation for women in executive positions over the next few years.

Best Options and Practices

Options for Change

Without systematic collection and analysis of data on the representation of diverse groups in Canada and other countries, we will be talking about this topic in a vacuum. It is only with evidence (such as diversity data) in hand that we can start to examine the status of diverse groups in leadership positions, identify patterns and trends, and think through the implications of findings. A few examples show how diversity data collection, analysis, and monitoring could be done successfully.

Figure 2.1. How best to determine the representation of diverse groups in leadership

Data collection	→	Establish a comprehensive data system with cross tabulation capability	→	Tabulate data to find patterns and trends
⊹				⊹
Data analysis	→	Adopt an agreed-upon research methodology, measuring tools, and indicators	→	Compare with external benchmarks and peer performance
⊹				⊹
Data monitoring and review	→	Develop regular monitoring process and records	→	Review extent of progress regularly

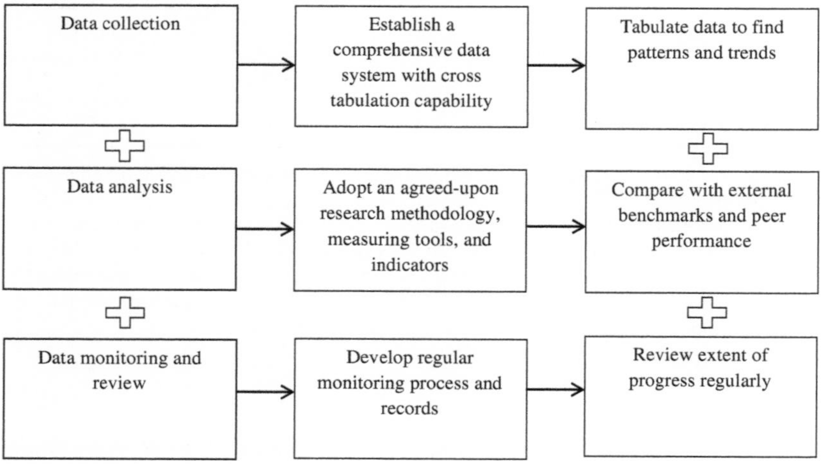

Data Collection

In this chapter, a pattern of underrepresentation of diverse groups in leadership positions in Canada has emerged. To monitor and measure the degree of representation, it is advisable for corporations to collect and analyse diversity data on board directors and senior executives.

It is a standard observation in business that we cannot manage unless we measure (Branson 2007, 183). This very much applies to human resources management. Businesses can manage their workforces well only when they measure them. Accordingly, whether a corporation has information on a diversity gap in leadership positions depends largely on whether it has collected workforce data based on Indigeneity, ability, race, and gender.

The success of workforce data collection depends largely on leaders' firm commitment, allocation of sufficient funds, staff expertise in informational technology and data systems, clear communication of its purposes from the top, and substantial employee engagement.

Collecting workforce data is not a one-time exercise: they have to be updated regularly in response to resignations or new appointments of board members as well as hirings, promotions, or terminations of employees. It is a fluid process. Mechanisms are needed to facilitate ongoing data updating. To ensure their optimal use, data need to be monitored regularly so that the organization has current information on its board directors and workforce.

The discussion of the comparability and benchmarking of the representation data of diverse groups (Appendices I and II, available online on utorontopress.com) illustrates several data and related methodological problems. Being cognizant of these problems, there are a few things we can do to improve data collection. Organizations across jurisdictions should come together to determine a variety of data issues and reach a consensus or a formal agreement. These issues include:

- How diverse groups are defined.
- How board directors and senior executives are defined.
- How data are collected – "self-identification" or "other-identification."
- Whether hiring, promotion, termination, and training/development data can be collected.
- Who will collect these data.

Data Analysis

After workforce data on diverse groups have been gathered, they need to be compared with external data gathered from, for example, segments of the population or labour force, or pools of the qualified and available labour force in the larger society. These external data will serve as benchmarks for the corporate data. Through this comparison, diversity gaps can be identified and the degree of representation can be determined.

Again, joint efforts by organizations or jurisdictions would help achieve commonalities in several analytical areas:

- What data should be used as external benchmarks – population data, working-age population data, labour force data, or pools of qualified and available labour force?
- What are the key analytical areas: Proportion of diverse groups among leaders? Proportion of organizations without individual diverse groups as leaders? Duration of tenure of diverse group members in leadership positions? Training/development opportunities for diverse groups? Proportion of diverse groups in new hires, promotions, and termination? Intersectionality of diverse groups?
- What software for data analysis could be used by other organizations as well?

Given the different priorities that jurisdictions or organizations assign to this area, achieving a consensus may not be easy. However, agreement on the basic analytical areas is a first step toward developing a more accurate picture of the status of diverse groups in leadership positions and toward comparing organizational or jurisdictional findings.

Data Monitoring and Review

Data monitoring and review is related to data collection and analysis. Organizations may join forces to track, analyse, monitor, and review the status of diverse groups in leadership positions within a timeline agreeable to all. Then information could be shared and they could identify progress (or regression) with regard to interpretations, unresolved problems, and solutions.

Several measuring tools are available to enable organizations to compare their findings. The most recent is the gender diversity index adopted by European Women in Boards, which measures the status of women on the boards of directors of 200 larger organizations in Belgium, the Czech Republic, Finland, France, Germany, Italy, the Netherlands, Spain, and the United Kingdom (Zillman 2018). The Canadian Board Diversity Council has its own measuring instrument for board directors and executives in *Financial Post* 500 companies that addresses the following parameters: industries, functional areas of expertise, management experience, geography, education, international experience, age, ethnicity, Indigenous peoples, persons with disabilities, visible minorities, LGBTQ, and gender (Canadian Board Diversity Council 2018). These instruments may not be methodologically perfect, but they could be improved or enhanced.

Practices for Change

Data collection, analysis, and monitoring is not an abstract process. The examples below highlight the efforts of organizations in Canada and the United States to implement it for workforces. Tha following accounts are not exhaustive, but they illustrate the value such mechanisms offer for fostering diversity in the workforce and in leadership.

Canadian Private Sector Companies

The Royal Bank of Canada was one of the Canada's Best Diversity Employers in 2016, reflecting its long history of collecting and analysing workforce data. It has established a Diversity Leadership Council comprised of senior executives, who discuss workforce profiles based on quarterly diversity scorecards and determine what actions are necessary to tackle new findings or to modify initiatives. The workforce metrics also focus on leadership diversity; hiring, promotion, and termination; and diversity representation in every occupational group. At the operational level, the bank has created a special diversity and inclusiveness office to monitor these workforce data, and analyses are conducted regularly (MediaCorp Canada 2016a). Similarly, Telus Corporation has established a regular diversity data collection mechanism in, and Xerox has a global diversity survey. These two corporations were named Canada's Best Diversity Employers in 2016 (MediaCorp Canada 2016a).

Canadian Public-Sector Organizations

The City of Toronto was recognized as one of Canada's Top 100 Employers in 2017 and as one of Canada's Best Diversity Employers in 2016 (MediaCorp Canada 2016b). Although the city is not required by provincial or federal statute to collect workforce data, it has a long history of collecting data on diversity. In 2000, the City Council approved the collection of employment equity data from employees in order to monitor the workforce profiles of Indigenous peoples, persons with disabilities, racialized minorities, and women (City of Toronto 2000). In 2014, to increase the response rate of employees, it developed a new employment equity workforce survey, which collects data on employees' identities, including gender, aboriginality, race, disability, and sexual orientation. It is not an anonymous survey, but it is confidential and voluntary. Results of the survey are stored in a confidential database with very limited staff access. In addition to employees' data, data on job applicants are collected. Analyses of the data are reported to City Council and provide an overview of the proportion of diverse groups in the organization as a whole as well as within each city division. The data are used to create strategies for raising the representation of diverse groups at different occupational levels and are benchmarked with the population of the city as a whole (City of Toronto 2014, 10; City of Toronto n.d., 17).

Canadian Advocacy Organizations

The Canadian Board Diversity Council began its annual surveys on board directors in 2001. It started by focusing solely on women; but since 2010, the scope of data collection has expanded to cover Indigenous peoples, persons with disabilities, and racialized minorities. In 2016 the council began collecting data on senior executives based on gender only – "FP500 C-Suite Analysis," in addition to data on board directors (Canadian Board Diversity Council 2016). These survey data provide valuable information on the changing representation of diverse groups in Canada. It is not known whether any Canadian companies have volunteered to collect diversity data on their board directors. However, some companies collect workforce data on "senior managers" to comply with legal requirements under the federal employment equity legislation.

American Companies

AT&T, headquartered in Texas, has more than 230,000 employees worldwide. It was ranked fourth among Top Diversity Employers in 2016. To ensure better representation of minorities, including persons with disabilities, AT&T launched the "iCount Self-ID" campaign to collect workforce data and to track its employees' demographic and social backgrounds (DiversityInc. 2016a).

Sodexo is an American-based global company with close to 300,000 employees. In 2016, it launched a data collection program in all of its global entities, covering 30,000 managers, to determine the relationship between gender balance in management and financial and non-financial performance. Preliminary findings suggested that having gender balance in management improved performance. This is an indication that Sodexo sees value in using measurement to develop diversity. It also reflects the corporate philosophy that, as Lorna Donatone, regional chair for North America and CEO of Schools Worldwide, said, "diversity and inclusion is at the heart of our business strategy and our brand promise" (DiversityInc. 2016a).

Conclusion

This chapter reviewed research studies and Statistics Canada's data on the representation of diverse groups. It is clear that all of these groups are underrepresented in leadership positions in Canada, both on the boards of directors and among senior executives. The representation rates of diverse groups among board directors and senior executives and the labour market availability rates of these diverse groups in Canada showed two noteworthy patterns.

First, the external labour market availability rates of diverse groups in Canada are all higher than the representation rates of diverse groups among board directors and senior executives. The availability rates denote the availability of qualified pools of diverse groups with experience in senior management. This indicates that there are qualified pools in all four diverse groups who could be appointed to leadership positions. Therefore, it is not for lack of qualified talents from diverse backgrounds, but rather that these diverse group members do not appear on the radar of those who are in a position to appoint or hire them.

Second, as will become apparent later in this book, the fixation of current board chairs, CEOs, and board members on proven senior executive experience often precludes the appointment of members of diverse groups. With the exception of Indigenous peoples, the representation rates of diverse groups among senior executives are all higher than those same rates among board directors. For example, among women, "24.8%" (female senior executives)

Table 2.7. Representation and availability rates of diverse groups, Canada, 2014 and 2015

	Representation rates among board directors 2015* (%)	Representation rates among senior executives 2014** (%)	Benchmark (availability rates)*** 2011 (%)
Indigenous peoples	1.3	0.8	2.9
Persons with disabilities****	1.3	2.6	4.3
Racialized minorities	7.3	8.1	10.1
Women	19.5	24.8	27.4

*Data on board directors based on *Financial Post* 500's boards of directors (Canadian Board Diversity Council 2015, 4, 9)
**Data on senior managers in the federally regulated private sector (Canada 2015, Appendix A, Table B)
***Benchmark – National labour market availability rates of senior managers in Canada are based on the 2011 National Household Survey (Canada 2015, Appendix A, Table B).
****Benchmark data of persons with disabilities are based on the 2012 Canadian Survey on Disability (Canada 2015, Appendix A, Table B; Canada 2016a, Appendix A, Table B).

is higher than "19.5%" (female board directors). This suggests that the talent pools of diverse group members with senior executive experience are large enough to provide qualified candidates to boards of directors. The only exception is that Indigenous peoples' representation among senior executives (0.8%) is smaller than that among board directors (1.3%). The implication is that greater effort is needed to employ Indigenous peoples at the senior executive level, so that their numbers will grow enough to supply and sustain talents for board directorship.

Data from Canada on the low representation of diverse groups and the existence of diversity gaps give impetus to actions to address this issue. The private sector may need to consider the best strategies for meeting the challenges of a changing world (see chapter 1). The business case for diversity (also discussed in chapter 1) summarized the benefits of leadership that includes diverse groups.

Toward the end of this chapter, several organizations were cited to illustrate the value of diversity data collection, analysis, monitoring, and review as an approach to managing and promoting diversity in the workforce and in leadership. Diversity data provide systematic evidence to support or dispute any arguments over diversity representation in leadership positions.

chapter three

Concepts of Leadership

Chapter 2 provided data on the underrepresentation of the four diverse groups in leadership positions (board directors and senior executives) in Canada and in other countries. To understand why diverse groups are underrepresented among leaders, it is helpful to examine four areas: how leadership is defined (chapter 3), how diverse groups are perceived (chapter 4), how human resources are managed (chapters 5 and 6), and how inclusive the workplace is for diverse groups (chapter 7). This chapter examines the first of these four areas: concepts of leadership.

This chapter discusses concepts of leadership as revealed in three sources: primary sources such as job advertisements for leadership positions; secondary sources such as published social science studies on leadership in general; and published articles on the views of diverse groups on leadership. We begin with a discussion of the concepts of leadership in the literature; this is followed by a comparison of mainstream concepts of leadership held by current leaders with those held by diverse groups.

Analysis of these three sources suggests that mainstream concepts of leadership often held by corporate leaders do not align well with those held by diverse groups. Current leaders' concepts of leadership determine the attributes that future leaders should possess; thus they constitute a framework for leadership identification, selection, hiring, appointment, promotion, and retention. These leaders view any deviations from these concepts as secondary and marginal in their decisions.

Concepts of Leadership in the Literature

Conceptual Subjectivity

In leadership studies, there are many ideas about the nature of leadership, but generally these concepts have been poorly defined and give way to personal preferences. As W.G. Bennis (1959, 259) observed, over a period of fifty years, "of all the hazy and confounding areas in social psychology, leadership theory undoubtedly contends for top nomination. Probably more has been written and less is known about leadership than any other topic in the behavioural sciences."

Bennis's unflattering view of leadership studies was echoed by R.M. Stogdill (1974, vii), who noted that "four decades of research on leadership has produced a bewildering mass of findings ... It is difficult to know what, if anything, has been convincingly demonstrated by replicated research. The endless accumulation of empirical data has not produced an integrated understanding of leadership."

Despite the vast literature on leadership, there is little consensus among scholars who have studied it as to what characterizes a leader. Personal preferences and expectations may explain why concepts of leadership are subjective and ambiguous (Harvey and Riggio 2011, 3–4; Fairholm 2004, 579). Yet leaders today generally use these concepts to identify leadership candidates and select, hire, appoint, promote, and retain leaders. It is important to keep this subjectivity in mind as we learn about the attributes that have come to define contemporary mainstream concepts of leadership – we should approach those concepts critically, with an eye to how they exclude diverse groups.

Four Themes of Leadership

The literature on leadership outlines various attributes from which today's leaders may pick and choose when assessing leadership candidates. Four themes emerge from this: characteristics, styles, competencies, and cultural contributions. It seems that no clear, persistent importance has been given to any of these four leadership themes over time. In the 1950s, in the literature, leadership was defined rather narrowly, in terms of personal characteristics and styles. Over time, definitions came to focus on other aspects, and now the shift is toward competencies and cultural contribution to corporations.

Leadership Characteristics

Historically, various personality characteristics have been associated with the "Great Man" school of leadership, on the assumption that leaders are born and that their personalities are innate rather than acquired. In this school of thought, leaders' personal traits are relatively fixed and rigid, lending them an aura and substance of leadership. Leaders induce people to follow them voluntarily (Kirkpatrick and Locke 1991). Many descriptors have been attached to leaders: "endurance," "determination," and "decisiveness" (Flores 1981); "stamina" and "vision" (Hartman 1999); "excel" (Benimadhu and Gilson 2001); "emotional

Figure 3.1. Four themes of leadership in the literature

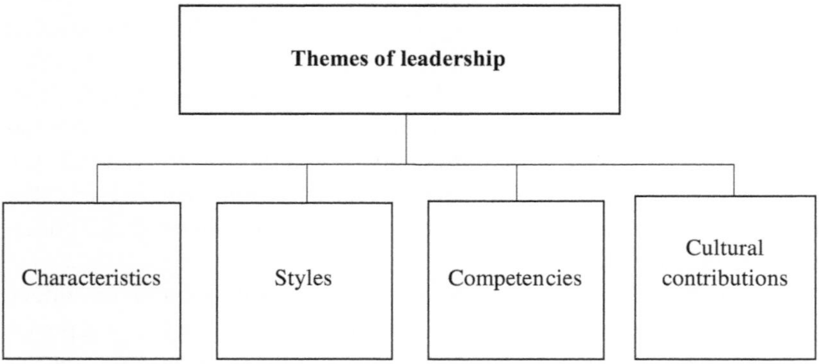

```
┌─────────────────────────────────────────┐
│           Themes of leadership            │
└─────────────────────────────────────────┘
```

| Characteristics | Styles | Competencies | Cultural contributions |

toughness" (Mills 2005); and "inspiring," "courageous," and "resilient" (Lafley 2011). Other words are more modest: "humility" and "self-knowledge" (Mills 2005); and "compassionate," "calm," and "cool" (Lafley 2011).

Leadership Styles

Another theme in leadership studies is leadership styles. In simple terms, leadership styles are approaches used in leading people. Scholars have attempted to delineate leadership styles. Examples include Weber's (1947) and Hunt's (1999) concept of charismatic leadership; Avolio and Gardner's (2005) categories of leadership styles: "authentic," "transformational," "charismatic," and "narcissistic"; Mills's (2005)'s leadership styles: "directive," "participative," "empowering," "charismatic," and "celebrity"; and Bass's (1985; 1996) eight "full range leadership" styles, which Kirkbride (2006) condensed into three main ones: "laissez-faire," "transactional," and "transformational."

Leadership styles are ideal types and are quite fluid and multifaceted. In reality, any single leader may possess overlapping styles, deploying them according to the circumstances at hand. It is not clear which style is more acceptable to which segments of the population, is perceived as better than others in the given circumstances, or best aligns with particular stages of organizational or personal development. The preference for particular leadership styles is unstable – that is, it changes over time and according to the situation.

Leadership Competencies

The knowledge and skills of leadership acquired through formal education and work experiences are referred to collectively as leaderhip competencies. In summarizing the opinions of leading Canadian CEOs, Benimadhu and Gilson (2001) highlighted leaders' competencies in business knowledge, innovative thinking, learning, effective communication, team orientation, coaching and mentoring, decisiveness, and capacity to inspire. A former CEO of Procter & Gamble, A.G. Lafley (2011), maintained that senior executives must possess a multitude of competencies: "capability and capacity builder," "visionary and strategic leadership," "productive relationships with internal and external stakeholders," "institution builder," and leadership in "transformational change." Goleman (1998, 82–91) designated "emotional intelligence" as the defining feature of leadership, which, for him, included self-awareness, self-regulation, motivation, empathy, and social skills.

Leadership Cultural Contributions

The fourth theme in leadership literature is leaders' cultural contributions. Corporate culture is the essence that sustains and in some cases transcends the entire organization. It is a primary reason why people continue to work in an organization. Because it is so important to employee retention and business growth, this chapter highlights it as a separate theme.

Sergiovanni and Corbally (1984, viii, 14), Sergiovanni (1984a, 17), and Sergiovanni (1984b, 105–14) highlighted what leaders do to create order, purpose, and meaning so as to bind people together – to weave together "various strands of symbolic and subtle aspects of organizational life." Because leaders are responsible for the life of organizations, their intuitive judgment (Schon 1984, 36–63) and transformative ability (Bennis 1984, 64–71) are of utmost importance. They resort to symbolism to brand the corporate culture (March 1984, 18–35) and to bind people together through "purposing" (Vaill 1984, 85–104). Collard and Normore (2009, vii–viii), Mills (2005), and Collard (2009, 3–22) viewed leaders as cultural agents who bring established values and interface them with other cultures in organizational decisions.

Cultural features – be they values, symbols, norms, or approaches – are often abstract, and defining them in concrete, measurable, and observable terms may be difficult. People who work in the organization may take these cultural features for granted, so it often takes new hires from outside to identify the cultural features of an organization.

Contemporary Mainstream Leadership Concepts

Sources

We can explore contemporary mainstream concepts of leadership by examining the language used in primary sources generated by companies, board directors, and senior executives. These can be speeches or public statements by CEOs or executives, verbal or written instructions by board directors to search firms, internal job descriptions, internal minutes from board or executive meetings, records of conversations or interviews, internal job postings, or external job advertisements. Or we can look at secondary sources such as research studies and publications on leadership. In this section, we will rely on a single primary source: external job advertisements for leadership positions published by companies in the *Globe and Mail*.

Job ads in newspapers were selected as the sole source for this study because information on what today's mainstream leaders look for in leadership candidates is seldom transparent and is typically difficult to obtain. The private sector uses a number of methods to recruit leaders. A survey of *Financial Post* (FP) 500 boards conducted by the Canadian Board Diversity Council (2018, 28–30) found that most boards utilized search firms to help them recruit board directors. However, job descriptions for leadership positions and information on leadership attributes for individual companies are guarded tightly –companies and search firms treat them as proprietary material. Access to this information is difficult. Another popular way that boards of directors recruit candidates for directorship is through word of mouth, including phone calls, emails, and social media, which often tap into the "directors' personal network," "shareholder referrals," and "alumni of director education programs." These methods seldom provide readily available written records on leadership attributes that researchers can scrutinize. Traditional media ads (such as in newspapers) are another way to recruit leaders. These often yield a wealth of information on leadership attributes that leaders are looking for.

Job Advertisements in the *Globe and Mail*

The author of this book examined external job advertisements for board directors and senior executives in the *Globe and Mail* – a national newspaper in Canada – and analysed the leadership attributes mentioned in those ads as indicators of contemporary mainstream concepts of leadership. There is no reason to believe that the contents of the job ads in the *Globe and Mail* are substantively different from those used by search firms or in informal recruitment methods. Search firms often complement their searches by turn-ing to printed or social media as well as their own internal databases of lead-ership candidates. Placing job ads in the *Globe and Mail* is yet another way to make vacant positions more public and transparent. What distinguishes the *Globe and Mail*'s job ads from internal job descriptions used by search firms is that the former are concise, public, readily available, and transparent, whereas the latter are detailed, proprietary, exclusionary, and opaque.

The following review analyses the content of these job ads in order to pro-vide a comprehensive and systematic account of what leadership attributes are most in demand. Such information is seldom available through interviews or observation. An added benefit of content analysis is that it enables us to quan-tify the frequency of word usage and thereby measure the popularity of certain leadership attributes. The review covered the entire year 2013.

During that year, in the *Globe and Mail*, there were 266 job postings for senior executive positions: 26 in the public sector, 193 in the broader public sector, and 47 in the private sector. The term "leadership" was mentioned in almost all executive postings (Siu 2016b). Given how many corporations there are in Canada, the number of job postings for senior executive positions in the *Globe* confirmed that it is not common practice for companies to advertise such positions in newspapers. Even so, the ads yielded insights as to which leadership attributes were most sought after. Among the job titles in these 47 job advertisements were chief executive officer, vice-president, and chief risk officer. There were only 12 job postings for board directors, of which 11 were in the broader public sector and only 1 in the private sector. The lack of job postings for private sector board directors precludes any meaningful analysis, so the focus of the present analysis will be on the senior executive positions.

The 47 ads for senior executive positions in the private sector covered a range of industries but were concentrated in educational services (29.79%) and manufacturing (19.15%). The rest were spread thinly among finance and insurance (8.51%), utilities (8.51%), transportation and warehousing (6.38%), construction (4.26%), professional, scientific, and technical services (4.26%), arts, entertainment, and recreation (4.25%), accommodation and food ser-vices (4.25%), health care and social assistance (4.25%), information (2.13%), mining (2.13%), and retail trade (2.13%).

Leadership Attributes

Patterns
The leadership attributes listed in these job advertisements focused largely on competencies rather than on personality traits, leadership styles, or cultural

Figure 3.2. Patterns of leadership attributes as portrayed in the *Globe and Mail*'s job advertisements

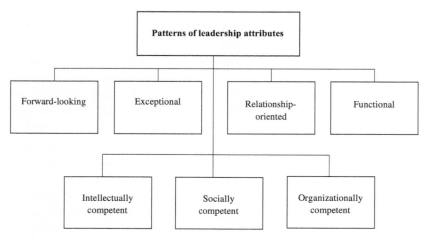

stewardship. They portrayed leaders as forward-looking ("proactive," "visionary"), exceptional ("dynamic," "exemplary"), relationship-oriented ("diplomatic," "people-oriented"), functional ("financial," "operational"), and rich in experience ("established," "proven"). They should have multifaceted competencies in the intellectual sphere ("analytical," "innovative"), the social sphere ("communication," "partnership"), and the organizational sphere ("change," "growth").

Popular Words

A large amount of space and a large number of words in the job ads in the *Globe* were devoted to preferred competencies. In all, 296 different leadership attributes appeared in the 266 job postings. The five most popular ones (as measured by frequency of appearance) were "strategic" (94 times), "communicative" (81), "relationship-oriented" (59), "strong" (55), and "collaborative" (55). Their high frequency suggested that these attributes were greatly desired by the current leaders. These five words can be categorized into two types: militaristic ("strategic," "strong"), and diplomatic ("communicative," "relationship-oriented," "collaborative"). The militaristic attributes were goal-focused, individualistic, and masculine; the diplomatic were people-oriented, collective, and feminine.

Note that the most popular attribute ("strategic") has a military connotation. It has long been associated with warfare and battle; more recently, it has

Figure 3.3. Popular words for leadership attributes in the *Globe and Mail*'s job advertisements

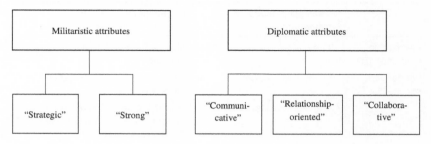

been associated with competition and conflict. This mix of militaristic and diplomatic attributes suggests that the leaders being sought today are ones who can both fight for business survival/growth and work with people. They are simultaneously tough combatants and smooth collaborators. These two attributes do not mix easily in one person. Because they are to a certain degree ambiguous, they are subject to personal preference and can be used to screen out candidates who are simply not "liked" by some leaders. However, these attributes can be put in more measurable terms without inherent biases often connected with attributes, which may make the selection more objective.

Education, Knowledge, Experience, and Reputation
Two other leadership attributes are more measurable and quantifiable: knowledge and experience. That is, leadership competency is a function of knowledge and work experience. Accordingly, the private sector looks for leaders who have "business acumen," "working knowledge," or "sound knowledge" in specific industries or fields and who are "informed" and "talented." Academic credentials may not be as important one might think. Of the forty-seven senior executive job postings, only nine clearly indicated the need for a bachelor's or master's degree and professional credentials. Long years of executive experience were more important. Words related to experience such as "accomplished," "experienced," and "extensive" were noted in job ads. Of the sample of forty-seven senior executive job ads, fourteen indicated clearly the number of years of executive experience required for the job: four postings mentioned five to ten years and ten mentioned ten or more years. Knowledge is a measurable attribute and can be operationalized in more concrete terms, whereas the requirement for long experience may work to the detriment of diverse individuals looking to enter leadership circles. It constitutes

Table 3.1. Contemporary mainstream concepts of leadership as a continuation of leadership characteristics, styles, competencies, and cultural contributions in literature

	Concepts of leadership in literature	Contemporary mainstream concepts of leadership
Leadership characteristics	"Great Man"	Modest form of "Great Man" attributes
Leadership styles	"Charismatic leader"	Militaristic attributes of leaders ("strategic," "strong")
	"Transformational leader"	Diplomatic attributes of leaders ("communicative," "relationship-oriented," "collaborative")
Leadership competencies	Leaders are to be competent in a broad range of knowledge, skills, and experiences related to their industries	"Functional" and "exceptional" competencies (in intellectual, social, and organizational domains); high educational level, deep knowledge, long history of rich executive experiences, and reputation
Leadership cultural contributions	Leaders are cultural agents with their values and symbolism, which are transformative for the organization	Descriptions of attributes such as "forward-looking," "visionary," "inspiration," "innovation," and "change" denote cultural contributions of leaders

a "Catch-22" for members of diverse groups, for they have not been given opportunities to lead and so have not accumulated years of experience. A requirement like this essentially erects an obstacle for them to be qualified even to apply for leadership positions.

Also important was the candidate's reputation in the industry, as reflected in words such as "credibility," "reputation," "respected," and "trusted" in the job ads. This leadership attribute is vague and inherently subject to interpretation. Clear indicators for these attributes could allow a more objective selection and appointment processes.

Comparison of Leadership Concepts

In sum, competency is front and centre in contemporary mainstream concepts of leadership. Leaders are expected to be exceptionally competent in working with ideas, people, and organizations. They must blend militaristic with diplomatic strengths. They need to be visionary, well-educated, knowledgeable, experienced, reputable, and multi-skilled. A comparison of the leadership concepts presented in the literature and those specifically mentioned in job ads in the *Globe and Mail* indicated that the concepts were interconnected.

Analysis of Leadership Concepts

Leadership Attributes Are More Than Just Competency

Contemporary mainstream concepts focusing on competency are linked with leadership characteristics, styles, and cultural contributions, although the last are not mentioned explicitly in job advertisements. In other words, the mention of specific competencies has implications for what some leaders look for in leadership candidates' characteristics, styles, and cultural contributions.

On leadership characteristics: The use of words such as "communicative," "relationship-oriented," and "collaborative" denotes leaders with a softer character. In addition, words like "strong" (read "decisive") and "strategic" (read "sound judgment") appeared frequently in job advertisements, implying that a desirable leader is both strong and likable.

On leadership styles: As with leadership characteristics, the contemporary mainstream concepts are not explicit about leadership styles. However, competency words such as "communication," "growth," "encouraging," "motivating," "relationship," "support," "team building," and "understanding" are often associated with a transformational leadership style – a style that seems to denote an interest in empowering people. Words such as "inspirational," "driven," "dynamic," "relentless," and "unassailable" may point to a charismatic leadership style. Suffice here to say that charismatic and transformational leadership styles emerged from the job ads in the *Globe and Mail*.

On cultural contributions: Job ads in the *Globe and Mail* did not explicitly require that candidates maintain or change the corporate culture, but emphasis on the need for particular competencies such as vision, innovation, inspiration, collaboration, partnership, and change may implicitly underscore the importance of leaders as cultural change agents.

It appears from these observations that while leaders may be focusing on candidates' level of competency, they are likely looking at candidates "as a package" – that is, at those with the right mix of characteristics, styles, and cultural contributions.

Leadership Concepts Are Abstract and Subjective

Concepts of leadership are abstract and subjective in the leadership literature and contemporary job advertisements. This creates space for current leaders to exercise their discretion and their personal leanings when determining which people are qualified for leadership positions. Current leaders are in a position to prioritize a broad range of intellectual, social, and organizational competencies, and the subjectivity and abstractness of the competency terms used only increase the latitude available to them when making decisions.

In the leadership literature, most of the words used to describe personal characteristics, styles, competencies, and cultural contributions are hard to measure. Educational credentials and years of executive experience are more concrete measurements in job ads. These factors are proxies for leadership competencies in quantitative terms. But it is not clear how important these factors are when leadership candidates are being assessed. We will discuss this later in the context of the backgrounds of diverse groups with regard to education, experience, and reputation.

Competencies Are Acquired, Not Innate Attributes

Leadership characteristics and styles are often viewed as innate and authentic. By contrast, leadership competencies denote acquired knowledge and learned behaviour. Such distinctions imply that leaders are not born that way. Theoretically, anyone could be trained to be a leader.

According to this concept of leadership competency, individuals can acquire competencies and organizations can "grow" potential leaders. Competency is a function of accumulated working knowledge and a long history of executive experience. This means that anyone who aspires to be a leader needs coaches, mentors, and sponsors to provide regular advice, encouragement, and supports as well as opportunities to engage in assignments and developmental education and to be promoted to positions that are building blocks to becoming a leader. These essential ingredients for developing leadership are contingent on many psychological, organizational, and cultural factors, which will be examined in the remaining parts of this book.

Diverse Groups' Concepts of Leadership

Contemporary mainstream concepts of leadership are the reference points for leaders to identify candidates' attributes and the extent to which they possess them. But do diverse groups hold the same leadership concepts as current leaders? The short answer is "not exactly." Which raises this question: How are their concepts different from or similar to those of the contemporary mainstream?

A discussion of diversity runs the risk of ascribing the same attributes to all members of a diverse group. In much the same way, a discussion of mainstream attributes may be construed as relating solely to those of white, non-Indigenous, able-bodied men. These two perceptions incorrectly assume the homogeneity of individual members in diverse groups and non-diverse groups, respectively. In fact, there are variations among individual diverse group members, just as there are variations among white, non-Indigenous, able-bodied men. These variations may relate to age, ethnic origin, marital status, education level, and economic status, among many other variables. Variation in social identities is part of the reality of any group. So it is important to point out that when, in this book, certain attributes are mentioned as related to a group, there is no intention to stereotype that group. It is merely to point out a tendency for that group to exhibit such attributes collectively rather than individually. This tendency may or may not have statistical meaning. There are always individual variations, notwithstanding the collective findings or statistical data.

Indigenous Peoples

Indigenous peoples define leadership differently than non-Indigenous peoples (Grahn, Swenson, and O'Leary 2001; Foley 2010). Non-Indigenous peoples have a tendency to view leadership as an individualistic matter, while Indigenous peoples see it as collective or communal (Sveiby 2011). The essence of Indigenous leadership is a close relationship between leaders and community, and leaders have communal responsibilities (Metoyer 2010). This communal nature of leadership is confirmed in McLeod's (2002) study of American Indigenous leadership.

Indigenous peoples see a leader as merely one among many people working together as equals. This is analogous to the people of a community holding a fishing net. When people hold a fishing net communally, they are interconnected. "Sometimes one person pulls harder than another. Sometimes a person pulls for another. Leadership is like that. Leadership moves around the circle." It follows that everyone in the circle is a leader at certain points in time (Wakshul 1997). Leaders adopt a holistic approach in connecting with others. Thus, Indigenous leaders reject the notion of top-down leadership (often practised by non-Indigenous peoples), for it is at odds with traditional Indigenous values and the Indigenous circular communal approach (Coyhis 1995; McLure and Stanco 1996; McLeod 2002). According to Thompson (2008), Indigenous female leaders in Nunavut exhibit participatory and communal styles (sharing responsibilities with other people equally) and are respectful and cooperative.

All of this illustrates how Indigenous peoples shift leadership roles among themselves as circumstances dictate, leading and supporting one another at different times. Leadership is a rotationally shared responsibility, and leaders lead and follow at the same time. This is very different from the non-Indigenous approach, in which leadership hinges on one individual. The Indigenous concept therefore requires ongoing learning and skills development among all people, to ensure successful leadership (McLeod 2002).

In addition, Indigenous peoples' image of a leader is that of a selfless person devoted to caring for others. In contrast to mainstream concepts of leadership, Indigenous leadership is not authoritarian or authoritative in character – rather, its style is caregiving and consultative (Miller 1978). A leader is an enabler who facilitates others to take action, who consults with people, and who participates in community life.

Indigenous leadership, with its focus on collective, communal, holistic, rotational, and egalitarian approaches, is different from contemporary mainstream leadership. Because the latter focuses largely on vision, experience, and individual achievement in specific functional areas, Indigenous peoples may not score well in that milieu. But when *Indigenous* concepts of leadership are used to assess the leadership capabilities of Indigenous peoples, they are likely to score higher. This divergence in conceptual frameworks is one overarching reason why Indigenous peoples are seldom viewed as leaders or potential leaders – their perspectives on leadership are too different from the contemporary mainstream.

There are some similarities in leadership concepts between Indigenous peoples and the contemporary mainstream. Both include "people-orientation," that is, working with other people is a priority for both. That said, Indigenous peoples focus on the community, white people more on individuals. Some Indigenous concepts of leadership align somewhat with mainstream ones: "collaboration," "teamwork," "consultation," "participation," "communication," "partnership." These common grounds should enable the two to share space in the leadership circle. However, often they do not.

Persons with Disabilities

The leadership perspectives of persons with disabilities are much harder to determine because there have been few studies in this area. These persons value leaders who are inclusive, collaborative, caring, compassionate, and collective (McGee 2003; Foster-Fishman et al. 2007; Tremblay 2011; Bixby 2008). They also value leaders who empower their followers (which is a distinctive attribute of "transformational leadership") (Pointer 2001), but they also accept leaders who adhere to formal policies and procedures (a distinctive attribute of "transactional leadership") (Hill 2013). After studying deaf female leaders in higher education and not-for-profit organizations, Larew (2011) noted that they consider team leadership and strategic leadership. Also, they are resilient and have a strong sense of self-efficacy (Ewing 2002; Shuey and Jovic 2013; Torres 2002; Taub, Fanflik, and McLorg 2003).

These findings suggest that persons with disabilities lean strongly toward a people-orientation. This means that their notions of leadership are consistent with a contemporary mainstream concept. But in general, people-orientation is seen as only a "nice to have" attribute, not as a core requirement for leadership. The general view is that this trait on its own is not enough to make a leader (Burke 2010a, 2010b; Dennis 2012; Fondas 2010).

The traits of being visionary, strategic, and competent in working with ideas, people, and organizations have not surfaced in leadership studies on persons with disabilities. "Transformational leadership" – the leadership style respected by persons with disabilities – is gaining ascendence in the mainstream but does not yet occupy an important place in contemporary mainstream concepts.

Overall, the perspectives of persons with disabilities do not align well with contemporary mainstream views about leadership. If today's mainstream leaders were to give more weight to leadership concepts favoured by persons with disabilities, there might be a greater chance for them to join leadership circles.

Racialized Minorities

Race, ethnicity, and culture all play an important role in leadership development (Ospina and Foldy 2009; Ford 2010; Flores 2012). Leadership studies show that racialized minorities and whites share some concepts of leadership, others not as much. Racialized minorities are not a monolithic group, and Asian, black, and Latino leaders all have different attributes. Because Canadian studies in this field are limited, this book will use findings from American research to illustrate the leadership attributes of racialized minority leaders. Two themes emerge: people orientation, and transformational style.

People orientation: There is heavy emphasis on people orientation among Asian-American managers (Ahn 2009); among Asian-American female leaders specifically, there is emphasis on relationship building, intercultural efficacy, and respect for equity (Almandrez 2010; Somer 2008; Ramsundar 2006; Benham 1997). After reviewing 646 studies from peer-reviewed publications on leadership approaches, King and Zhang (2010, 1–21) noted that Chinese leaders strongly emphasize relationships. African-American female leaders are also people-oriented (Picou-Broadnax 2010). They are known for their perseverance, inclusiveness, and transformational leadership style (Stewart 2010; Scales 2011; Bright 2010; Scinto 2006). Latinos in the United States view compassion and community orientation as leadership attributes (Ramirez 2005–6; Sullivan 2006; Flores 2012, 217). While people-orientation is integral to contemporary mainstream concepts of leadership, the emphasis is on being forward-looking, exceptional, functional, and experienced. Intersectionality of gender and race further confirms its importance in shaping leaders' concepts of leadership (Pollard 1997; Dujon 2010; Brinson 2007; Roby 1998; Davies 2011; Littrell and Nkomo 2005; McAdams 1991).

Transformational style: Coleman (2010) noted that East Asian American executives in the private sector have transformational styles with competency in innovation, communication, mentoring, and guidance and that they focus strongly on improving employees. Similarly, African-American female leaders exhibited the transformational leadership style (Picou-Broadnax 2010; Ramsundar 2006). They placed their priority on consensus building, empowerment, and the nurturing of subordinates (Stewart 2010; Scales 2011; Bright 2010; Scinto 2006). Empirical studies, such as Biggles (2007), confirmed the transformational attributes of racialized minorities.

These two leadership concepts of diverse groups align with a certain segment of contemporary mainstream concepts (collaboration, people-orientation, diplomacy). Missing from the concepts embraced by diverse groups are militaristic ones ("strategic," "strong"), which some current leaders look for in leadership candidates.

Women

Much has been written about female leadership. Three key patterns have emerged from these publications: female leaders are strongly people-oriented; they embrace a combined transformational and transactional style; and they are strongly committed to organizational change.

People orientation: Female leaders follow a leadership model different from that of men. They exhibit people-oriented traits, focus on teamwork and consensus building, and maintain an effective work/family balance (Cheung and Halpern 2010). Also, they are noted for their interpersonal and intercultural skills, and they handle emotions and relationships differently than men (Boon 2003). A US study of women in middle and upper management found that female leaders have a unique humanizing style, especially in interpersonal relations (Edlund 1992). This focus on human relationships was also noted in a study by Zulu (2011) on female heads of academic departments of universities in South Africa and the United Kingdom. Zulu found that they are characterized by strong communication and interpersonal skills, servant leadership, and participatory and collaborative leadership.

Combined transformational and transactional styles: Another hallmark of female leaders is that they mix transformational with transactional leadership, as evidenced in Belasen's (2012) study of female leaders in corporate America, and also in studies by Scott and Brown (2006) and McDaniel (2007) of female police leaders in the United States. The same leadership styles are noted in the United Kingdom (Dodd 2012).

Change agents: Female leaders are more likely to be "agents of change," for they recognize the patriarchal nature of traditional leadership and are more tuned into discrimination at work (Archard 2013; Estler 1975; Griffiths 2012). In this context, female leaders in Canadian and Australian university faculties of education were found to exhibit a strong commitment to "making a difference" (Wyn, Acker, and Richards 2000). A study by Stainback and Kwon (2012) of South Korean organizations found that female leaders acted as "agents of change" in their organizations.

In terms of contemporary mainstream concepts of leadership, on the surface women seem strong on people-orientation and weaker on other attributes valued by current leaders. Contemporary mainstream concepts are often interpreted in a skewed manner by current leaders, who unconsciously ignore or overlook attributes of women that could properly be included among these concepts. In chapter 4, we will examine perceptions and attitudes and how the lenses worn by some current leaders may filter out some valuable attributes of women is such a way as to render them unworthy of leadership. The alignment of women's concepts with those of the contemporary mainstream is not perfect. While some features possessed by women are rearing their heads more and more strongly in mainstream concepts of leadership, they remain abstract notions (Brady and McLean 2002, 6). For some conservative leaders, being "agents of change," especially in the area of gender, may not be a desirable feature: they are concerned about a "women's agenda" being promoted at the executive or board director level (Davidson and Cooper 1992, 93). Mainstream leaders of business organizations often view a people-orientation, inherent in the transformational leadership style, as less directional, instrumental, and commanding (Parker 2005, 69–71). In sum, it appears that, with the exception of a people-orientation, current leaders view some attributes of female leadership as secondary in importance or even as problematic.

Discussion

There is a modest distinction between contemporary mainstream leadership concepts and those of diverse groups. By "modest distinction" I mean that the demarcation of contemporary mainstream concepts and those of diverse groups is not clear-cut, but that some differences are noted, especially when those of Indigenous peoples are compared. The other three diverse groups' concepts shared some attributes with those of the contemporary mainstream (such as people-orientation and social competencies), but the diverse groups' concepts were not broad or balanced enough to meet all of the attributes exhibited in contemporary mainstream concepts. For example, Indigenous peoples have a collective and community-based approach to leading, whereas persons with disabilities, racialized minorities, and women opt for more individualistic approaches, similar to those of the contemporary mainstream.

Other research findings suggest that leaders from diverse backgrounds are strong in people-orientation and relationship-building and have a transformational style. Diverse groups value these attributes in a leader. Contemporary mainstream concepts include these attributes but also emphasize militaristic ones. They also stress intellectual, social, and organizational competencies that are usually associated with deep knowledge, high education, rich executive experience, and reputation in the industry.

Overall, there are some discrepancies and some overlaps among these concepts of leadership. Hence the distinctions among them are not as overwhelming as might be expected. The discrepancies may largely be due to the frame of mind of some current leaders, who prefer – often unconsciously – to utilize an exclusionary lens when determining how qualified leadership candidates are. As a result, candidates from diverse group backgrounds may find themselves at a disadvantage.

Diverse groups' concepts of leadership value a "softer" people-orientation and its related transformational styles and do not display or highlight the "stronger" strategic and combative attributes. The literature seems to suggest that the intellectual and organizational competencies of diverse groups are largely unnoticed and ignored by current leaders, or they come to light only when a more inclusive lens or more precise measuring instruments are used. As a result, the competencies of diverse groups are perceived as occurring narrowly in the social sphere, while contemporary mainstream concepts of leadership define competencies in a broader and more balanced way.

In themselves, the theoretical differences between contemporary mainstream concepts of leadership and those of diverse groups are not enough to exclude diverse groups from rising to leadership positions. Additional psychological factors (such as perceptions of and attitudes toward diverse groups), as well as organizational and cultural factors (such as recruitment, selection, and succession management), may place diverse groups at a disadvantage in competition for leadership positions. The remaining chapters will discuss the interplay of these factors and how they affect the life chances of diverse groups.

Best Options and Practices

Options for Change

Review of Current Corporate Concepts of Leadership

As this chapter has noted, there are elements in contemporary mainstream concepts of leadership that do not align with diverse groups' concepts of leadership. The latter, which focus largely on people relationships, are narrower, segmented versions of contemporary mainstream ones. As long as contemporary mainstream concepts are used to define what a leader should be, diverse groups will find it difficult to become leaders. If companies that do not have diversity parity on their boards of directors or in their executive teams decide to find out why, they might begin by reviewing of how "leadership" in their organizations is defined and whether barriers built into these concepts hinder appointments of people from diverse groups. In the course of this review, organizations may find that contemporary mainstream concepts are too narrow, skewed, or restrictive and need to be made more inclusive.

Steps for Conceptual Review and Re-imagination of Leadership

A review might begin with a discussion among leaders about the desirable attributes of a leader in their organization. This discussion might be facilitated by an expert in diversity and inclusiveness. The discussion will help leaders identify how they view leadership, whether there are biases in their concepts of leadership, whether these concepts are in tune with the changing world, and whether they are fluid enough to incorporate other elements. Leaders might determine that their identification and selection criteria are screening out diverse groups or that current leadership attributes are hindering their search for appropriate talents.

A closer examination of job descriptions and job advertisements with the assistance of an expert could help identify hidden biases in these documents. The discussion might dwell on indicators that leaders have been using to identify potential candidates. For example, how can the concept of "strategic leadership" be operationalized in a way that leaders can clearly identify persons who have such a competency?

Second, if search firms are contacted, leaders might wish to closely review their track records to ascertain whether they are using contemporary mainstream concepts of leadership without being aware of their biases. For example, how can these firms operationalize "strategic leadership" and translate it into identification and selection criteria in such a way that diverse groups

Figure 3.4. Steps in reviewing the concepts and operationalization of leadership

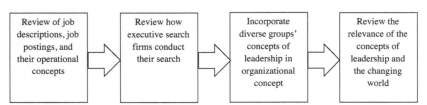

| Review of job descriptions, job postings, and their operational concepts | Review how executive search firms conduct their search | Incorporate diverse groups' concepts of leadership in organizational concept | Review the relevance of the concepts of leadership and the changing world |

are not excluded? It is also important to discover whether these search firms utilize mechanisms to ensure they do not rely solely on traditional screening criteria, which may not be aligned with the changing labour force.

Third, diverse groups have their own ideas about the characteristics, styles, competencies, and cultural contributions of ideal leaders, so it might be innovative to examine those concepts to see whether any of their leadership attributes could be incorporated into job descriptions, job ads, and identification and selection criteria and indicators. Some diverse groups' concepts of leadership are not all that different from contemporary mainstream ones and could be used either to supplement or to replace the mainstream ones. This would enlarge the scope of the search and would be more likely to result in diverse group members being included on short lists of potential candidates.

Fourth, this review of leadership concepts would best be done in association with a review of the changing world – changing economic landscapes, shifting demographic patterns, new technological trends, and emerging industrial trends. Ultimately, a leader is effective in leading only to the extent that his or her leadership aligns with the changing world and the new international order. Leadership concepts are relevant only to the extent that they reflect what is going on in the world and what is expected to emerge in the future. A conventional routine of finding a replacement for previous or current leaders will not do the job.

Practices for Change

Top companies in leadership often have the above "rethinking" process built into their leadership search and selection practices. With its annual survey of global companies (the "Best Companies for Leadership" survey), the Hay Group (2014) identifies the top twenty companies at identifying and developing potential leaders. The top companies, such as Procter & Gamble, General Electric, Coca-Cola, IBM, and Uniliver, assessed their external and internal changing environments and identified new attributes that new leaders would need for the next ten to fifteen years. Through this exercise, they identified new attributes and directions for leadership development. Attributes for these new directions could be in the realms of customer services, global expertise, complexity management, innovation, and collaboration.

These top twenty companies took a more structured approach than others in developing leaders and managing successions. These assessments produced good results in leadership recruitment and selection. In 2014, half of the top twenty companies had special leadership development programs for women, compared to 13% of all other companies. Also, 40% of the top twenty companies had programs aimed at employees with diverse backgrounds, compared to only 11% of all other companies. When assessment of leadership attributes in the context of social and organizational changes is associated with the opening up of leadership opportunities for diverse groups, it can produce remarkable results.

Conclusion

The concept of leadership has many meanings. As the leadership literature suggests, there are many ways to view leadership, including its characteristics, styles, competencies, and cultural contributions. There is a broad range of leadership attributes in each of these categories. No single leader has all of the attributes; each has a unique configuration of attributes. Furthermore, there is no consensus on universal leadership attributes that would fit all circumstances and meet everyone's expectations. The reality is that leaders are as good as the way their followers define them in their own specific circumstances. When circumstances change, so should the attributes of leadership.

Given that diverse groups in Western societies have had little opportunity to become leaders, the attributes that have become entrenched in leadership identification and selection are in line with the preferences of white, able-bodied, non-Indigenous men – that is, men who have always dominated leadership positions. Character traits such as determination, decisiveness, vision, energy, toughness, inspiration, and compassion; styles such as authenticity, charisma, and narcissism; competencies such as strategic thinking, innovation, communication, and relationship-building; and cultural contributions such as meaning, purpose, and symbolism, which bind people together, are generally associated with the term *leadership*. These attributes may even be seen as the "gold standard" of leadership.

One indication that these attributes are accepted as the essence of leadership may be found in the executive job advertisements in the *Globe and Mail*. These ads may provide only a small window through which to view leadership, but they are relevant in Canada, as some senior executive positions in the private sector are posted there. In those ads, leadership competency words such as *strategic, visionary*, and *innovative* are popular ones to describe leaders. These words are usually associated with white, able-bodied, non-Indigenous men, yet these men do not necessarily monopolize them.

In the leadership literature and in the job ads that were examined in this chapter, attributes such as *relationship, team-building, transformational, collaboration, consultative, support*, and *emotional intelligence* were more in line with the concepts of leadership as expounded by diverse groups. These attributes are gaining ascendency in Western societies (as indicated in the leadership literature as well as in the job ads) and should favour diverse groups in their quest for leadership. But ascendency is not linear: these attributes are competing for dominance and are not as valued as the more common militaristic attributes of leadership (such as *visionary* and *strategic*).

Lack of alignment in the concepts of leadership between contemporary mainstream leaders and diverse groups illustrates that when contemporary mainstream concepts of leadership are used to identify and select top candidates, the misalignment works against diverse group members. The mindset shaped by contemporary mainstream concepts prevents current leaders from seeing diverse group members as top-quality candidates for a variety of reasons, including the conceptual partial alignment of "leadership," as well as issues related to social perceptions and attitudes (see chapter 4).

While some companies have begun to rethink or reimagine the concepts of leadership, the process remains slow and sporadic. A major reason for this slow change is the persistent dominance of the white, able-bodied, non-Indigenous men in leadership, because they are the key decision-makers in corporations. The most important implication of this chapter is that these men's overall mindset is too exclusionary and that a change in it to a more inclusive mode is necessary and desirable. This will require current leaders to see the benefits of reimagining what new leadership would look like as well as the downsides of not keeping up with the changing world.

So far, we have examined the larger context of economic, demographic, and labour force changes and how these changes affect the labour force. This in turn highlighted the value of diversity in leadership (chapter 1). We have also examined the leadership echelon in the private sector and noted the homogeneity in leadership and the magnitude of diversity gaps (chapter 2). In this chapter, we began to find answers to the problem of homogeneity in leadership by drilling deeper into the concepts of leadership.

The discrepancy between contemporary mainstream concepts of leadership and those of diverse groups may shed more light on the current homogenous leadership pattern (chapter 3). In the next chapter, we look deeper into the psychological components (perceptions and attitudes) of how diverse groups are viewed.

chapter four

Perceptions and Attitudes

This chapter argues that the perceptions and attitudes of current leaders may be acting as "psychological filters" when they identify and select leaders. These filters determine how they view, assess, categorize, rank, and feel about diverse groups' leadership characteristics, styles, competencies, and cultural contributions. Perceptions and attitudes are subjective and often deeply embedded in decision-making processes and in corporate culture more generally. In the corporate world, they are often referred to as "unconscious biases," because those who have them are often unaware of it. These views and feelings may limit the work performance and social interactions of diverse groups and their entry to leadership positions.

Perceptions and attitudes have been studied extensively, but corporate leadership and diversity is not often the focus of such studies, and when it is, women are the main focus. Also, these studies typically examine media coverage and public opinion to illustrate stereotypes of and prejudices toward diverse groups. After all, the corporate world is part of the larger society.

This chapter outlines negative perceptions (i.e., stereotypes) and negative attitudes (i.e., prejudices) in order to show that they are largely at odds with contemporary mainstream concepts of leadership. When current leaders hold these negative images of and feelings about diverse groups, there is a strong chance that diverse groups will not be viewed as leadership material. Research studies have found that this negativity persists over time. The term "unconscious biases" is often used in the corporate world to denote both stereotypes and prejudices without pointing out that these terms mean two different things: stereotypes are *images* of diverse groups, and prejudices are *feelings* toward them. This cognitive and emotional distinction wil be valuable as we try to understand what some leaders see in and feel about diverse groups, so that we can create solutions for addressing bias in hiring and promotion.

In discussions of negative perceptions and attitudes, it is easy to assume that all members of non-diverse groups (white, non-Indigenous, able-bodied males) possess them. But some of these people do *not* have these views and feelings. Research studies on stereotypes and prejudices present a *pattern* of views and feelings of people; these studies do not deny that some individuals think and feel otherwise. This pattern reflects a social phenomenon, not individuals' behaviour. When we live in a social context in which prejudices and negative stereotypes are engrained, they tend to become embedded in our mindsets and may influence our behaviour.

Perceptions

Stereotyping is a form of cognitive simplification that helps people organize their thinking and manage information. When people simplify what they see and start grouping people on the basis of visual differences such as gender, race, or ability, they tend to gloss over unique individual features and generalize particular attributes on the basis of those differences. Such simplification is often the source prejudices that disadvantage individuals on the basis of their group affiliation rather than on their actual performance (Gardenswartz and Rowe 1998, 80). Stereotypes tend to demarcate the boundaries of diverse groups, so that non-diverse people constitute an "in-group" and diverse people form "out-groups." In-group members view themselves as belonging to the same group, and those who are excluded are viewed as members of an out-group (Gibbins and Ponting 1986; Langford and Ponting 1992).

How do non-diverse people perceive diverse people? Answering this question will bring us closer to understanding why diverse groups are relatively absent in leadership positions.

Indigenous Peoples

Werhun and Penner (2010, 899–900) summarized research findings on how Indigenous peoples are perceived: "lazy," "uneducated," "primitive," "ignorant," "stupid," "undependable," "aggressive," "dishonest," "disloyal," dirty," "poor." These adjectives emerge from public opinion and have been associated with crime, suicide, alcoholism, poverty, and social threats (Harding 2006, 205–6). Their sources include parents, peers, schools, and the mass media.

These negative perceptions place Indigenous peoples at a disadvantage when it comes to employment by undermining their performance as well as their self-confidence. The result is that in a corporate environment in which productivity, performance, reliability, and results-orientation are given high

Figure 4.1. Impacts of negative perception of Indigenous peoples

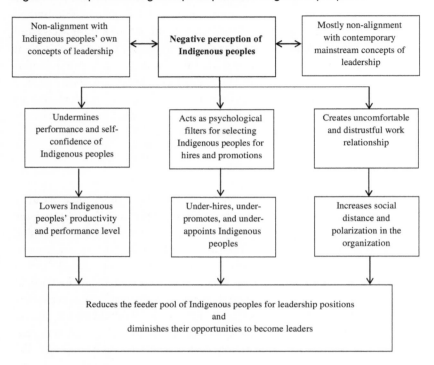

priority, Indigenous peoples are viewed as unreliable, sloppy at their jobs, and often absent from or late for work. Negative stereotypes of Indigenous peoples put others on guard, create an uncomfortable and distrustful work relationship, and foster social avoidance and social distance in the workplace. This can foster a polarized in-group/out-group environment in the workplace. These views may also act as psychological filters when Indigenous peoples are being selected for hiring, promotion, or appointment to a board. As a result, Indigenous peoples may be underhired, underpromoted, or underappointed, making it unlikely they will ever rise to leadership positions. Indeed, these negative perceptions may discourage Indigenous peoples from even applying for jobs, and if hired, they may leave those jobs sooner than other employees.

These stereotypes do not correspond with Indigenous peoples' own concepts of leadership. Their visions of leadership are holistic, collective, egalitarian, community-oriented, people-oriented, partnership-oriented, collaborative, consultative, participatory, and communicative.

As well, these negative stereotypes do not align with contemporary mainstream concepts of leadership, whether they refer to personal characteristics, styles, competence, or cultural contributions. The negative stereotypes held against Indigenous peoples do not at all align with mainstream leadership competencies as they relate to ideas ("strategic," "visionary"), people ("collaboration," "partnership"), or organization ("directorship," "planner"). The competencies generally viewed as required for executive positions are largely militaristic (as in "strategic") and diplomatic (as in "collaborative"), and Indigenous peoples are largely stereotyped as lacking these and as incompetent workers and leaders.

As a result of negative stereotyping, Indigenous peoples are largely viewed as lacking those leadership characteristics so often encountered in the literature on leadership ("endurance," "determination," "decisiveness"). Their communal, rotational, participatory, and circular styles of leadership are at odds with the hierarchical, individualistic, and directive styles of mainstream leadership. Indigenous peoples are known for their cultural sensitivity and are able to foster intercultural connections among people, but current leaders may not view such contributions as essential to the corporate culture.

In essence, there is no compatibility between mainstream concepts of leadership and the stereotypes of Indigenous peoples. According to the mainstream concepts, the negative stereotypes of Indigenous peoples are profoundly different from what leaders should be like. Clearly, this poses a barrier for Indigenous peoples as they look for employment in the first place, then seek promotion, acceptance in social networks, and appointments to senior executive positions or directorships (Canada 2016a; Canadian Board Diversity Council 2016).

Persons with Disabilities

Persons with disabilities face overwhelming negativism in public perceptions, including in media portrayals. They are viewed as innately incapable or as less capable than others, which places in doubt both their relationships with customers and colleagues and the quality of their work. Disabilities are often associated with dependence, unreliability, and helplessness (Bogdan and Biklen 2013, 1–5; Shier, Graham, and Jones 2008, 68). Some persons with disabilities are viewed as "erratic" or "dangerous and bizarre." Media images of them committing violent acts, and the association of criminality with some forms of disability (such as "mentally ill") may lead some employers to view them as a workplace safety risk (Bogdan and Biklen 2013, 7–9). Unless disabilities are invisible or hard to detect, there is a tendency for negative perceptions to make disabled people hard to employ or promote.

These negative stereotypes undermine the confidence of persons with disabilities. Some current leaders unconsciously interpret their work behaviours

Figure 4.2. Impacts of negative perception of persons with disabilities

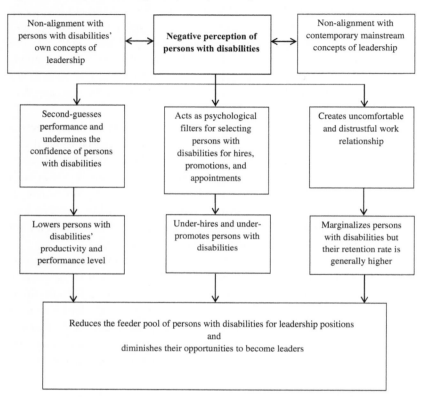

(including how they answer interview questions during hiring and promotion processes) and second-guess their performance, thus fostering uncomfortable workplace relationships (in-group versus out-group) among employees. In this way, stereotypes act as psychological filters and encourage bias when assessing performance and developing relationships.

A joint Ryerson University–Royal Bank of Canada study of employees with disabilities found that the most critical employment barrier for them is that managers and co-workers simply do not know how to work with them. Church and colleagues (2007) found that persons with disabilities spent most of their time trying to "look normal" and hide their disabilities. They became marginalized and less productive, and some took their work home to complete lest management and colleagues view them as slow or unreliable.

The negativity faced by persons with disabilities clashes with their own concepts of leadership. As noted in chapter 3, persons with disabilities see ideal leaders as inclusive, compassionate, empowering, collaborative, and people-oriented. Overall, leaders with disabilities have these same attributes. They are usually transformational leaders, with some inclined to be transactional. But this is not how others perceive them. There is a perception gap between how persons with disabilities see themselves and visualize leadership and how the public does.

Mainstream concepts of leadership are far from current stereotypes of persons with disabilities. Persons with disabilities are viewed as incapable, dependent, helpless, risky, and criminal; none of this aligns with the demand for high leadership competency in idea formation ("creative," "analytical"), in relationships ("communicative," "inspirational"), and in organization ("change agent"). The characteristics that current leaders look for in leadership candidates are "dynamic," "effective," "relentless"; yet persons with disabilities are often viewed as incompetent, weak, unpredictable, and unreliable. Some of these views carry stigma, which affects their integration into the workplace, never mind leadership circles (Barg et al. 2010; Garcia, Barrette, and Laroche 1999).

Regarding leadership styles, persons with disabilities may focus on collaboration, growth-orientation, empowerment, and care (aligning with a transformational leadership style), but the mainstream concepts are more inclined to styles such as inspiring, rational, goal-focused, and hierarchical (aligning with a "transactional" or "charismatic" style). Because their inclination is to empower, motivate, and consult employees (attributes of a transformational leader), persons with disabilities can glue their organizations together when given a chance to be leaders. However, the stereotype so often held of them may work against this positive view. Cultural contributions are often associated with strong, influential, and persuasive leaders, and those descriptors are not associated with persons with disabilities.

In sum, the stereotypes of persons with disabilities have made some current leaders feel uneasy about hiring/promoting them or appointing them to leadership positions (Canada, 2016c; Canadian Board Diversity Council, 2016). The negativity expressed by these stereotypes poses a real barrier for persons with disabilities. These stereotypes are very different from what leaders should look like according to the contemporary mainstream concepts of leadership. Unless some current leaders become more self-reflective and prepared to challenge these stereotypical views, we will not see broad representation of persons with disabilities in leadership positions.

Racialized Minorities

The stereotypes of racialized minorities vary. For Asians, those stereotypes tend to focus on characteristics that are perceived as incompatible with leadership, but these stereotypes also include positive ones related to their professional or technical competencies, which are not necessarily management skills. For blacks, the stereotypes focus on their characteristics and their lack of competence. This negativity fosters a tense and distrustful "in-group versus out-group" environment, which marginalizes and undermines them, creates social distance, and acts as a psychological filter in hiring and promotion.

Racialized minorities have been perceived as unfit for management. Powell's study on executives' perceptions in the United States (1969, 209–25) noted that when executives compare racialized minorities with their white counterparts, they are seen as inferior in managerial capability. These negative perceptions have persisted since the 1960s. Racialized minorities still have problems meeting the expectations of executives in terms of leadership attributes (Chung-Herrera and Lankau 2005). Most Canadians view racialized minorities as less competent than whites (Li 2008, 21–33), and media portrayals of them tend to marginalize and disparage them (Henry and Tator 2002).

Asians are often viewed as competent but untrustworthy (Kulik and Bainbridge 2006, 34, 45); as meek, modest, and "good in math" or "good with computers" (Askarinam 2016); as hardworking, custodial, authoritarian, inscrutable, and keeping to themselves (Wong, Horn, and Chen 2013); as "relatively competent, cold, and non-dominant" (Berdahl and Min 2012, 141–52); as obedient, unassertive, cooperative, humble; or as not good at taking charge. East Asians who deviate from these stereotypes tend to find themselves ostracized, resisted, or harassed by colleagues, for they are not conforming to expectations.

Blacks are perceived as too direct in their communication style or as having a poor work ethic (Kochman 1981). To counter this stereotype, some black professionals work longer hours. This may lead other employees to see them as lacking in intellectual capabilities (Wingfield 2015). "Aggressiveness" is negatively associated with black people, who have been stereotyped as confrontational, pushy, athletic, direct, and abrasive (Dixon and Rosenbaum 2004; Mayovich 1972).

Stereotypes of racialized minorities seem to be based on their perceived competence and personalities. These negative stereotypes are at odds with their own concepts of leadership. As noted in chapter 3, Asians view leadership as transformational and situational, people-oriented, and intercultural. Blacks see leadership as transformational (consensus-building, empowering, networking), people-oriented, and inclusive. They see themselves as having these leadership attributes.

These stereotypes of racialized minorities are incompatible with most leadership attributes, according to contemporary mainstream concepts and the leadership literature. For example, Flores (1981, 6–8, 16) listed endurance, determination, integrity, and decisiveness as key ingredients for leadership. Hartman (1999, 122, 127, 133) defined leaders as those who have vision, energy, insight, tenacity, and stamina. The stereotypes of racialized minorities as such that they are not seen as leadership material.

The stereotypical perceptions of racialized minorities fit poorly with many styles in the leadership literature, except for the "transformational," "empowering," and "servant" styles. These attributes align well with the nurturing, caring, enabling, motivating, and people-oriented competencies attributed to racialized minorities. However, it is not clear whether mainstream leaders view these "transformational" attributes as a priority in leadership selection. Furthermore, other negative stereotypes of racialized minorities may undermine leaders' confidence in them as potential leaders.

In addition, leaders expect leadership candidates to have exceptional personal competencies ("dynamic," "passionate") and to be forward-looking ("visionary," "proactive") and relationship-oriented ("diplomatic"). These expectations are in contrast with the stereotypical views and media portrayals of racialized minorities. A review of the most common descriptors in the *Globe and Mail*'s senior executive job advertisements – "strategic," "communication," "visionary," "lead," "management," "innovative," "relationship" – found that the stereotypes of racialized minorities do not include these competencies, the exception being "relationship-oriented." In contemporary leadership literature, there is a push for greater focus on relationship-building, as found in fashionable terms such as "transformational leadership," "relationship marketing," "employee engagement," and "customer relations." However, in general observations about how corporations function, relationship competency, while high on paper, remains low as a priority when resources are allocated (as witnessed in training and development), as well as weak in practice (evidenced by the relative absence of measurement indicators or criteria in performance management). It is unlikely that the attribute "people-orientation" noted among racialized minorities is given much weight.

On the surface, contemporary mainstream competencies seem to be value-neutral, but people tend to attach stereotypical images to them. While competency in relationships is included among the leadership concepts valued by racialized minorities, stereotypical views on this competency vary. Some

Figure 4.3. Impacts of negative perception of racialized minorities

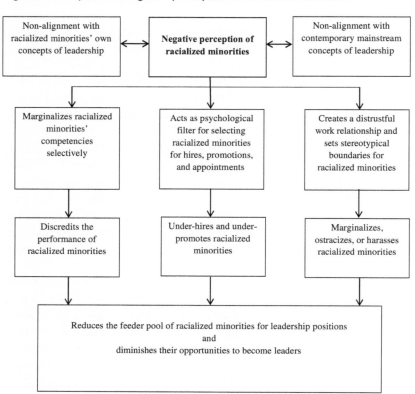

whites view racialized minorities as having good relationships with people or clients of similar status, but they are not viewed as good in relationships with people who are influential or have higher status. Some whites tend to see themselves as better at building relationship teams with other senior executives or CEOs than with racialized minorities. According to mainstream concepts of relationship-building, a competency that enables stronger relationships with people in higher echelons is viewed as more suitable for leadership positions than one that enables stronger relationships with people at similar or lower levels. Thus, even though relationship-building is seen as a strength of racialized minorities, this does not help racialized minorities get closer to leadership positions.

In a diverse workforce, it is crucial to have leaders who can build bridges to diverse communities (Eng 2009). The cross-cultural experiences of racialized minorities are expected to foster a better intercultural environment and bind people together (Ayman and Korabik 2010). But in spite of today's demographic changes, general awareness of business globalization, and organizational commitment to diversity, and in spite of the intercultural advantages provided by racialized minorities, some leaders view them as "useful" solely in terms of intercultural contributions and not in other aspects of corporate culture. Such views seem consistent with tribunals' findings in human rights cases – that management views intercultural competency as only marginally important in the performance evaluations of employees and even as "crowding out" the time needed to perform core tasks at work (Human Rights Tribunal of Ontario 2017). Given that they hold these views of intercultural competency, current leaders have little confidence in handing leadership roles to racialized minorities (Lowe 2013).

Women

Masculine Instrumentality and Feminine Collaboration

Women are viewed as nurturing, sharing, passive, caring, gentle, kind, supportive, affectionate, expressive, non-hierarchical, people-oriented, gentle, passive, sensitive, problem-solving, team-playing, consensus-building, motivating, and empowering (Avolio and Gardner 2005; Mills 2005; Kirkbride 2006). Women are also seen as more "emotionally intelligent" than men, which means they are introspective and empathetic. Women are often associated with a lack of self-confidence, which is viewed as a sign of incompetence (Chamorro-Premuzic 2013).

These stereotypical characteristics are perceived as soft and weak and as at odds with strong leadership (Helgesen 1990; Rodler, Kirchler, and Hölzl 2001, 827–43). Men are usually associated with endurance, determination, decisiveness, stamina, and integrity (Flores 1981, 6–8; Northcraft and Gutek 1993, 220–1; Heilman 1995, 3–26; Hartman 1999, 122, 127, 133).

These perceived gender differences correspond to Parker's (2005, 4) typology of leadership styles – masculine instrumentality and feminine collaboration. The masculine instrumentality type of leadership is based on the ideology of the rugged individualism of white men in the Western industrial environment (Bennis and Biederman 1997). This masculine model of leadership is exemplified by authority, rigidity, instrumentality, control, assertiveness, aggressiveness, and directedness (Parker 2005, 7). Men are stereotyped as independent, assertive, self-protective, goal-oriented, power- and fame-seeking, inspirational, relentless, poor at listening, aloof, ruthless, courageous, and competitive (Fishbein 1979; Basow 1992; Huddy and Terkildsen 1993; Shively, Rudolph, and De Cecco 1978;

Charles and Davies 2000; Maher 1997; Boyce and Herd 2003; Rodler, Kirchler, and Hölzl 2001). These attributes fit well with the narcissistic, directive, inspirational, and charismatic styles of leadership, which are variations of the school of the "Great Man."

The feminine type of leadership views human relationships as "a web ... with leadership at the centre of the web" (Parker 2005, 9–10; Webster et al. 1999). The stereotypes of women align with the attributes found in the "transformational leadership" style, which contrasts with the more charismatic, narcissistic, or directive styles usually associated with men (Devarachetty 2013). This demarcation may hurt women in their pursuit of leadership positions (Eagly and Johannesen-Schmidt 2001).

The transformational leadership style is likely to foster a more engaging corporate culture. It has been suggested that female managers are viewed by their leaders as more transformational than their male counterparts, but less so by the employees who report to them (Carless 1998). The gender differences in cultural contributions are therefore inconclusive, at least when it comes to people's perceptions. Type of industry, gender stereotyping, race, and other factors may further or hinder the extent to which female leaders can contribute to the organization (Garcia-Retamero and Lopez-Zafra 2009; Eagly, Karau, and Makhijani 1995; Ecklund 2006; Sanchez-Hucles and Davis 2010).

Some male leaders tend to see women as less interested in or less committed to leadership positions. According to this perception, women are more committed to their families and children because they give a higher priority to "marrying and/or starting a family" (Davidson and Cooper 1992, 119–20). Some men see women as "universal mothers," that is, supportive, nurturing, passive, and seldom challenging or critical of others (Heller 1982). They are perceived as less committed to their organizations. Accordingly, female employees with MBAs are given less challenging jobs than their male counterparts (Dobson 2014, 3–9). Women are often viewed as less committed or less trusted to lead an organization (Brady and McLean 2002, 9).

As a result of these stereotypes, some current leaders do not believe that women can take on the responsibility of steering an entire organization. When male leaders assess women through the psychological filters of female stereotypes, they are likely to see women as too weak or soft to be leaders. As Heilman (1995) noted, activities believed necessary for jobs of power and authority – such as taking leadership roles, competing for resources, "toughing it out," and making hard-nosed decisions – are all activites inconsistent with the stereotypic view of women.

Stereotypes and Contemporary Mainstream Concepts of Leadership

As noted in chapter 3, competency is integral to contemporary mainstream concepts of leadership. On the surface, the term denotes a set of objective skills that enable leaders to perform well. But how these skills are defined is often loaded with personal biases. Intellectual and organizational competencies are more associated with men and are more valued than social competencies, which are more associated with women (Steffens and Mehl 2003; Page and Meretsky 1998; Bobbitt-Zeher 2011; Boldry, Wood and Kashy 2001).

As noted earlier, the stereotypes of men largely correspond in a more balanced manner with contemporary mainstream concepts of leadership without skewing heavily toward diplomatic attributes (such as people-orientation). As a result of binary gender stereotypes, however, women are placed in the feminine collaboration type of leadership and do not cover the fuller spectrum of leadership attributes encompassed in contemporary mainstream concepts of leadership. When male leaders perceive diplomatic attributes as more feminine than militaristic ones, the chances of women becoming leaders are limited (Perez, 2013; Eisenhart, 2006).

One competence is "relationship-building." Women are viewed as good at building relationships because they have been stereotyped as caring and nurturing and as having an ability to reach out, connect, and reciprocate with people. They are seen as better than men in this realm (Stead and Elliott 2009). For this reason, women are often found clustered in public relations, human resources, media relations, and customer service. As noted in chapter 3, even women's own concepts of leadership encompass people orientation, inclusiveness, teamwork, collaboration, and participation, and these attributes are in line with some of the female stereotypes described above.

Female stereotypes can become problematic because men (who dominate leadership circles, as shown in chapter 2) have defined women's strengths with relationships as secondary and unbalanced. Male leaders tend to see women as neither "strong" nor "strategic" nor "tough" enough to withstand organizational and external challenges.

In 2019, Plan International Canada commissioned a survey of 2,200 young Canadians (aged fourteen to twenty-four) to determine how they viewed girls and women. Fifty-three per cent of boys and young men viewed girls and women as "emotional," and only 10% of them applied that term to describe a good leader. Also, 57% of them chose "strong" as an adjective for a good leader, and less than one-third viewed girls and women as strong. Only 10% of these young Canadians visualized a woman when they thought of a CEO.

These stereotypes of women remain a barrier for girls to advance to leadership roles (Canadian Press 2019).

These stereotypical images of women undermine the value of women and set up barriers against their rise to leadership positions. This is because contemporary mainstream concepts of leadership encompass a broad range of leadership attributes covering both diplomatic attributes (being communicative, relationship-oriented, and collaborative) and militaristic ones (being strategic and strong), in addition to competence in the intellectual, organizational, and social domains. Furthermore, female stereotypes are at odds with some of these concepts and cast women as having a much narrower spectrum of attributes. These stereotypes do not align well with contemporary mainstream concepts of leadership and fall short of meeting some current leaders' expectations for potential leaders. Even when some female stereotypes (such as being caring and collaborative) seem to align well with contemporary mainstream concepts of leadership, some male leaders often resort to those stereotypes to cast doubt on the social competency that women have in relationship-building. They argue that women may be at a disadvantage even in building relationships because, as most leaders are men, they may be less comfortable working with them and may not be able to develop a trusting rapport with them.

In addition, men are viewed as developing better networks of influential or higher-status people. If current leaders aim to build better relationships with CEOs or executives (who are predominantly white males) in other companies, women (who may not have such networks) may be viewed as disadvantaged (Troffer 1975; Unger 1975; Ward and Balswick 1978). When current leaders are mostly men, female relationship-building skills are thought to have limited scope. Some current leaders may even view this skill as "nice to have" rather than mandatory for leadership. Thus, at the top echelons, the utility of women's skills in relationship-building is questioned. Again, this twisted interpretation of relationship-building puts women at a disadvantage.

"Strategic" competency is often included in mainstream concepts of leadership. The term "strategic" is militaristic and has long been associated with combat, although contemporary usage covers a much broader range of human activities, including those in the political, economic, business, and social domains. Because of its past associations with military activities, people tend to perceive men as more strategic than women. As a result, men are more likely than women to be viewed as leadership material (Stump 1985; Thompson 1985; Dennis 2012).

"Communication" competency is well-embodied in contemporary mainstream concepts of leadership. It has various meanings: an ability to exchange

Figure 4.4. Impacts of negative perception of women

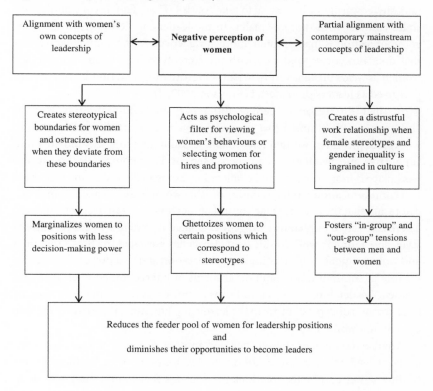

information, the art of transmitting verbal or written messages, skill at raising people's awareness and understanding, or an ability to influence others through words. Women may be viewed as better public communicators, while men are viewed as better orators who are able to influence more people (Valentine and Hoar 1988; Creedon and Carmer 2007; Carter and Spitzack 1989; Sullivan and Hoar 1996). Such gender stereotypes make it harder to give an edge to women in communication skills. As leadership is dominated by men, what men perceive and interpret matters, and some may even downgrade what seems to be one of women's strengths.

Another stereotypical view of women's communication is that they have a particular method of expression. When women communicate in a gentle and indirect manner, using modal verbs such as "may," "might," or "could" and verbal hedges such as "kind of" or "to some extent," "I think" or "I suppose," men see this way of communication as indecisive, unclear, and lacking self-assurance. Moreover, when women raise their intonation or remain silent in conflicts, men interpret such ways of communicating as emotional, uncertain, shy, cowardly, or hesitating to take control. These female communication styles contrast with those of males. In the leadership literature, ideal leader communication is inspirational, motivating, encouraging, and dynamic, and that does not correspond well with the stereotypes of women. So men see women as weak, unstable, subservient, subordinating, and timid. They are not perceived as leadership material (Branson 2007, 4).

In their discussion of gender differences in communication, Kendall and Tannen (1997) noted that men and women interact differently. During workplace meetings, women tend to talk less and interrupt less and are more supportive and facilitative than men. Men's style of communication in the workplace is more assertive and challenging. Some male leaders may see these two communication modes as indicators that women are "weaker" communicators and that they cannot take control of meetings or even decision-making. There is a wealth of literature on gender-related differences in conversational style, and Tannen's work in this field (1994) has enriched the thesis that men and women signal their meanings in conversation and that power plays a critical role in communication and other forms of interaction between men and women. Leadership, expressed in terms of power, as found in contemporary mainstream concepts or those in the leadership literature, is clearly on the side of men, not women.

Another competence often included in contemporary mainstream concepts of leadership is "innovation." Being "innovative" in business means finding newer and better solutions to problems that inhibit market growth, technological breakthroughs, product improvement, or process efficiency. In contemporary mainstream literature it is considered essential for increased business competitiveness in a global economy (Kadeřabková et al. 2007). It has been noted that men and women innovate in different ways, but the *types* of innovation most valued in the business sector seem to cluster around technology, business processes, and product manufacturing, which have long been male domains (Catling 2013). Innovation in these fields has been prominent in the media, and it is men (not women) who are often associated with innovation. This places men in a more advantageous position in competition for leadership positions.

Men and women are equally capable of contributing to the organization; it is just that they do so in a different ways. With their stamina and strategic strength, men can induce order, stability, and organizational change, while women's intuitive judgment and relationship-building can bind people together and handle intercultural issues better (Stead and Elliott 2009). Each sex has its own strengths, and their cultural contributions vary in kind. The issue is, which types of strength are valued by current leaders, who are pre-dominantly male. It seems that some current leaders view women's stereo-types as less desirable.

Currently, none of the above female stereotypes are conducive to their access to leadership positions. Some women may view leadership as gender-neutral; some men seem to view it as gender-based, with negatives attached to women (Kanter 1977; Davidson and Cooper 1992, 90–4; Bosner 2008). These stereotypes are often projected irrationally and harm women by pro-moting biases. They create obstacles to women's progress to top jobs, convince women to avoid leadership roles in favour of subordinate positions, lower women's level of performance (as women adopt the poorer images and lower expectations), make women more vulnerable and more hesitant to aspire to leadership, and taint the judgments of board directors and senior executives (Heilman and Parks-Stanton 2007, 47–77; Davies, Spencer, and Steele 2005).

Overall, some men see women as incapable of becoming leaders because female stereotypes are at odds with notions of leadership in today's main-stream (Cann and Siegfried 1990; Boyce and Herd 2003; Sczesny et al. 2004; Fuegen 2007; Archer 2013). In reality, the behaviours of men and women may well be similar, but gender stereotyping (by some male leaders) affects how their behaviours are interpreted (Heilman 1995). These female stereotypes, which work subtly and often unconsciously, harm women.

Discussion

All four diverse groups under examination are stereotyped or perceived nega-tively. There are five main impediments to their advancement to and retention of leadership positions.

First, the negative images of these four diverse groups may act as psycho-logical filters in terms of current leaders' expectations of their performance, irrespective of their individual attributes. Stereotyping is subtle, subjective, and automatic. People too often reach conclusions without extensive analysis, sacrificing objectivity for the sake of speed (Kulik and Bainbridge 2006). Neg-ative stereotyping harms diverse groups in many different ways; when added together, they likely pose an insurmountable hurdle for them to become leaders.

Second, negative stereotypes marginalize these diverse groups and place them in a no-win situation in the workplace. These stereotypes lower lead-ers' expectations of their performance or their potential; they also reduce the opportunities for them to move up the organizational hierarchy and to be con-sidered for executive positions or board directorships. They also may reduce

Figure 4.5. Summary of adverse impacts of negative stereotypes on diverse groups

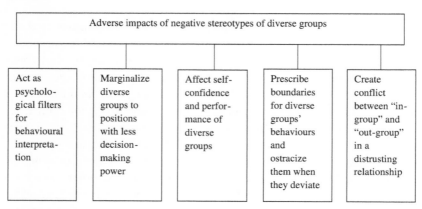

their chances of getting hired, even at occupational levels lower than that of leadership, and this shrinks the feeder pool for leadership positions.

Third, negative stereotyping damages the performance of these diverse groups, as has been suggested by numerous research studies (Shih, Pittinsky, and Ambady 1999; Aronson and Inzlicht 2004; Walton and Cohen 2007; Codjoe 2001). Poor performance (often below their potential) affects scores on performance evaluations; it also limits the opportunity for members of diverse groups to "shine" at work and to be selected for leadership development, awards, coaching, mentorship, and sponsorship. As they perform below their potential, diverse groups may find themselves more isolated and less engaged in work-related and social networks necessary for their advancement.

Fourth, stereotypes serve as reference points according to which the work behaviour of diverse groups is judged. These are what Berdahl and Min (2012) called "prescriptive stereotypes." When diverse group members do not fit their stereotypes, they often encounter still more negativity from people who hold these stereotypes, in the form of annoyance, anger, resistance, or intervention. For example, when women do not behave in a traditional feminine manner (e.g., when they speak with confidence or act assertively or dominantly), they are subject to more harassment or discrimination. In other words, stereotypes define social boundaries within which diverse groups are allowed to behave; in essence, they are a social control mechanism for keeping the ambitions of diverse groups in check. When diverse groups lead teams, projects, or committees, colleagues who stereotype diverse groups without knowing it often find leadership by diverse groups uncomfortable. Diverse groups feel the resistance of their colleagues. Stereotypes thus create roadblocks for diverse groups to "shine" as potential leaders and to excel in performance, even among their peers.

Fifth, stereotypes often divide (rather than unite) people in the workplace. The lines between in-groups and out-groups are often drawn along racial, ethnic, religious, linguistic, gender, and cultural lines. In-group members feel comfortable with one another but uncomfortable with people outside their own groups. Social distance, discriminatory behaviour, favouritism, or conflict may develop as a result of the perceived differences between an in-group and an out-group and the perceived similarities among in-group members. Some diverse employees may be shut out from insider information on new a business direction, a forthcoming organizational restructuring, or pending staff changes because they are not part of the network. Leaders from diverse backgrounds may not be a part of the inner circle of senior executives or board directors so that they can know whether some of their innovative ideas are acceptable to senior members (Tajfel, Sheikh, and Gardner 1964; Tajfel 1982; Tajfel and Turner 1986; McLeod 2008).

Another aspect of stereotyping is "stereotype threats." The perceived differences and stereotypical images of diverse groups pose threats, real or unreal, to the dominant group. White, able-bodied, non-Indigenous men may see them as competing for positions. Such threats lead to an in-group versus out-group relationship (Stephan and Stephan 2000, 23–8). These relationships create social distance between the dominant group and diverse groups (Goff, Steele, and Davies 2008; Aboud, Mendelson, and Purdy 2003).

Solutions must be found to rectify this situation, lest the harm inflicted by stereotypes reduce the chances for diverse groups to be hired, to stay put, and to gain access to the pipelines to leadership. There are at least two steps to minimizing stereotyping: raise everyone's awareness of the prevalence of unconscious biases, and find ways to eliminate those biases. This will be discussed later in this chapter.

Attitudes

Stereotypes shape attitudes and behaviours (Dovidio et al. 1996, 276). Prejudices and negative stereotypes and often go hand-in-hand and may affect people's beliefs, feelings, experiences, and behaviours (Haddock, Zanna, and Esses 1994, 83–4). An attitude is a feeling toward a person, thing, place, or event that may affect a person's thoughts or actions. Negative attitudes may be formed through negative perceptions or experiences. Let us examine public attitudes toward diverse groups.

Figure 4.6. Impact of negative attitudes toward Indigenous peoples

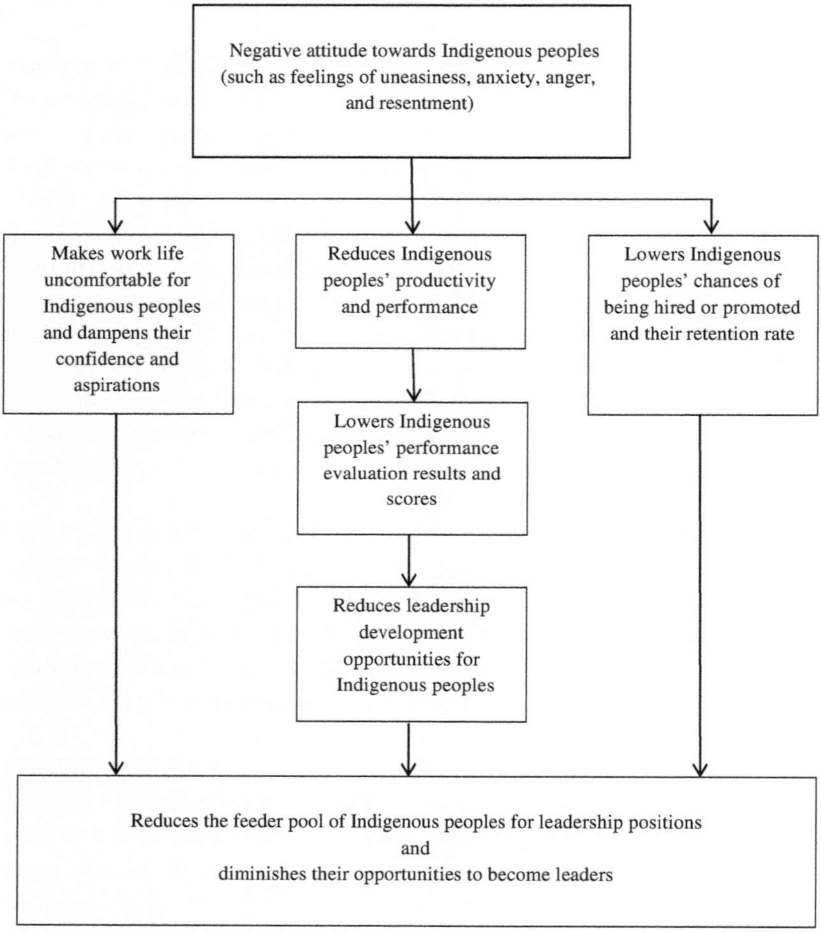

Indigenous Peoples

Canadians hold ambiguous attitudes toward Indigenous peoples: they are proud of Indigenous peoples' history and heritage, yet at the same time they harbour negative feelings about their behaviours and ways of life. It is unfortunate that attitudes of distrust and anxiety toward Indigenous peoples persist (Werhun and Penner 2010, 900; Bell and Esses 1997; Dunk 1991; Langford and Ponting 1992, 140). These negative attitudes may spring from media portrayals or from the stereotyping of Indigenous peoples as alcoholic, lazy, and uneducated. These stereotypes evoke anger and uneasiness (Trimble 1988; Angus Reid Group 1991).

The Environics Institute for Survey Research (2016, 11–13) conducted a national public opinion survey of non-Indigenous persons across Canada in 2016 and found that public attitudes toward Indigenous peoples appear to have improved: one quarter of non-Indigenous Canadians have a better appreciation of them than before; only one tenth have a less favourable opinion (APTN National News 2016).

The author's consulting experience – which includes time spent in focus groups and interviews with executives and non-management employees in a variety of organizations – has been that negative attitudes appear in pockets of these organizations. According to some employees, Indigenous peoples do not take punctuality and time management seriously; they are not reliable; their community lives take priority over work; and they do not do their share. Systemic biases were also noted in the performance evaluations of Indigenous employees by executives and managers, irrespective of the occupational groups they were in and whether they were middle-level managers, professionals, technicians, or clerical personnel. The ratings of Indigenous employees were consistently lower than those of non-Indigenous employees. Furthermore, Indigenous employees were not given opportunities in leadership development programs.

For Indigenous peoples, a work environment with negative attitudes, subtle or blatant, is not conducive for work. It may make their working lives uncomfortable, reduce their productivity and work quality, or even discourage them from staying on. It may have a detrimental impact on their hiring or promotion as well as explain why they are generally underrepresented in middle management, which is the feeder group for leadership positions (Canada 2016a).

Persons with Disabilities

Persons with disabilities have to reckon with employers' attitudes (Unger 2002). American employers who employ persons with disabilities have a more favourable attitude toward them than those who do not (Hannon n.d., 17–20). In the United Kingdom, public attitudes toward persons with disabilities are still negative – in one survey of the British public, 67% of respondents felt "uncomfortable talking to disabled people," 36% thought "disabled people as not as productive as everyone else," 13% thought that "disabled people are getting in the way some or most of the time," and 85% believed that "disabled people face prejudice" (Aiden and McCarthy 2014, 3, 7).

Figure 4.7. Impact of negative attitudes toward persons with disabilities

```
┌─────────────────────────────────────────────────────┐
│        Negative attitude towards persons with         │
│      disabilities (such as feelings of uneasiness,    │
│            anxiety, anger, and resentment)            │
└─────────────────────────────────────────────────────┘
```

Makes work life uncomfortable for persons with disabilities and dampens their confidence and aspirations

Reduces persons with disabilities' productivity and performance

Lowers persons with disabilities' chance of being hired or promoted and their retention rate

Lowers persons with disabilities' performance evaluation results and scores

Reduces leadership development opportunities for persons with disabilities

Reduces the feeder pool of persons with disabilities for leadership positions and diminishes their opportunities to become leaders

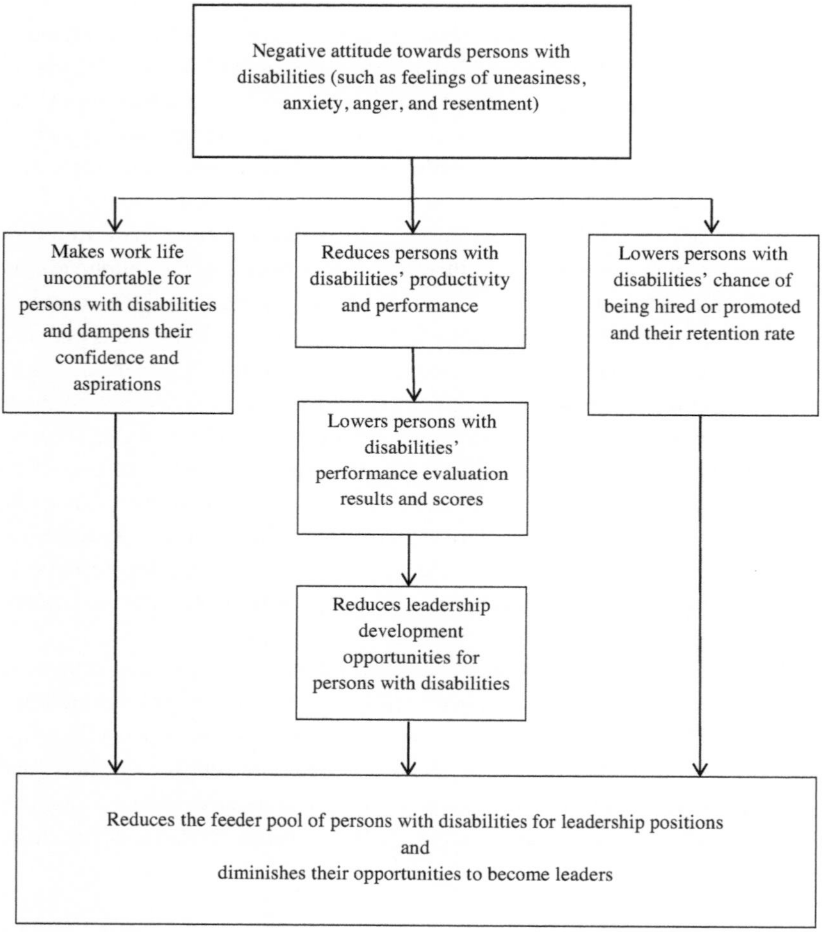

In Canada, attitudes toward persons with disabilities are mixed. According to the 2004 Canadian Benchmarking Survey (Office for Disability Issues), 82% believed that persons with disabilities are less likely to be hired for a job than those who are abled, even when they are equally qualified. Among the employed respondents in the same survey, 73% agreed that persons with disabilities contribute as much to the organization as others (Hannon n.d., 17–20). A study by Church and colleagues (2007) about bank employees in Canada found that persons with disabilities detected unease and discomfort with them among managers and co-workers. Such attitudes harmed their work quality and productivity as well as their working relationships, their self-confidence, their chances of promotion, and even their retention rates.

The author of this book tabulated data on performance evaluations of persons with disabilities and compared them with those for persons without disabilities in large corporations in Canada. He found that the evaluation scores of persons with disabilities were lower than those for able-bodied colleagues throughout the enterprise. Persons with disabilities attributed their lower scores to these factors: managers and supervisors do not listen to them well, do not know how to work with them, and offer them accommodation measures that are inadequate or inappropriate to enhance their performance. Some managers second-guessed their work and sought co-workers to review and revise their deliverables. Such tactics undermined their confidence and affected their performance. And when competing for promotions to management or leadership positions or for leadership development opportunities, employees with disabilities may face more challenges. A few employees with disabilities reported that they had simply given up applying for promotion lest they be disappointed one more time.

Racialized Minorities

An early national study of Canadians by Berry, Kalin, and Taylor (1976, 106) noted that Canadians tended to rank people of European backgrounds higher than racial minorities. A national study by the Angus Reid Group (1991) on Canadian attitudes found that European Canadians continued to enjoy a higher social standing and that people felt more comfortable with them than with racialized minorities. A survey of 1,500 Canadian adults conducted for CBC News (2014a) found that 79% felt comfortable "working for someone of a different ethnic background," which suggested that their attitude had improved somewhat over the past twenty years. Here, the term "ethnic background" included racial minority backgrounds.

Another way to determine attitudes toward racialized minorities in Canada is to review how people feel about their arrival as immigrants, because most immigrants over the past few decades have been racialized minorities. A review of research studies in Canada between 2006 and 2009 found that Canadians express "strong but conditional" support for multiculturalism and immigration (Soroka and Robertson 2010, iv, 6–8). In its survey of Canadian attitudes, Ekos Politics (2013) noted that while 42% of respondents reported that the number of racialized minority immigrants coming to Canada was "about right," 37% reported that it was "too many." The latter respondents showed signs of "apprehension around unfamiliar cultures" or "an expression

Figure 4.8. Impact of ambivalent or negative attitudes toward racialized minorities

```
┌─────────────────────────────────────────────┐
│   Ambivalent or negative attitude towards    │
│   racialized minorities (such as feelings of  │
│  uneasiness, anxiety, anger, and resentment)  │
└─────────────────────────────────────────────┘
```

| Makes work life uncomfortable for racialized minorities and dampens their confidence and aspirations | Reduces racialized minorities' productivity and performance | Lowers racialized minorities' chances of being hired or promoted and their retention rate |

Lowers racialized minorities' performance evaluation results and scores

Reduces leadership development opportunities for racialized minorities

Reduces the feeder pool of racialized minorities for leadership positions
and
diminishes their opportunities to become leaders

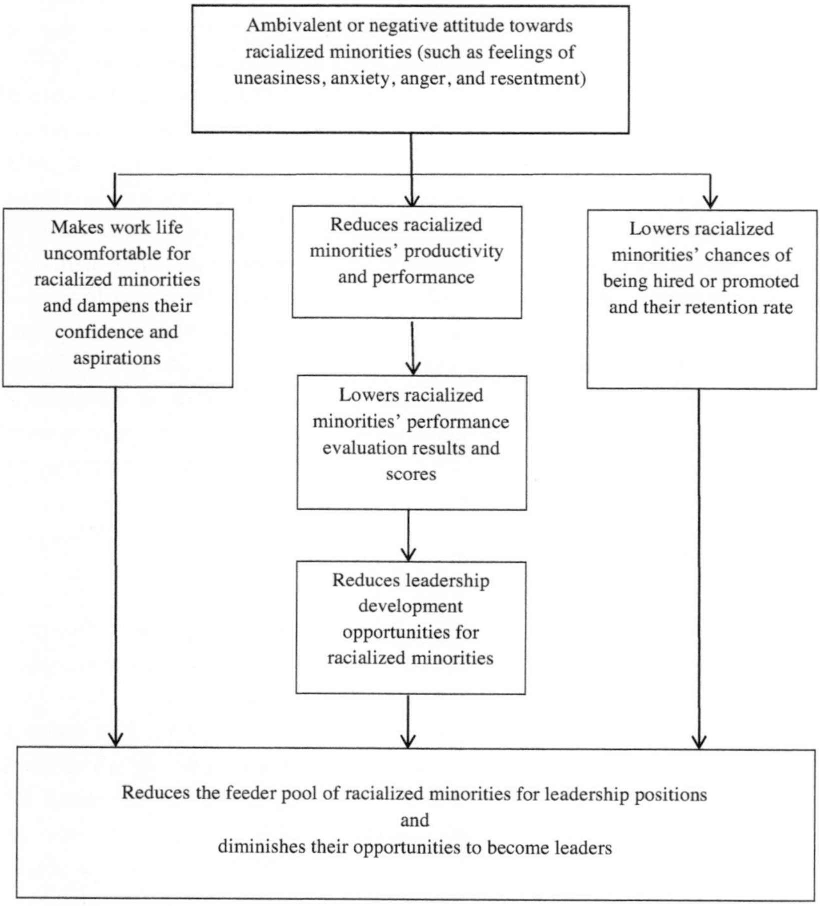

of racial prejudice." American and European survey results showed higher negativity in attitudes toward racial minorities and immigrants (European Monitoring Centre on Racism and Xenophobia 2005, 12; Coenders, Lubbers, and Scheepers 2003).

The author of this book has conducted focus groups and interviews in workplaces in the private sector over the past twenty years. He has found that while negative stereotypes and prejudices against racialized minorities persist, there have been improvements. Improvements in attitudes were found mainly in hiring practices, especially in urban centres in Canada. However, there was reluctance to promote those employees to management and executive positions. The general attitude among senior executives was that racialized minorities were still not leadership material and that they were uncomfortable when interacting with them. Results from performance evaluations were mixed, and racialized minorities complained about their lack of opportunities for leadership development. This suggested that stereotypes and prejudice played a role in their lack of opportunities.

Women

In the 1970s and 1980s, American and British studies found that male attitudes toward women were "think manager, think male." Some male managers had the attitude that women were inferior to men and that managerial qualities were found mainly in men (Davidson and Cooper 1992, 130). Antal and Izraeli (1993, 63) stated: "Probably the single most important hurdle for women in management in all industrialized countries is the persistent stereotype that associates management with being male." Male dominance in management remains prevalent, it reinforces the male attitude, and it dies hard. There are still men who say that it's okay to have women in senior-level positions but they personally do not want women on their boards (Holton 2010).

In general, CEOs have long been uncomfortable about the idea of female board directors. A Catalyst study in 1993 found that 44% of board directors were concerned that women might have a "women's issue agenda" (Mattis 2010, 50–1). CEOs were concerned that gender diversity might complicate or slow how business was run on the board. They worried that women would not play by the conventional rules and would disrupt the board by raising "women's issues" (such as family care and health benefits) (Bilimoria 2010, 30–2). In Bradshaw and Wicks's (2010, 206) study of female board directors, one woman director remarked that women were appointed "because companies thought it was important to have a female on the board, but they wanted a female who did not rock the boat. So they wanted women to keep their mouth shut." This summarizes the anxiety felt by male board directors as well as their attitude that women should play traditional passive and supportive roles.

The Conference Board of Canada's national survey of 876 women and men and additional in-depth interviews with 29 women found that "male senior executives were the least likely of all management groups to agree that there is a need to increase the number of women in leadership roles," although the vast majority of female senior executives agreed that the need was there. Attitudes were polarized along gender lines (Conference Board of Canada 2013).

Figure 4.9. Impact of negative attitudes toward women

```
┌─────────────────────────────────────────┐
│   Negative attitude towards women (such as │
│   feelings of uneasiness, anxiety, anger, and │
│              resentment)                  │
└─────────────────────────────────────────┘
```

| Makes work life uncomfortable for women and dampens their confidence and aspirations | Stigmatizes women's roles and reinforces their "double jeopardy" | Lowers women's chances of being appointed, hired, or promoted to assume traditionally male roles |

Ignores women's contributions and marginalizes them

Reduces leadership development opportunities for women

Reduces the feeder pool of women for leadership positions
and
diminishes their opportunities to become leaders

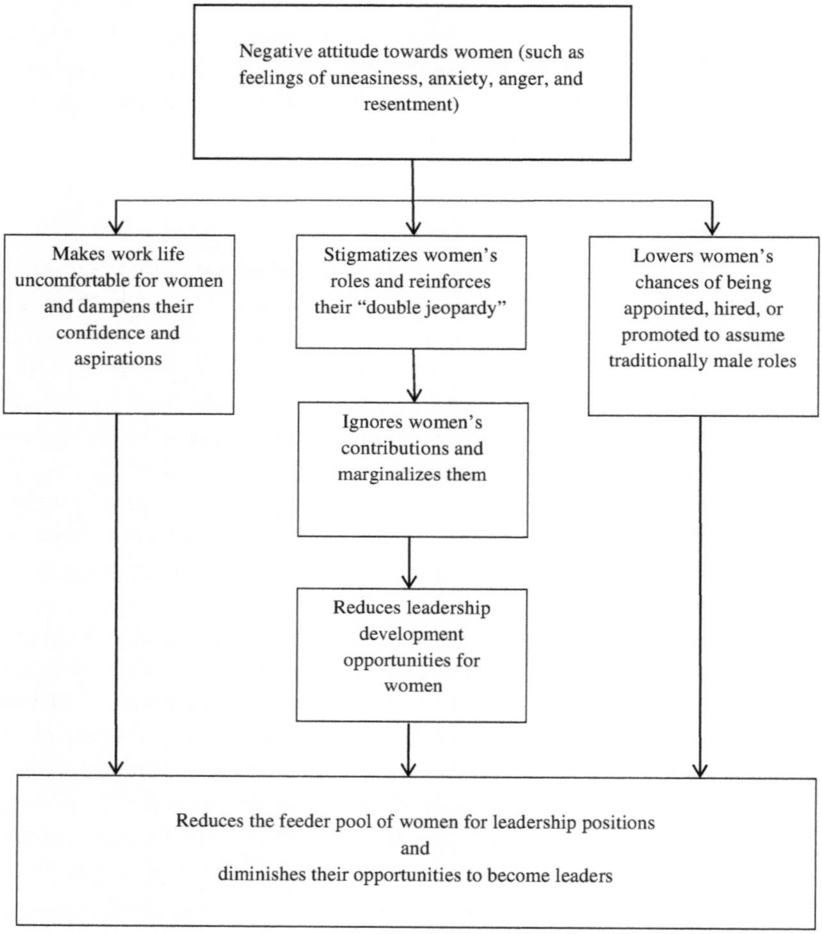

The polarized situation had changed little by 2018, when the views of FP500 board men and women on diversity were surveyed: 52.4% of men and 76.1% of women perceived diversity as very important (Canadian Board Diversity Council 2018, 18).

The above research studies indicate that despite improvements in male attitudes toward women in leadership, biases are still engrained in the mindsets of current leaders. It has gradually become easier for women to break into management positions, but they still have difficulties joining executive circles (Canada 2016a).

Discussion

This section has shown that there is prejudice toward diverse groups and that it has relegated them to an inferior status. That prejudice, however subtle it may be, tends to manifest itself in exclusionary conduct that marginalizes diverse groups. This has hindered the hiring or promotion of diverse groups. There are two seemingly harmless prejudices worth noting. One involves the legitimization of prejudice – that is, it is justified by the need to make money, grow the business, or expand customer base. The other is the myth of "benevolent prejudice," which puts diverse groups in their "proper" place. Both forms of prejudice work against diverse groups, no matter how gentle and subtle they are.

And contemporary prejudice *is* largely subtle. People who are subtly prejudiced see themselves as not prejudiced at all. They also reject the stereotyping of minority groups, at least on the surface. Yet it has been observed that it *is* possible to legitimize prejudice and discrimination on business grounds when those with authority, including managers or executives, provide a seemingly rational justification for it. One such justification might be that customers dislike being served by persons with disabilities; another is that co-workers prefer working with people who look like themselves (Petersen and Dietz 2006).

This suggests that in the business sector, when prejudice can be rationalized in business terms, diverse groups' upward mobility can be impeded. For example, women may be denied promotion to leadership positions because they have been stereotyped as emotional, unassertive, and more committed to their children than to their companies. Leaders consider these attributes as not advantageous for business because an emotional outburst is unprofessional, or taking time off to take care of sick children neglects business matters. When employees are influenced by this "business" rationale, at a subconscious level they may believe that women should not assume leadership responsibilities. They would not see themselves as prejudiced against women, but they indirectly support leaders' decisions not to appoint women to leadership positions. This example shows how prejudice can be legitimized and even endorsed when business rationales are provided and formalized.

Such legitimization of prejudice also applies to the work experiences of Indigenous peoples (on the business grounds of their "unworkable" communal or holistic approaches to leadership), persons with disabilities (on the business grounds of their "inability" to get things done quickly enough), and racialized minorities (on the business grounds of their "confrontational" or "direct" style of communication). It seems that these dislikes of stereotyped leadership attributes and these prejudices against the work approaches or human relations of diverse groups are acceptable as long as the business reasons are considered legitimate.

Second, not all prejudices are perceived as negative: some are seemingly positive and are referred to as "benevolent prejudice." This is a special kind of bias whereby diverse groups are viewed as having positive attributes, but those in power use these attributes to undermine their status. In an organizational setting, this kind of prejudice may enable majority groups to hide their negative feelings and subordinate these groups without guilt (Werhun and Penner 2010, 900).

Little research has been done on these benevolent prejudices. Several stereotypes of women (people-orientation, nurturing and caring attributes) may be viewed as benevolent, but the result is that that women are often assigned to responsibilities that are traditionally in line with femininity or motherhood.

Similarly, some racialized minorities are stereotyped as good in technical and computer skills or professional knowledge but not in strategic management and inspirational leadership. Such stereotypes create a mindset that is receptive to a narrow view of what racialized minorities are good at, thus denying them leadership responsibilities. These positive images of diverse groups are a form of prejudice that allows current leaders to feel that diverse groups may not be up to becoming leaders. In the end, such feelings work against diverse groups in their quest for leadership.

Prejudice can be blatant and direct, but it works just as well when it is subtle and indirect. It is often associated with stereotypes of diverse groups. In the context of understanding leadership, prejudice often narrows the roles and responsibilities of diverse groups in occupations that are not in the leadership domains. It casts diverse groups in a negative light so that people do not feel that they are suitable and desirable as leaders. When they try to work toward securing leadership positions, prejudice makes people feel that those pursuits are not legitimate. And when current leaders are prejudiced against diverse groups, the opportunities for diverse groups in leadership diminish.

A study by Billan and Humber (2018) of high-achieving professional women in Canada (1,501 respondents in the sample) illustrated the power of stereotypes of women. This study found that women in the workplace cannot be seen as "too" ambitious or "over"-achieving, for fear of being ostracized or undermined by their superiors and even by their peers. This view is confirmed by the testimonies of achieving women in the workplace in Canada. When a woman accomplishes more than men at work, she is a threat to be checked and contained. Efforts are made to show that her performance is unacceptable. In other words, her ambition and competitiveness have caused her to deviate from the boundaries placed around women. She must be returned to her "proper" place, for she has gone beyond her stereotype as a woman.

Perspectives of Diverse Groups on Negative Stereotypes and Attitudes

How do diverse groups view and feel about these negative perceptions and attitudes and their implications for their work experiences?

Indigenous Peoples

Indigenous peoples have not been perceived in a positive light for many years (Gibbins and Ponting 1986). They are aware that negative stereotypes and prejudice, intercultural ignorance, racism, and discrimination affect their self-esteem and self-identity. All of these heighten their sense of being an out-group and act as "fundamental barriers" for them in "getting a job and remaining in the job" (Joseph 2013; Centre for Social Justice n.d.; Ontario Federation of Indian Friendship Centres 2013; Werhun and Penner 2010, 899–900).

There have been few studies about the perspectives of Indigenous peoples in the private sector. However, in his focus groups and interviews with employees on their work experiences in large corporations in Canada, this author found that Indigenous employees are cognizant of the disadvantages they face in the workplace once their Indigenous identity is known. These disadvantages may include negative stereotypes, prejudice, social distance, isolation, perceptions of incompetence and unreliability, and a lack of opportunities for promotion and career development. So they find the workplace not particularly safe for them and work hard to conceal their Indigenous identity. Some of them working in federally regulated companies do not even declare themselves to be Indigenous in the self-identification confidential workforce survey required by the federal government for employment equity purposes. The fact that some Indigenous peoples choose not to identify themselves as such amounts to a statement of how unsafe or insecure they feel about being Indigenous in the workplace and how far they have to go to protect themselves in order to survive in the workplace or get a promotion.

Indigenous peoples recognized how unlikely it was that they would be promoted to management. They came to believe they had reached their "job plateau" sooner than other employees, and they grew frustrated at work as they saw non-Indigenous employees promoted faster. Indigenous employees came to have a defeatist attitude: there was no point applying for a promotion because they would not get one. To avoid disappointment, they screened themselves out by not applying for middle management or senior executive positions.

The experiences of Indigenous peoples in other sectors confirmed these observations. A study of Canadian federal government employees found that Indigenous peoples are aware of the negative stereotypes they face and of the discriminatory practices and prejudicial treatment they encounter from their superiors. These factors had an impact on their work experiences and their promotion chances (Dwyer 2003). Similar findings have been noted among police services in Canada (Jain, Singh, and Agocs 2000).

Persons with Disabilities

Persons with invisible disabilities learned from their physically disabled counterparts who experienced negative stereotypes and prejudice. They spend as much time hiding their disabilities as they do performing their work. They do not wish to have their co-workers or managers find out they have disabilities. These were the findings of the joint research project of the Royal Bank of Canada and Ryerson University (Church et al. 2007, 7–9). They viewed concealing their disabilities as their "second job" at the bank. In this way, they avoided negative reactions, secured their personal privacy, and facilitated their own integration into the workplace. They observed that as soon as they made known to their managers or co-workers that they had disabilities (even though the disabilities were not visible), the negative labelling process began and managers and co-workers start focusing on their disabilities and not on what they were able to contribute to the organization. This may explain why they were underrepresented in all of the occupational groups, including the "middle management" category, which is the feeder pool for leadership positions (Canada 2016c).

This concealment of disabilities and ongoing "never let your guard down" pressure have generated work-related stress for them and affected the quality and productivity of their work. Persons with disabilities make other efforts besides to manage their working lives. They reported that they very often have to take their work home so that they do not give people the impression that they are less competent because of their disabilities, and they do not wish to have poorer performance evaluations.

The stigmatization and marginalization of persons with disabilities has severely limited their acquisition of management skills and experiences. Although the data from the federally regulated private sector (reported in chapter 2) indicated that there are middle managers with disabilities, the negative stereotypes and prejudice hovering over them often make them screen themselves out of applying for senior executive positions. Overall, persons with disabilities in Canada have a higher level of job dissatisfaction than those who are able. Such dissatisfaction seems to relate to their lower incomes, poorer interpersonal relations, fear of job loss, experience of harassment and discrimination, and lack of accommodation in the workplace (Uppal 2005, 335–49).

Similarly, in the United Kingdom, persons with disabilities are cognizant of the public prejudice. Aiden and McCarthy's (2014, 9–11) study found that "they have been talked to in a patronizing way," "have been stared at due to their disability," have been "called you names," and have experienced people "act[ing] in an aggressive or hostile way" toward them. In relation to employment, they "faced challenges around work and employment" and reported that people do not understand their needs, "expecting less of me because of my health condition or disability," "treating me like I'm a nuisance," "thinking I can't make my own decisions," "being awkward around me," and/or "ignoring me or pretending not to see me." Their experiences pointed to a lack of respect and support from people around them, which made them feel unsafe. In this kind of work environment, they were likely to lower their aspiration to be leaders, and others were unlikely to see them as potential leaders.

Racialized Minorities

Racialized minorities are cognizant of the workplace barriers, some more than others. This author found, based on the focus group discussions and interviews conducted with employees in the past, which compared to their white counterparts, that racialized minority employees were less positive about corporate inclusiveness, promotion practices, development opportunities, and meeting their career goals in their organizations. As sources of these problems, they cited management's negative stereotypes and attitude toward them.

These findings are consistent with those of other empirical studies. Deitch, Barsky, and Butz (2003, 1299–324) noted that in the area of promotion, negative attitudes often express themselves as physical avoidance, uneasiness during interactions, or discriminatory actions, and that all of these have adversely affected the occupational mobility of racialized minorities. Studies in Toronto found that racialized minorities reported more prejudice and discrimination than whites in many contexts, including when it came to being promoted to managerial and executive positions (Dion 1989; Dion and Kawakami 1996).

The Ethnic Diversity Survey 2002, conducted by Statistics Canada, noted that racial minorities perceived more discrimination than whites. While 10.7% of whites perceived experiences of racial discrimination (and felt uncomfortable or out of place in Canada), 35.9% of racial minorities had that perception. In addition, when perception of vulnerability to discrimination (worried about being a victim of a hate crime) was singled out for the survey, 16% of whites and 37.3% of racialized minorities acknowledged that perception. These statistics showed the discrepancies in racial perceptions (Reitz and Banerjee 2007). Banerjee's (2008, 380–401) studies of Canadian racialized minorities noted that close to one quarter (24.3%) of them had perceived workplace discrimination in the past five years. Racialized minorities had much the same aspirations as their white counterparts but felt that their negative stereotypes and attitudes were hindering their advancement (Olsen, Maple, and Stage 1995, 267–93). They also felt like outsiders because they did not have the same social or cultural interests as white men (Silva, Dyer, and Whitham 2007, 10–11).

In its groundbreaking reports on racialized minorities in corporate Canada, Catalyst reported that racialized minorities in forty-three large publicly traded and privately held corporations and professional service firms were "less satisfied with their careers, less likely to report positive experiences and perceptions regarding their workplaces, and more likely to perceive workplace barriers" than their white counterparts. Racialized minorities working in these organizations tended to believe that their organizations were not committed to cultural diversity. They also felt there was a lack of fairness in advancement, in performance standards, and in getting high-profile assignments (Catalyst and the Diversity Institute in Management and Technology 2007).

In the same study, racialized minority executives, managers, and professionals noted barriers in their career development because of an apparent lack of corporate fit. They perceived cultural, ethnic, racial, and linguistic barriers. Negative stereotyping abounded – East Asians were viewed as "hardworking but not social," South Asians as "foreigners" or "outsiders," and blacks as "lacking the skill or motivation to work." Some racialized minorities felt socially isolated and lamented that they were not fully accepted by the white majority (Giscombe 2008, 2–5; Giscombe and Jenner 2009, 2–8).

Studies in the United States found that racialized minorities felt they had been discriminated against, had often been given menial tasks even in professional firms, had been unfairly treated and overlooked for promotion, felt marginalized and unwanted by their employers, felt that they were being treated as "tokens," and experienced low job satisfaction (Irizarry 2012, 9–11). Elliott and Smith's (2004, 376) study found that in the United States, black men were about half as likely as white men to be managers and supervisors. They concluded that black men were increasingly unequal to white men as they moved up the hierarchy; also, black women suffered from direct discrimination more than other groups. Other studies found that African-American women (such as professionals and managers) of higher status experienced more pronounced barriers to upward mobility than their lower-status counterparts (Hughes and Dodge 1997, 581–6).

In sum, racialized minorities found that they were aware of the implications of negative stereotypes and prejudice against them and of the negative consequences on their work. They realized there were many employment hurdles between where they were now and leadership positions.

Women

More than 20 years ago, *Business Week* (1992) reported that women were pessimistic about the future of women in corporations. Of the 400 female managers surveyed, 70% felt that the culture of male dominance was a barrier to their success. Also, 56% believed that "a glass ceiling exists for women, and that in five years' time, the number of senior women executives at their companies will have remained the same or fallen."

Since then, women have not become much more optimistic. Forty-five per cent of Canadian female senior executives identified men's stereotypical notion that women are less committed to management positions and that their priority is children and family as one of the top three barriers to their advancement. The Centre of Excellence for Women's Advancement noted that 69% of the female executives in its survey felt they had not been taken seriously at work; 50% agreed that female managers are often viewed as having "less organizational commitment and professional capability" than male managers (Brady and McLean 2002, 9).

Negative stereotypes and prejudice against women are commonplace and have been an immense hurdle to their entry to leadership circles. Branson (2007, 56–62) argued that some of the stereotypes of women (such as that they lack confidence and assertiveness) may be the result of men's interpretation of how women speak or act. Some men also think that women's priority is in taking care of their children and family and that they are not willing to work beyond their regular working hours. Many of them hope to change their full-time status to part-time and to take longer leaves. Some men viewed that lack of commitment to the organization as a stigma (Branson 2007, 37). With this stigma, it would be difficult for women to land leadership positions, given that work commitment and long working hours appear to be a basic requirement for these positions.

The study of prejudice toward female leaders by Eagly and Karau (2002, 573–98) suggested that when the roles of leaders are different from those of women, two forms of prejudice may emerge: women will be viewed less positively than men in leadership roles; or, female leaders' behaviours will be assessed more negatively than those of male leaders.

Female leaders may find themselves criticized for being too aggressive, for trying to be a man, or for not being feminine enough. The incongruence between the stereotypes of women and the expectations placed on leaders often gives rise to prejudice. Female leaders' competence is constantly debated in the workplace because of this incongruence. Sheridan (2013, 260–88) even suggested that women's voices may trigger prejudice by enabling people to identify the sex of the speaker, which activates a number of socialized gender-based beliefs. Those gender-based beliefs resulted in a less favourable attitude toward female leaders and a reduced opportunity for women to succeed as leaders.

There are mounting data in the literature indicating that historically, women have much the same aspirations, skills, and productivity as their male co-workers; also, that they resent not being promoted to the highest management levels merely because, as noted earlier, there is a tendency to ascribe to them attributes that make them ill-suited to be managers (Olsen, Maple, and Stage 1995, 267–93). In many cross-cultural studies, women in management have reported that prejudice and discrimination have impeded their career development (Gitek and Larwood 1987; Marshall 1984; Nicholson and West 1988). Davidson and Cooper (1992, 119–20) found that

> nearly every woman … interviewed believed that she had encountered some type of discrimination or prejudice throughout her career. Indeed, the general consensus was that women who secure managerial positions are usually better qualified than men, and have to be twice as good at the interview and the jobs.

Moreover,

> woman managers across all sectors and organization sizes were more likely to say that prejudice against them as a group affected their promotional prospects. Some of the women quoted examples of less qualified and less experienced male colleagues achieving considerably faster promotion, and even hav[ing] a female boss did not always appear to prevent this.

For those women with more than one social identity, Mahtani's (2004, 91–9) study of racialized minority women working in universities in Britain, Canada and the United States found that they felt "out of place," "unwanted, unappreciated and unwelcome," and "discouraged." Their legitimacy was

Table 4.1. Reactions of diverse groups toward negative perceptions and attitudes

Indigenous peoples	Persons with disabilities	Racialized minorities	Women
*Lower their self-esteem and confidence *Cognizant of people's perceptions of incompetence, laziness, and unreliability *Feel discriminated against, belittled, and second-guessed *Feel unsafe and isolated at work *Conceal their Indigenous identity	*Aware of others' negative labelling *Experience work-related stress and job dissatisfaction *Add more efforts and time to manage their working lives *Feel isolated and disrespected by others *Fear of job loss, harassment, and discrimination *Conceal their disability identity	*Aware of employment barriers *Feel discriminated against *Dissatisfied with their careers and work experiences *Feel a lack of fairness in treatment and advancement *Feel overlooked for promotion *Feel not accepted *Feel marginalized and unwanted *Feel like "tokens"	*Feel pessimistic about their future *Feel that they have not been taken seriously *Feel "out of place" *Resent their lack of promotion to management positions *Feel the "double burden" *Feel unwanted, unappreciated, unwelcome, discouraged, and isolated

questioned by their colleagues, who believed they had been appointed owing to their "double" minority status or affirmative action rather than on the basis of the quality of their academic work. Overall, racialized minority women felt deeply that they were outsiders. They felt that they are neither part of the sexually dominant group (men) nor part of the racialy dominant group (whites). In other studies, racialized minority women reported feeling isolated and that they had difficulty gaining access to influential networks. However, they viewed that as more a gender issue than a race one (Silva, Dyer, and Whitham 2007, 10–11). Indigenous women, too, felt that they were carrying a "double burden": "We're sometimes discriminated against because we're women and additionally because we're indigenous women" (Sweetgrass 2016).

All of these studies suggest that when race or ethnicity and sex intersect, stereotypes and prejudices based on social identities change depending on the context. Some feel the "double jeopardy" of being racialized minorities *and* women; others perceive that race or ethnicity takes on more importance than sex. Whatever the consequences of intersectionality, they are negative not only for the work experience and for well-being but also for advancement in an organization.

Discussion

All of the diverse groups being examined here are aware of the negative ste-reotypes and prejudices that are being imposed on them and that do so much to define them. Some internalize these negative perceptions, believing that this negativism has had a detrimental impact on their employment oppor-tunities and career development, in that these stereotypes and prejudices act as psychological filters for current leaders. In addition, prejudice saps them of self-confidence. They often experience social isolation and job dissatisfac-tion, along with a sense that they are "out of place." They also feel that they have not been accepted in the work environment and that their careers do not offer them much of a future. All of them believe that their workplace is discriminatory.

They are pessimistic about rising to leadership positions. Employees of diverse backgrounds working as mid-level managers, professionals, techni-cians, and administrators aspire to be leaders, but negative stereotypes and prejudices have had a chilling effect on their aspirations, work performance, and well-being; all of this in turn hinders their mobility within the organi-zation. As long as these stereotypes and prejudices are perceived and felt by diverse groups, their working relations with the current leaders will be strained. Trusting relationships are unlikely to develop between them and their leaders, and this is not conducive to diversity in leadership.

Diverse groups' awareness of stereotypes and prejudices does not make their working lives easier. Indeed, it increases the strains between them and others, including executives. It does not help them get closer to leadership positions. Knowing the perspectives and experiences of these diverse groups is a first step toward solving the problems they face. Consulting them regard-ing how best to utilize their talents would make human resources systems fairer. This is discussed in the following section.

Best Options and Practices

Options for Change

There are at least three approaches that employers could take to identify and remove negative perceptions and attitudes between diverse groups and leaders. Many companies, especially (in Canada) those that are federally regulated, have put these options into practice. Other companies besides have embraced diversity and inclusiveness as part of their human resources strategy.

Consultation with Employees from Diverse Backgrounds

When seeking ways to build a more representative board of directors and senior executive team, it is important to consult employees from diverse backgrounds. At least from their perspectives, they would be able to provide information on the barriers they face when competing for leadership positions; they would also be able to suggest how barriers could be removed so as to establish a work environment and human resources mechanisms that are more conducive to fairness and equity.

Without going into too much detail, consultation could focus on a sample of diverse employees who would likely be in the potential pools of candidates for mid-level management positions, executive positions, and board directorships. Internally, candidates for mid-level management positions are likely to be professionals; those for executive positions are likely to be mid-level managers; and those for board directorships are likely to be executives (or former executives). Consultation could be conducted on a one-on-one basis or in a focus group setting. It is advisable to hire an outside consultant who specializes in equity, diversity, and inclusiveness to facilitate group discussions and interviews. An external consultant signals professionalism, neutrality, and objectivity and encourages employees to be frank. To state the obvious, it is vital to build a trusting relationship between leaders and their diverse employees before launching the employee consultations, and building those relations may require a long time.

Through these consultations, a series of human resources mechanisms (such as training, development, selection, and performance evaluation) could be identified as having inherent biases in policies and procedures and even in the manner of how they have been carried out, and suggestions or recommendations could be solicited from employees regarding how best to develop a system of human resources development in such a way that leadership positions will be within the reach of diverse groups.

Another area for consultation is stereotypes and prejudice. Employees are to be encouraged to talk about their observations and experiences in the workplace as well as how their work life has been affected by negative perceptions and attitudes. A review of their comments would enable leaders to determine the priority areas in human resources that need immediate attention for system adjustment or reform as well as how to incorporate the results into education and training for their employees (see the following discussion on educational sessions).

Armed with these consultation findings and working with diverse employees, leaders and managers would be able to change the human resources mechanisms, the corporate culture, and the work environment for the better.

Educational Sessions on Stereotypes and Prejudice (Unconscious Bias)

Negative stereotypes and prejudice can play a damaging role in the recruitment and selection of diverse groups for board directorships and senior executive positions. Therefore it is important to develop educational sessions for the existing board directors and senior executives improve their awareness, knowledge, empathy, and skills in relation to diverse groups. A variety of educational resources have been developed to help people recognize their unconscious biases. For example, the Implicit Association Test, developed at Harvard University, enables participants to identify their own implicit attitudes and beliefs about other people as they relate to race, age, gender, and other variables (IAT Corp., n.d.). Also, various organizations offer readily available training courses on diversity and inclusiveness, both classroom-style and online. Those organizations include the Canadian Diversity Initiative, the Indigenous Leadership Development Institute, and CorporateTraining-Materials.com. DDI, a global leadership consulting company, has developed a series of educational and consulting programs that enable corporate leaders to reflect on unconscious bias, develop skills to interact with people, and establish human resources mechanisms that are free of bias and that utilize assessments so as to improve hiring and promotion practices (Busine, Byham, and Neal 2018).

These sessions should also be cascaded to mid-level managers, supervisors, and the rest of the employees in the organization. These educational sessions might emphasize the roles of non-Indigenous peoples, able-bodied persons, whites, and men in diversity work (Reynolds 2016). Professional experts specializing in diversity and inclusiveness might be invited to run these educational sessions, experiential workshops, and role-playing exercises for the purpose of identifying and removing conscious or unconscious biases.

To maximize the impact of these educational efforts, they should be conducted regularly, not just once. Refresher sessions should be provided at least annually. These educational efforts should ensure that board directors and senior executives connect their individual progression in removing negative stereotypes and prejudices to corporate diversity and inclusiveness policies, programs, and activities, if they are already in progress. In other words, organizational changes must be integrated with those to individuals.

In Canada, a number of financial institutions (such as the Royal Bank of Canada) and other large corporations have rolled out training workshops on unconscious bias, mainly for their leaders. Business Development Bank of Canada (BDC) is coordinating training sessions on the same topic across

Figure 4.10. Identifying and removing negative perceptions and attitudes

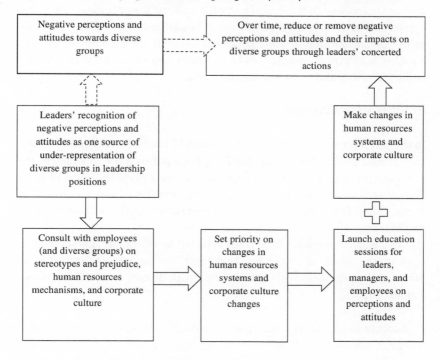

Canada. These workshops and sessions are not limited to gender issues; they include diversity issues (such as race, weight, and age) as well.

Changes in Human Resources Systems and Corporate Culture

During educational sessions, bias can also be addressed at the organizational level. Individual perceptions and feelings can be explored and analysed, and organizational policies and practices can be examined and assessed as to their impacts on people and businesses. There are often close links between stereotypes and prejudices and human resources activities. For example, human biases may permeate interview questions (such as questions on family obligations), rigidity in job application procedures (such as in online applications), and other human resources areas (such as recruitment, selection, training, development, and employee relations). Once identified, they can be set in priority sequence, and changes can be made in these systems.

Furthermore, the above-mentioned consultations may result in a series of concerns expressed in the area of corporate culture: the prevailing values and approaches in the treatment of employees or customers, how things get done in the organization, how complaints and requests for accommodation are handled, how work is assigned, and a variety of issues that would best tackled at the leadership and corporate culture levels.

Practices for Change

In the corporate world in the United States and Canada, there are many examples of educational procedures that have been put in place to augment the development of diversity and inclusiveness in the workplace. Some of these educational sessions are found in companies that have been nominated as Canada's Best Diversity Employers. The listed paragraphs below highlight several of them.

In Canada, companies have often resorted to education and training to open up the minds of employees, help them become aware of unconscious biases, and equip them with skills to work with diverse groups (MediaCorp Canada 2016a):

- **Accenture**, a Canadian management consulting firm, was recognized as one of this country's Best Diversity Employers in 2016. It participated in the Partners for Mental Health "Not Myself Today" campaign to highlight issues related to mental health.
- **Loblaw Companies Ltd.**, a supermarket and grocery company, has provided training for its members on unconscious biases and gender intelligence training.
- **Shell Canada**, a petroleum and natural gas extraction company, has launched training sessions in managing inclusiveness, cross-cultural skills, and gender balance. It has organized International Day of Persons with Disabilities recognition events and an annual Aboriginal awareness week.
- **Toronto Dominion Bank** has mandatory diversity and inclusiveness training sessions, mental health awareness training sessions, and cultural competency training sessions. Quarterly reviews of these training sessions and other diversity initiatives have been conducted to ensure progress.
- **Telus Corporation**, a telecommunications firm, has in-house training sessions on building an inclusive workplace, gender awareness, and generational diversity, as well as a diversity and inclusiveness website.

- The **Centre for Addiction and Mental Health (CAMH)**, a research-based hospital in Canada, provided full-day training sessions on diversity for all employees.
- **TransCanada Corporation** is a national gas distribution company in Alberta. The firm has required employees to complete mandatory online diversity training.

Education on diversity and inclusiveness has also been very popular in American companies (such as Novartis Pharmaceuticals, Johnson and Johnson, Ernst & Young, and PricewaterhouseCoopers). Such training helps highlight the subtle stereotypes and prejudices that people experience on a daily basis (DiversityInc. 2016a).

The above list of organizations and companies is not exhaustive, but they serve to illustrate the prevalence and popularity of educational sessions as a means of improving the awareness, knowledge, empathy, and skills of managers and employees. Education in diversity is quite common in organizations that have won awards as best diversity employers. Furthermore, each organization may customize its training topics and approaches based on its corporate needs. If disability (e.g., mental health) is a pressing issue at work, a company may develop educational sessions for raising the awareness and skill levels of managers and employees in working with persons with disabilities.

It may well be impossible to eradicate people's long-entrenched stereotypes and prejudices in a single educational session of a few hours; the effects of this sort of training are much longer-term when it is conducted regularly and in tandem with other diversity initiatives. In addition, an experiential/practical approach in these sessions is more effective than a classroom/theoretical approach because people can relate to the diversity messages better when those messages are applicable in the workplace. Not all of the examples cited here are experiential/practical, but more and more companies now recognize the value of that approach and have adopted it in their educational sessions.

In the past few years, large corporations in Canada have become increasingly aware of the need to raise the awareness of their leaders and managers regarding their unconscious biases (prejudice). These biases have been studied systematically, and educational modules have been prepared based on those studies. Leaders and managers could get together to explore and self-reflect on their hidden thinking and feelings related to gender, race, and disability and find ways to apply their learning to their work. Ideally, these educational sessions on unconscious biases should be cascaded from the leadership level down to middle management so that managers, who interact daily with their staffs, can apply their learning. Still later, the educational sessions could be cascaded down to all employees. To minimize the cost of education, some organizations could opt for online learning. And to make these educational sessions more effective, these sessions could be mandatory for all employees, with refresher sessions arranged at least once a year.

Conclusion

This chapter has illustrated the types of negative stereotypes that have evolved around diverse groups: Indigenous peoples (lazy, unreliable, dishonest), persons with disabilities (incompetence, dangerous), racialized minorities (untrustworthy, socially awkward), and women (lack of commitment, competence, assertiveness, and confidence). Feelings toward these diverse groups range from uneasiness to resentment. These negative stereotypes and attitudes highlighted at least three issues:

First, stereotypes and prejudices are different and unique for each diverse group, but all of them allege that members of those groups are not fit for leadership positions. These justifications may be unproven, but they are part of the collective mindset in the workplace and the broader society. Workplaces seem to be a microcosm of the larger society.

Second, irrespective of the variations in these negative perceptions and attitudes, they all have detrimental impacts on the well-being of diverse groups. Those impacts include ambivalence toward diverse groups, which often creates anxiety, uncertainty, and discomfort among employees and between management and non-management employees. Job dissatisfaction has been cited as a common state of mind for diverse groups and may lead to poor morale (often associated with work stress, group conflicts, and a lack of belonging and commitment among employees), poor work performance (often associated with poor job quality), and low productivity (often associated with cost ineffectiveness and inefficiencies).

Third, negative stereotypes induce discomfort among current leaders. As noted, most of them are white, able-bodied, non-Indigenous men. They do not interact with or feel at ease with these diverse groups. Because they feel uncomfortable and guarded with them, they avoid interacting with them. In this way, social distance develops between employees of different backgrounds. This further disadvantages diverse groups because leaders and colleagues have less chance to get to know them, which increases their chances of being misunderstood or suspected. This discomfort also makes it difficult for white, able-bodied, non-Indigenous men to find out what diverse groups can contribute to the organization with their knowledge, skills, and experiences. In these circumstances, diverse groups may find themselves shut off at the entry level; and once hired, they may have problems getting promoted to higher-echelon jobs. They may also find the workplace discouraging, which makes it more likely they will leave the organization before they have any chance to move up. It is difficult to imagine leaders being motivated to lift members of these diverse groups to leadership echelons or that they would feel comfortable doing so, where they would be working and making decisions as a team. Overall, for diverse groups, negativity has an corrosive effect on opportunity.

The adverse impacts of negative stereotypes and prejudices are often overwhelming. Because they are engrained in organizational structure, corporate culture, and the human psyche, it will take a long time to reduce and eradicate them. Prior to making any changes, organizations may organize consultation meetings with diverse employees to find out what stereotypes and prejudices they have noted in the workplace, how they feel about them and address them, and what changes they recommend to the organization. The results of consultations would help leaders identify priority areas for educational sessions for leaders and executives as well as improvements in human resources mechanisms and in the corporate culture as a whole.

Conducting regular education sessions on diversity and inclusiveness, in tandem with organizational changes in policies and practices, is a sure way to address the cognitive and emotional aspects of perceptions and attitudes. Education sessions are not the only method for addressing the issue of underrepresentation of diverse groups in leadership positions, but they can be an effective, sustainable, and long-term solution when combined with other systematic and structural means to effect changes in human resources mechanisms and corporate culture. When diversity education or training is the sole method used for tackling perceptual and attitudinal biases, it is unlikely to be effective in the long run. The reason is simple: the relative absence of diverse groups in leadership positions is not grounded solely in stereotypes and prejudices; its roots go deeper, into organizational structures and processes as well as their cultures.

In the first four chapters, we placed diversity in leadership in the context of the larger social and economic context and changing demographic trends. We provided evidence to demonstrate the lack of representation of diverse groups in leadership positions and started the analysis of such phenomena in the context of psychology: at the cognitive level, various concepts of leadership were examined; and at the perceptional and emotional levels, stereotypes and prejudice were discussed at length. These are the *psychological* barriers preventing diverse groups from becoming leaders.

That is only a beginning at dissecting the issue of diversity in leadership. More than thirty years ago, Sergiovanni (1984a, 1–11) suggested that one may have to look more broadly and deeeply to understand leadership. The conceptual framework of leadership and the negative perceptions and attitudes of people toward diverse groups are not the only barriers to the advancement of diverse groups in the workplace. In the next few chapters, we examine organizational and cultural factors in the workplace and gain greater insights into why current leadership is homogenous.

chapter five

Moving In – Recruitment and Selection

As noted in chapter 2, diverse groups in Canada are underrepresented among board directors and senior executives in the private sector. Finding out why is becoming increasingly pressing because, as noted in chapter 1, having diversity in leadership is more aligned with the changing world and has so many benefits for organizations. There are no compelling reasons why leaders should miss any opportunities to ensure diversity in leadership. Indeed, our society has fallen behind in economic growth and productivity because it has not sufficiently utilized the talents of diverse groups.

Chapters 3 and 4 provided insights into why diverse groups are unlikely to become leaders: it has to do with the concepts of leadership that current leaders use and the (probably) negative perceptions and attitudes they have developed unconsciously. First, contemporary mainstream concepts of leadership are based largely on attributes that some current leaders view as unlikely to be possessed by diverse groups. This has happened because negative stereotypes have been attached to those groups that are incompatible with what current leaders consider to be leadership qualities – members of diverse groups are not associated with vision or foresight, exceptionally strong leadership competencies (both diplomatic and militaristic), and proven executive experience. Their characteristics, styles, competencies, and cultural contributions do not quite resemble to what current leaders seek. The only competence that diverse groups have and that is close to what some current leaders expect is "people-orientation." The communal characteristics of Indigenous leadership and the transformational features of leadership valued and practised by persons with disabilities, racialized minorities, and women correspond well with the "people-orientation" of contemporary mainstream concepts of leadership. Unfortunately, today's current leaders consider such qualities to be either too narrow or too secondary on the hierarchy of leadership attributes they seek.

Second, prejudices directed toward these diverse groups play a role in their exclusion from leadership echelons. Some current leaders do not trust diverse groups enough to hand over stewardship to them; they also feel ambivalent, uneasy, and anxious when working with them. These negative feelings lead to social distance, marginalization, and avoidance between current leaders and diverse groups. This negativity, while subtle, affects the confidence and performance of members of these diverse groups, who generally see prejudice as prevalent and persistent. In this kind of work environment, where feelings are negative on both sides, it is unlikely that members of diverse group members will be hired as leaders.

When we keep these findings in mind, and understand how they define leadership and how prevalent negative stereotypes and prejudices are, we will be better positioned to recognize the forces acting against diverse groups as they attempt to rise to the leadership echelons. These findings suggest that diverse groups are not even the prime targets for recruitment or selection, let alone leadership identification. Over and above these forces, other factors are at play that hinder them from becoming leaders – in particular, the recruitment and selection mechanisms utilized in organizations.

Before discussing recruitment and selection, let us examine three contextual issues – the availability of (a) qualified leadership candidates, (b) a critical mass of diverse groups among leaders, and (c) vacancies at the leadership level. All three conditions must be present before recruitment and selection can be equitable. In this chapter we examine whether externally, there is a sufficient pool of qualified and available diverse group members from outside the companies from which organizations can draw for leadership, and whether internally, the number of diverse group members is large enough to constitute a critical mass in corporate leadership and whether there are vacancies in leadership positions for new members. If the answer in each case is "no," then finding diverse group members to become leaders will be difficult.

In the area of recruitment, our discussion will focus on three recruitment methods commonly used by corporations: word-of-mouth, job advertisements, and external search firms. In the area of selection, we will highlight three components in selection: selection panels, selection criteria, and interview processes. Recruitment and selection mechanisms are highlighted because they can have an immense impact on diverse groups outside the organization. The application of contemporary mainstream concepts of leadership and the psychological filters of negative perceptions and attitudes, when interfaced with the human resources mechanisms at the leadership level and the absence of a critical mass of diverse group members, will tend to bar these group members from joining the leadership echelons. Toward the end of the chapter, I will suggest various best options and practices for addressing the problems arising from these human resources mechanisms.

Representation and External Availability of Qualified Diverse Groups

A business organization can be viewed as a hierarchy of occupational groups. Board directors and senior executives comprise the top two layers of the hierarchy. The board of directors provides the organization with policies and strategies; senior executives (including the CEO) translate those policies and strategies into actions and execute them on a daily basis.

This chapter focuses on recruitment from outside the organization. Promotion from within will be discussed in chapter 6. The reality is that most board directors come from outside, and most senior executives from within.

First, we need to ascertain whether there is a strong external supply of qualified candidates. For this, the data sets on the external labour market availability of qualified diverse groups and on the representation of senior executives in the federally regulated private sector in Canada for 2014 provide the data we need. That sector consists mainly of the banking, communications, and transportation sectors. This is a robust data set that has workforce data on 501 employers and a total of 740,740 employees (4% of the Canadian workforce) across Canada for 2014. The data set is also longitudinal, which allows us to look at trends in representation since 1987 (Canada 2016c). For benchmarking purposes, we will be using the external labour force availability rates of diverse groups. Those rates will tell us how many qualified diverse group members in senior management are available to fill positions at this level. It is based on the National Household Survey of 2011 and earlier censuses. Whether people are deemed "qualified" is a function of their reported work duties and experiences in senior management. Some of them were working as senior managers during the census period.

The external availability data indicate that there is a rich supply of external qualified and available diverse group members who are ready to rise to senior management. Yet it seems that this external pool has yet to be tapped for leadership candidates.

Three patterns emerge from table 5.1:

- First, all diverse groups are underrepresented among board directors and senior executives in Canada.
- Second, the external availability data of all diverse groups in Canada indicate that their numbers are higher than the numbers of their internal

Table 5.1. Representation and availability of diverse groups in senior managers group, Canada, 2011, 2014, and 2015

	Indigenous peoples			Persons with disabilities			Racialized minorities			Women		
	Internal representation* (2014, 2015)	External availability rates** (2011)	Diversity gaps	Internal representation* (2014, 2015)	External availability rates** (2011)	Diversity gaps	Internal representation* (2014, 2015)	External availability rates** (2011)	Diversity gaps	Internal representation* (2014, 2015)	External availability rates** (2011)	Diversity gaps
	%	%	%	%	%	%	%	%	%	%	%	%
Board directors	1.3	2.9	**-2.6**	1.3	4.3	**-3.0**	7.3	10.1	**-2.8**	19.5	27.4	**-7.9**
Senior managers	0.8	2.9	**-2.1**	2.6	4.3	**-1.7**	8.1	10.1	**-2.0**	24.8	27.4	**-2.6**

*Statistics on the internal representation of board directors are based on 2015, and that of senior managers are based on 2014.

Source: Canada 2016c. *Employment Equity Act: Annual Report 2015. Appendix A, Table B* and Canadian Board Diversity Council, 2015: 4, 9.

**Benchmark – National labour market availability rates of "senior managers" in Canada are based on the 2011's National Household Survey.

Bolded values denote diversity gaps in which the percentages of all four diverse groups in both the board directors and senior managers are below those of the external availability rates.

Source: Canada 2015: Appendix A, Table B

"senior managers." This means that the external pool of qualified and available diverse group members is ready to be recruited, selected, and hired for "senior management" positions.

- Third, however underrepresented they are at the senior management level, some diverse group members are qualified to serve as board directors or senior executives and are available externally and/or internally. In other words, senior managers are ready for board directorship positions. But as noted in chapter 2, diverse groups continue to be underrepresented on boards of directors. This implies that they have yet to be sufficiently tapped by the current boards.

Indigenous Peoples

In 2014, Indigenous peoples comprised only 0.8% of senior managers in the federally regulated private sector. Plainly, they were underrepresented relative to their external availability rate in senior management (2.9%). The latter showed clearly that there is a strong supply of qualified Indigenous peoples from the broader community to take on senior management roles in the private sector. Incidentally, there is also a large external supply of Indigenous peoples at the middle management level (2.2%) ready to take senior management roles (Canada 2014b; 2016c). An external supply of qualified Indigenous peoples is there waiting to be utilized.

Persons with Disabilities

In 2014, persons with disabilities were underrepresented at the senior management level (2.6%) in the federally regulated private sector. Given that the external availability rate of persons with disabilities at that level (4.3%) is higher than what has been identified internally in the private sector, it is clear that in the broader community there is a strong supply of qualified persons with disabilities to take on senior management roles. Equally important, there is a large external supply of persons with disabilities at the middle management level (4.3%) ready to serve as senior managers and board directors (Canada 2014b; 2016c).

Racialized Minorities

In 2014, within the federally regulated private sector in Canada, racialized minorities comprised 8.1% of senior managers in the federally regulated private sector. This underrepresentation, relative to the external availability rate, indicates that in the broader community there is a large supply of racialized minorities at the senior management level (10.1%) ready serve as senior managers and board directors (Canada 2014b; 2016c).

Women

In 2014, women comprised 24.8% of senior managers in the federally regulated private sector. Given that their external availability rate at the senior management level is 27.4%, it is clear that they are underrepresented, even though there is a strong supply of qualified women with senior management experience in the broader community to take on senior management or board directorship roles in the private sector (Canada 2014b; 2016c).

Overall, diverse group members at the board and senior executive levels are not underrepresented because supply of them is lacking; the problem is that private sector leaders are not utilizing them. This is for a number of reasons, discussed later in this chapter.

Lack of a Critical Mass

"Critical mass" refers to the minimum number of people it takes to make and drive change in an organization or a community. In the social sciences, the term often relates to group dynamics, collective behaviour, public opinion, innovation, or politics. Different social situations seem to require different degrees of critical mass for change to come about. In politics, some people have observed that 30% is the "magic number" – that is, women need to achieve 30% representation before they can affect substantive political change. Other people argue that the proportion may be smaller – as low as 15%. There is no consensus on this (Dahlerup 1988, 2006; Tremblay 2006). For our working purposes, a mass of 30% is critical for diverse groups in leadership positions in an organization. Given the current demographic profiles of diverse groups in Canada, Indigenous peoples, persons with disabilities, and racialized minorities cannot reach their "critical mass" on their own. It may be that the only way for them to reach a critical mass will be to combine all four diverse groups. Women, however, have the potential to reach the critical mass of 30% on their own if the diverse composition of the organization's workforce reflects the larger population.

The importance of having a critical mass of diverse groups in leadership positions is that it usually enables them to acquire a sustained voice when new ideas or solutions are being advanced. It also makes possible a more comprehensive review of issues. And it makes it easier for them to influence peers, make connections, and make decisions in their areas of responsibily. It also facilitates liaison with diverse groups outside the organization for marketing, recruitment, and community or public relations purposes. Note that human resources planning is one area in which a critical mass of diverse group members is pivotal. With 30% or over and with a united voice, they find it more possible to make diversity a key strategy in human resources planning. They can also exert influence on their peers and break traditional modes of thinking, thereby making group decisions in favour of diversity.

Some political scientists are uncertain about the substantive impact of a critical mass of women on policy changes and outcomes, wondering how useful or relevant it is. They point to additional factors such as institutional mechanisms, types of parliamentary proceedings, party allegiances, and party status (Chaney 2012; Childs and Krook 2006, 2008; Grey 2006) In other words, a critical mass in itself does not guarantee organizational change.

While there may still be questions about how a critical mass interfaces with other factors to effect substantive changes, its value remains noteworthy in public opinion, politics, innovation, social trends, social networks, and group dynamics. So it is important to cast diversity at the leadership level in this light and to examine how critical mass can play a role.

Senior Executives

None of the four diverse groups being examined here have a critical mass at the senior executive level. To recap, among senior executives in the federally regulated private sector in 2014, the representation rate of Indigenous peoples was 0.8%; for persons with disabilities, 2.6%; for racialized minorities, 8.7%; and for women, 24.8% (Canada 2015; 2016c). Clearly, none of these diverse groups has reached the critical mass of 30%. Given the diversity gaps in Canada, they are unlikely to reach it in the foreseeable future.

When we compare the representation rates of France and Canada, we gain a better perspective on present-day gender parity in both countries. The relevance of a critical mass at the executive level is illustrated by the performance of France. In 2019, the country commanded the highest degree of gender parity in board directorships, with over 40% women, which met its quota of 40% set by the government in 2011. At the board level, women have reached a critical mass. Canada is lagging behind France, at 24.8%.

According to one global gender-balance measurement, at the executive level, women constituted 19% at the Top 20 companies in France, and these companies were above the 15% mark reached by the Global Top 100. At the executive level, Canada's TSX companies were at 15.8% in gender parity, a few percentage points behind France but still a bit ahead of the Global Top 100. If three or more women on the executive team are considered to be a critical mass, nine companies in France among its Top 20 companies have reached that stage. In Canada, data on gender parity at the level of individual companies have not been broadly studied or released. A preliminary examination of executives in large companies found that they do not fare well on this front: Scotiabank (with 3 women among 30 executives), Royal Bank of Canada (1 woman among 10), Canada National Railway (5 among 30), Nutrien (2 among 10), Suncor Energy (1 among 9), BCE (1 among 13), Imperial Oil (1 among 6), and Power Corporation (no woman on the executive team) (Schachter, 2019).

There are many possible reasons for the relative absence of women and other diverse groups at the executive level in Canada. One of these relates to the feeder pool for executives, the feeder pool being an organization's middle managers and professionals (from which future senior executives are likely to emerge). Canadian data indicate that at the middle management level, the representation rate for Indigenous peoples is 1.2%, that of persons with disabilities is 2.9%, and that of racialized minorities is 20.4%. At the professional levels, the representation rate for Indigenous peoples is 1.1%, that of persons with disabilities is 2.7%, and that of racialized minorities is 28.3%. It is clear that these groups have not achieved critical mass at the middle management and professional levels (which serve as pipelines to senior management). The lack of a critical mass at levels immediately below the senior executive level suggests that companies are in a poor position to promote diverse groups from within. If the internal pipelines are not there, raising diverse groups to the leadership level will require recruitment from outside (Canada 2016c).

Meanwhile, women's representation rates in the middle-management (42.0%) and professional (45.5%) levels are indicative of their critical mass. This has expanded the feeder pool of talents for senior executives available within an organization (Canada 2016c). It appears that the lack of women among senior executives is not so much because there is no internal feeder pool; rather, they are not being promoted and retained. These issues will be discussed in chapters 6 and 7.

Board Directors

None of the four diverse groups examined here have achieved a critical mass among board directors. The Canadian Board Diversity Council's survey (2015, 4, 9) of *Financial Post* 500 organizations found that only 1.3% of board directors were Indigenous peoples, 1.3% were persons with disabilities, 7.3% were racialized minorities, and 19.5% were women. In 2016, the percentages for women (21.6%) and persons with disabilities (1.8%) were slightly more than the year before, but those for racialized minorities (4.5%) and Indigenous peoples (0.6%) had declined (Canadian Board Diversity Council 2016).

Based on 2016 data from the Corporations Returns Act, along with other administrative data and gender probability data based on first names in Canada, Statistics Canada's 2019 study of the share of female board directors in public and private corporations and public/private enterprises found that women constituted 19.4% of all board directors. The difference between this percentage and other percentages cited earlier is likely due to the sample size that Statistics Canada used: around 13,000 corporations reporting on more than 44,000 directors. The data showed one interesting pattern – private corporations had the lowest share of female directors, and government/business enterprises the largest. This suggests that governments are more vigilant in ensuring gender parity on boards in anticipation of public scrutiny (Grant 2019).

The Canadian Board Diversity Council's 2018 survey found that efforts toward diversity had stagnated somewhat, except when it came to women, whose percentage on boards had risen to 24.5%. This pattern of stagnation or pause in the linear progress of women at the board level is of concern to people who are pushing for gender parity. These concerns are grounded in some evidence, beginning with the peak appointment of women to 45% of all non-executive directors in 2015, as demonstrated in a report released by Spencer Stuart on the 100 largest companies in Canada. After 2015, the proportion of women among new board appointments steadily declined until it reached 30% in 2018 – the year the study was conducted. Because of this decline, the 27% representation of women on boards may not be sustainable (Milstead 2019). Furthermore, compared to other Western countries, Canada's gender parity record was weak to begin with, and even large firms are uneven in their performance in terms of increasing the proportion of women on boards. Some women are openly concerned about the mindsets of some board members who believe in a self-congratulatory manner that having one female board director on a board means "task accomplished" (Schachter 2019; McFarland 2019; Bouw 2019).

The other three diverse groups examined here may not achieve critical mass for a long time due to their small population sizes and the lower external availability of qualified senior executives. As the progress report cards of the Canadian Board Diversity Council showed, the pace of progress has slowed, stagnated, or even regressed at times. Meanwhile, women have the potential to reach a critical mass due to their larger population size and the increased external availability of female senior executives.

The underrepresentation of women on boards (19.5% of current boards compared to the availability rate of women in senior management at 27.4%) and the lack of a critical mass of women (benchmarked as 30%) call for a change in the status quo. According to the Canadian Board Diversity Council (2016, 19), only 37.8% of board directors reported that their boards had a target for female directors. In other words, 67.2% still did not have a target. The good news is that among those board directors whose boards did not have a target for female directorship, 35% would personally support a target of either 33% or 50%. However, nearly one out of four directors in this group would not support any target. The resistance to gender targeting remains high.

The lack of critical mass makes it difficult for diverse groups to develop an effective voice at the senior executive and board directorship levels. This may make it impossible for them to show other leaders what they can accomplish. It also makes it harder for them to advocate for more diversity. A contrast worth observing is the sheer numbers of Indigenous peoples and women on boards. There are far more women than Indigenous peoples on boards, and this is reflected in their influence and decision-making power on those boards.

According to Leighton's study of 500 corporate boards (2010, 254), the average number of directors on Canadian boards is 11, and only 1.3% of them are Indigenous based on the Canadian Board Diversity Council's survey results cited earlier. Calculations based on these figures indicated that there were only 71.5 Indigenous persons on boards among a total of 5,500 board directors (i.e., 11 directors/board x 500 boards). So on an average, there were only 0.14 Indigenous persons on each board (i.e., 71.5 Indigenous directors divided by 500 boards). While this is a rough estimate, the statistics on the participation of Indigenous peoples are consistent with a special study on companies listed on the TSX60 conducted by the same council in 2013. Of the 428 seats on their boards, 5 (or 1.2%) were held by Indigenous peoples – that is, there were 0.08 Indigenous persons on each of the TSX60 corporate boards (Canadian Board Diversity Council 2013, 18).

The above estimates of the number of Indigenous persons sitting on boards – 0.08 or 0.14 – are merely averages for the companies in the samples. The reality is that Indigenous persons are concentrated on boards of directors in natural resources and utilities (Corporate Knights 2012b). So it is very likely that most organizations outside of these industries in Canada do not have any Indigenous peoples on their boards.

The Conference Board of Canada's 2001 study on female board directors found that having two or more women on a board of directors is likely to strengthen advocacy for female representation on boards and to increase recruitment of more women to the boards through an external search company (Brown, Brown, and Anastasopoulos 2002, 10). The study also found a positive correlation between more women on boards and a higher proportion of women among senior executives of the same organization. This suggests that the appointment of diverse group members to boards (so that they can get closer to critical mass) may be key to driving more representation both on boards and at the senior executive level.

When Indigenous peoples are underrepresented and do not have a critical mass on private sector boards, there is less chance for more of them to be appointed to directorships. As Leighton (2010, 257) observed, the current homogeneity of boards "begets more homogeneity." As was demonstrated earlier, there are hardly any Indigenous senior executives in Canada, so it is to be expected that CEOs and other board directors will find it hard to appoint Indigenous executives to directorships, especially given the relative absence of an Indigenous voice to "advocate" for greater representation for Indigenous peoples.

Discussion

All four diverse groups in the federally regulated private sector lack a critical mass at the senior executive and board directorship levels. Indigenous peoples and persons with disabilities face an additional problem: they lack a critical mass at occupational levels below the senior executive level. As a consequence, there are no internal pipelines for them to the senior executive level in the federally regulated private sector, and therefore, their entry to the senior executive and board directorship levels has to rely more heavily on outside routes.

The good news is that there is a strong supply of qualified and readily available diverse group members from outside who can take on the responsibilities of senior executives or board directors in the private sector. Their relative absence from leadership positions over time is not due to the lack of external feeder pools; rather, the pipeline to bring them on board is not there or is simply blocked by various other barriers (a factor that will be explored later in this chapter). Clearly, one solution for rectifying the problem of underrepresentation is to look outside the organization and start developing networks (pipelines) to draw these people in. We will discuss this later in the chapter.

Lack of Board Vacancies

Trophy Directorships

Certain traditions on boards of directors may explain why progress in the representation of diverse groups has been rather limited. Board directors have long tended to accumulate board appointments to create an aura of reputation and credibility (often known as the "halo effect"). They solicit or encourage more invitations to sit on other boards of directors. In the process, they gain more board experiences and more extensive comprehension of various industries, besides garnering more media coverage (through announcements of their appointments), credibility, reputation, and supports from other board members. Directors with these cross-appointments to numerous boards have been referred to as "trophy directors."

"Trophy directors" present multiple disadvantages from an organizational perspective. They are more exposed to liability or conflict of interest, for they represent different business interests. They also have to manage their time well, given that preparing for board meetings requires extensive reading of briefing notes and documents. Multiple seats on boards necessarily means less preparation time for board meetings, which in turn often weakens the quality of board discussions and decisions. More pertinent to the issue of representation of diverse groups on boards is that having trophy directors sit on numerous boards means they are occupying seats that could be opened for others, including diverse group members (who are waiting to join the boards).

Board Tenure and Term Limits

Another traditional practice that is detrimental to fairer representation of diverse groups is board tenure. In most organizations, board directors can stay on boards until they retire or resign. There are no set rules for their tenure, nor are there limits to the number of reappointments of directors or to the number of years they can serve. This likely means that board directors occupy board seats for a long time, which makes it harder for new directors to join.

According to the Canadian Board Diversity Council's 2016 survey, only 45.8% of board directors reported that their boards had term limits. Close to 30% (29.1%) of them expressed no inclination to adopt term limits unless this became a legal obligation, and only 25.1% were prepared to place term limits on directorships. Close to half the directors (47.7%) believed that term limits might enhance diversity in the boardroom. But among those directors who did not face term limits, only one quarter (25.1%) believed they should be adopted. This suggests there is no consensus among current board directors regarding term limits and that there is still resistance to them from within. Apparently, if diversity in leadership is to be achieved, this area will need some changes.

The dearth of board vacancies owing to the clustering of trophy directors, lack of term limits for board seats, and resistance to opening up board membership may explain why better representation of diverse groups at the board level has been so slow to develop. This slow pace makes it even harder for diverse groups to achieve equitable representation and a critical mass to effect changes in board membership and, indirectly, the appointment of diverse group members to senior executive positions. To address the issue of underrepresentation of diverse groups on boards, it may be necessary to eliminate trophy directorships, set term limits on board tenure, and develop board policies or even legislation on these issues. This will be discussed later in the chapter.

Human Resources Mechanisms

"Human resources mechanisms" refers to the structures, processes, systems, and tools used when developing people in an organization. These mechanisms cover various aspects of how an organization gets its people from outside, helps them work in the organization once they are in it, and grows and retains them. The term covers a range of human resources functions such as recruitment, selection, promotion, training, development, performance appraisal, succession management, compensation, and benefits. These mechanisms, known collectively as "talent management," are used for recruiting, managing, and developing "the right people with the right capabilities in the right roles" to meet the organization's business goals (Humber 2014, 7–8). Companies utilize the latest methods and tools for doing all of this effectively. It is the contention of this book that human errors or biases are often embedded in these policies, procedures, tools, and methods – often unknowingly – as they are developed and practised. These mechanisms need to be reviewed for the purpose of finding more equitable ways to develop human resources.

This chapter examines human resources mechanisms related to senior executive positions and directorships. In organizations in which diverse groups are underrepresented in middle management, a review of human resources mechanisms below the senior management level is in order. This is because a persistent pattern of underrepresentation or an absence of diverse groups in certain occupations at any level of an organization points not only to the ineffective and inequitable utilization of talents, but also to a lack of pipelines, or to a pipeline blockage that prevents diverse groups from being mobile, be it laterally or vertically.

As our focus is on finding out why diverse groups have problems securing leadership positions, we will concentrate first on identifying common barriers that apply to all or most diverse groups; we will then examine specific issues related to each of the diverse groups. This author, having conducted many consulting and research projects in the private sector and examined the literature in this field, finds it apparent that diverse groups share a broad range of systemic barriers that hinder them from becoming leaders. Each diverse group also confronts barriers that are specific to it. These barriers are blocking them from becoming leaders over and above factors that were discussed in previous chapters (i.e., contemporary mainstream concepts of what a leader should be, and biased perceptions and attitudes towards diverse groups).

A discussion of common barriers pertinent to more than one diverse group is valuable because, being in common, they signal their prevalence and embedded nature. For this reason, they are of higher priority when it comes to finding solutions. Specific barriers applicable only to one specific diverse group call for the customization of solutions for that group in particular.

Recruitment

There are two sources of potential candidates for senior executives – internal and external. Observations indicate that most senior executives are promoted from within. Directors, by contrast, are usually recruited from outside. There is a distinction between "external" and "internal" board directors. "External" board directors have no working history as employees of the organization that has appointed them as directors, whereas "internal" board directors are either former or current employees of the organization that has appointed them. Canadian data from 1996 indicate that around two thirds of board directors in the *Report to Business Top 1000* Canadian companies were external, and one third were internal (Burke 2010a, 100–1).

Before we discuss recruitment methods, it is important to note that leaders tend to focus on potential leaders in their own industries and to ignore the supply pool of middle managers and senior executives from other industries. They also tend to believe that management and leadership knowledge and skills are not transferrable from one industry to another. This narrow mindset hinders the advancement of diverse groups to the board directorship and senior executive levels. For example, there is currently a sizeable supply of middle managers and senior executives with disabilities or of Indigenous and racial minority background in the public sector, yet their knowledge and leadership skills are seldom acknowledged or appreciated by the private sector because they are not deemed relevant or applicable to the business world. Another example is found in the natural resources sector in which some Indigenous executives are found. This is another feeder pool that other industries should tap. Recruitment methods are only as good as they are targeted properly. To diversify boards of directors and senior executive teams, the scope of recruitment must be broadened.

This chapter focuses on how candidates are recruited from outside and defers discussion about promoting candidates from within to the next chapter. Three main methods of recruiting senior executives and board directors are highlighted here: word-of-mouth, job advertisements, and executive search firms. These methods may be used one at a time or simultaneously, depending on circumstances, corporate policies, and need for special talents.

Word-of-Mouth

"Word-of-mouth" is a traditional but still prevalent method for recruiting senior executives and board directors – and indeed, other positions as well. Typically, the current CEO, board directors, and senior executives compile a short list of candidates whom they know and then contact them personally through their own social networks. They may also spread the word that an executive position has opened up and hope that qualified candidates will come forward. Who among these cadidates is actually "qualified" is an open question, but it is likely to be determined by each senior executive. Often (and this depends on the arrangement between the board of directors and senior management), the vacant executive position is made known to the board directors first, and they are encouraged to refer qualified candidates.

It has often been observed that this method is potentially biased, narrow in focus, and ridden with favouritism or even nepotism. But it is still considered quite effective in identifying candidates with the best "corporate fit" (Breaugh, 2000; 2008). The survey results of the Canadian Board Diversity Council (2016, 20) found that this method is quite widespread – 38.5% of board directors reported that they "always" tapped into their own personal networks, and 50.6% reported that they tapped into them "sometimes." Among those directors who tapped into their own personal networks in recruitment, 21.3% "always" and 57.1% "sometimes" used gender, race, and indigeneity as prime considerations. The same council's 2018 survey showed similar patterns (Canadian Board Diversity Council 2018, 30). In fact, when one includes tapping into the networks of others such as shareholders, the percentages of board directors using the word-of-mouth method is even higher.

CEOs play an important role in recruiting board directors mainly because they have knowledge and experience in the strategy/policy as well as the operational aspects of the organization. They are the "bridge" between the board and the organization's operations, as well as between the board and the external world. They know their colleagues in their own industry and in others, and they mingle with their peers outside their own organization. They are in a good position to contact people whom they believe are qualified for leadership positions, as well as to find people who can replace them and work with or for them. Historically, board directors have been invited to join a board through the personal contacts of CEOs, chairpersons, or senior executives. This reinforces the image of a "closed shop" and "old boys' club" (Holton 2010, 145–55). As time progresses, more board directors believe that the board as a whole is responsible for board diversity (60.2%) and that the responsibility should not be limited to the CEO (2.0%), the chair (14.8%), or the chair of the governance and nominating committee or equivalent (12.9%) (Canadian Board Diversity Council 2018, 22).

Board directors often provide names of potential candidates to external search firms for shortlisting candidates. They can definitely play a pivotal role in recruitment, and the "word-of-mouth" method has been perceived to work well in the past. However, given that most CEOs, senior executives, and board directors are not women or members of other diverse groups, name recognition of diverse group members for these CEOs is unlikely. Being unknown, diverse group members are seldom targeted by CEOs, existing board directors, or senior executives in recruitment.

Yet, as far as board directorships are concerned, CEOs have expressed a strong interest in recruiting female directors. Catalyst's 1995 survey found that 72% of CEOs reported that it was their "top priority" or "a priority" to have a female board director and that only 5% placed female directorship as a "very low priority." Eighty-six per cent of these CEOs also indicated that it was important to have higher representation of women on their boards, and only 14% believed that gender was not a relevant recruitment criterion" (Mattis 2010, 49). As far as the entire board was concerned, the results of the Canadian Board Diversity Council's (2018: 17) 2018 survey showed that 54.7% of them felt that board diversity was very important.

In practice, recruiting female board directors has been more difficult than expected. The Catalyst 1993 survey of 1993 on the *Fortune* 500/*Service* 500 companies noted that board directors have problems identifying and locating potential female board directors. Forty-six per cent of board directors surveyed did not know where to look for qualified women because they were not currently on boards, or that there were too few qualified women, and that too few women who *were* qualified failed to communicate their interest (Mattis 2010, 50–1; Burke 2010, 107). As late as 2010, one third of Canadian CEOs estimated that there were 50 or fewer qualified women for board directorships, and 80% of them thought the pool was fewer than 250. This perspective is also quite common in the United States and in other countries (Burke 1994; Balimoria 2010, 26; Bradshaw and Wicks 2010, 199). They may even find it uncomfortable to recruit other diverse group candidates because they are not certain that candidates from diverse backgrounds will be allegiant to them, or under their influence. Perhaps, too, they will be independent thinkers who are at odds with the traditional ways of running an organization.

In the context of board politics, a certain segment of board directors are outsiders (which means that they have not worked in the organizations they are now serving as board directors). When boards are composed mainly of outsiders, there is a great likelihood that new ideas or changes will be proposed and discussed, for these outsiders do not have much ownership of the present-day strategic direction or operation. When new ideas (not proposed by the CEO) are endorsed, this signals or implies a reduction of the CEO's power to exert influence on the board, and CEOs have to abide with the board's decisions. So CEOs are likely to resist the appointment of more outsiders. In the context of the existing composition of board directors, diverse groups are viewed as outsiders. As such, they are largely resisted. According to Fondas (2010, 173, 175–6), using the example of women, it is not so much their "femaleness" that places women at a disadvantage, but that they are outsiders, with unknown track records and little name recognition, and are perceived as independents – "It is not discrimination against women per se; it is a bias against independents and outsiders." Whether it is gender bias or outsider-bias that has excluded women from leadership positions for many years is still to be determined, but the likely scenario is that both factors play a role and, when combined, are a strong contributing factor.

The word-of-mouth method tends to benefit white, able-bodied, non-Indigenous men because that describes most board members, and always has. They are the first to know when vacancies have opened, and they know what types of candidates they want. They may also spread the word through their personal networks. In this way, they control who joins the boards or senior executive teams, and this tends to stabilize the board's composition, for they do not want the new members to disrupt the board. In essence, they are the gatekeepers. Most studies have found that when recruiting future senior executives or board directors, the existing ones reach out and contact their peers, who also sit on boards or work as senior executives. As previous chapters have shown, those peers (mostly other board directors or senior executives) are likely to be white, able-bodied, non-Indigenous, and male. Diverse groups are unlikely to be among them.

As Leighton (2010, 256) noted, "the corporate director universe in Canada is relatively small, so that most directors know each other, either personally or by reputation. It is a comfortable pew!" It seems likely that the word-of-mouth method will result in existing leaders looking for future leaders who are more or less like them. Admittedly, there have been some changes in the profile of leaders, but they have been too slow to alter the critical mass of the white, able-bodied, non-Indigenous men (Burke 2010a, 98).

Basically, the word-of-mouth method transmits information on open executive positions or board directorships through the current leaders' social networks. By resorting to word-of-mouth as the dominant means of recruiting future leaders, white, able-bodied, non-Indigenous men have been able to maintain their long-held grip on leadership circles.

Because current leadership is relatively devoid of the four diverse groups being examined here, diverse groups have very little opportunity to learn about job opportunities. Brown, Brown, and Anastasopoulos (2002, 10) found that more women were recruited to boards when two or more women are already on them. Compared to other diverse groups, women in Canada are in a much better position in terms of their critical mass at the board directorship level (19.5%) and at the senior executive level (24.8%). Even so, their voices are likely to be be crowded out by their male counterparts. It is essential for there to be a critical mass of diverse groups at the leadership level if word-of-mouth methods are to sustain the growth of diverse groups in the leadership echelon. As noted, other diverse groups may never have the opportunity to reach the critical mass they need.

The dearth of members of diverse groups in the social networks of current leaders is another factor that works against them when the word-of-mouth method is used. Various factors may explain the relative absence of diverse groups in those social networks; chief among them are negative stereotypes and prejudice. As noted in the previous chapter, negative perceptions of diverse groups do great harm to their well-being and performance. Most importantly, in the context of recruitment, those perception create social distance and discomfort between Indigenous and non-Indigenous persons, persons with and without disabilities, whites and racialized minorities, and men and women. Current leaders are largely socially separated from diverse groups; their social networks are rather homogeneous. For these leaders, diverse groups are essentially "out-groups."

Research studies have found that people are uncomfortable and unsure of themselves when interacting with persons with visible disabilities, especially those with physically disfiguring conditions. In fact, they try to avoid them physically. This social avoidance behaviour is similar to that of people who try to avoid people with visible symptoms of disease (Park, Faulkner, and Schaller 2003, 65–7). Furthermore, negative perceptions and attitudes often translate in observable behaviours such as physical avoidance, uneasiness, and discriminatory actions. All of these have implications for social networking. They encourage diverse group members tend to stick to themselves and maintain their own circles of friends. According to Deitch, Barsky, and Butz (2003, 1299–324), blatant racism has been replaced by more subtle forms, such as avoidance of racialized minorities, unfriendly verbal or non-verbal communication, and exclusion from social networks and group activities. Because of social avoidance and distancing as a behavioural response to negative stereotypes and prejudice, the word-of-mouth method can only benefit those within the boundaries of social networks of senior executives and board directors.

Related to social distancing and avoidance is people's tendency to be suspicious of outsiders. This psychological trait is not limited to white, able-bodied, non-Indigenous men; indeed, it is rather common among people of whatever their race, sex, indigeneity, and ability. As noted in chater 4, due to negative stereotyping, people tend to see those who are similar to themselves (often based on physical attributes or appearances) as an in-group and those who are dissimilar as an out-group. This distinction results in distrust of the out-group. So when board directors or senior executives are recruited from outside the organization, the existing leaders find it more difficult to recruit diverse groups, for they are often viewed as out-groups in addition to having outsider status.

Job Advertisements

Job ads for executive positions or board directorships may be used by an organization or by an external search firm that has been contracted by an organization. Essentially, a job ad announces a job vacancy for an executive position or board directorship, laying out the position's duties and responsibilities as well as the desired qualifications and experience. In the private sector, sometimes these leadership positions are not advertised. Most such ads are placed by the broader public sector. On rare occasions, if and when these vacancies are advertised, they are posted on the organization's website. In the past, job ads were not commonly used to recruit senior executives, but due to increased social pressure for transparency and accountability, they are becoming more common now.

The wording of job ads varies greatly. That said, a review of the *Globe and Mail*'s job postings (see chapter 3) suggested that today's mainstream leaders are looking for change agents, advocates, catalysts, champions, developers, consensus-builders, ambassadors, problem-solvers, motivators, coaches, organization-builders, diplomats, and visionaries as their future leaders. Many of the *Globe and Mail*'s job postings indicated that current leaders are looking for people with a long list of competencies. Job ads tend to describe the "ceiling" (ideal features) and not the "floor" (basic features) of job requirements.

This discourages diverse groups from applying and competing for the advertised positions. Take persons with disabilities as an example. Church and colleagues (2007, 7–9) noted that these people devote a significant portion of their time to managing their disabilities, visible or not. Those with invisible disabilities expend a lot of energy and effort in their work lives hiding their disabilities to avoid stigmatization and labelling by the people around them. So when job ads focus on "ceiling" requirements and the demands of executive jobs and board directorships, instead of attracting more persons with disabilities to apply, they often discourage them for applying.

Men and women typically respond differently to job ads. Men are more inclined to apply for jobs when they barely meet the qualifications, whereas women apply for jobs only when they are certain they meet all or most of them. Women read the required qualifications in ads as basic requirements that candidates must have. They do not apply because they see no point, given that they will likely fail. Men are more risk-taking and opportunity-seeking than women. Women also feel that they are wasting their time and energy in applying if they do not meet the requirements. They see the requirements as rules with which they must comply. This suggests that they are unfamiliar with how hiring actually works, perhaps because of differential gender socialization processes (Mohr 2014; Hannon 2014). As a result, job ads that outline ideal candidate's attributes (often with high-sounding words and messages) may discourage women from applying even when they may be objectively qualified.

Some job ads list a broad range of competencies and requirements that make persons with disabilities think twice about applying. A few job postings may emphasize the enormous responsibilities of executive work and the broad range of executive activities: liaising and working with stakeholder groups, taking responsibility for a broad range of tasks, travelling widely. Some job ads stress multitasking, making oneself available 24/7, working in a fast-paced work environment, and other "discouraging" work conditions for persons with disabilities. Usually there is nothing written in the job ads about accommodation (upon request), accessibility, work flexibility, or other work-related supports.

Without these kinds of statements, job advertisements may discourage persons with disabilities, as well as women, from applying. Persons with specific disabilities may be concerned about their mobility, capacity to handle workloads, the availability of accommodation, and many other issues related to their physical or mental health. Meanwhile, women may be concerned about their work/life balance, family obligations, and work supports. They have to consider their overall obligations to their children, families, and communities, and ponder whether they would still be able to perform their responsibilities as advertised. These concerns may induce self-screening on the part of diverse groups, who shy away from applying for positions perceived as demanding.

Job ads are often written in such a way that diverse group members are discouraged from applying. There is one job requirement that most diverse groups view as especially insurmountable – a long history of executive experience (preferably ten or more years). In narrative terms, these job ads use the terms "established," "proven," and "senior" to describe leadership, executive, or board experiences.

For all four diverse groups, the requirement for extensive executive or board experience tends to discourage them from applying. Job ads that emphasize experience discourage diverse groups from applying and are ineffective at recruiting them. A small number of diverse group members may have experience sitting on boards of not-for-profit or community organizations, or may have worked as executives in those organizations (i.e., not in private sector companies). Ads that do not explicitly state the relevance or even the desirability of such experience can only discourage diverse group members from applying.

Indigenous peoples face yet another hurdle: job ads for executive positions or board directorships often require a strong academic record – for example, one or more university degrees and professional credentials. Most Indigenous peoples with post-secondary education are college-educated (i.e., not university-educated) (Canada 2014b, Table 8), so this requirement essentially removes from the running three quarters of Indigenous peoples who have a post-secondary education. The requirement for high educational credentials often acts as a barrier, especially when those credentials are not job-related.

The issue to be resolved here is whether sitting on a board of directors or working as a senior executive requires a university degree or professional credentials. The conventional argument is that board directors and senior executives make business and organizational decisions and that strong academic qualifications are important to high-quality decision-making. Yet in the sample of executive job ads examined in the *Globe and Mail*, none stated that a PhD was required for these positions. This suggests that current leaders may actually see a limit to the utility of the highest academic degree for a senior executive. Many job ads state that knowledge and skills based on a combination of a bachelor's or master's degree, established business experience, and a good reputation will suffice.

The final hurdle posted in some job ads is the requirement that leadership candidates have a proven and well-known track record. This may be difficult for diverse groups to acquire, for they have been given few opportunities to "shine" in executive jobs and have received few business awards. They also do not have much media exposure in the form of professional awards, community leadership awards, or even personal achievements, and their networks are often weak. As a result, diverse groups suffer from a "fame deficit," so that current leaders may not recognize their names or their accomplishments. Therefore, the requirement of a good reputation may not be fair to diverse groups.

External Search Firms

Search firms are often called "head hunters." Many search firms focus on different types of occupations in a specific industry (such as health care, marketing, or information technology); others specialize in senior executives and/or board directors. They charge retainer fees for their services, and the higher and more specialized the positions, the higher the retainer fees. For senior executives (including CEOs) and board directors, fees are in the thousands. Some companies are prepared to pay a great deal of money to recruit high-quality candidates; others are not. If existing board directors and senior executives can encourage their peers outside their organizations to apply through word-of-mouth, they can save a lot of money. For this cost-saving reason alone, word-of-mouth is more common than utilizing the services of external search firms. Indeed, even when the services of search firms are retained, leaders still use word-of-mouth to recruit candidates and then refer them to the search firms. Not all boards use search firms to recruit board members; the survey results of the Canadian Board Diversity Council (2018, 28) found that only 18.6% of board member respondents "always" use search firms for director recruitment and that 41.5% "sometimes" use them. When these statistics are compared with those noted in 2016 (where 22.3% always used these firms, and 46.4% sometimes used them), a slight decline is noted (Canadian Board Diversity Council 2016, 19) More longitudinal studies are needed to verify whether this signals a trend. It has been observed that some organizations prefer to use word-of-mouth instead of paying a retainer fee to search firms.

Search firms specializing in finding candidates for directorships and executive positions usually do not have systematic up-to-date human resources databases on indigeneity, disability, race, or gender. In the past, given their focus was not on the social identity of candidates, these attributes were not included in their databases and were not part of their search filters. External search firms today are increasingly equipped to create a database for women, but they remain quite weak regarding databases for other diverse groups. Their databases on diverse groups depend largely on word-of-mouth (referrals from executives), names of board directors, mentions of executives and managers in mass media and social media, internet presence, conference programs, and the websites of academic institutions, professional associations, and not-for-profit organizations that list the names of their board directors and executives. With the exception of women, diverse group members are seldom appointed as executives or board directors or invited to speak at public events, and their names are seldom mentioned in the media. As a result, external search firms are unable to accumulate sufficient names from diverse groups for them to then refer to their clients. Some external search firms specialize in recruiting persons with disabilities, but they focus largely on clerical, administrative, technical, or professional jobs. It is hard to find a search firm that specializes in reaching out to persons with disabilities for executive positions or corporate board directorships for a retainer fee.

Yet increasingly, clients are showing interest in finding candidates based on their social identity in addition to their qualifications, experience, specialties, and so on. The 2016 survey results of the Canadian Board Diversity Council (2016, 19) found that, of the board directors who responded, 42.2% "always" and 29.1% "sometimes" required the external search firms to include qualified and diverse individuals in terms of gender, race, and/or indigeneity.

A few search companies are now paying more attention to women and racialized minorities, albeit less so to Indigenous peoples or persons with disabilities. Organizations seeking assistance from search firms regarding diverse candidates may find themselves disappointed in their capabilities in the area of diversity.

The influence of search firms retained to find qualified candidates for board directorships or senior executive positions does not usually overshadow the strategic roles played by CEOs in recruitment. The deliverables of external search firms depend on the preferences of their clients, that is, on what they are looking for in terms of characteristics, competencies, qualifications, and experiences. Branson (2007, 149–50) studied how CEOs are selected and found that the corporation's search committee usually provides a specification sheet for the CEO position to an executive search firm or through word-of-mouth. Instead of a set of skills, this sheet focuses on individual attributes such as "executive presence," "proven leader," "able to balance risk with rewards," "decisiveness," and "motivator"; the term "charisma" is also sometimes used. External search firms then use these attributes to recruit candidates.

On this specification sheet, high educational qualifications are often named as a job requirement. Such credentials are not an issue for racialized minorities or women. But as noted earlier, the requirements for proven executive experience may pose a problem for Indigenous peoples and persons with disabilities. Compounding the problems arising from this requirement, current leaders commonly prefer to recruit people from the same industries as they are in – yet another barrier, and one that makes already short lists of diverse groups in specific industries even shorter, when it does not reduce them to zero.

As search firms have to work with the CEOs or with the search committees of the boards, there is a strong chance that CEOs' and search committees' picks will appear on the short list. Even when a search firm has identified qualified diverse candidates to sit on a board, the CEO and the search committee may not give them a fair chance unless the board has decided to prioritize appointing a member of a diverse group. The centrality of the preferences of current board directors, CEOs, and senior executives (whose picks typically come from word-of-mouth) gives people the impression that search firms are often used as a mere gesture at fairness, as professional cover for hiring decisions that are actually based on word-of-mouth – a method that diverse groups have criticized as biased and exclusionary.

External executive search firms are quite adaptive to the realities of board politics. It is commonly understood that CEOs, board directors, and majority shareholder(s) have powerful say in the selection of new board directors. For an executive search firm to recommend that a woman or other diverse group member to be placed on the short list, it has to have a solid grasp of how prepared these stakeholders (CEOs, board directors, and majority shareholders) are to welcome directors or executives with diverse backgrounds. Perhaps they have even specifically requested them. Otherwise, unless the diverse group members on the short list are trusted by CEOs, board directors, and majority shareholders as "one of us," the submission of names of diverse group members by the search firms will be viewed as outlandish (Leighton 2010, 258). For this reason alone, external search firms usually seek confirmation from current leaders regarding their commitment to diversity at the leadership level. Reading between the lines may not enough.

Selection

Selection is another important stage in the process of appointing senior executives or board directors. This process determines who the successful candidate will be. In this section, three areas will be highlighted for discussion: the composition of selection panels, selection criteria, and the interview process.

Composition of Selection Panels

The selection of an executive candidate is usually conducted through a panel of the CEO and executives. Only rarely are external persons (such as board

Figure 5.1. Recruitment methods and their biases

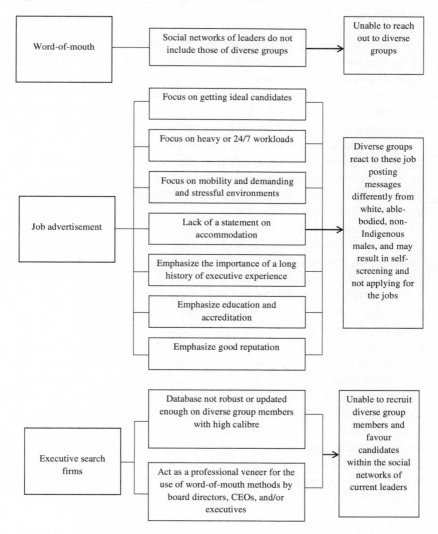

directors) invited to sit on the panel. This small group is often called the selection panel (or search committee), and the panelists are tasked with selecting and/or nominating the successful candidates for the vacant positions. The selection panel is sometimes one and the same as the search committee. Once an internal decision on the successful candidate has been made, the panel makes its recommendation to the full executive team and the CEO.

Depending on the internal policy, the CEO may then place the name before the board of directors for final approval.

Our previous findings on the small number of executives and board directors with diverse group backgrounds and the overwhelming proportion of white, able-bodied, non-Indigenous men at that level suggest that this panel is likely to be largely homogeneous. The panelists may have minimal experience working closely with people from diverse backgrounds. They may not know much about diverse groups, may not have them as peers or connect with them in their networks, and probably do not know much about what diverse executives have accomplished or could accomplish. Essentially, they are dealing with the unknown when deciding whether to appoint or hire a person from a diverse background. From their perspective, they will be taking a risk if they do so. All of this may place diverse candidates (if indeed there are any) at a disadvantage in job competitions.

Take persons with disabilities as an example. Their work experiences are quite different from those of able-bodied persons. As Church and colleagues (2007) noted, persons with disabilities confront a labelling process in which managers and co-workers tend to define them as incompetent; because of this, they hide their disabilities and work extra hard to ensure they do not get labelled as such. When the selection panel is comprised of able-bodied executives or board directors, these panelists may not fully realize how well persons with disabilities can perform in the right kind of work environment when proper accommodation measures are provided. Very likely, the negative stereotypes about persons with disabilities (discussed at length in the previous chapter) serve as psychological filters for the able-bodied panelists, who thus view candidates with disabilities as inadequate or incompetent and are likely to exclude them from further consideration. Absent the perspective of at least one panelist with disabilities, they may not see the competency of these applicants and instead focus on what they cannot do. Yet the reality is that not all persons with disabilities are visibly disabled; some have invisible disabilities. At the selection stage, the panelists may not visibly identify any persons with invisible disabilities, and that is good news for these candidates.

Studies have found that the presence of more female board directors increases the likelihood that more women will be considered for directorships and senior executive positions. They may emphasize the value of increasing gender representation. Conversely, it has been found that boards with fewer than two female directors rank gender representation as a low priority (Brown, Brown, and Anastasopoulos 2002, 10). When a board has female directors, it is possible they will be part of the selection panel, and this may increase the likelihood of having stronger female representation on boards. While these studies have focused on women, the same logic may apply to other diverse groups as well. A homogeneous selection panel may reduce the chances for more diverse representation both on boards and among senior executives (Moran, 2019).

Selection Criteria

"Proven Senior Executive Experience"

At the conceptual level, there are some commonalities between contemporary mainstream concepts of leadership and those of diverse groups. For example, Indigenous concepts of leadership share some ground with contemporary concepts of human relationships and collaboration. Both embrace "servant leadership," which places leaders at the service of the people they lead. However, there are many other components to contemporary mainstream concepts of leadership that carry far less weight in Indigenous styles of leadership. It is in these aspects of leadership that selection panels of CEOs and executives may require more concrete evidence from Indigenous peoples regarding how they lead.

So, some components of diverse groups' concepts of leadership align well with mainstream ones. But these alignments will remain abstract unless diverse groups can provide some tangible evidence that they can lead. Mattis (2010, 49) noted that CEOs look for particular work experiences for board directors, such as "significant general management," be it line, industrial, or international. Measuring against these preferences, CEOs cited "small number of women with appropriate business experience" and "women have not been in the pipeline long enough" as the top two reasons why women are not well represented on boards of directors. In other words, few women have long enough business experience to be leaders. "Approximately half of the CEOs surveyed reported that female candidates for corporate boards were 'difficult to find.'"

The perspective that women do not have appropriate or demonstrated business experience is reinforced by Dalton, Hill, and Ramsey's (1997, 29–50) observation that women in the accounting profession seem to have a greater tendency to quit their management positions or even the accounting profession sooner than men. As CEOs are looking for people with long work experience, this tendency of women to leave their positions may work against their chances of being appointed to boards.

D'Aveni (1990) viewed the dearth of women on corporate boards of directors a little differently. According to D'Aveni, women have very limited experience in monitoring and control, resource dependence, and service/

expertise functions. They are seldom in occupations that require them to oversee and direct businesses, utilize resources to produce and add value to companies, and/or serve as advisers in specialized areas. These experiences are usually gained through executive work. CEOs view board directors as sounding boards and advisers, and without such executive experience, it is unlikely that women can make positive contributions; as a consequence, they are not seen as suitable for directorships (Daily, Certo, and Dalton 2010, 14–15)

In the 1990s, the Glass Ceiling Commission in the United States found that three out of four male CEOs of large companies did not believe there was a glass ceiling for women. Catalyst's research found that 80% of CEOs believed that women lack experience in line positions or positions in which profits are made and risks are inherent (Branson 2007, 11–12). In essence, male CEOs believe that women are not in leadership positions because they are simply not qualified and experienced enough; it is not because they are discriminated against on the basis of gender.

Given that the selection panels tend to be homogeneous, it is difficult for their members to acquire knowledge about the achievements of candidates with diverse backgrounds. However, concrete executive experiences and accomplishments are hard to come by, given that historically, diverse groups were seldom given the opportunity to take on executive responsibilities (Mattis 2010, 51). Executive search firms confirmed that few women had senior executive experiences such as those of former or current CEOs, COOs, or chairs of major corporations (Mattis 2010, 48). Some CEOs and board directors place the stringent requirement on board directors that they must have executive experience in leading blue-chip companies. Without those experiences and accomplishments under their belts, it is an uphill struggle for diverse groups to compete for directorships or executive jobs.

As the review of the *Globe and Mail*'s job ads indicated, leadership hinges on some key attributes such as being "strategic," "visionary," "strong," "excellent," and "innovative." Leaders' ability to connect with people through "communication," "relationships," "collaboration," and "management" is crucial. Some diverse group members may well have these attributes, but without tangible executive experiences and accomplishments, how can selection panelists be confident of this? That is the hurdle that diverse groups have to overcome.

The selection of an executive candidate boils down to "trust" – that is, how much trust can the selection panelists place on candidates of diverse backgrounds as revealed in their résumés, prior to their face-to-face interviews? Trust is often based on tangible indicators that the panel of the CEO and executives can see; or better still, it is based on experiences of actually working together. In the contemporary context, a leader's competency is tightly intertwined with his or her extensive executive work record and executive accomplishments, as these are written down on paper, or it is manifested in the candidate's public reputation, third-party testimonials, or media coverage. When selection panelists know or have worked with the candidates and have gained a positive impression of them, that will increase the panelists' level of trust.

Unfortunately, members of diverse groups face a "Catch-22": they do not have executive experience because they had not have the opportunity to serve as executives, which means they have less executive experience. In addition, they lack strong social networks that would enable them to generate teamwork opportunities with existing executives or board directors, credible third-party testimonials, public profiles, and media coverage.

Another factor is at work: boards of directors tend to strive for unity, stability, and harmony on boards and in organizations. Board directors don't want to "rock the boat." This is because CEOs have a dual responsibility: to manage organizations, and to report to boards. The latter tend to be comprised of former CEOs, and they prefer that their friendship networks not be disturbed. From their perspective, anyone who lacks CEO experience is "out of place." Introducing a woman or a member of a diverse group would disturb the stability of these networks, especially if that person lacks CEO, executive, or board experience. As a consequence, diverse groups are perceived as outsiders and their involvement as likely to destabilize the board (Bradshaw and Wicks 2010, 198; Burke 2010, 97–8; Patton and Baker 1987). In addition, some CEOs and board directors cling to an old-fashioned mentality about women's roles, believing that "it is OK to have women at senior level but I don't want a woman on my board" (Holton 2010, 145–55).

Visibility and Reputation

Simply having the right kind of business experience may not be enough; reputation, credibility, and a social profile are also viewed as paramount for board directorship (Humber 2014, 8). Qualified women need to have a public profile. Visibility is vital for women to be nominated to boards of directors. Specifically, to be named to a board of directors, a woman must be visible to male leaders (Mitchell 1984). As Burke (2010, 105) noted: "Being visible to male CEOs, male board chairman and male board members was the most common route to board nomination. The 'old boys' network' is still alive and well. Personal contacts and visibility to these gatekeepers was critical."

This is confirmed by women themselves, who were surveyed about the factors that led to their success in business. Variously, they named a high community profile (23%), the increasing representation of women (21%), and their business expertise (14%) (Burgess and Tharenou 2010, 113). It seems that women saw their profile as more important than their business expertise.

It has been observed that women's work tends to be less visible, which brings them minimal exposure to CEOs and senior executives (who are the decision-makers when it comes to appointments to leadership positions). Men's work is apparently more visible and provides greater external exposure (Daily, Certo, and Dalton 2010, 14). However, the nature of the work may not be the determining factor in visibility. The more crucial factor is whether managers and executives provide opportunities for women to be visible to senior executives. The feeder pool for senior executive positions is middle management. Accordingly, female middle managers have exposure to leaders when executives or senior executives provide opportunities for them to make presentations, act as experts in front of other executives, or assign them to working teams, task forces, or committees in which senior executives are present. These opportunities are crucial for senior executives to know the names of these female managers and have a chance to work with them, observe how they conduct themselves, and evaluate their performance.

One suspects that, given that a significant percentage of senior executives are men, they are more comfortable with other men. This may make them more reluctant to invite female managers to accompany them to senior executive meetings unless those female managers are in the core business functions. Even after reaching the management level, women tend to cluster in corporate affairs areas such as human resources, communications, public relations, and information technology. These functions play a supportive role for an organization's core business: they keep the organization going but they do not directly develop the business or manage its risks. Unlike line positions, these functions are viewed by CEOs and male executives as secondary because they do not deal with day-to-day business risks or bring in profits or higher market share (Brady and McLean 2002, 7; Schachter 2012, B15). Because of this, female managers seldom have the exposure to CEOs and senior executives that they need for career advancement.

"One of Us"

Negative stereotypes and prejudice play a role in the selection of candidates. As noted in chapter 4, Indigenous peoples bear the stereotypes of laziness and unreliability. Persons with disabilities carry with them the stereotypes of helplessness, unreliability, incapability, dependence, risk, and danger. However, people's attitudes are inconsistent toward persons with disabilities: some employers are more concerned about persons with mental disabilities than about those with physical disabilities. Other employers are concerned variously about their performance, productivity, reliability, turnover rates, and/or social skills (Unger 2002, 2–10). Depending on whether they are Asian or black, racialized minorities face the stereotypes of being untrustworthy, inferior, socially awkward, aggressive, or abrasive. Women are perceived as less competent, less assertive, less qualified, and less committed to leadership than men. Some male executives seem to worry that women are disloyal.

These stereotypes and prejudices tend to seep into leadership selection processes, with the result that diverse groups are viewed as poorer leadership material (Bosak and Sczesny 2011). They are unlikely to be perceived by current leaders as "dynamic," "effective," "proactive," or "visionary" – the types of attributes that contemporary mainstream leaders should have, according to job ads found in the *Globe and Mail*. Negative perceptions like these do not instil confidence about the competency of candidates of diverse backgrounds, and indeed generate distrust and ambivalence toward them.

Negative stereotypes and prejudices may go hand in hand, thus placing candidates from diverse groups as an "out-group" – a group that is not seen as belonging to existing leadership circles. If they are external candidates, they are "outsiders," for they have not previously worked in the organization as executives or managers. Studies of female representation on boards of directors may shed some light on this aspect of selection.

In theory, a board of directors is to be responsive to the shareholders. Unless individual shareholders collectively push for women to be appointed to a board, the board's decision will lie largely with the CEO and the present directors. In practice, however, when there is a majority shareholder or a shareholder with a controlling interest, the decision to appoint a new board director is likely to hinge on the approval of that person. No controlling shareholder is prepared to approve the appointment of a new board director who is likely to challenge the company's owner or custodian. In these circumstances, the selection criteria boil down this: the new board director must be "one of us."

It is indeed a common practice that names submitted to boards for directorships will be those of colleagues, friends, or close acquaintance of the chair or a major shareholder, that is, "someone who will not 'rock the boat.'" Women, who have long been outside the old boys' club and are viewed as members of an out-group, may find it difficult to break into the club unless they are invited to join the board (Leighton 2010, 257–8). Furthermore, if they are from outside the organization, they are "outsiders" unless they are reputable and have been in the industry for a long time. While other diverse groups have not been as well-researched as women on this matter, given the mindsets of current leaders and their views and feelings toward diverse groups, their fates are unlikely to be that different from those of women.

"Cultural Fit"

Another informal selection criterion, usually not mentioned in job ads, is "cultural fit." Some Indigenous peoples and racialized minority members have cultural traits that may not align well with contemporary mainstream concepts of leadership and are likely to be misunderstood by current leaders. Indigenous applicants may have been brought up in unique cultural environments far from urban centres. Racialized minorities may bring with them cultural traits from abroad (if they are immigrants) or that they learned from their parents and relatives (if they were born to immigrant parents). Some racialized minorities are brought up to be respectful and not to challenge those in authority; but some are socialized to be upfront about their views and are prepared to maintain their independent thinking. Some are more collective and communal, others more individualistic. Girls and boys are usually raised with different cultural values and norms. Women tend to follow socially acceptable feminine roles, whereas men tend to follow a masculine culture, notwithstanding their efforts to adjust. The gender demarcation lines may not be rigid, but they are subtle. When cultural values and norms in a corporation are largely developed and moulded in terms of how leadeers view them, the traits related to white, able-bodied, non-Indigenous, male cultures tend to prevail and dominate. These values and norms are often engrained in the corporate culture.

To varying degrees, these cultural traits (based on gender, race, and indigeneity) may not fit well with the corporate culture in which diverse groups work. For example, the religions of some racialized minorities prohibit drinking alcohol, and as a result, they find it difficult to mingle comfortably at social functions where alcohol is served. This may even limit their opportunities to get to know the executives. Some women may find that the sports culture of men dominates conversations, office decor, and workplace events; and some find male language and styles of interaction too direct and assertive for comfort. All of these relatively "small" cultural traits, when prevalent on a daily basis, may create social distance between groups. Diverse groups may try to "live with" these cultural elements, but the discomfort remains.

Some of these cultural traits (and they are not limited to racialized minorities and women) give executives the impression that some diverse groups are socially awkward or unsociable, too direct and straightforward, too shy and introverted, too indirect in communication, too technical in their approach, too concerned about families or communities, undiplomatic in social interactions, too unwilling to take risks, not decisive enough, and so on. Some of these cultural traits, when they persist, evolve into stereotypes of particular diverse groups. As a result, these groups may come to be defined as unsuitable for leadership because their behaviours are at odds with the expected norms of the current leaders and do not fit the image of a contemporary mainstream leader. As white, able-bodied, non-Indigenous male executives have problems placing some diverse groups' behaviours in their own cultural contexts and cognitive maps, they may find working with them uncomfortable. When the relationship is not comfortable, it becomes socially more awkward, which makes it harder for executives to include them in their leadership circle.

"Corporate Fit"

"Corporate fit" is a subjective concept and usually works against the hiring of diverse groups from outside. People from the outside usually do not know much about the organization's corporate culture – whether it is open and inclusive, transparent, authoritarian, results-oriented, proactive, customer-driven, performance-driven, conservative, employee-centred, and so on.

More important, because diverse groups from outside have not worked for the organization before, CEOs and executives do not have direct experience working with them. Because they are not part of the organization's established network, all they know about how they will fit into the corporation comes to them from third parties or the media. As such, they are ambivalent or even distrustful about diverse group members joining the leadership circle. An external diverse group member will have a more difficult time being appointed than an internal diverse group member who has worked in the organization for years. CEOs as a rule are extra-cautious when selecting leadership candidates. Mattis (2010, 47–8) found that CEOs insisted on finding not just *any* woman to sit on the board, but finding the *right* woman "with appropriate skills and demeanor" (Mattis 2010, 47–8).

The process of recruiting a new board director can be stressful. As Long (2016) noted, it is not easy to recruit and appoint the right candidate for a directorship, and it is even harder to terminate a new director. Terminating a new director, or having a relatively new director resign before his or her tenure ends, is costly in both financial and reputational terms for the organization. That is why existing board directors agonize over whether to appoint an external person to the board. This question is about more than résumés. The board members have to determine whether the candidates have the right "chemistry" to work with the existing directors and senior executives (including the CEO), in addition to having the proper "balance" of characteristics, styles, that will enable the candidate to integrate well with the organization's existing culture, corporate values, thinking modes, and operational approaches. This "chemistry" and "balance" constitutes the "corporate fit" that existing directors seek in new candidates. This determination usually goes beyond objective evaluation; it often becomes partly a matter of intuition (or "gut feeling").

Large corporations usually develop leadership profiles as formal criteria for assessing the potential performance and behaviour of leaders. These profiles may include values – such as integrity, transparency, passion, teamwork, consensus-orientation, respect, and creativity – and are sometimes adopted as identification and selection criteria for leadership candidates (Humber 2014, 8). When candidates' characteristics or past performance exhibit these profiles, they are viewed as corporate fit.

However, behavioural traits found in these profiles are culturally tainted. Diverse groups, based on their past socialization and cultural conditioning, attach different meanings to these profiles. Management approaches depend to some extent on how people view reality and how people express themselves. Some racialized minorities tend to contextualize an issue in communication instead of stating it directly. This type of expression can easily be misinterpreted by current leaders as indirect, imprecise, or just "beating around the bush." Similarly, some racialized minorities tend to take a long-term view on developing business relationships, and such behaviour may be misinterpreted by current leaders as an inability to seize the moment for short-term gains (such as making a quick business deal). This generalization of differences between Asian, African, and white business people has been well observed and documented (Mills 2005; Parker 2005, 74). Similarly, men and women have different approaches in relationship-building and leadership – women are more caring, while men are more assertive (Helgesen 1990). These differences impact how leadership profiles are measured and how the performance of diverse groups is viewed.

There is also an individual dimension in interpretations. Any profile can mean different things to different persons. For example, "passion in work" may mean a positive, "can do" attitude or a good work ethic (such as hard-working and uncomplaining), or a willingness to be relocated for work even if it requires personal sacrifice. Depending on the meanings, women may be assessed as less passionate or less committed to work if they do not wish to relocate and spend more time with their children; Asians may be seen as too family-oriented, and Indigenous peoples may be viewed as too community-oriented if they prefer to take time off for family matters or community gatherings. As such, they may be perceived by current leaders as less passionate about their work. The multiple meanings of each leadership profile allow a lot of latitude for decision-makers to select their candidates based on their own selective perceptions or personal preferences, whether or not they are aware of their own biases.

The reality is that all of these leadership profiles are vague and at times ambiguous, and senior executives or board directors on the selection panel may act on their personal discretion to determine what they mean by leadership. This discretionary power of board directors and executives, when exercised, is likely to determine who will get appointed or hired. When contemporary mainstream concepts of leadership are mixed with racial or gender stereotypes and prejudices, even though Indigenous peoples, racialized minorities, and women may exhibit compatible behaviours, the latter may be interpreted through tainted filters. The problem is that very often, formal criteria are not formally defined and the selection criteria are mixed with personal preferences, group dynamics, and business practices. All of these combine to make formal selection criteria secondary even though on paper, they are the official yardsticks of selection. As a result, the term "corporate fit" is often seen as a criterion for "screening out" some candidates and "screening in" others. This flexibility can have an immense impact. Diverse groups are often assessed as fit or unfit for leadership based on stereotypes and prejudices, or it is left to the personal discretion of current leaders. "Corporate fit" is a fluid selection criterion, yet it often carries great weight in hiring decisions.

The Interview Process

The objectives of the interview process for board directors and senior executives are similar to those for other occupational groups. While there are many questions to be resolved, the selection panel needs answers to these key ones: Can the candidate do the job? Is that person fit to work in the organization? What contributions can he or she make to the organization?

The formats for interviews for leaders are different from those for other positions. One might be tempted to say "conversation" rather than "interview," for an "interview" suggests formality and a question-and-answer format. The formats for selecting senior executives and board directors are more fluid, informal, and conversational. Candidates may have lunch or dinner with the CEO, board directors, or senior executives, one at a time, several at another. Interviews may take place variously in offices, boardrooms, or restaurants or on golf courses. These interviews may follow a sequence starting with the selection of candidates by the panelists. The short list may then be submitted to the CEOs or the board chairs, who will conduct further interviews.

Interviews are usually conducted by one executive or board director at a time; for that reason, the criteria for selection are more informal. Each interviewer usually examines different aspects of the candidate by posing different questions (again, depending on personal preferences or priorities).

The selection panelists may agree to focus on certain central issues; but as the interviews are conversational, they are fluid, which allows the panelists to probe deeper into issues as they arise. These panelists may elect to interview the candidates one-on-one – a format that allows flexibility in the direction of interviews. Board members, CEOs, and other senior executives may sometimes have a chance to interview the candidates even though they are not a part of the interview panel. All of this fluidity give rise to a non-standardized array of interview questions and flows of topics that make it difficult to develop a set of agreed-upon selection criteria and interview questions.

This fluidity has been confirmed by several studies of board selection. According to Leighton (2010, 256), the interview process has been largely "informal, unplanned, and lacking in rigor." It is stacked against women because the selection criteria are often unfocused and the methods are spontaneous. Personal discretion and subjectivity may play a significant role in them. Also, given the informality of these interviews, no written records on the interview questions and responses are required or kept. Instead, information on the leadership candidates is reported verbally. Decisions are made based on discussions among senior executives, selection panelists, and board directors. Personal preferences often play an increasingly pivotal role in these discussions, and which personal preferences will win out depends on how well one communicates and convinces others.

More importantly, this fluidity creates a situation in which the choice among candidates often depends on the power relations among board directors (in the case of appointing a board director) or among senior executives (in the case of appointing a senior executive). When selection criteria are not clear and agreed upon before the interviews begin, this fluidity enables people of higher rank to have more weight in the decision (Adams 2015; Rogers and Senturia 2013; Wood 1973). Furthermore, when a consensus on a decision cannot be reached among the panelists and other board directors or senior executives, given that the CEO will have to work with the successful candidate, very likely he will have the last word, pending the board's approval (if board candidates are to be decided).

The role of the CEOs in this matter is crucial, because they are the strategic links between board directors and senior executives, the highest-ranking among all senior executives, and the persons who know the policy *and* operational sides of the organization. CEOs know both the boards of directors and their senior executives who execute board directions. Because of this, they play a much larger role in bringing to the attention of the entire board the "qualified" candidates for directorships and senior executive positions.

A study of female board directors found that being visible to and having personal contacts with board directors (including CEOs) was of paramount

Figure 5.2. Selection and its biases

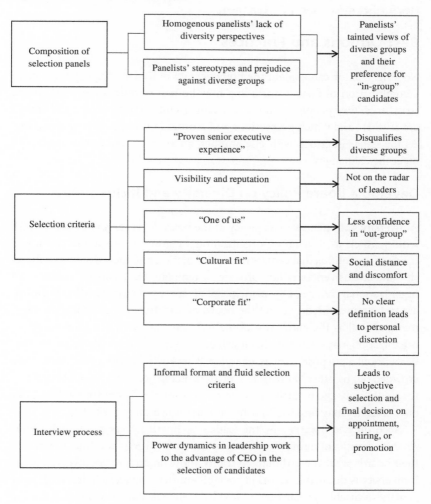

importance (Burke 2010, 105). The same logic may apply to the appointment of other diverse group members, if the latter have a close relationship with the CEO. As noted earlier, this is unlikely happen often. Diverse groups have a disadvantage here because of the negative stereotypes and attitudes that are part of the social context and the resultant social distance and avoidance between the board directors (who may be white, able-bodied, non-Indigenous, and/or male) and the diverse groups. Social distance and avoidance behaviours tend to minimize awareness and knowledge of diverse groups, which in turn creates further discomfort between them.

Best Options and Practices

No single factor can explain the homogeneity of leaders. Explanations lie in a combination of factors, including how human resources mechanisms are structured, how people put these mechanisms into action, what social factors are at work, and which perceptions and attitudes underpin decision-making. As the issues interlock with one another, an array of solutions is needed to meet the challenges.

Develop a Board Policy on Diversity and Inclusiveness

A diversity and inclusiveness policy at the board level serves as a framework within which to develop an organizational culture, strategic direction, and mode of operations that centres on representation and inclusiveness. A diversity and inclusiveness policy provides a template for business strategy and organizational changes. One principle of diversity policy is that diverse groups are to be represented both on the board of directors and in senior management, as well as the entire workforce. Without such a policy framework, an organization may be lost, in that it will be carrying out diversity-related activities without a purpose, a focus, or a plan. These activities may find themselves crowded out by other, more urgent matters on the board agenda. A board policy on diversity and inclusiveness represents the board's commitment; without one, diversity may find itself pushed further down the priority list.

According to a survey by the Canadian Board Diversity Council (2018, 17, 20), significant numbers of current directors (81.5%) continue to feel that their boards are diverse, though in reality, those boards are not diverse *enough* if diversity is defined in terms of social identities (such as gender, race, indigeneity, or disability). Chapter 2 provided statistical data showing that diverse groups are seriously underrepresented on boards. Regarding the importance of board diversity, 61.3% of the survey's respondents viewed it merely as "very important," and 33.6% viewed it as "somewhat important." The term "somewhat" signifies a lukewarm attitude toward diversity. An additional 5.1% viewed it as "not really important" or "not at all important."

The Canadian Board Diversity Council found that current directors viewed "ethnicity," "visible minorities" (i.e., racialized minorities), "Aboriginal people," and "people with disabilities" as least significant among the twelve indicators of diversity. Management experience, functional area of expertise, industry experience, and education were all highly rated as indicators of diversity. Unless markers of diversity such as indigeneity, ability, race, and gender are clearly established in a corporate diversity and inclusiveness policy statement, board diversity may tend to remain skewed to the disadvantage of diverse groups (Canadian Board Diversity Council 2016, 10–13; 2018, 20).

The 2018 survey results found that only 57.0% of boards today have adopted a written diversity policy and that 17.2% do not but are open to considering one. Only 8.2% expressed no interest in writing a diversity policy unless it became a legal obligation. A sizeable percentage (17.6%) simply did not know whether their board had adopted such a policy or not. This suggets that more educational work must be done on this front and that some additional impetus is needed to drive 17.2% of boards to adopt a diversity policy instead of sitting on the fence (Canadian Board Diversity Council 2018, 23). The council's survey results showed that the proportion of boards with a written policy had "ups and downs" between 2010 and 2018, from 62% in 2010 to 86% in 2017. This suggests that such policy adoption has been uneven and unsteady. Also, most board directors (50.4%) opposed the imposition of written diversity policies by governments, which was slightly more than favoured this step (43.0%).

Organizations that decide to develop a diversity policy may need to consult with their peers in industry that have experiences in diversity management or employment equity. Consultations can also be conducted with the management team and with other segments of the organization's workforce. This sort of effort creates a sense of ownership among employees; it also highlights relevant diversity issues that may serve as focal points in the diversity policy. Once this process is completed, the resulting policy framework can be placed on the board's agenda for approval.

Following are examples of companies with a diversity commitment and/or policy:

- **Hong Kong Shanghai Bank of Canada** (HSBC) has a board policy on diversity and inclusiveness and has had a gender-based board of directors and executive committee since 2013. Its diversity and inclusion council is comprised of senior leaders, who sponsor employee resource groups. The diversity policy serves as the framework for human resources development (Stuart 2019).
- **Corus Entertainment**, a media production and broadcasting company, was one of the Top 100 Best Diversity Employers in Canada in 2016. It has more than 1,500 employees. It has established a diversity and inclusion policy whose translation into program activities is overseen by an

equity and diversity committee. That committee is comprised of management, non-management, and unionized staff (MediaCorp Canada 2016a).

• **Marriott International** was the ninth of the Top 50 Diversity Employers in 2016 as compiled by DiversityInc. (2016). In 2003 it established a Committee for Excellence to carry out its commitment to diversity and inclusiveness. The committee is comprised of senior executives, and board directors meet regularly to discuss diversity objectives at all levels of the organization (DiversityInc. 2016a).

Develop an Action Plan with Goals and Timetables

A big problem among companies that do have diversity policies is a lack of specific actions in line with the policy. So it is important to remember that once a diversity policy has been developed, an action plan must be prepared to translate an abstract idea like diversity into concrete and measurable activities with goals and timetables for diversity representation on boards and among senior executives. A board policy on diversity and inclusiveness indicates leadership commitment; a plan to put it into action is a further step forward.

This action plan should state the corporate strategy for moving the organization from a relative absence of diverse groups in leadership toward fair representation and the provision of human resources mechanisms and processes to make it happen. In developing such a plan, the organization's vision and the business strategy as well as the issues of talent management, succession management, and leadership develop are to be integrated at the board and senior executive levels. Risks related to changing circumstances, alignment with evolving business priorities, and transition are to be considered and incorporated. Some benchmarks may be needed for measuring progress over time, and each activity and its implementation steps are to be monitored and reviewed regularly. Needless to say, adequate resources are valuable for the implementation of the action plan (Streifer 2016). Given the shortage of women in the tech industry overall and the problems that industry has in recruiting and selecting them (and then promoting and retaining them), Jodi Kovitz (2019), founder and CEO of #movethedial, a Toronto-based global organization that advances the participation and leadership of women in tech industry, even recommends having a gender diversity strategy with a chief gender diversity officer. This person would focus on addressing the biases in the industry, albeit without ignoring the broader multipronged strategy on diversity and inclusiveness.

Here are some examples of companies with action plans:

- **Rogers Communications**, a communications and cable company, has more than 23,000 employees across Canada. Its Diversity Leadership Council launched a subcommittee to implement action plans to increase female and racialized minority representation in leadership and to build pipelines for this purpose. It also plans to increase the representation of Indigenous peoples and persons with disabilities (MediaCorp Canada 2016a).
- **Information Services Corporation**, a medium-sized company with more than 300 employees based in Regina, Saskatchewan, has crafted a five-year diversity strategic plan with quarterly and annual diversity and inclusion goals (Globe and Mail 2013).
- The **Hong Kong Shanghai Bank of Canada** (HSBC) has an action plan for diversity and inclusiveness. It begins with an accountability framework that has measurable targets for leaders and managers to achieve. Under the plan, for every senior role, a diverse slate of candidates (ensuring at 50% are women) must be prepared for consideration. The plan offers educational sessions on unconscious bias for leaders. It also reviews systemic biases in human resources mechanisms such as parental leave (Stuart 2019).
- **Nudge Rewards**, a Toronto-based company specializing in retail technology that links restaurant, retail, and hospitality companies to front-line employees, takes ownership of diversity work at all levels. It has a policy framework on diversity and inclusiveness and is able to actualize its principles in the company's action plan (Scarborough 2019).

Set Limits on Trophy Directorship and Board Tenure

"Trophy directors" sit on multiple boards, occupying seats that could be for new directors. To open up boards and create vacancies, boards could start establishing a "no trophy directors" policy. This would open up many more opportunities for diverse groups. Current trophy directors might start resigning or retiring from their posts, and their seats could be reserved for diverse groups. Boards would have more vacancies, and qualified diverse group members would be able to fill those seats at faster rates. If something like this is not done, it might take many years or even decades for board seats to come available for qualified diverse group members.

The long-standing practice of allowing directors to stay on a board for an unlimited time has restricted the availability of vacancies for new board directors, thus shutting out qualified candidates from diverse groups. Boards of directors could start limiting the number of years and the number of appointment renewals so that new directors could be appointed. When opportunities for appointments are opened up, qualified diverse group members will have a chance to join more boards (Burke and Mattis 2010, 8–9). Even when some current board directors believe that eliminating trophy directors is a good idea, there may well not be enough of them to force the issue. Setting time limits on board directorships may be more common, but examples of this are hard to find.

Outreach to Diverse Groups

The three methods for recruiting diverse groups being examined here – word-of-mouth, job ads, and external search firms – have their shortcomings. Board directors and senior executives need to prepare the ground for increasing the representation of diverse groups in leadership positions by establishing a solid profile and reputation in diverse communities and positive working relationships with community leaders, as well as by teaming up with organizations and associations that advocate stronger representation of diverse groups in the workforce and in leadership. To increase diversity in the workforce (including in leadership), an organization must reach out to diverse communities in a proactive manner. Some companies are using artificial-intelligence software to identify pools of diverse candidates (Moran 2019).

In reaching out to diverse groups and other organizations, private-sector organizations may need to abandon or at least minimize the requirement of work experiences specific to their own industries. As leadership attributes are highly transferable from one industry to another and some are even transprovincial and transnational, current leaders could trust leadership candidates to acquire the unique capacities their industries require if appointed to the job. Better still, they could utilize their experiences in other industries to help their new companies develop innovative strategies once they become leaders. This change of mindsets among current leaders would greatly expand the feeder pool of leadership candidates.

Companies need to do more active recruitment by working closely with business associations and management organizations. Those diverse group members who have been able to rise to middle-management and senior executive positions see the value of forming associations of their own. In Canada, women executives and professionals have organized a number of groups. Examples are the Women's Executive Network (Toronto, Vancouver, Calgary, Edmonton, Mississauga, Ottawa, Montreal, Ireland) and Women in Capital Markets. Organizations like these are also found in the United States and in other countries (Northcraft and Gutek 1993, 224). They may publicize leadership opportunities on their websites and in their newsletters; establish and maintain working relations with diverse communities; and sponsor public events (such as festivals) held by diverse communities.

Since 2012 the Canadian Board Diversity Council has published a Diversity 50 list every year to publicize the availability of qualified candidates from diverse backgrounds for board directorships. So far, that list has led to twenty-nine appointments on *Financial Post* 500 corporate boards and three on *Fortune* 500 corporate boards. This list has been useful for corporate boards that are interested in recruiting more candidates from diverse backgrounds. Canada's Most Powerful Women: Top 100 is an award program that may also serve as a reference point for potential female board appointments (Canadian Board Diversity Council n.d.).

Some not-for-profit organizations provide online inventories of diverse groups to increase their opportunities to sit on boards. Some not-for-profit organizations focus on advocating diversity and inclusiveness. In Canada, Catalyst Canada, the Canadian Institute for Diversity and Inclusion, and the Canadian Board Diversity Council play that advocacy role. These organizations may be able to connect leaders to potential candidates or have ideas on how best to recruit qualified diverse group members.

One such not-for-profit organization is the Canadian Board Diversity Council. It has twenty-five corporate members representing the financial, energy, housing, transportation, legal, utilities, consulting, retail, telecommunications, and academic sectors as well as several not-for-profit organizations. By joining this council, these organizations raise their reputation as diversity-friendly and inclusive; they are also able to connect themselves with well-qualified diverse groups regarding board directorships and senior executive positions.

One of the least utilized ways to reach out to diverse communities is by developing in-house role models. Organizations have to start promoting their diverse employees to leadership positions so that they, as leaders, will act as magnets to attract members of diverse communities. For example, to reach out to Indigenous peoples, one or more senior executives or board directors have to be Indigenous themselves. These people can act as living proof that the organization is opening up its leadership "club" and that Indigenous peoples can succeed at that level. In this way, they will serve as role models for other Indigenous peoples. These role models from diverse backgrounds could also act as ambassadors to their communities.

A number of companies have developed these outreach practices:

The **Canadian Imperial Bank of Canada (CIBC)**, one of the Top 100 Best Diversity Employers in 2016, collaborated with several national Indigenous employment organizations to develop "Pathways to Opportunity." Workshops, community networking sessions, mock interview sessions, and other methods link Indigenous peoples with bank recruiters and hiring managers. This program does not reach out directly to potential Indigenous leaders, but it does build a profile in their communities (MediaCorp Canada 2016a).

Similarly, **Blake, Cassels & Graydon LLP** reaches out to diverse communities through its Blakes/Juriansz Inclusivity Fund, which supports student-led organizations that promote diversity, inclusion, and accessibility. The firm also provides volunteer services to diversity-related organizations. Partnerships with other organizations are another way to reach out to diverse communities. Partners include the Law Firm Diversity and Inclusion Network, the Black Law Students Association of Canada, the Iranian Canadian Law Association, and the Canadian Association of Black Lawyers. All of these engagements help consolidate the company's efforts to make its name known to diverse groups and to reach out to them (MediaCorp Canada 2016a).

The best way to build diversity in leadership is to ensure that the pipeline to leadership is not blocked. So it is important to ensure there are enough diverse employees in the professional and middle-management feeder pools. **Limelight Platform** is a Canadian marketing automation software company. Only 20% of tech engineers are women, yet seven of the thirteen employees of Limelight are women, who hold development and quality assurance engineering jobs. Central to Limelight's recruitment strategy is outreach to communities through event sponsorships (Midanik and Roy-Boulet 2019).

Similarly, **IBM** has identified the low participation rate of girls and women in the information and communications technology workforce in Canada. They constitute only 27% of the workforce, and that percentage has not changed much over time – indeed, it has actually declined from its peak of 29% in 2011. To build up a reservoir of female professionals in this field and related professions, Ayman Antoun (2019), president of IBM Canada, has launched three major outreach programs for Canadian girls and women. The first of these is a STEM program for 29,000 girls in more than twenty Canadian cities in Canada to inspire and coach them in the STEM fields. The second is the Six Nations Polytechnic STEAM Academy – the first secondary school in Canada focused on a STEAM curriculum (science, technology, engineering, arts, and mathematics). It leads to an integrated Ontario Secondary School Diploma and a tuition-free two-year computer software engineering technician college diploma. The third is the Pathways in Technology Early College High School. This is a six-year educational model that starts in grade nine with a combination of secondary school and college course work. Through it, several companies, including IBM, offer internships and mentorships that combine academics, skills training, and work experience without cost to students.

Many other companies have reached out to diverse groups, mainly at the occupational levels below senior executive. They include Home Depot of Canada, Lefarge Canada, Loblaw Companies, National Bank of Canada, PepsiCo, Royal Bank of Canada, Rogers Communications, Shell Canada, and the Toronto Dominion Bank (MediaCorp Canada 2016a). Telus Corporation and the National Bank of Canada have reached out to higher occupational levels – for example, through the Women's Executive Network, Women of Influence, Out on Bay Street, the Canadian Women's Foundation, and Catalyst (MediaCorp Canada 2016a).

Establish and Enrich Databases on Diversity

Today's search firms lack robust databases on diverse group members. Organizations would find it useful if these firms made a more concerted effort to develop and enrich those databases (Holton 2010, 153). Once these search firms have strengthened their databases, the organizations that use them will find it easier to locate qualified diverse group members.

Organizations with enriched databases could help CEOs and board directors connect with female candidates. Holton (2010, 154) has suggested that an international Web-based *Harvard Business Review* database of female candidates would be a useful tool with a prestigious brand image. Another option is for wide-circulation publications such as *Der Speigel*, the *Australian Observer*, *Le Figaro*, the *Times of India*, and the *Malaysia Daily News* to develop their own registers of female candidates for board directorships or executive positions. Major newspapers such as the *Globe and Mail* and its *Report on Business*, in consultation or collaboration with various boards of trade or chambers of commerce across Canada, could establish a robust database of diverse group members who are likely candidates for leadership positions.

Alternatively, prominent management/business schools and professional institutes could collectively develop a database of diverse candidates for board directorships and executive positions. In addition, the public sector has a large reservoir of leaders (such as deputy ministers, assistant deputy ministers, and directors) who have executive skills. The Institute of Public Administration of Canada, the Professional Institute of the Public Service of Canada, and other institutes in the public sector could develop their own databases for diverse group members with strong leadership potential.

Rahul K. Bhardwaj (2016), president and CEO of the Institute of Corporate Directors (ICD), has reported that the institute has more than 3,500 women in its Directors Register. Close to a thousand of them have their ICD Directors' Designations. They are ready to take on board directorships and the responsibilities that come with them. This is a good example of how a robust database can help build better representation of women in the leadership echelons. The database could extend to other diverse groups of similar calibre.

A new online database – Film in Colour – has just been announced by Pavan Moondi. This database does not deal with leadership talents in the private sector per se, but its idea could be modelled. The database is diversity-focused and provides names, résumés, and contacts for talented directors, writers, producers, editors, and so on. This database enables people with diverse talents to find one another (Hertz 2020).

Catalyst, an advocacy research organization, established Corporate Board Placement to serve the business sector in advancing women. Corporations retain its services to find women who are qualified to be board directors. It has clients in multiple industries such as finance and insurance, retail, manufacturing, technology, communication, and transportation. It has a large database of potential female leaders and claims to be the only women-only director-ready database in the United States. Some companies are expanding their searches for "high level" women, including "executive and senior vice presidents, division presidents, chief financial officers, entrepreneurs, and other candidates with strong managerial and operational skills." Data from its database can be cross-tabulated in many different ways, including by race, industry, function, and geography (Pollak 2010, 263–7).

Review and Address Issues Related to Recruitment and Selection

Policies and procedures related to hiring and selection could be made more equitable through regular reviews and evaluations. Often, even after policies and procedures have been reviewed and biases have been removed, how leaders and managers carry them out may be perceived as biased. So it is essential for leaders and managers to regularly examine the operations side of recruitment and selection (Scarborough 2019).

Word-of-Mouth

The actual mechanisms for recruiting and selecting candidates also need to change. Given that a critical mass of diverse groups (except women) at the leadership level is not attainable, diversity policies must include a principle of diversity representation. Accordingly, following this principle, existing leaders should commit themselves to use word-of-mouth when recruiting candidates of diverse backgrounds. If there are diverse group members among the leaders, they should play an active role in spreading the word about recruiting talent from diverse backgrounds. When diverse group members can utilize their networks of diverse group members, they naturally reach out to more people, something that non-diverse leaders cannot do (Midanik and Roy-Boulet 2019).

Given that current leaders do not have strong connections with diverse group members, especially those with proper qualifications and experiences, they will need to rely on closer liaison with the college and university sectors, public sector organizations, the business associations of diverse communities, and the international business sector. At present, the public sector in Canada is more advanced than the private sector in promoting diverse group members to higher positions such as deputy minister, assistance deputy minister, and executive director. These people are potential leadership candidates for the private sector as well. Through liaison and word-of-mouth, the pool of leadership candidates from diverse backgrounds may be broadened.

Job Advertisements

Job ads should be reworded to focus only on the basic requirements for leaders (i.e., the "floor"), and not on the ideal requirements (i.e., the "ceiling"). In other words, job ads need to be written so as to be more encouraging and appeal to the wider audience. This would encourage more diverse group members to apply, not because they are of poor calibre or have lower qualifications, but because diverse groups interpret "ideal" attributes or qualifications as "requirements."

Also, instead of focusing on educational credentials or executive experiences and accomplishments, job ads might focus on alternative educational qualifications (such as international learning institutes or internships) and board or executive experiences and accomplishments in the entrepreneurial (as opposed to corporate) and/or not-for-profit executive worlds. Even running or helping parents to run a family business should be counted as an accomplishment.

To attract more diverse groups to apply for high-level positions, more welcoming statements may be needed. (Scarborough, 2019) Job ads with an offensive or misogynistic tone are discouraging to diverse groups, so it is worthwhile to have a specialist in diversity and inclusiveness vet the ads prior to their release (Kramer 2019). Every ad should include a statement on the availability of reasonable accommodation upon request, as well as a statement of the corporate principles of diversity and inclusiveness and human rights. Organizations keenly interested in raising the representation of diverse groups at various levels to broaden the pool of recruits could also include a statement on the availability of coaching, mentorship, internship, and other initiatives that enable employee growth and engagement.

Executive Search Firms

When resorting to an external executive search firm, the board directors or senior executives should insist that the firm have a good, up-to-date inventory of executive candidates from diverse backgrounds as well as a proven record of recruiting diverse candidates of high calibre. They should also insist on paying the retainer fees only once a successful candidate from a diverse background has been hired. This would signal to the search firm that the current leaders are serious about their commitment to diversity.

Furthermore, although many executive search firms have enormous databases worldwide and a million assessment files broken down by job roles, organizational level, and industrial type, they are usually still operating under contemporary mainstream concepts of leadership that (as earlier chapters demonstrated) adversely impact diverse groups. These firms need to revamp their leadership profiles.

Several popular search firms such as Korn Ferry, RHR International, Spencer Stuart, and Egon Zhender may be updating their assessment methodologies and tools, leadership profiles, and search processes to facilitate searches based on principles of diversity and inclusiveness. They may also be refining their leadership development approaches to unlock potential candidates' capabilities. Current leaders may need to provide clear instructions regarding their commitment to recruiting qualified leadership candidates from diverse backgrounds. They may also need to examine the modes of operation of these search firms in terms of identifying leadership candidates and working with leadership candidates from diverse backgrounds.

Composition of Selection Panels

Historically, members of selection panels were all white, able-bodied, non-Indigenous men (Moran 2019). Panels with that composition have a limited perspective on leadership candidates of diverse backgrounds. Broadening a panel's composition to include diverse groups would provide multiple perspectives and innovative approaches. Unfortunately, the current make-up of board directors and senior executives may not allow such alternative composition.

During a transitional period (i.e., before more diverse group members are included in leadership circles), organizations with homogeneous leadership could "borrow" leaders of diverse backgrounds from other industries or not-for-profit diversity councils to sit on their selection panels so that alternative perspectives might be fostered. Or, instead of allowing the CEOs to play a crucial role in the selection of board directors (with all the biases that accompany this), it might be best to have a panel of existing directors, ideally comprised entirely of "outsider" directors, to ensure the independence of the selection process (Burke and Mattis 2010, 8–9).

This model is recommended by the Toronto Stock Exchange Committee in Canada, by the Business Round Table in the United States, and by organizations in other countries. This selection panel then develops the terms of reference for new leadership candidates. The terms of reference are to be viewed as integral to a longer-term plan for the composition of the board based on an in-depth analysis of the current board structure. This analysis will enable the organization to carry out its strategic plan. This selection panel has the option of working with an external search firm or working among themselves in compiling a list of potential candidates based on these terms of reference. These potential candidates must have the qualifications and competencies specified. The selection panelists then use a variety of selection methods to sound out and evaluate these candidates. As the end of this process, a shorter list of candidates is compiled by the selection panel (Leighton 2010, 256).

Establishing shareholder groups is another way to create a more inclusive process for nominating board directors. Shareholder groups may nominate potential candidates for board directorships and may be independent of the existing boards. Much like selection panels, they can submit their slates of directorship candidates for approval at annual general meetings (Mattis 2010, 54–5). All of the above proposed mechanisms for addressing the issue of skewed selection panelists are based the model of utilizing the assistance of outside persons. In the eyes of current leaders, they are just that – "outsiders" – and this may radically upset the framework of past recruitment and selection processes. It is precisely this radicalness that can consitute a break from the past modes. Without it, change at the leadership level may be perceived as too slow, too timid, or too reluctant.

Selection Criteria

The biases arising from selection criteria may be summarized as follows: criteria are often devoid of agreed-upon indicators and measurements; the requirement for "proven senior executive experience" has exclusionary impacts on diverse groups; and informal (often below the surface) criteria (such as "must be one of us," "cultural fit," and "corporate fit") often replace formal criteria. Needless to say, these informal criteria tend to reflect "gut-level" decision-making and need to be kept in check. Though this does not specifically address the issue of selecting leaders, Thomson Reuters Canada usually does a blind baseline coding test to determine candidates' skills, comparing the results with the decision-makers' impression of their résumés. The idea behind this is to reduce the likelihood that decisions will be based on someone's gut feeling or intuition (Moran 2019).

These biases could be removed by requiring a set of agreed-upon selection criteria (such as transparency and integrity) with concrete indicators and measurements prior to the interviews. "Proven senior executive experience" could cover a broader range of executive, small-business, and/or not-for-profit executive experiences and a broader range of management portfolios, including risk management, business development, and compensation and benefits (Mattis 2010, 54–5).

It has also been noted that too much focus on Canadian work experience as a selection criterion is a great barrier for immigrant men and women in spite of their higher-than-average educational levels. Canadian companies may also overweigh the value of Canadian academic credentials and undervalue those from abroad. These two hiring barriers are likely to reduce the pool of immigrants joining the professional occupations, further diminishing the supply of diverse talents at the middle-management level that is the feeder pool for the senior executive ranks. Accordingly, these biased criteria should be removed (Maher and Luongo 2019).

All criteria should be formalized and made measurable, with clear, agreed-upon indicators prior to the interview process. Informal criteria (e.g., "cultural fit," "corporate fit," "one of us") should be examined in light of the principles of diversity education and assessed as to whether they are acceptable or not.

This revamping of selection criteria does not preclude the adoption of objective criteria that may prove detrimental to some diverse group members. For example, the criterion "strategic thinking" when selecting candidates is objective and of high value for selection; however, it depends largely on the indicators the selection panelists use when assessing candidates. Clearly, a discussion of what panelists mean by "strategic" is necessary, and the indicators they intend to use should be examined to determine whether they are inherently biased against diverse groups. Each of these revamped criteria (and their indicators for measurement) has to be examined in light of human rights laws and diversity and inclusiveness principles prior to their adoption.

Xerox Corporation was one of the Canada's Best Diversity Employers in 2016. It is a computer equipment manufacturing company with more than 3,000 full-time employees in Canada. It has examined its recruitment policies to ensure they are consistent with corporate priorities. It provides a bias-neutral selection guide for hiring managers (MediaCorp Canada 2016a).

Figure 5.3. How best to remove barriers in recruitment and selection

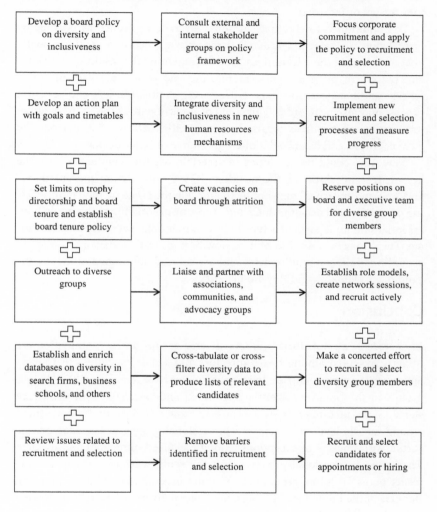

Interview Process

A fluid interview process, with CEOs playing an increasingly important role, enables personal preferences and power relationships to drive decision-making. So it is important to make the interview process more structured (Scarborough, 2019). When selection criteria are formalized, personal preferences and discretion are minimized though perhaps not completed eliminated. It may be harder to address the biases associated with power relationships, be they formal or informal.

One solution is to eliminate personal discretion as much as possible by formalizing the selection criteria, democratizing decision-making, having observers during the selection process, documenting the results of decisions, and putting in place a regular monitoring and review mechanism. Some "checks and balances" in terms of overseeing the recruitment and selection process may also be in order. This could be done in part by the board of directors, the human resources department, or the office of the ombudsperson. The lack of "checks and balances" is often the source of systemic biases.

New ways could be developed to ascertain whether candidates have the knowledge and skills for the position. "Q&A" interviews, "presentations," and "making speeches" may not be the most appropriate methods for selecting diverse candidates. If influencing others or negotiating with people is an essential skill for a particular type of leader, then role plays may be appropriate. There may be a need to rethink how best to "test" leadership candidates according to the job requirements and the cultural upbringing of the diverse candidates (Midanik and Roy-Boulet 2019).

Conclusion

In chapter 2, we noted that the four diverse groups under examination are underrepresented among board directors and senior executives in Canada and other Western countries. In this chapter, we have focused on how diverse groups in the broader society are recruited and selected. From workforce statistics, the picture emerges that diverse groups are also underrepresented among middle-level managers and professional groups in Canada's private sector, with pockets of exceptions among racialized minorities and women. These two occupational groups below the senior executive group are the feeder pools for future generations of senior executives and board directors. Because of the limited feeder pools, the issue of diversity has to be addressed not only at the middle-management level but also at the occupational levels below it. Overall, all diverse groups lack a critical mass at the leadership level (though women are edging closer to it).

A review of the recruitment and selection mechanisms suggested that the lack of a critical mass of diverse groups at the leadership level can be attributed in part to the ineffectiveness of the word-of-mouth method to reach out to them. Nevertheless, it remains a method for reaching out to the peers of existing leaders. Given that current leaders' peers are seldom of diverse backgrounds, the method is not likely to recruit candidates from those backgrounds. The job ads posted in the media tend to focus on the attributes that ideal candidates should have, and such focus tends to discourage diverse groups from applying. There is also a requirement for demonstrated rich executive experience and visibility, and many diverse groups have neither. Meanwhile, external search firms follow the direction of the leaders, and this results in similar biases in recruitment and selection criteria. As its stands now, the word-of-mouth method, job ads, and external search firms are ineffective at recruiting diverse groups. Even if a few diverse group members do get recruited through these methods, they still have to go through the selection process, which is equally fraught.

When a critical mass of diverse groups is not present in the selection panel, the homogeneity of the panelists has a major impact in determining selection outcomes, and this often penalizes diverse groups. As the selection process for future leaders is fluid and unstructured, formal selection criteria may not be firmed up and may provide an opportunity for informal selection criteria to take their place. Informal criteria often work against diverse groups, for the latter do not have the historical advantages that other groups have. Given their powerful position, CEOs play an important role in recruiting, assessing, and selecting candidates, for they carry a disproportionate amount of decision-making weight. This also works against diverse groups.

Social and organizational contexts also play an important role in recruitment and selection. Negative stereotypes and prejudices may permeate the mindsets of the leaders involved. These perceptions and feelings often lead to social distancing or avoidance between leaders and diverse groups, which makes it still more uncomfortable for leaders to select diverse group members as fellow leaders.

Overall, it seems that a multitude of organizational and psychological factors have embedded themselves in recruitment and selection mechanisms, resulting in the exclusion of diverse groups from leadership positions. Now that we know how the entry to leaders' circles works, we need to seek solutions in human resources mechanisms. This chapter has proposed a series of solutions, all of which are practices that have been put in place by various organizations, with some wonderful results. These practices include the development of a board policy on diversity and inclusiveness; the translation of this policy into actions complete with goals and timetables; the elimination of "trophy directors" and unlimited tenure on boards; the development of diversity-rich databases on diversity; outreach to and partnership with diverse communities and specialized agencies; and the reviewing and addressing of biases related to recruitment and selection.

chapter six

Moving Up – Promotion, Performance, and Succession

Chapter 5 focused on the recruitment and selection of diverse groups for leadership positions from *outside* an organization. This chapter focuses on their advancement *within* an organization.

As with recruitment and selection from outside, promotion from within is best understood in terms of the mindsets of current leaders – that is, how they define what a leader should be and how they view diverse groups. These issues were discussed at length in chapter 3 and 4. Suffice to repeat here that the contemporary mainstream concepts of leadership used by current leaders to identify and select leadership candidates do not fit with their stereotypes of diverse groups. One of these concepts, "people-orientation," aligns well with the diverse groups. However, some current leaders look for a broader range of competencies in leadership candidates, so it seems that when only "people-orientation" matches these concepts, it may be too limited or peripheral for an all-encompassing leader. Current leaders expect more from leadership candidates – an inspiring vision, exceptional quality, established experience, and so on.

In addition to negative stereotypes, there is also prejudice against the four diverse groups under examination that causes current leaders to distrust them and feel uncomfortable around them. These feelings increase the social distance between them, besides reducing the confidence and performance levels of diverse groups. We have to keep in mind this context – the interfacing of contemporary mainstream concepts of leadership with negative stereotypes and prejudices toward diverse groups – when exploring how human resources mechanisms related to promotion impact diverse groups.

First, though, let us review the representation status of diverse groups in the workforce and how it affects their pipelines to leadership positions. "Pipelines," a fashionable term in the private sector, denotes internal occupational routes (or career pathways) leading to senior executive positions and, in some cases, to board directorships. In reviewing data on the internal representation of diverse groups in business organizations and their external availability in Canada, we will focus on three occupational groups: senior executives, middle managers, and professionals. Senior executives are the most likely candidates for board directorships in the private sector, middle management is the most likely feeder pool for senior executive positions, and professional groups are the most likely feeder pools for middle managers. While this is a common pattern as far as internal promotion is concerned, each organization has its own configuration of occupational groups that act as pipelines for rising to leadership levels.

To get the big picture, some organizations look at the organization's entire workforce and see how representative diverse groups are at each occupational stratum. When the entire workforce of an organization does not reflect the diverse composition of the larger society, active recruitment of diverse groups is needed if an equitable workforce is to be attained. However, the issue of diversity in leadership has to be addressed in terms of having qualified employees rise from one layer of management to the next, and this involves an examination of the feeder groups within an organization. When the supply of qualified candidates is inadequate for the next level of management, we have to go lower in the hierarchy and see whether there are more feeder pools below so that the organization is not short of diverse groups at each occupational level in the long run. As far as promotion is concerned, this "cascading" approach in identifying qualified diverse group members is forward-looking and has been adopted in larger corporations.

This chapter focuses on the dearth of equitable representation of diverse groups in senior management and in the feeder groups below. We will find out whether the feeder groups for senior executives are adequate and whether the pipelines are blocked. After reviewing data in this area, attention will shift to three human resources mechanisms – performance evaluation, succession management, and supportive measures – and determine the inherent biases built in those mechanisms. Both mechanisms have implications for leadership positions. Toward the end of the chapter, a series of best options and practices will be put forward as ways to remove the employment barriers.

Diversity Representation

The data on the federally regulated private sector in Canada suggested that all four diverse groups are underrepresented at the senior management (senior executive) level; also, that women and racialized minorities are the only two groups that are overrepresented at the middle-management level – the feeder group for senior executives. This implies that the pipeline for senior executive positions is available and that it is not the lack of talent of racialized minorities and women that has prevented them from becoming senior executives.

As for Indigenous peoples and persons with disabilities, their internal representation in middle management and professional positions is disproportionately low, which suggests there is an internal pipeline issue for them, not only between the senior- and middle-management levels but also between the middle-management level and those below, most likely in the professional fields.

Meanwhile, as far as the entire workforce in the federally regulated private sector in Canada is concerned, three diverse groups – Indigenous peoples, persons with disabilities, and women – are underrepresented. This suggests there may be additional pockets of underrepresentation of these groups in the sector.

Indigenous Peoples

Overall, Indigenous peoples are underrepresented throughout the federally regulated private sector in Canada. Indigenous peoples represented only 2.1% of the workforce in that sector, whereas they constituted 3.5% of the Canadian workforce. This underrepresentation has been noted since 1987, with some variations through time; however, it is getting better. Their representation increased from 0.7% in 1987 to 2.1% in 2014 (Canada 2016c).

In 2014, Indigenous peoples were underrepresented in the senior management group (0.8%), the mid-level management group (1.2%), and the professional group (1.1%). The external availability rates for these three occupational groups (2011) were higher than the above percentages: 2.9% for senior managers, 2.2% for middle managers, and 2.1% for professionals. In other words, there were more qualified Indigenous persons in these occupations outside the private sector workforce than were utilized by the private sector. Indigenous peoples are being underrepresented and underutilized. These occupations were feeder pools for the occupational group one level up. These underrepresentations have implications for promoting Indigenous peoples internally (Canada 2016c).

Persons with Disabilities

Persons with disabilities constituted 4.9% of the Canadian workforce. However, they were only 2.8% of the entire workforce in Canada's federally regulated private sector. This means they were underrepresented in that sector.

Table 6.1. Representation and availability of diverse groups in total workforce and selected occupational groups, Canada, 2011 and 2014

	Indigenous peoples		Persons with disabilities		Racialized minorities		Women	
	Internal representation (2014)	External availability rates (2011)	Internal representation (2014)	External availability rates (2011)	Internal representation (2014)	External availability rates (2011)	Internal representation (2014)	External availability rates (2011)
	%	%	%	%	%	%	%	%
Total workforce*	**2.1**	3.5	**2.8**	4.9	20.4	17.8	**41.4**	48.2
Senior managers	**0.8**	2.9	**2.6**	4.3	**8.7**	10.1	**24.8**	27.4
Middle managers	**1.2**	2.2	**2.9**	4.3	20.4	15.0	**42.0**	38.9
Professionals	**1.1**	2.1	**2.7**	3.8	28.3	19.9	**45.5**	55.0

*Total workforce covers only workforce in the federally regulated private sector.

Underrepresentations of diverse groups in selected groups are in boldface.

Source: Canada 2016c. *Employment Equity Act: Annual Report 2015.*

Since 1987, persons with disabilities in the private sector have been under-represented, with only a slight improvement over time in recent years – their representation increased from 1.6% in 1987 to 2.8% in 2014 (Canada 2016c).

In this sector, underrepresentation is also found at different occupational levels. In 2014, persons with disabilities represented 2.6% of senior manage-ment, 2.9% of middle-level management, and 2.7% of professionals. The external availability rates for these three occupational groups (2011) were 4.3%, 4.3%, and 3.8% respectively. Clearly, persons with disabilities are under-represented in all three occupational groups, and this poses problems in pro-moting persons with disabilities, for the feeder pools for those occupational groups below are limited (Canada 2016c).

Racialized Minorities

Racialized minorities constituted 17.8% of the Canadian workforce. However, they represented 20.4% of the workforce in the federally regulated private sec-tor. This means that they are overrepresented in that sector. Since 1987, the representation of racialized minorities in this sector has increased: from 5.9% in 1987 to 20.4% in 2014 (Canada 2016c).

In 2014, racialized minorities represented 8.1% of senior management, 20.4% of the mid-level management, and 28.3% of professionals. The exter-nal availability rates for these three occupational groups (2011) were 10.1%, 15.0%, and 19.9% respectively. A comparison of these statistics indicates that while racialized minorities are underrepresented at the senior management level, they are overrepresented at the middle-management and professional levels. This overrepresentation of racialized minorities in the feeder groups implies that racialized minorities are well positioned for promotion to senior executive positions.

Women

Women constituted 41.4% of the workforce in the federally regulated private sector in Canada, and they are underrepresented compared to their external representation rate of 48.2% of the entire Canadian workforce (2011). Since 1987, women in this sector have been underrepresented, and the data suggest that their status is getting worse. Their representation in the workforce has declined from a peak of 46% in 1993 to 41.4% in 2014 (Canada 2016c).

In 2014, women represented 24.8% of senior managers, 42.0% of mid-level managers, and 45.5% of professionals in the federally regulated private sec-tor in Canada. Their external availability rates for these three occupational groups (2011) were 27.4%, 38.9%, and 55.0% respectively. This means that while women are underrepresented at the senior management and professional levels, they are overrepresented at the middle-management level (a feeder group for senior executives). Internally, in the private sector, there is an adequate supply of women at the middle-management level ready to take on the roles of senior managers, but the feeder pool (from the professional groups) is considered weak.

Discussion

The workforce data showed that Indigenous peoples and persons with disabilities are underrepresented in their feeder groups (middle managers) for executive positions; however, racialized minorities and women are overrepresented in the feeder group (middle managers) for executive positions. In a longer run, women may need to have a higher representation rate at the professional level so as to provide a pipeline to middle management. Overall, for Indigenous peoples and persons with disabilities, more corporate efforts are definitely needed to make their feeder groups (middle management and professionals) more representative. Otherwise, corporations may need to depend more on external hires to get their senior executive positions filled, an option not especially favoured by the current practices of many organizations, which prioritize internal promotions rather than external hires.

The significant underrepresentation of Indigenous peoples and persons with disabilities in the workforce of the federally regulated private sector is also an eye-opener, for it points to the general deficiency in employing these two diverse groups. Such deficiency also reflects the lack of corporate focus on diversity in the past. One may argue that this has immense implications for establishing pipelines for them to access leadership positions, and also for mapping career paths for them in the hierarchy of occupations from front-line workers to senior executives and beyond. If indeed the private sector is serious about diversity in leadership, they may have to approach this issue holistically and systemically, so that the noted diversity gaps in leadership positions do not become a large gap, given that the time required to rectify this situation is lengthy.

Human Resources Mechanisms

In this chapter, three human resources mechanisms related to promotion are highlighted for discussion: performance evaluation, succession management, and supportive measures. Our focus here is on middle managers' advancement to senior executive positions, for this is the most common approach that corporations take to fill these leadership positions. Executives are sometimes recruited from outside, but for many companies this is not the principal method. These mechanisms, as they are currently carried out, have built-in biases, for subjectivity and personal discretion seep into them. When negative stereotypes and prejudices toward diverse groups exist, these mechanisms are often tainted, adversing impacting middle managers of diverse backgrounds. When succession management does not include supportive measures (such as mentoring, sponsorship, and networking) for diverse groups, those groups do not receive the much needed boost they require to advance to leadership.

Performance Evaluation

Performance evaluation for middle managers is different from that for non-management employees. Middle managers are directly responsible for their own competence, performance, achievements, and adherence to corporate values; they are also responsible for the performance of their teams, work units, branches, or departments. Indirectly, they are responsible for the organization's reputation and overall business performance. Clearly, senior executives want to know how well middle managers are carrying out their responsibilities.

In Karakowsky and Kotlyar's (2012, B5) survey, the vast majority (90%) of respondents used performance reviews as a tool for measuring candidates' potential for leadership. However, the job performance of lower-level employees (which here refers to middle managers) has not been a reliable predictor of job performance at higher levels (i.e., senior executive jobs). The Washington, DC–based Corporate Leadership Council of the Corporate Executive Board noted that fewer than one-third of candidates for leadership identified as "high potential" actually had the ability to perform well at higher levels. Even so, studies have found that organizations that do conduct effective performance evaluations outperform those that do not (Tyler 2013, 18). Performance management is now coming under greater scrutiny as more and more leaders and human resources managers/professionals grow dubious about its effectiveness.

Also debatable is whether performance management is an appropriate tool for determining leadership quality. One contemporary mainstream concept of leadership relates to the capacity for vision. A leader must be forward-looking and act as a steward, captain, and driver for the organization. Obviously, he or she must be able to perform well, but that is not a core attribute of leadership. As long as the followers can perform well, so will the organization overall.

However, the essence of leadership is to *lead*. The contemporary mainstream definition of leadership tells us what leadership attributes are. Good performance is not one of those attributes. Leading is not the same as performing, being productive, or ensuring quality. A performance management system, then, with all its "bells and whistles," is more appropriate for managers and employees than for leaders.

Merit and Limited Opportunities

In North America, "merit" has been viewed as the golden principle for human resources. The term relates to the effectiveness and efficiency of middle managers and their overall contributions to the organization. These contributions may be in the areas of innovation, productivity, market share, strategic alignment, partnership, reputation, or sustainability. Whether middle managers have opportunities to "shine," and to demonstrate their merit and contributions, depends on whether senior executives provide them with those opportunities.

Senior executives may assign racialized minority managers peripheral projects that are not of high priority or strategic significance. As a result, they do not acquire experience with more complex and strategic tasks and are not given the opportunity to establish a higher profile. Or they are asked to accomplish more with fewer resources, with the result that their performance suffers. The work assignments they *are* given may limit their opportunity to shine and thereby undermine their long-run chances to advance (Werhun and Penner 2010, 901). In reviewing the practices of some corporations in Canada, this author found that some racialized minority managers complained that high-profile responsibilities (such as "blue ribbon task forces") were usually not assigned to them, which essentially deprived them of the chance to demonstrate their capabilities and raise their profile among senior executives. Other diverse groups have voiced similar concerns. It appears that personal discretion and favouritism can effect how managerial responsibilities are assigned, to the disadvantage of ambitious middle managers.

Seemingly Objective Evaluation

A typical formal performance evaluation system has a set of evaluation criteria, measuring tools, and a scoring scale. The evaluations may be conducted online or on paper, and the evaluation results may be computerized. The formal criteria may include the performance level (such as sales volume or productivity) of the team or branch the middle manager works in, their competency (e.g., as innovators or team players), and their leadership values (e.g., integrity and transparency). These criteria are operationalized through concrete indicators and measurement tools. Performance levels are scored on a scale (from high to low, or excellent to poor). For each indicator, a high score means good performance and a low score means poor performance. The scores for each criterion are then totalled, and middle managers' overall ratings are thus determined. When the total ratings of middle managers are compared, a ranking of the middle managers' performances is possible across the organization's lines of business.

Some organizations use "organizational citizenship behaviours" (OCBs) as markers of competency. OCBs consist of employees' activities that go beyond what their job descriptions require. These activities benefit other employees or organizations, but they are not formally required and may not be acknowledged by the formal rewards system. OCBs include altruism (e.g., helping other employees), courtesy (e.g., respect and diplomatic behaviours to minimize workplace conflicts), conscientiousness (e.g., doing work that exceeds minimal requirements), civic virtue (e.g., defending the organization's policies and practices from external challenges), and sportsmanship (e.g., tolerance of difficult situations without complaining) (Organ 1988; Organ, Podsakoff, and MacKenzie 2006).

Evaluations of Indigenous peoples and racialized minorities based on OCBs may be problematic, for many OCBs could be viewed as culturally based. Diverse groups often have different expectations of what management and non-management employees should be doing in the workplace (e.g., managers, but not non-management staff, are expected to have "civic virtue") as well as different perspectives on the organizaton's minimal standards (e.g., non-management employees are expected to "complain" to managers regarding difficult situations). Unless Indigenous peoples and racialized minorities, male or female, are acculturated and have internalized the organization's cultural and citizenship values, their scores may not be as high as other employees'. OCB evaluations, then, do not strictly measure performance; rather, they measure employee behaviours based on their cultural values and norms (Lillevik 2007, 85–102).

Formal evaluation systems may look sophisticated, but their results are too easy to interpret subjectively. Performance as measured by revenues and outputs is easy to quantifiable; competency and leadership values are much harder to quantify properly and are more subject to personal discretion. Very often, when these latter criteria are interpreted both by executives (the evaluators) and by managers (the ones being evaluated), disagreements surface as to their meanings. For example, "judgment," as a criterion, could be indicated by the process a middle manager follows to make a decision or by the results the decision yields. There are gender differences in interpretation.

Compounding this weakness, scores are often subject to personal inter-pretation. The lines between scores are not as clear as they may seem. For example, the distinction between "excellent" and "good" could refer to the quality of the existing management team members, to a reference point yet to be defined by individual senior executives, or to a "textbook" standard of what "excellent" or "good" performance means. Some scoring demarcations have been developed by human resources professionals after limited consulta-tion with people at various levels or occupations; the resulting scales may be artificial and have questionable applicability.

Middle managers of diverse backgrounds, with their different notions of how a leader should behave, and their different cultural upbringing (which has inculcated different values and norms), may have different reference points and standards than those of senior executives with regard to compe-tency or leadership attributes, and this may affect the results of performance evaluations. If leaders harbour negative stereotypes of and prejudices against diverse groups, this too may taint the performance evaluation results. This blend of cultural references and performance standards is hard to untangle.

Some American studies have examined how racialized minorities feel about performance evaluations. Greenhaus, Parasuraman, and Wormley (1990, 64–86) compared black and white managers in the United States and found that black managers felt they were less accepted, enjoyed less discre-tion in their jobs, scored lower in performance evaluations, had less chance of being promoted or had reached their career plateau, and had less career satisfaction. Another study found that racialized minorities among university faculty "often experienced … a chilling and alienating environment." These managers were often expected to focus on enhancing diversity on campus, but that role performance was ignored or not evaluated properly and was not recognized and rewarded under the faculty reward system (Aguirre 2000).

In organizations that practise formal scoring, the magnitude of scores may have repercussions for middle managers. This author compared the internal scores of Indigenous managers and non-Indigenous managers at two large corporations in Canada and found that the percentage of Indigenous manag-ers with scores at the high end of the scale was consistently lower than for non-Indigenous managers; conversely, the percentage of Indigenous manag-ers with scores at the low end of the scale was consistently higher than that of their non-Indigenous counterparts. This suggests that Indigenous manag-ers were viewed as poorer performers than non-Indigenous managers. The implication is that they may be less "in the running" than non-Indigenous managers when it comes to promotion to senior executive ranks (on the assumption that performance evaluation scores are used for job competitions for those positions). Similarly, at the middle-management level in the same organization, compared to able-bodied persons, persons with disabilities were proportionately fewer at the higher end of the rating scale. This implies that, if performance evaluation scores are used for determining the promotion of middle managers with disabilities, they may not compete well with their able-bodied counterparts.

In general, assuming that each performance evaluation method measures a particular aspect of employee performance, using a single method for evaluating performance may not be as effective as using multiple methods. Several current methods on the market – 360-degree performance appraisal, the critical incident method, management by objective, the checklist method, the self-evaluation method, performance tests, and performance rating scales – are utilized in one way or another by some organizations, and they all have their strengths and weaknesses. In combination, they can provide a more holistic picture of employee performance. Yet they do not help leaders much in determining leadership candidates, for several reasons: (a) they do not measure leadership potential, they measure mainly performance; (b) they only measure people's opinions (including those of the employees themselves); (c) they are unable to shake off the subjective elements of evaluation; and (d) they do address the issue of built-in biases as related to diversity and inclusiveness.

Formal Systems Become Dysfunctional and Informal

Formal performance evaluation systems are developed on the premise that information about employees' performance is confidential. Managers may know their own scores, but they are not told their colleagues' scores. So individual managers never know how their scores compare with those of their colleagues. There are exceptions, though – some organizations aggregate colleagues' scores, so individual managers know where they stand relative to their colleagues.

This system is dysfunctional. It appears that, in some organizations reviewed by the author, it is common practice for every manager to receive a high performance score. This happens because many senior executives do not wish to antagonize their middle managers or create "bad feelings" among them. When all managers are score high, they all raise their expectations and come to believe they are high on the promotion chain. Most are disappointed when, despite their high scores, they are not promoted to senior executive positions.

When a formal performance evaluation system moves away from providing proper and genuine feedback to middle managers, it becomes dysfunctional and ineffective. Executives are increasingly relying on an informal system of daily observations, which are not written down, scored, or ranked. Performance evelauations are kept confidential by the executives themselves or are shared only among executives. As a result, formal performance evaluation systems, while they continue, are becoming increasingly irrelevant as far as executive promotion is concerned. Some middle managers of diverse backgrounds view how they have been treated by executives as an indicator of their performance. This too points to the dysfunctional nature of formal performance evaluation systems.

An additional problem is that formal performance evaluation results are not often taken at face value. They are often supplemented with recommendations from senior executives who work with those who are being evaluated. These recommendations carry more weight in career advancement than the formal results. Unfortunately, these recommendations may not be as reliable as they should because proper and more objective methods for identifying and selecting potential leaders are lacking. The recommendations of senior executives may be based largely on observations of the candidates' job performance, subjective appraisals of their potential, and personal preferences.

All of this has implications for the promotion of members of diverse groups. When informal performance evaluations are relied on, the personal discretion of executives plays a much larger role in promotion despite the existence of a formal system. Under an informal system, it is unclear what additional factors have carried weight when middle managers are promoted. This lack of clarity and transparency, when coupled with personal discretion, has an adverse impact on diverse groups because of the prevalence of negative stereotypes and prejudices (see chapter 4) and a host of other factors to be discussed later.

Adverse Impacts

The discussion of negative stereotypes and prejudices in chapter 4 highlighted the prevalence of in-group versus out-group mindsets. The "in-group" is the senior executives, who are overwhelmingly white, abled-bodied, non-Indigenous men. The "out-group" includes those who do not have backgrounds similar to the senior executives, who view them as peripheral or outsiders. Empirical studies have found that negative stereotypes and prejudices are consistently attached to out-groups. For example, Indigenous peoples are perceived by the in-group as untrustworthy, disloyal, dishonest, and unreliable. Non-Indigenous executives see Indigenous peoples as an out-group that is missing the corporate values of integrity, honesty, transparency, diplomacy, respect, and loyalty. Because of this mindset, non-Indigenous executives may feel uncomfortable when interacting with Indigenous peoples and distance themselves physically, psychologically, and socially. Some of these behaviours result in further closing of the door to leadership circles for Indigenous managers, thus marginalizing Indigenous peoples to the point that they give up on trying to advance their careers internally and look for outside job opportunities.

Similarly, the faulty perception that persons with disabilities are less than competent and reliable works against managers with visible disabilities. Physical avoidance and social distance may be common between persons with physical disabilities and able-bodied persons; those with *invisible* disabilities may be able to avoid stigmatization and the label of incompetence – up to a point.

It is in the interest of persons with invisible disabilities not to let other peoplle (including those in management) know about their disabilities because stigmatization and labelling begin as soon as those others are aware of their disabilities. Able-bodied persons tend to focus on what these persons with disabilities can*not* do as opposed to what they *can* do. This also affects their performance evaluations. Negative attitudes disadvantage persons with disabilities and affect their well-being, work quality, performance, training, development, and promotion. These ripple effects determine their fate when they attempt to rise to senior executive ranks or board directorships.

When executives evaluate the performance of middle managers, one area for consideration is whether the manager is ready for an executive position. Personal discretion plays an even larger role when the performance of middle managers is appraised with that in mind. Men dominate the executive level, so it is they who evaluate how well women are performing, and biases against women (such as the belief that they are not fit for decision-making or not really committed to the organization) may permeate the evaluation process, whether men are aware of it or not.

Also, executives may evaluate women using men's performance as a benchmark. For example, if risk management is a corporate value for evaluating managers, male executives may use how men manage risks (such as aggressive sales or acquisitions) as a benchmark for measuring how women operate in risky situations. There may well be discrepancies in behaviourial terms between the sexes, in which case the male style of risk management may be used as the standard, with the result that women's performance is viewed as weak by comparison (for they are more cautious about taking risks). When performance evaluation is conducted in this manner, it is difficult to see how women can be viewed as more fit than men for executive positions.

As noted earlier, when formal performance evaluation systems become dysfunctional and scoring practices have been misused, the organization may fall back on an informal system. That system is often heavily subjective and overreliant on personal discretion. There may be no clarity or transparency regarding how the performance of diverse group members is actually evaluated. In this way, accountability is lost, and the in-group (executives) versus out-group (diverse groups) division may become more deeply rooted, making it harder for diverse groups to be promoted to the in-group (i.e., the senior executives).

Note that biases in performance evaluation are not universally acknowledged. Some studies in the United States have found little evidence of sex bias in managers' performance appraisals. Other US studies have suggested that assessments of managers' job performance have not led to the unfair treatment of female managers in any major way (Davidson and Cooper 1992, 130–1). The verdict is still out regarding the neutrality, scientific value, and practical effectiveness of performance evaluations. It is, however, safe to say that as a human resources mechanism for promoting diverse groups, evaluation tools should be approached with caution, and senior executives' use of them needs a close look. They are potentially biased.

Succession Management

For an organization to grow, it needs to identify and develop leadership candidates internally so that they can one day move the organization forward. That is the purpose of succession management. For it to succeed, potential board directors need to be identified and effective pipelines need to be created within the organization. This is a "long haul" management system in that it focuses on creating paths for future advancement as well as a culture of leadership development. Succession management, if carried out effectively, benefits organizations by increasing their effectiveness and profitability, retaining talented employees, reducing turnover rates, making training and development resources more focused, and increasing commitment from employees (Yarnall 2011).

Knightbridge, the Clarkson Centre for Board Effectivenes, and the Institute of Corporate Directors (2011) found that 55% of senior executives had identified CEO successors, 40% were confident that current succession plans were seamless in terms of leadership transition, and 39% had identified successors for all top executive positions. These statistics are not ideal, but they suggest that a significant portion of organizations are ready for succession (Yarnall 2011). Unfortunately, these same statistics suggest that many are not.

Karakowsky and Kotlyar (2012)'s survey of organizations found the same patttern. Only 17% of respondents were satisfied with their company's succession management practices. Nearly half the respondents viewed their organization as either "highly ineffective" or "somewhat ineffective" at identifying high-potential employees who could be future leaders. For them, succession management did not guarantee that the leaders thereby selected were fit for leadership positions. In sum, they were unsure whether they were choosing the right people to develop as leaders. A significant proportion of organizations are unprepared for leadership succession (Kleinsorge 2010), have no succession management process (Sengupta 2012), or are not happy with their succession plans (Lafley 2011).

These studies illustrate the underdevelopment of succession management as a system for identifying and developing potential leaders as well as the general lack of its adoption for finding and grooming the next generation of senior executives and board directors. Candidates from diverse groups may be overlooked, screened out, or discouraged. Deliberate or not, the result may be a dearth of diverse groups in leadership positions. In what follows, we identify and discuss the barriers for diverse groups.

In some organizations, to simplify succession management, performance evaluations are integrated with succession management. The assumption here is that evaluations of middle managers' performances offer a lens through which to identify senior executives. This "clear lens" indicates how middle managers execute the organization's policies and strategies and contribute to the organization. In other organizations, performance evaluations are kept separate from succession management: the performance of middle managers is viewed as only one component of management, whereas succession management focuses on leadership. Leadership is about vision, strategy, and stewardship, whereas management is about operations, administration, and quality control. Performance evaluations are not designed to evaluate potential leaders.

Succession management usually entails an elaborate system for identifying and selecting potential leadership candidates. It involves classifying candidates according to their competence, potential, and readiness to assume leadership responsibilities, developing a database (inventory) of high-potential candidates, nurturing their leadership knowledge and skills in a systematic manner, and providing them with developmental and experiential experiences.

After potential candidates for promotion are identified and selected, they are categorized. Each organization will have its own categories. Essentially, though, there are three main categories: "high potential" (candidates who can assume leadership positions immediately with minimal leadership development), "medium potential" (candidates who need leadership development for one to two years), and "low potential" (candidates who need leadership development for much longer). The names of middle managers in the different categories are placed in an inventory of candidates, to which senior executives have access.

Approaches

There is no standard approach to managing succession. In this section, we highlight three approaches to identifying and selecting potential leaders.

Performance Evaluation Results

The first approach is based on senior executives' review of the performance evaluations of middle managers and their own personal experiences working with them. Based on these two sources of information, senior executives determine the extent to which middle managers' performance meets their expectations.

The basic premise is that middle managers' active roles in developing their own career paths geared toward higher levels of management and their high performance results indicate they have the potential to become senior executives. In this approach, performance evaluation results and the judgments of senior executives are important. But it has been found that performance evaluation results are often not in favour of diverse groups and that diverse group members tend not to be in the inner circles of senior executives, so it is unlikely that diverse groups will be in a position to command favourable judgments from senior executives.

Alignment with Leadership Profiles

The second approach does not rely at all on performance evaluation. Instead, it focuses mainly on how well middle managers' values and behaviours align with those of the organization's leaders (or its values). These profiles include the organization's ideal leadership profile or values (such as transparency, trust, and integrity). Once again, assessment of how well aligned middle managers' conduct and values are depends largely on the opinions of the CEO and senior executives, who review managers on a regular basis (perhaps once or twice a year). This judgment is largely a group effort that aims to arrive at some sort of consensus. As often happens at this level, power dynamics among senior executives play a crucial role in shaping the "verdicts" on middle managers and determining their advancement prospects. Here, proximity to the inner circle of the CEO and senior executives plays a pivotal role, and diverse groups usually do not enjoy that access.

Possession of Leadership Attributes

The third approach is to identify potential candidates based on whether they possess leadership attributes. These attributes are often found in job descriptions. Depending on the position, they may include "visionary," "strategic," and "innovative." Performance evaluation results usually do not reveal leadership attributes, for they focus on performance and productivity. In identifying and selecting leadership candidates, CEOs may also depend on the recommendations of senior executives who have worked with the middle managers as well as their own experience with them. This may amount to a variation of the second approach, especially when some leadership profiles overlap with the leadership attributes mentioned in job descriptions. This approach seems to have the same drawbacks as the previous approaches – that is, the diverse groups lack proximity to senior executives (the "inner circle"). Compound this with negative stereotypes and prejudice toward diverse groups, and the latter have an uphill battle to fight to get a favourable judgment from senior executives.

Whichever approach senior executives adopt when assessing potential leaders, diverse groups have a number of barriers to confront with regard to current succession management approaches and practices. These barriers are of two types: leadership barriers and management barriers. Leadership barriers are hurdles in succession management related to leaders' own mindsets, competency, and behaviours; management barriers are largely organizational and operational. The line between these two barriers in the real world may not be as clear as their conceptual differences because very often, human resources mechanisms are the products of an interface between human beings and the structures and processes they have created.

Leadership Barriers

Lack of Diversity Competency

Fundamental to succession management is the diversity competency of senior executives. Large corporations are paying ever more attention to diversity competency; however, the issue of how to apply a diversity perspective when managing succession has not been dealt with comprehensively. How are diverse groups to be included when contemporary mainstream concepts of leadership are tainted with biases and narrow in interpretation? How are potential leaders to be identified when diverse groups are often tainted by negative stereotypes and prejudice? How is the alignment of middle managers' behaviours with corporate leadership values to be assessed without an objective compass? Answers to these questions are sorely lacking, and as a result, diversity principles and guidelines are not prominent in succession management. In a survey of Canadian companies conducted by Katakowsky and Kotlyar (2012, B5), most of the respondents acknowledged that they had no real way of knowing whether their choices of candidates to succeed them were correct or not. While that study did not specify why they thought so, lack of diversity competency may be one of them. The authors concluded that "those who are charged with choosing which employees to groom for leadership need to be fully trained to make that call."

The lack of diversity competency among CEOs and senior executives may explain the anxiety and discomfort they exhibit in their working relations with diverse groups, and the perceived solitude between them. The author of this book noted in numerous consultations with employees with disabilities in a large corporation in Canada, that executives and managers do not have the knowledge and skills to work with them. Some executives and managers openly acknowledged as much, and that they were concerned about the unpredictability of some disabilities (such as epilepsy, attention deficiency, obsession, anxiety, and depression) and how this might affect the performance of executives or managers with disabilities and how customers react to them. They had not been trained to identify early signs of mental issues, to be cognizant of behavioural manifestations of disabilities, to work with such people, to enable other employees to work with them, to accommodate them, and to enable persons with disabilities to excel in their responsibilities and contribute to the organization. Instead, executives and managerial colleagues tended to avoid engaging with them, which further marginalized and alienated them. Social avoidance of this nature works against comfortable working relationships and further reduces the likelihood that persons with disabilities will be promoted to executive ranks.

Similarly, the lack of diversity competency results in social distance between Indigenous peoples and non-Indigenous peoples, for they have not learned to reach past the in-group/out-group relationship. This social distancing presents itself as minimal interaction time, avoidance of eye contact, lack of communication of work-related information, and spatial and social separation. The long absence of Indigenous peoples among senior executives makes it even more unlikely that senior executives will promote Indigenous peoples to their level. There may be token Indigenous executives among their ranks, but that rarely results in reduced social distance and avoidance, for they have not yet learned how to interact with one another.

Without competency in diversity and inclusiveness, working with women can be a minefield. Negative stereotypes of women and doubts about their capabilities are hard to abandon unless men develop a full understanding of and empathy toward the social environment in which women work. The work/life balance women seek is not really a women's issue. Men's general lack of support regarding familial, childcare, and eldercare obligations outside the workplace (but with direct implications for work) are largely the result of traditional social norms that relieve men of many responsibilities. Once they have developed diversity competency, senior executives can work with women to find accommodate these demands, instead of perpetuating negative perceptions and feelings that are obstacles to promoting women to leadership.

Cloning

Unless the board of directors has a firm, written corporate policy for diversity representation, especially at the senior executive level, the lack of board monitoring will allow CEOs and senior executives to play a leading role in determining who will fill vacant positions in their own echelon. Senior executives tend to select candidates who look and act like them, whom they trust and feel comfortable with, who have educational and executive work experiences similar to their own, and who share world views, business approaches, lifestyles, philosophies, hobbies, and so on (Smith 2002; Leighton 1983; Zajac and Westphal 1996; Kanter 1977). This is the very definition of cloning. Smith (2002, 509–42) concluded that there is a "tendency on the part of authority elites to reproduce themselves through both exclusionary and inclusionary processes."

The terms "homosocial reproduction" and "self-cloning" refer to similar processes (Bradshaw and Wicks 2010, 198). Whatever it is called, it ensures that new members of the senior executive will closely resemble the old. Smith (2002, 509–42) adds that, following Kanter's concept of "homo-social reproduction," people in authority create "management enclaves" comprised of employees from similar backgrounds and with a similar social orientation.

Cloning is psychologically attractive for senior executives because it reduces the risk of conflict with out-groups – that is, people who are different – and increases their own comfort (owing to commonly shared cultural values, philosophies, norms, and behaviours).

Cloning results in diverse groups – those who look different and have different social and cultural backgrounds and work experiences – being passed over for senior executive positions (Siu 2011b, 193). When racialized minorities are promoted to executive circles, white, able-bodied, non-Indigenous male executives lose their monopoly over their privileges and have to share their social space with racialized minorities. Their own negative perceptions and attitudes make it hard for them to trust racialized minorities. It is much easier for executives to choose their own kind and exclude racialized minorities and other diverse groups. Elliott and Smith (2004, 377) noted that white men are twice as likely to be promoted to managerial positions when those positions are overseen by white men rather than by other groups. Cloning behaviours are especially common at the top levels of an organization.

Cloning perpetuates itself because it rewards those who practise it. When leaders are largely homogeneous (as shown in chapter 2), bringing in a new person similar in background and appearance to the current leaders is an easy call because he is "one of us" and there is no reason to suspect that he is not "culturally fit" or a "corporate fit." By contrast, when inviting a new member from a diverse group – whether that person is a woman, a person with disabilities, an Indigenous person, or a racialized minority – unease and suspicion may arise. Such invitations require additional justifications – that is, current leaders need to have more "proof" that the person can do the job, fit in, and work well with them. Whatever the new candidate's qualifications, the current leaders are likely to focus on social, cultural, and reputational issues. This does not mean that his or her qualifications and experiences will not count, but it does mean they are in for extra scrutiny, which means in turn that the process may not be "smooth" as it would be if the leaders were engaging in cloning.

The "human capital" thesis maintains that educational attainment and other training investment may have rewarding results for people aspiring to occupy top positions. But this thesis may work mainly for white people, and not for Indigenous peoples, persons with disabilities, racialized minorities, and women. One study found that the return on human capital investment for racialized minorities was stronger at the lower end of the authority hierarchy than at the upper end (Smith 2002, 526, 530–2). This suggests that the higher up the ladder that racialized minorities hope to climb, the less likely are to translate their educational investment into financial or occupational rewards. Similar findings are noted for other diverse groups in terms of their compensation as well as their opportunities for promotion. Cloning may play a role in this skewed pattern of occupational rewards.

Prejudice and discrimination are more subtle today than in the past. Kopecki (2010) quoted Susan Estrich commenting on a case of work discrimination filed by female senior executives: "In the old days, the problem was conscious, explicit discrimination – the doors were literally closed and we had to put our heads against them and pound them in," but now "people who are doing the judging unconsciously prefer people they're comfortable with, people they know, people who look like them, people whose experience they recognize" (Sheridan 2013, 269–88). The feminist take on the dearth of women in leadership roles is that male dominance in the leadership echelons makes it almost impossible for women to rise to the same. The critical mass that men have attained seems to perpetuate itself. In the corporate world, men will rule in perpetuity until they are persistently challenged (Martin 1993, 278).

When the majority of board directors are white and male, it is more likely that the CEOs and senior executives will be "cloned" (Brown, Brown, and Anastasopoulos 2002, 4). This relationship between board directors and senior executives is noteworthy.

Another aspect of cloning merits attention: it draws CEOs and senior executives toward people who *think* like them. According to a Conference Board of Canada study, men and women do not view their contributions to an organization the same way. CEOs' priority is for their executives to make strong contributions to financial performance (such as profitability, operating performance, and internal efficiencies) and marketplace/product performance (such as consumer-perceived value, quality, and market acceptance). By contrast, female executives believe they make their strongest contributions in innovation, internal efficiencies, and employee relations. For women, profitability ranks fifth on their list. This research also found that over 90% of CEOs rate profitability contribution as important, yet only 60% of female executives indicated that they were strong on that dimension. This discrepancy between CEOs and female executives may explain CEOs' decisions not to consider women for developmental programs that may lead them to top jobs (Brady and McLean 2002, 7). These findings are confirmed by Schachter (2012, B15), who reported that the definition of "executive accomplishments" seems to be gender-based – women view internal employee and organizational wellness and customer service as executive accomplishments, whereas men viewing high profits, larger market share, more acquisitions, and risk management as executive accomplishments. Clearly, the leadership concepts are different for men and women. For a homogeneous group of white, non-Indigenous, able-bodied male executives, the desirable accomplishments of women are not on par with those of men.

Brady and McLean (2002, 7) explained such disparities by suggesting that women are predominantly in human relations areas and thus contribute largely to internal business processes, human capital, and stakeholder relations, which in turn improve financial results. Furthermore, women' style of decision-making and approach to organizational issues focuses largely on long-term business success rather than on short-term rewards. As most CEOs are male, it is difficult for them to adopt the female perspective on long-term investments in organizational success. Women viewd indirect supportive functions as having higher value than immediate profits and direct financial payoffs. Given that the gender perspectives are so different on this issue and many others, the current leaders may find it psychologically more comfortable to hire, groom, and promote people who think and act like them.

Suspicion of Out-Groups

The effectiveness of succession management in ensuring diversity in leadership is often hindered by current CEOs' and senior executives' suspicion of out-groups – that is, people with a different appearance (i.e., social identity) or background (in education, work experience, world view, values, norms) as the senior executives.

Senior executive teams in the private sector have long been "old boys' clubs" whose members all belong to friendship networks of former and current board directors, CEOs, and senior executives. They want to maintain the status quo within those clubs and continue to do business with one another undisturbed. Anyone who is not white, able-bodied, non-Indigenous, or male is viewed as not belonging to the club. Those clubs are consistently reluctant to end their homogeneity, no matter what the pressure to do so (Bradshaw and Wick 2010, 198). That reluctance reflects an effort to reduce uncertainty and conflict, to safeguard the privileges of membership (Hill 1995; Zajac and Westphal 1996), and to preserve the elite and interlocking power relations among organizations (Pettigrew 1992). This process has also been noted among senior executives and board directors in the broader public sector (Jain, Singh, and Agoc 2000, 46–74).

Some team members are likely to contend that letting out-group members "join the club" would risk destabilizing the status quo, that is, "rock the boat." Traditional out-groups, such as persons with disabilities (i.e., visible ones), are often viewed as lesser human beings. As an out-group, they may raise the level of distrust among existing senior executives.

Similarly, women have been viewed as not belonging to the club. The men who are already members generally do not know them as well as they do other men. Promoting women thus runs the risk of bringing unwelcome change to the organization. Out-groups do not have much ownership of or allegiance to an organization's current strategic direction or modes of operation. When out-groups propose changes at meetings, this amounts to a challenge to the CEO's authority. Fondas (2010, 173–6) has argued that it is not so much their *femaleness* that places women at a disadvantage; rather, it may be that they are simply outsiders with unknown track records.

Perceived Risks in Accommodation

Effective succession management considers the unique challenges encountered by diverse groups in order to smooth their transition from mid-level management to senior executive positions. However, senior executives may not understand or empathize with the special needs of diverse groups, and some have expressed concern that accommodating them would be too risky for their organizations.

Take disabilities as an example. Not all disabilities are accommodated in the same way, and not all accommodation measures are acceptable to all executives. Some such measures require additional persons (e.g., note-takers, sign-language interpreters, or personal assistants) to accompany those with disabilities in their daily work. Some executives are concerned that company secrets will be exposed by those who assist mid-level managers with disabilities (who could be promoted to executive ranks). These personal assistants are not an actual part of the executive team and are usually not even part of the organization. They are, in essence, outsiders. Yet due to the accommodation requirements, they have to be present at executive meetings and on other occasions when confidentiality is vital. Some executives view this as exposing the organization to some risks.

Still other senior executives are concerned about the required accommodation measures needed for communications about complex issues (such as financial statements, be they digital or in print form) for persons who have a visual impairment. Concerns like these often limit the opportunity for persons with disabilities to gain access to executive positions. Assistive devices may help overcome these difficulties, but current leaders are very often unaware of them. In this sense, their anxiety over promoting persons with disabilities may be misplaced.

Lack of Governance and Accountability

Succession management's weak record for promoting diverse groups to senior executive positions is compounded by the lack of monitoring and review on the part of boards of directors. Here, the crux of the problem is the distant working relationship between board directors and senior executives with regard to board governance and accountability. Almost all large private sector boards are policy and strategy boards that focus solely on policy-making and strategizing, not on operations. Board directors are more concerned about getting results than about how policies and strategies are executed and how results are obtained. Those things are the responsibility of the CEO and the senior executives. Most board directors, then, are "hands-off" from day-to-day operations. They are generally shielded from individual senior executives and seldom work with or mingle with them. This easily leads to a gap in terms of monitoring and reviewing how succession management is implemented, which, in effect, grants CEOs and senior managers autonomy in such decisions.

Most boards are interested in succession management, but rarely enough to prioritize it on their agenda. Succession questions regarding board directors and senior executives are usually decided in a rush. Succession is often viewed as a form of replacement, especially at the CEO level, rather than as a form of leadership renewal or transformation. It is also probable that the CEOs have a vested interest in delaying the process of finding their own replacements, because this maximizes their own flexibility and because they fear being viewed as "lame ducks." Also, the responsibility for finding the successors to outgoing board directors is often not clearly laid out. Unless there is a firm policy to increase diversity at the board level, the filling of vacancies is likely to be less than vigorous, and at times it will be left to the CEO. CEOs have a close working relationship with the senior executives as well as board directors, and this gives them immense influence on appointments. Studies have suggested that those who are closer to the CEO have a greater chance of being appointed. Given that diverse group members are socially distant from these CEOs, their chances of promotion are remote (Burke 2010a, 105).

As for the succession of senior executives, board directors often leave it to the CEOs and keep their own "hands off." They do little to scrutinize CEOs in this matter, leaving succession management to the CEOs and their senior executive teams. Thus CEOs enjoy a lot of autonomy when selecting candidates for senior executive positions, and the existing senior executives often defer decisions to the CEO, who is seldom challenged by senior executives or board directors. Unless a board establishes a strong policy promoting diversification on the board and in senior executive ranks, diversity in leadership is highly unlikely to be monitored, reviewed, or enforced. It may be advisable to place diversity in leadership as a regular agenda item at board meetings. This would establish it as a priority and enable board directors to hold CEOs accountable.

Lack of Role Modelling

A lack of diverse group members among the current senior executive in itself deters the development of a diverse senior executive. Middle managers as well as non-management employees of diverse backgrounds are discouraged from aspiring to senior executive positions when they see no one like them at that level. While working for the organization, they may observe many promotions of employees who are white, able-bodied, non-Indigenous, or male to senior executive positions, while none or only a few from their own diverse groups have risen to those positions. This discourages them from believing they have a chance to rise to that level, so they self-screen themselves out of the application process. When asked why there are hardly any diverse group members in leadership positions, present-day leaders often reply that diverse group members seldom apply (and that when they do apply, they are usually not that qualified). The self-screening of diverse group members may at least partly explain this phenomenon.

More and more organizations have formally announced their commitment to fostering diverse, equitable, and inclusive workplaces. But when the current executive is homogeneous (i.e., white, able-bodied, non-Indigenous men), such announcements send a double message to diverse groups. The gap between formal announcement and actual practice only shows them how hypocritical the organization can be. This causes diverse groups, as well as other employees who notice that gap, to distrust the organization and those who run it. This in turn generates increased social distance, poor morale, and low employee engagement, which only widens the gulf between the current senior executive and diverse groups in the organization.

Having persons with disabilities in executive positions is important for both able-bodied executives and persons with disabilities who aspire to be executives. Executives with disabilities make executives without them more used to working with them, which can help dispel some of the myths surrounding disabilities. For persons with disabilities, the presence of executives with disabilities makes them more confident that they can learn from their role models and rise to executive positions. Unless there are role models at the executive level, persons with disabilities may not even bother to apply for promotions.

The lack of racialized minority models will dampen how these people view their prospects by sending the message that the glass ceiling starts at the executive level. The Catalyst's survey findings of employees found that those who felt there were not enough role models for them were also less likely to agree that "talent identification processes were fair" and that "they have an equal chance of finding out about promotional opportunities" (Silva, Dyer, and Whitham 2007, 16–17).

White, able-bodied, non-Indigenous senior executive teams have long deprived women of the female role models they need. Female middle managers – the most likely feeder pool for executives – do not know what the best way is to become executives, how to prepare themselves for executive work, and how to act once they reach that level. In contrast, when there are female role models at the executive level, they can serve as role models, or even mentors or champions, for other women aspiring to be executives. Several studies have found that having female role models in senior executive positions is important for the career aspirations of other women (Davidson and Cooper 1992, 87).

Management Barriers

Lack of Transparency

Some organizations do not have a formal succession management system in place. When they do not, it usually means that candidates for succession are chosen on a personal basis and that a limited number of people have the authority to do the choosing. This sort of informal system is inherently opaque. Usually only the person with the authority to appoint senior executives knows the selection criteria, which could include personal traits, knowledge, skills, and/or experiences the decision-maker views as relevant, not to mention favouritism and nepotism. Given that these criteria are informal and sometimes personal, an observer can never be sure what they are.

In some organizations, succession management is more formal, though not necessarily transparent. While this is slowly changing in the private sector, many organizations continue to opt for secrecy. As a result, middle managers do not know what they actually have to do to rise to executive ranks, and they wonder how those who got promoted managed to do so. Middle managers will be familiar with the formal performance evaluation system for their own staff as well as for themselves, so the rating of employees based on performance has become the "default" mode of thinking about promotion, especially when the processes and criteria for promotion are not clear to them. In other words, improving oneself from an average performer to one of high performance is often perceived, rightly or wrongly, by middle managers as a legitimate and certain approach to rising to senior executive ranks.

In reality, performance evaluations matter less than other attributes. In some organizations, senior executives determine the potential for promotion based on how well they have worked together with middle managers. For senior executives, a strong leadership profile and the display of core corporate values are more important than performance. Middle managers may not realize this because succession criteria are not meant to be transparent. It is unclear to them precisely how senior executives assess their leadership potential, how often they are being assessed, and who is doing the assessment.

Furthermore, in some organizations, senior executives keep the shortlist of potential candidates close to the vest. Even those candidates who are on it may not be certain they are. They can only guess they are because they are being offered developmental opportunities and exposure to the inner workings of senior executives. The shortlist is kept hidden for a variety of reasons: it eliminates the sense of entitlement, avoids raised expectations, allows maximal flexibility for CEOs and senior executives, maintains cohesiveness among the candidates, minimizes accusations of favouritism, and makes the process look more fair.

In the interviews and focus groups this author has conducted, diverse groups have consistently pointed to their lack of information on the criteria and processes of succession management. This is often a result of their social distance from the senior executives. Diverse groups are generally less connected than others to the higher echelons. Their networks are limited, and they have few links to influential people in the organization. As a result, they are not well informed on the "ins and outs" of how the system works, on recent developments in the organization (including potential job opportunities), and on "who has been selected for what assignments." All of this reflects their social marginalization in the workplace. Because they lack information on succession management, they find it hard to judge or critique the process. They simply do not know how it works, formally or informally. Negative stereotypes about and attitudes toward diverse groups often manifest themselves in tainted judgments of some senior executives and missed promotion opportunities for diverse groups. Needless to say, they find all of this frustrating and disenchanting.

Because of this lack of transparency in succession management, those who have forged the closest connections with executives have the best and latest information. They know what it takes to be noticed and appreciated by executives, what criteria executives use in identifying candidates for top jobs, what processes they have put in place, what opportunities are coming up, and other important information. Those with the least connections – such as diverse groups – are in no position to compete with those who do have connections.

Selective Communication

The issue of who learns about vacant senior executive positions is a contentious one. Some organizations make it a point not to publicize these vacancies. Instead, existing senior executives restrict their communication to "word-of-mouth" directed to only one person and basically give that person the position. Or, senior executives contact a handful of these people (i.e., those they already consider the most qualified) and meet them over meals to discuss upcoming opportunities for promotion.

This selective method, which injects bias into the seccession system, has implications for diverse groups. Absent a real job competition for senior executive positions, middle managers of diverse backgrounds who are not "in-group" members are seldom aware of pending short- or longer-term vacancies at the senior executive levels because they have been deprived of advanced knowledge about new business strategies and directions, executive retirements or relocations, job reassignments, reorganizations, and acquisitions or mergers. Without this sort of advance knowledge, they are unable to position themselves for advancement. Furthermore, as noted earlier, diverse groups are not within the comfort zone of senior executives and are unlikely to be among the top few "high potentials" destined for "shoe-in" in executive positions.

Selective communication has other adverse impacts on diverse groups: it impacts their self-esteem, self-confidence, self-doubt, mental health, and well-being. Over time, all of this undermines performance and productivity as well as motivation and engagement, to the detriment of group morale and the organization as a whole.

Identification Issues

A key ingredient of succession management is identifying people who are qualified to be future CEOs and senior executives. As the feeder pool of senior executives is middle management, the onus for identifying potential candidates for executive positions is on the CEOs and other executives.

Identifying potential leaders is not easy. The three approaches described earlier in this chapter have many shortcomings. The first of these – using performance evaluation results – focuses on management capabilities, not on leadership capacity. The problems associated with this approach range from the personal subjectivity inherent in indicators and measuring tools to the dysfunctionality inherent in informal practices. Clearly, evaluation results are not reliable enough to determine which middle managers have leadership potential.

The second and third approaches – utilizing leadership profiles and attributes as benchmarks – also have shortcomings. Profiles, values, and attributes (such as "visionary," "strategic," and "innovative") are abstract terms that are hard to concretize and translate into measurable indicators. Also, middle managers have never been senior executives or board directors and do not have the executive work records or tangible accomplishments to prove their capabillities. Because leadership profiles, values, and attributes are rather subjective, promoting employees to the executive level on the basis of them allows "more room for unconscious prejudice" (Branson 2007, 15).

When concrete evidence is lacking, identifying potential leaders among middle managers becomes a matter of trust. The trust factor becomes the determining one when candidates for leadership are being determined. Trust between two parties takes a long time to develop, and that is why, when leaders identify potential leaders, they tend to be risk-avoidant and select people who are similar to them ("cloning"). Because they are similar in background, executives are more comfortable around them and thus more confident of them.

Leadership profiles, values, and attributes are subject to the personal interpretations, biases, and selective perceptions of those who are tasked with identifying potential leaders. For example, "visionary" ideas coming from men may be viewed as cutting-edge; but when those same ideas come from women, they may be viewed as flights of fancy. A white person's bluntness in a difficult conversation may be viewed as a positive sign of leadership; whereas a racialized minority who just as blunt may be viewed as simply abrasive. Similarly, men who act decisive and confident may well be viewed as strong crisis managers; women who act the same may be viewed instead as stubborn or inflexible and thus poor crisis managers.

Leadership profiles, values, and attributes are not culture- or gender-neutral. Some leadership profiles and attributes may well be interpreted differently depending on the candidate's gender or cultural background. As was noted in chapter 3, diverse groups have their own ideal types of leadership, which are different from contemporary mainstream ones. The collective leadership concept of Indigenous peoples is different from the individualistic leadership concept of the mainstream. Men and women may have different interpretations of what "strategic" or "collaborative" means. This points to the subjective nature of leadership profiles and to how difficult it is for senior executives to perceive their own biases.

Human resources practitioners have begun working harder to measure knowledge, skills, and experiences. Even so, these tasks are still quite underdeveloped. Given that different configurations of profiles and attributes are needed for different leadership positions at different points in time, the "science" of identifying potential leaders is still a challenge.

The identification of leaders among middle managers continues to be based largely on long-term observations and working experiences rather than on short-term encounters (as in job interviews). Historically, leaders have been almost entirely white, able-bodied, non-Indigenous men, which means that opportunities for these people to observe or work with diverse groups has been rather limited. This makes it even harder for current leaders to identify leadership candidates from diverse groups. For them, it is more comfortable as well as less risky to identify other white, able-bodied, non-Indigenous men as potential leaders.

Selection Biases

In chapter 5 it was discussed at length how selection works and the adverse impact that process has on diverse groups. Suffice here to say that present-day selection panels, selection criteria, and interview processes have much the same adverse impacts on diverse groups whether they are recruited from outside or promoted from within. Selection barriers are often the result of a lack understanding of diversity, personal discretion (due to the lack of objective selection criteria and a dearth of "checks and balances"), skewed power relations (due to a hierarchy of authority among CEOs and senior executives), and a lack of documentation for the decisions made (because the selection process is so informal and unaccountable).

While they are mentioned in the context of diverse groups entering organizations from outside (i.e., as external job applicants), these biases also arise during promotions from within. Here too, negative stereotypes and prejudices complicate the selection process, acting at times as unconscious filters when senior executives are selected. Lack of clear, measurable criteria agreed upon by senior executives prior to selection reduces the selection process to a more subjective process, with negative implications for diverse groups.

Of all the selection criteria discussed in chapter 5, "corporate fit" seems to be the most prominent one, for it is often linked to all other selection criteria. It is also the most subtle one and is seldom broached formally as a selection criterion. The term is also subjective, that is, it means different things to different people at different times. Whether candidates are a corporate fit or not is often on minds of selection panelists – indeed, it can amount to the central question. But given the complexity of many selection criteria and the difficulties associated with measuring them, any discussion of the corporate fitness of candidates is likely involve a personal imputation of what individual candidates are or do based on personal observations or intuition, sometimes without much grounding in facts. Moreover, the term is relative when different candidates are compared. Contemporary mainstream concepts of leadership may further affect the selection process, for these concepts may be used as subtle informal benchmarks for "corporate fitness," without having been formally agreed upon by the selection panelists prior to the selection.

The following section highlights three further biases that may manifest themselves when selections are being made for senior executive positions: (a) negation of transferable skills, (b) emphasis on personal mobility and relocation, and (c) the requirement of seniority. These biases are often not broached as formal selection criteria, but they often arise when determining a candidate's suitability.

(a) Negation of Transferrable Skills
It is generally acknowledged that management and leadership skills are largely transferrable, yet some executives seem to have a "silo" bias – that is, they

believe that management and leadership experience gained in one line of business or industry is not transferrable to another.

The prevalence of this belief affects both men and women who wish to find executive positions in other lines of business within an industry or in another industry. However, this bias harms women more because they tend to be restricted to a much narrower range of traditional female work domains such as human resources, public relations, communications, education, clerical and administrative services, and personal and health care services. These domains are crowded with women. The male perspective tends to be that these are corporate functions and do not involve business risks or operational know-how. Women tend to be concentrated in health care, retail, educational, and not-for-profit community services. Male executives tend to "look down" on these gender-based sectors and to look more favourably on executive candidates who have demonstrated work experience in operational lines of business and in profit-based industries. This narrows the field of potential good candidates; it also negates the management and leadership knowledge and skills that women have accumulated over the years. In this manner, executives' lack of confidence in transferrable skills may impede women's progress toward executive positions. It also hinders their entry to boards of directors, for their risk management skills are perceived to be limited. This "silo" mindset may also slow the advancement of other diverse groups to board directorships and senior executive levels.

(b) Emphasis on Personal Mobility and Relocation

When new leaders are being chosen, a high priority is often placed on personal mobility – that is, willingness to relocate. The assumption is that the ability to relocate to another region is essential to being a senior executive. This is likely to have an adverse impact on diverse groups.

Some board directorships and executive responsibilities do include attending meetings and conferences, but proper accommodation measures (e.g., walkers, wheelchairs, guide dogs) can address this job reqirement. A high priority placed on this requirement poses an employment hurdle for some diverse group members, especially those with mobility or visual impairments or other limiting disabilities, for they usually rely on local supports such as WheelTrans, medical assistance, or personal caregivers. It can be difficult for these people to relocate, for their supportive networks may not be easily portable. Because of all this, middle managers with disabilities often screen themselves out of the promotion process, having perceived that ability to relocate is a requirement, even if it is not explicitly stated in job descriptions.

Some Indigenous employees assume that some positions, including in senior management, would require them be flexible about relocating to other regions. They will thus hesitate to apply for promotions, preferring to stay close to their own communities. They will choose not to apply for positions if they will probably be expected to relocate.

Some women, especially those who are married and those who have children, face special challenges when it comes to relocation (Davidson and Cooper 1992, 123). Women have long been less likely than men to relocate to further their careers. They are more likely to move to help a spouse advance *his* career. Men are less likely to follow women who have been relocated (Northcraft and Gutek 1993, 235–7). For women with children, familial arrangements make relocation even more difficult because the entire family has to be uprooted from one community and transplanted to an unfamiliar one; they worry that their children will have problems adjusting. So when relocation is a job requirement (implicitly or not), it tends to discourage women from applying for executive positions.

There is also the issue of short-term assignments in other parts of the country or the world. Women may find it difficult to decide whether to take on these executive responsibilities. Their lack of eagerness may suggest to to male leaders that they are less committed to the organization (Davidson and Cooper 1992, 126). This perception hinders some men from appointing women as leaders.

(c) Requirement of Seniority

Some organizations have made it their formal or informal policy not to promote employees who have not been at their current positions for a certain period of time. The rationale behind this is that employees must "learn the trade" and gain experience in their current positions before applying for higher ones; moreover, too much job-hopping could jeopardize client relationships. When these rationales apply to management and executive positions, it delays the succession process for diverse groups. As a result, diverse group members, whose career progression is usually slow, are often underutilized. Policies like this one tend to lengthen further their period of underutilization. Studies have found that diverse group members usually progress slowly in their careers because they have difficulty getting promoted. This requirement of job residency thus has an adverse impact on them.

With executive positions, there is an emphasis on high-level management experiences, especially in multiple portfolios. This usually requires applicants to have actual work experiences or, at least, developmental experiences in several business domains over a period of time. Given their underrepresentation in many occupations and management positions, diverse groups may be more junior than white, able-bodied, non-Indigenous men and thus find it harder to rise to executive positions.

Negation of Familial Obligations

Familial obligations include caring for children and the elderly. This issue needs to be addressed in succession management; if not, it will continue to restrict women's opportunity to rise to senior executive positions. Society still expects women (not men) to take care of children and to do much more than their share of unpaid household work. This can place psychological stress on them to the point that they have to treat paid work as a second priority (Martin 1993, 279). It has been observed that women with children under sixteen are less likely to get executive positions (Smith, 2002, 530–2). Nicola (2019) maintained that childcare is one of the most crucial issues for women in their lives, both at work and at home. Concerns about how to take care of children in an affordable manner may explain why few senior executives are women. Nicola has termed this the "motherhood penalty."

Family obligations place constraints on women that clearly demand attention. Unfortunately, succession management, as it stands now, largely ignores this matter. More importantly, the private sector (which has "rewarded" women with childcare obligations with partial benefits and reduced opportunities for promotion) and various levels of government in Canada (which benefited heavily from unpaid childcare for economic growth) are not doing much to address this issue. Childcare has been viewed as a women's issue when actually it is a societal one that has worked against the full utilization of women's talents (Nicola 2019).

Women tend to be in their thirties or forties by the time they reach middle management; these are also the years they are raising children. This means their professional and domestic workloads have increased at the same time, so that they have to think twice before applying for executive positions that would increase their workloads even more. Once the children grow into teenagers, their needs become even more unpredictable. That unpredictability on the home front creates stress. When that stress is combined with the stress of executive work (which is equally unpredictable, if not more so), women find that they are bearing the burden more than men because society expects caregiving to remain predominantly women's responsibility (Brizendine 2008), For these biosocial reasons, the feeder pool of women at mid-level management may be smaller than the demographic numbers would indicate. Neutral and gender-friendly succession management will factor in this reality, making it integral to its formulation and implementation.

It has long been demonstrated that women spend more time doing domestic work than men. Women who work outside the home are basically holding two jobs – unpaid work at home, and paid work in an organization. Executive women who are married may have the luxury of hiring nannies, housekeepers, or cleaners to take on various traditional female roles such as childcare, laundry, and grocery shopping, but they are still expected to play the primary role at home as mothers and spouses. It has been noted that "the more a woman is succeeding in management, the more she may be viewed as neglecting or even failing in her family obligations" (Northcraft and Gutek 1993, 230–2).

Then there is the issue of the high expectations placed on senior executives. For them, devotion and attentiveness are paramount, given that executive work is viewed as pivotal for an organization and that many employees' daily tasks depend on executives' decisions and directions. Thus, executives' absence from work, inattentiveness to business and employee relations issues, and delays in making decisions may have a great impact on the business's activities and productivity, as well as its good name. This perception may be exaggerated because executives usually work as a team, and any short-term absence or inattentiveness may be addressed in a timely manner by other members of that team. However, physical presence, attention to strategic directions and operational details, participation in planning and meetings, and responsiveness in teamwork all indicate commitments to work that have been treated as a given by executives, most of whom are male. Thus, female executives who need time off because of childcare and other family issues are often viewed as lacking commitment to the organization. These high expectations on the part of other executives often raise questions about women's commitment to the organization when female candidates are being considered for executive positions.

Maternity leave is yet another issue. Some men view it as an indication that women are less committed to the organization, and that misperception often permeates the succession management regime. Women who take maternity leave may miss out on developmental or job opportunities. These leaves, whether long or short, may affect their career mobility. It has been observed that on average, it takes a woman without children three to four years longer than a man to climb one rung on the corporate ladder. Add to that two or three more years for each maternity leave. These leaves do affect the daily operations of an organization, especially if women occupy key positions. When women have babies, people tend to assume they will have still more babies. Consequently, in corporate planning, women may be overlooked as potential candidates for newly open positions (Asplund 1988, 24–5).

There is yet another factor to consider: eldercare is increasingly falling on women's shoulders. Their parents, as a result of medical advances and healthier lifestyles, are living longer, often with a protracted illness or age-related disability in their later years. Women who are contemplating executive jobs have to include eldercare on their list of responsibilities outside work, over and above their childcare responsibilities if they have a family. It has been observed that executive women are increasingly single and have few (if any) children in their care. Married women may find it difficult to carry all these familial responsibilities and still be able to perform executive duties well (Northcraft and Gutek 1993, 233–4). The author of this book asked one executive why there were so few female executives in his organization. He replied: "female executives tend to be single or divorced with no children." Then, in the same breath, the same executive commented that it was such a waste of female talents because women either did not apply for executive positions or quit after a time working as executives.

Succession management often ignores the family demands placed on women. Karakowsky and Kotlyar (2012) noted that in their survey, close to 50% of respondents rated succession management in their organizations as "highly ineffective" or "somewhat ineffective." With regard to women, part of the reason for this ineffectiveness may have to do with how they are selected and their orientation, training, and development thereafter. Until succession management addresses the issue of family obligations, it will be difficult for women even to apply for executive positions or consider taking them when encouraged or asked. In Canada, self-screening by women is more prevalent than in other countries when it comes to executive positions (Smith, 2002, 530–2).

Orientation, training, and development have focused on the business aspects of leadership – on character-building, leadership competency, staff motivation, risk management, stakeholder communication, change management, media relations, customer relations, and so on. Little or no attention has been paid to specific issues confronting female leaders, such as how to balance family obligations with workplace responsibilities. Furthermore, during orientation, training, and development, the curriculum is usually heavy with academic learning, assignments, homework, teamwork, and business activities, to the point that candidates' stress or fatigue, especially women's, is not addressed. More importantly, the challenges of childcare and eldercare are not met with changes in workplace supports and accommodations. In the end, it is difficult for women to perceive that succession management is effective as presently designed and implemented.

Selective Access to Leadership Development Opportunities

A key component of succession management is leadership development. This reflects a shift away from replacement planning for board directors or executives toward creating pipelines for future leaders (Yarnall 2011). Leadership development is an important transitional phase for potential candidates. Nadim and Singh (2008) noted that billions of dollars have been spent on leadership development in the United States. This suggests that senior executives expect leadership development to benefit the organization as a whole, not just its leaders.

Leadership development is essentially a stage of succession management. It involves giving selected high-potential candidates or high performers opportunities to develop their whole persons and to acquire additional knowledge, skills, and work experiences (Pernick 2001). Organizations vary in their approaches to leadership development, but generally, they include self-assessment, personality tests, coaching, performance appraisals, 360-degree feedback, team project management, homework, personal journal keeping, departing leaders' presentations, and/or e-learning (Green 2002; Kleinsorge 2010).

Access to these developmental opportunities is based on the recommendations of senior executives. The names of middle managers have by then already been included on the list of high-potentials or high performers. But in some organizations, not all high-potential candidates are offered these developmental opportunities. Middle managers of diverse backgrounds are often concerned that this process is too exclusionary. Unless they have the leadership development opportunities, it is difficult for them to showcase their leadership potential, network with influential people, and acquire additional knowledge, skills, and experiences; without these, they are less likely to be promoted to executive positions.

The most difficult developmental opportunity to get is not training or academy learning, but actual experience in a leadership position (such as a "bridging position," a "stretch" assignment, or an "acting" assignment). Due in part to the rarity of these opportunities at the top level, decisions by senior executives to assign them are discretional and are limited to the top high-potentials or high performers. Because there is no competition for these assignments, their doling out is often perceived as unfair.

Take persons with disabilities as an example. Depending on the type and severity of the disability, middle managers with disabilities may have a lower chance of getting a promotion to a senior executive position because they not only have to perform well in previous years but also need to showcase their leadership qualities. These qualities can only be developed over time as more developmental opportunities come available to them in the form of project leads, presentations to senior executives, acting executive assignments, bridging positions, and high-profile committee involvement. It has been perceived that such developmental opportunities are seldom provided to them because they are stereotyped as less reliable and their performance is often second-guessed. Middle managers with disabilities felt that developmental opportunities were not being fairly distributed and that able-bodied colleagues were more favoured. Persons with disabilities believed that an accumulation of these developmental experiences came in handy when actual executive positons came open. Without them, promotion was less likely.

Supportive Programs

Current succession management practices do not seem to prioritize making job competition a more level playing field. The prevalent position is that companies view merit as an overarching principle and that as long as diverse groups are just as qualified as white, able-bodied, non-Indigenous men, they have the same chance in securing senior executive positions as anyone else.

Many studies (some of which have been cited in previous chapters) have demonstrated that diverse groups do not have a level playing field in terms of employment in general and promotion to senior executive positions in particular. Negative stereotypes and prejudices are engrained in people's psyches and affect decision-making. Diverse groups have to combat these things in their daily work lives, as well as the lack of accommodation that would enable them excel in their current positions.

It has also demonstrated that the mainstream concepts of leadership are at odds with the ideal leadership concepts of diverse groups, but diverse groups are often judged from the mainstream perspectives. There are also indications that certain human resources mechanisms such as recruitment, selection, performance evaluation, and succession management place diverse groups at a disadvantage, with the result that diverse groups have fewer job opportunities as well as fewer chances of success in job competitions. Also, their expectations are lower. Sometimes, recognizing their disadvantage, they even screen themselves out, choosing not to applying for promotions, which suggests to the current leaders that they lack interest in leadership positions.

Little is being done to encourage diverse group members to compete for promotions or to prepare them for doing so. This is suggested by the general lack of supportive measures (or programs). In this section, three supportive measures are discussed to illustrate the problems: mentoring, sponsorship, and networking.

Lack of Formal or Informal Mentoring

Mentorship describes a relationship between a person who has more work experience ("mentor") and a person who has less ("mentee"). This relationship is created for the purposes of personal development: the less experienced person learns from the more experienced one. The mentor is expected to provide knowledge, psychological support, and/or connections that will benefit the mentee. Studies have found that mentorship benefits mentees: they gain more self-confidence and drive, they cope with stress more easily, they become better connected, and they experience greater job satisfaction (Cranwell-Ward, Bossons, and Gover 2004; Wang and Odell 2002).

Persons who wish to join boards of directors or senior executive teams need to acquire some knowledge about how to prepare for job competitions. Indigenous peoples, persons with disabilities, racialized minorities, and women have much to learn from people at the top corporate level. They may need to learn what leadership attributes and competencies they need, how to prepare themselves to work at senior levels, what personal connections they need to make, what networks would smooth their advancement, and what they need to do to rise in the organization.

Diverse groups seem to lack self-marketing skills. Some members of diverse groups may have to unlearn old mindsets. Indigenous peoples, persons with disabilities, racialized minorities, and women tend to be weak at self-promotion, and this works against their advancement. Racialized minorities in Canada are uncomfortable at promoting themselves. So are Indigenous peoples. Women still find it a challenge, for they are socialized to be modest (Silva, Dyer, and Whitham 2007, 1, 7, 25; Northcraft and Gutek 1993, 235–7). Mentors with more executive experience or from other backgrounds are able to identify this cultural habit of shying away from the limelight and hiding one's accomplishments and capabilities, and they point it out to diverse group members. They understand the value of mentorship. Whether their mentees are prepared to self-promote as a career enhancement tactic is another issue.

A number of factors have hindered diverse groups in their efforts to find mentors. Organizations may not recognize the importance of creating a level playing field for diverse groups and may not have established formal mentorship programs for them. The presence of a self-protective "old boys' club" may make it difficult (at least psychologically) for them to mentor diverse groups. Negative stereotypes and prejudices often heighten social avoidance behaviour between senior executives and diverse groups, so that it is hard to develop mentoring relationships between them. Also, North American culture tends to inhibit male executives from showing too much interest in mentoring women to join executive circles: gossip and rumours may develop and spread throughout the organization when the mentor is a man and the mentee is a woman. This may partly explain why young women in the Conference Board of Canada's surveys (2012) did not get much support from their organization in advancing their careers. They had fewer opportunities to be mentored, coached, assigned for job rotation, gain access to professional or leadership training, and gain line management experience (Hawkins 2013; Dobson, 2014 9).

Lack of Formal or Informal Sponsorship

Sponsorship – often referred to as championship – sometimes evolves from mentorship: the mentor speaks highly of the mentee to other people as a means to support or advance the mentee's career. Mentorship can prepare mentees to succeed; it does not secure leadership positions for them. Through sponsorship, middle managers can get an extra push from sponsors to secure leadership positions. Sponsorship involves actively promoting mentees in ways that go beyond mentoring.

Sponsors are usually influential executives. They can play an active role in the advancement of racialized minorities, providing them developmental assignments, recommending them for high-profile task forces, and nominating them for promotions. They can advocate on behalf of racialized minorities and promote their merit and accomplishments. Sponsors can also provide relevant information on advancement opportunities (Silva, Dyer, and Whitham 2007, 21–2). The extra push these executives can give is often a deal-maker, given that the competition for executive appointments is intense. An influential executive's sponsorship can add immensely to the prospects for promotion of racialized minorities.

Yet some factors work against sponsorship for diverse groups. As with mentoring, male executives may be reluctant to support or confide information to women due to risk avoidance, the "cloning" tendency, the need to safeguard the "old boys' club," personal discretion, and the need to avoid sexual gossip. All of this may reduce opportunities for women to be promoted to senior executive positions. Negative stereotypes and prejudices, and the distrust, social avoidance, and social distancing associated with these, may cause senior executives to hesitate to sponsor middle managers from diverse backgrounds. This results in diverse group members having less chance of being promoted to senior executive positions.

Sponsorship is usually informal, but some organizations have made it more formal, with designated executives responsible for "grooming" specific high-potential candidates. Most organizations do not have this sort of formal system; instead, sponsorship is more clandestine. The problem with informal sponsorship is that it is often perceived as favouritism, which benefits mostly "clones" of the current CEO or senior executives. When sponsorship is informal, there is no transparency in terms of the criteria for selecting sponsorship candidates and the practice is conducted. Given the historical biases built into career advancement at the executive level, the lack of a formal sponsorship program means that diverse groups do not have much of a chance to be sponsored.

Ineffective Networks

Networking has long been crucial for employees' career advancement. It is how career development information is transmitted and social connections are forged. But networks are not all equally effective. The networks developed by diverse groups are often locked out of the organizational networks that count.

First, diverse groups' networks are different from those of their white, non-Indigenous, able-bodied male counterparts in "composition and characteristics of their relationships with network members" (Ibarra 1993, 56–87). As diverse group members move up the hierarchy, their diverse status makes them more visible to the smaller homogeneous circle of leaders. Thus, as an out-group in the organization, diverse groups become *more* excluded because of the resistance to allowing them into the "old boys' club." Networking is important for advancement, yet it has been found that the effectiveness of Indigenous peoples' networks diminishes as they move up (Elliott and Smith 2004, 368–9). Indigenous networks have difficulty gathering information on promotion opportunities and resources, development and training opportunities, organizational strategies and policies, and executive connections. All of these are crucial to promotion. Due to the social distancing between persons with disabilities and those without, persons with disabilities are more socially isolated, and they tend to network among themselves. They do not find it easy to develop effective networks with able-bodied persons. As able-bodied persons still dominate the executive ranks, persons with disabilities have little contact with these executives. As a result, persons with disabilities are deprived of important information on job or developmental opportunities (Park, Faulkner, and Schaller 2003, 65–7).

Racialized minorities reported similar experiences (Davidson and Cooper 1992, 129), Ibarra's (1995, 673–703) study of informal networks of white and racialized minority managers found that racialized minority managers had more networks than white managers with racially heterogeneous groups but that their relations with them were less intimate. At the same time, high-potential minorities balanced same- and cross-race contacts besides having more contacts outside their own groups, fewer contacts with high-status people, and less overlap between their social and instrumental networks.

Diverse groups find that mainstream networking is not inclusive enough. In its study of forty-three large corporations in Canada regarding the experiences of racialized minorities in that country, Catalyst noted that racialized minorities were at a disadvantage when attempting to move up the career ladder by means of critical connections. They felt that they had been excluded from effective networking activities. They often felt uncomfortable participating in activities such as drinking in taverns and playing or watching sports. Racialized minority women felt that the "club" was excluding them because, very often, networking tends to take place in male-dominated spaces such as sports events and bars, and they were usually not invited (Silva, Dyer, and Whitham 2007, 11–13).

The Catalyst study also found that women and racialized minorities experienced increasing inequality higher up the ladder of power. At those higher levels, black women experienced direct discrimination. They pointed to the exclusion of racialized minorities and women from networks that could have provided them with information and resources to help them advance in the workplace. Such networks, which are often informal, enable employees who have access to them to gain knowledge and skills as well as connections.

Other studies found that members of these networks often used gender and race to rank other network members; also, that such ranking made minorities and women feel that crucial assistance for advancement (such as connections or informal training) was less accessible to them. Still other studies found that female managers find it difficult to break into male networks. They are not as effective as men at getting early information about decisions and policy shifts. Men tend to use extensive networking systems, including external contacts and high-level executives, for information on job opportunities; whereas women's networks are narrower (Davidson and Cooper 1992, 129).

Besides affecting how connected and informed racialized minorities are, networking affects their perceptions of fairness. They viewed the talent management process (including talent identification, acquisition, and development) as less than inclusive and fair, and they felt they had less chance to learn about career advancement opportunities. Racialized minorities tend, more than their white counterparts, to view "who you know" or "who knows you" as more important than "what you know" (Giscombe 2008, 2–5; Giscombe and Jenner 2009, 2–8).

Networking remains a major factor in advancement, especially for diverse groups. There have been few studies about the rise of diverse group members to senior executive positions. One such study, conducted by Elliott and Smith (2004, 377) in the United States, found that when networks were available to black women, their chances of rising from supervisor to manager increased

Figure 6.1. Biases in performance evaluation, succession management, and supportive programs

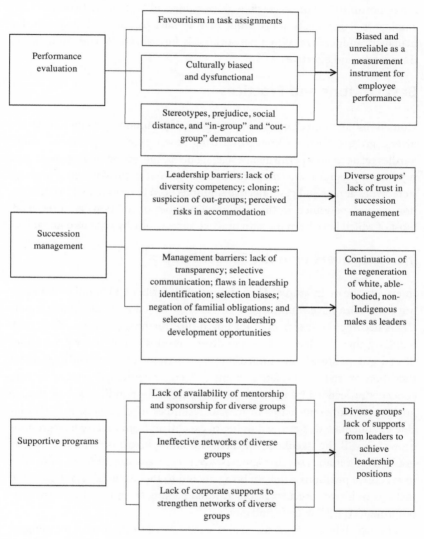

500 per cent. However, networking may not be as valuable for women and racialized minority groups as they approach the executive level, which has long been highly exclusive.

All of these studies suggest that networks of diverse groups are not as effective as they should be at higher levels; they also imply a need to make these networks more effective, perhaps with assistance from senior executives.

Furthermore, there would be value in making networking a formal corporate arrangement – that is, in a concerted effort by leaders to make networking opportunities more accessible to *everyone* and to make networking with employees – especially those from diverse backgrounds – mandatory for managers and leaders. When networking is formalized, it tends to be more transparent and effective.

Best Options and Practices

Human resources mechanisms in the matter of promotion present hurdles for diverse groups when it comes to securing senior executive positions. Those hurdles relate to how performance management, succession management, and supportive programs are structured and carried out in the context of negative stereotypes and prejudices. Effective solutions need to be executed in conjunction with one another. In this section, a number of solutions are presented, most of which have been put into practice successfully by various companies.

Increase Diversity in the Feeder Pools

Internally, the main source of board directors is former CEOs and senior executives. Studies have found that when more CEOs are female, those female CEOs become the feeder pool for board directorships (Branson 2007, 148). Similarly, there are few members of diverse groups in the feeder pool. Other diverse groups are seldom studied comprehensively, but one would expect that they share much the same fate as women, given the contemporary mainstream concepts of leadership, negative stereotyping and prejudice against diverse groups, and inherent biases in human resources mechanisms. It is reasonable to anticipate that as the number of executives from diverse backgrounds grows, so will the likelihood of them becoming board directors. This may not be as automatic as it first appears; even so, increasing numbers of women in executive positions will help bring an end to the "excuses" that CEOs and incumbent board directors resort to when passing them over for board appointments (i.e., "We can't find any").

The usual feeder pool for senior executives is mid-level management. Diverse groups are underrepresented at that level, especially when it comes to Indigenous peoples and persons with disabilities. So it is important for organizations to find ways to increase the number of qualified diverse group members in mid-level management. To do that, organizations need to monitor and review the composition of diverse groups in various occupations leading to mid-level management.

Women are largely found in the "pink collar" sector – that is, in the clerical and administrative occupations, which are viewed as "ghettoized" or "feminized." Studies have found that women's opportunities for promotion in that sector are limited (Branson 2007, 63). To increase the number of women and other diverse groups in mid-level management, organizations need to decluster – that is, open up ways for them to enter occupational groups that provide access to mid-level management (i.e., the feeder pool). This is often termed "occupational desegregation," and it requires an organizational plan (Asplund 1988, 127). One possible approach is to provide cross-training and skills-upgrading programs for women so that they can move out of pink-collar jobs. Another is to encourage women to use tuition reimbursement schemes so that they can gain new technical or professional skills in colleges and universities. The road to middle-management positions may be long, but special supports of this kind help.

More and more diverse group members, especially women and racialized minorities, are now employed in the professions, where they have greater chances to succeed when competing for middle-management positions (although women are still not faring equitably). Again, this is not automatic, for pipelines are often blocked by mainstream concepts of leadership, negative stereotypes and prejudices, and biases embedded in human resources mechanisms. Every organization needs to review its own environment and its own configuration of those jobs that serve as the feeder pool for mid-level management. After they have done that, it is important for companies to prepare, grow, promote, and transfer diverse groups to those occupations. This would increase opportunities for them to compete for mid-level management jobs.

Providing career planning and counselling to all employees, *including* diverse groups, is likely to result in more diverse group members joining the feeder pools. Members of diverse groups often complained that they did not know how to make career moves or navigate the promotion system at their workplaces. They expressed interest in learning how to prepare themselves for advancement. Companies that provide these services are helping their employees become leaders. But before launching services like these, it is important to research this field and update the counsellors/advisers regarding the actual paths to the top jobs and to train them in providing services to diverse groups. When employees do not see clear ways forward and are not being helped to advance their careers, they find themselves stalled. Currently, the best way to broadcast information on career paths is online.

Employment equity and affirmative action programs increase the participation of diverse group members in feeder pools that can lift them to leadership circles. Such programs assess the representation of diverse groups in various occupational groups including senior management; review employment policies and practices to see whether there are barriers inherent in them; and develop and implement action plans to address the underrepresentation of diverse groups in these occupational groups (Davidson and Cooper 1992, 162–3).

Canada's federal employment equity legislation requires federally regulated private-sector employers and federal contractors to monitor the representation of diverse groups in various occupations and to develop action plans for expanding the feeder pools for senior management. Federally regulated private companies in the financial, transportation, and communications sectors are required to do much the same, as are government-sector employers. In the United States, under various affirmative action programs, firms are similarly obligated to increase the representation of diverse groups by ensuring that their feeder pools are deep enough to fill leadership positions.

Johnson & Johnson, a global company with more than 120,000 employees, headquartered in New Jersey, has been acting robustly to promote women to leadership roles. In preparing the pipeline for women to become leaders, Johnson & Johnson joined ten global partnerships to increase female representation in undergraduate studies in science, technology, engineering, mathematics, manufacturing, and design. This is an excellent way to prepare women for professional jobs that are the feeder pools for middle managers and senior executives. Wanda Bryant Hope, J&J's chief diversity officer, remarked: "Diversity and inclusion is an integral part of the way we work at Johnson and Johnson. We embed it in our businesses, promote equal access to opportunity for all our employees and have leaders who hold themselves responsible for the growth and success of every team member" (DiversityInc. 2016a).

Make Performance Evaluation Objective, Fair, and Regular

Current performance management systems and their scoring mechanisms have long been viewed as ineffective and dysfunctional. They have been a source of anxiety and stress among managers and employees, and it is debatable whether they actually help employees perform better. A 2010 survey by Sibson Consulting Inc. found that nearly 60% of human resources executives graded their performance management system "C" or below. According to *2013 Mercer's Global Management Performance Survey*, only 3% of the 1,050 organizations from 53 countries stated that their performance management program provided exceptional value (Mercer 2013; Bernier 2013a, 2).

At least 1% of companies have already gotten rid of their formal performance appraisal systems. It remains to be seen whether the current performance management systems will survive at all. Atlassian Inc. – a software company with 450 employees in Sydney – ended its traditional performance review system and replaced it with weekly one-on-one meetings between managers and employees regarding performance goals. Glenroy Inc. – a Wisconsin manufacturer with 200 employees – has had no formal performance reviews for more than twenty years (Silverman, 2011, B16).

By 2015, around 6% of *Fortune* 500 companies had stopped doing performance ratings. Companies like Adobe Inc., Morgan Stanley, Kimberly-Clark, and Goldman Sachs Group, Inc., no longer conduct annual reviews and employee ratings. Companies that have dropped formal ratings have noted a concomitant drop in employee performance: their replacement review systems may not be as good and functional as hoped, and the newer performance review software programs have not been found to be better than the old methods. Absent better performance evaluation systems, some organizations (e.g., General Electric Co.) have created their own. Various informal systems have emerged to replace the old, formal ones, but they are more prone to personal biases and discretionary judgments (Greenfield 2016).

Given that present-day performance evaluation systems are clearly not working well, it is important to make them fairer, which means more objective. To that end, performance evaluation criteria, indicators, and measuring tools need to be assessed to ensure that biases against diverse groups have not been built into them. Indicators of performance can easily be biased in terms of gender, ability, culture, and race, and they need to be assessed properly by professional experts before application.

Performance evaluation has become increasingly interactive between managers and leaders, so both parties require extensive orientation and training. More importantly, the evaluator and the evaluated need to develop trust. That trust is what drives an effective performance management system, as shown in Mercer's report mentioned earlier and in Willis Towers Watson's *2012 Global Workforce Study*, which surveyed 32,000 employees worldwide (Willis Towers Watson 2012; Bernier 2013a, 8). An open discussion is needed between management evaluators and diverse group members regarding the appropriateness and acceptability of criteria, indicators, and measuring instruments. That discussion must focus on how stereotypes and prejudices may impact how performance is interpreted and how performance evaluations' indicators and measurement tools could be used to improve performance, not only for employees but also for the organization. Ideally, greater awareness and understanding will be achieved. This is easier said than done, but it is advisable to make the effort early. By the end, both parties must agree on the core framework for performance evaluations and have clear expectations.

Lastly, almost no one enjoys ritualistic annual performance evaluations. An ongoing approach is much better practice, for it provides middle managers with continuous input and feedback on their performance from their leaders, and poor performance habits can be addressed more quickly, thus increasing productivity. A consistent message from diverse groups is that they don't get enough face time with their leaders. When senior executives meet face-to-face more often with middle managers from diverse backgrounds, and communicate with them about their performance, diverse groups can improve more rapidly. Regular feedback from leaders and input from middle managers could be daily, weekly or monthly rather than annually.

3M Canada is a technology manufacturing company with more than 1,700 full-time employees. It was one of the Canada's Top 100 Employers in 2017. Its managers receive training in performance evaluation. Employee performance is tied to rewards: the firm has on-the-spot rewards, peer-to-peer recognition awards, long service awards, peer-to-peer recognition program ("We are 3M"), sales awards, and performance awards for business personnel ("Star of Q") and management employees ("Leaders of the Q"), as well as an annual awards gala for long-time employees (MediaCorp Canada 2016b).

Toronto Dominion Bank (TD) has more than 43,000 full-time employees across Canada. It too was named one of Canada's Best Employers in 2017. TD conducts employee performance evaluations every six months, and managers receive training in performance evaluation. In addition to this, employees are reviewed by co-workers and other managers who are familiar with their work. Employees may also provide confidential feedback on the performance of their managers. Exit interviews are conducted with employees who are leaving the company. TD provides bonuses and on-the-spot rewards to individual employees who perform well. Awards are also given to employees by peers ("peer-to-peer recognition awards"). TD also has long-service awards, a Vision in Action Award of Distinction that recognizes outstanding achievement, and unique performance recognition programs in each line of business (MediaCorp Canada 2016).

The Town of Pelham, Ontario, set out to revamp its performance evaluation system by involving employees in the design and implementation of a new system that would entail regular monitoring and linking results with rewards. This new system was to focus on building trust and meeting the needs of both individuals and the organization. The process began with a clarification of goals and a linking of performance evaluations to corporate plans, strategies, goals, and timetables. An employee task force was created with representation from different lines of business. A meeting of all employees was conducted to solicit ideas for performance management. Through this process, the corporate values of respect, communication, professionalism, teamwork, and innovation were determined; these are now used for benchmarking performance. A pilot phase was introduced, with regular review meetings and training sessions for management. Annual planning was done for both individual employees' and organizational goals, which were synched. Monthly goals are now monitored, and employees are provided with incentives. This grassroots engagement of employees from start to finish and the attention paid to aligning individual and organization goals have made this new performance management system for Pelham a success (Tyler 2013, 18).

Increase Leadership Development and Employee Growth Opportunities

Lifetime learning is part of working life. As society evolves and changes come to how products are made and servies are delivered, organizations need to adapt and innovate, employees need to learn new knowledge and skills, managers need to learn how to manage new workplaces, and leaders need to learn how best to lead. This is why education and training are both so important for organizations to survive and thrive.

To improve the chances for diverse groups to enter leadership circles, organizations can expand the education and training opportunities available to them. These are opportunities for personal growth as well as competency growth. These opportunities may include on-the-job training or seminars on leadership skills or the reimbursement of tuition for employees who have enrolled in executive development programs such as MBA programs. Very often, it is not so much that organizations do not have these programs; rather, it is the lack of opportunities for diverse groups to be a part of these programs.

One aspect of education and training is diversity training, which can involve every employee in the organization, including senior managers. Leaders would benefit from initiatives that open their minds to unconscious biases and to stereotypes and prejudices in the workplace. They would also benefit from skills training in working with diverse groups (Davidson and Cooper 1992, 162–3).

There are various ways to develop leaders among members of diverse groups and to expose them to boards and senior executive teams (Holton 2010, 153; Brady and McLean 2002, 3, 9). Some of these are discussed below.

(a) Job Shadowing

Job shadowing involves diverse group members being offered opportunities to team up with individual executives for a set time. It could be a few hours or a day or longer. The duration depends on the arrangement between the executives and the members.

The purposes of job shadowing are specified upfront. Some job-shadowing sessions are meant for diverse group members to observe how daily tasks are carried out so that they gain a sense of what it is like to be an executive. Some sessions are more specific: the focus is on tasks the executives actually delegate to them and involve some coaching.

Often, job shadowing is viewed as a minor component of leadership development and is conducted early in the development process. It often serves as an orientation session except that it is hands-on and on-site.

Job shadowing provides diverse group members with direct connections to individual executives, who in turn form first-hand working relationships with them. These opportunities are quite valuable for diverse group members, not just because of these connections, but also because they provide insights into the working lives of executives. More importantly, job shadowing exposes diverse group members to other executives, thus improving their name recognition.

(b) Secondment

In a secondment, diverse group members are reassigned to work in another capacity for a period of time ranging from a week or two to one or more years. These openings are the result of temporary or short-term vacancies because of, say, a maternity/paternity leave. Secondment enables diverse group members to acquire new knowledge and skills in another work environment. The learning for them is experiential.

When a secondment is at the executive level, in the form of a time-limited assignment or covering for an executive who is temporarily away from his desk, diverse group members can work more closely with other executives; this provides the latter with plenty of opportunities to know the diverse group members in an executive capacity. Clearly, secondment is a useful way to develop new leaders.

(c) Project Task Forces

Task forces are opportunities for diverse group members to shine. Task forces have a start date and an end date. At the executive level, they are usually "incubators" for high-potential candidates to develop their leadership skills. When diverse groups are provided with opportunities of this nature, they work alongside executives and learn their approaches, methods for handling risks, approaches to decision-making, and a range of executive skills.

(d) Developmental "Stretch" Assignments

Developmental "stretch" assignments is a term used by Brady and McLean (2002, 13–22) to describe "a challenging position or a cross-functional move to a different business area" in which high-potential candidates for leadership are placed so that they can learn new skills and gain experience in "complex management styles." These high-profile opportunities are usually loaded with challenges related to start-ups or problem-solving that require critical decision-making.

An assignment like this serves as a testing ground for diverse group members, for it forces them to learn quickly and they cannot afford many mistakes. When diverse groups seek out difficult job assignments and are able to complete them, their rise to the top is made easier. Unfortunately, women are seldom given opportunities of this nature. Canadian women tend to get smaller-scale assignments, Canadian men more challenging ones (Ohlott, Ruderman, and McCauley 1994, 46–67; Brady and McLean 2002, 14). Leaders are advised to reverse this tendency so that women can benefit from these opportunities too.

(e) Assignments with Line Responsibilities

As noted earlier, most CEOs have observed that women and other diverse group members have not been assigned enough line responsibilities – that is, jobs that involve expanding markets, managing risks, and generating profits and absorbing losses (Branson 2007, 81). It seems that there are "glass walls" around women that do not allow them to move around the organization and pick up knowledge and skills in functions that involve certain business risks. These "glass walls" prevent them from broadening their work experiences from corporate functions (such as human resources, communications, and financial management) to operational ones (such as product sales and running profit centres) (Branson 2007, 81–2). To enhance the chances for diverse groups to become board directors or senior executives, special assignments with line responsibilities need to be created for them to acquire these experiences.

(f) Classroom-Based Management Development Courses or Programs

According to a survey conducted by the Center of Excellence for Women's Advancement, 67% of Canadian women have pursued additional educational programs or courses in order to further their careers. Three quarters of these women reported that the additional education had a positive career impact. Yet female enrolment in MBA programs in Canada averages only 39%, and in executive MBA programs it is only 27% (Brady and McLean 2002, 21; Brown 2001, 105). According to Statistics Canada, women earned about 35% of MBAs awarded in Canada in 2011. Laurentian University had the highest proportion (60%) of female students of any business school in Canada. Overall, though, the number of women in Canadian MBA programs remains stubbornly low. This is for a variety of reasons, including women's slower career progression, high program costs, lack of female role models, concerns about work/life balance, lack of encouragement from employers, and lack of confidence in mathematics (McDiarmid 2016). CEOs view management courses as valuable for the advancement of women (Brady and McLean 2002, 19; Griffith, McBride-King, and Townsend 1998), yet women report that they have fewer opportunities than men to attend external development courses (Cianni and Romberger 1995, 440–59). If these courses are available for women to enrol and are financially supported or sponsored by corporations, the relative absence of women suggests a lack of transparency regarding enrolment opportunities within these corporations.

Most organizations do not have women-only management development programs. According to the Centre of Excellence for Women's Advancement, only 30% of the women it surveyed reported that their organizations provided women-only development programs (Orser 2000). The Centre for Creative Leadership and the Niagara Institute have customized programs for women (Brady and McLean 2002, 19). Women who participated in limited women-only programs reported positive experiences (Willis and Daisley 1997, 56–60). A supportive educational environment is necessary for such programs to succeed. This means that diverse group members should be encouraged to attend and should not be afraid to engage in frank dialogues on leadership and management issues related to diversity (Brady and McLean 2002, 9–10).

Some authors have suggested that diversity-specific programs be organized, but these come with their own problems, such as the lack of dialogue between diverse groups and non-diverse groups, as well as the perception that diverse groups are receiving preferential treatment (which can generate backlash) (Ohlott and Hughes-James 1997, 8–12). To maximize the benefits of leadership development and growth programs, participants are encouraged to spread the benefits of these programs among their peers through networks. If done properly, this can have multiplier effects. There are indications that some senior female executives have been doing this. In a survey conducted by Korn/Ferry, 78% of women reported that they were "actively grooming" women below them for top management positions (Northcraft and Gutek, 1991, 224).

Raising the Level of Diversity Competency

When rectifying the problems inherent in current models of succession management, the priority is to raise the level of diversity competency among board directors and senior executives. They are the organization's key leaders and decision-makers, so their policies and strategies and their day-to-day behaviour have an immense impact on those who work for the organization.

Diversity competency is a broad term that refers to values and behaviours as they relate to the principles of diversity and inclusiveness. These principles include respect, fairness, equity, inclusiveness, equal opportunity, and representation of diversity of all forms. These principles need to be spread throughout the organization, embedded in its culture, and manifested in its policies and procedures, strategies and tactics, programs and operations, as well as in the beliefs, norms, and daily behaviours of all who work there.

Diversity competency may take a long time and a concerted effort to achieve. Progressive organizations are advised to develop multi-year programs and activities for board directors, senior executives, and all employees. Educational sessions and skills development workshops on different topics related to diversity and inclusiveness could be organized as part of leadership development. Experts in this field are invited to speak on these topics and facilitate workshops. The first objective is to raise the awareness of senior executives regarding unconscious biases about gender, race, disabilities, and other identities. As the level of awareness is increased, senior executives then learn more about diverse groups and the barriers they face in the workplace and are able to relate to their experiences. As the level of empathy increases, senior executives may begin to acquire interaction skills for working with others. In this process, the issues of cloning, suspicion of outsiders, and anxiety over accommodation measures for persons with disabilities related to succession management barriers can start to be addressed. As knowledge and skill levels increase, senior executives can then develop policies and strategies, in consultation with diverse groups, to eliminate these barriers and create a more diverse and inclusive work environment. Specifically, they can then address the issue of homogeneity in leadership circles.

Since the 1990s, more and more organizations in Canada have been adopting diversity competency education as a tool to combat conscious and unconscious biases. These programs were launched mainly by large corporations for their senior executives and middle managers. Much of this work has since been cascaded down to employees through the intranet. This cascading could be more deliberate and comprehensive. Online courses on diversity could be provided for employees. They need not be mandatory; management and non-management staff members could embrace them on their own initiative.

Diversity education has sometimes been carried out as a one-time-only event, without regular follow-ups. It has focused strongly on eliminating stereotypes and prejudices, far less on skills for working with diverse groups and building a more structured, equitable, and inclusive corporate culture. So this training has not been as effective as it could be. Also, online courses on diversity and inclusiveness are focused too strongly on information and scenarios and are devoid of experiential learning. There is too little discussion among employees about diversity and inclusiveness. Put simply, these programs lack applicability.

To do better, organizations need to enrich the curriculum and rethink how they implement diversity education. These initiatives ought to be mandatory for all employees and carried out on a regular basis. They ought to elevate their educational content so as to focus on interactive skills, emotional empathy, and how to develop and implement policy. To those ends, diversity education ought to be carried out on an experiential basis, with as much interaction among participants as possible. There is also a need to emphasize the applicability and practicality of the information provided.

Extend the Time Frame of Succession Planning

Historically, many boards have relied on the CEO to find a successor. The CEO (most likely a man) is likely to want to avoid being labelled a "lame duck" and will try to hide from board directors his exact timeline for stepping down. Consequently, most board directors have no idea when he is stepping down, and as a result the recruitment effort is left to the last minute. Most boards do not start on succession planning until the final year or two of the sitting CEO's term (Lafley 2011). This leads to minimal planning efforts and a hasty succession conducted without due diligence or thoughtful discussion. When boards face this situation and time for succession is limited, CEOs and other board members tend to fall back on traditional methods of recruitment: "word-of-mouth," recruiting from a limited pool of peers they already know and are comfortable with. As a consequence, diverse groups are largely ignored.

To end this long-standing practice, boards of directors and senior executive teams must take succession planning seriously by allocating more lead time for it. More and more often, shareholders are demanding to see a succession plan. It is increasingly recognized that the process of appointing a new CEO must start at least five years prior to the actual succession. This is enough time to build pipelines for potential candidates, manage search firms, and effect a change in the organization's direction. Boards of directors are advised to establish a policy that requires, even while a new CEO is just starting, that a board committee be formed with a clear mandate to identify, select, and appoint the next CEO. The board and the CEO must collaborate in planning for the succession and handle the entire process (RHR International 2012, 1–2).

A.G. Lafley (2011), the former chairman and CEO of Procter & Gamble, recognized the importance of succession management. Under his leadership, CEO succession and leadership development were core responsibilities of the board. To allow maximum time, succession planning was started in the first year of the CEO, and one out of four board meetings each year focused on CEO succession. Procter & Gamble arranged regular meetings between board directors and internal functional or business leaders as well as annual meetings between board directors and regional and local leaders. To further the succession management process, a slate of internal candidates was developed. The board also implemented a transparent CEO candidate evaluation process that included job criteria, company and industry scenarios, and ideal experiences. Many potential CEO candidates were identified to address changes in circumstances.

Lafley acted as the leadership coach. He identified, trained, and evaluated potential candidates. He made sure that assessments of talent preceded reviews of business and financial results, strategies, and operational plans. He conducted these reviews with high-potential leaders every month on a one-on-one basis. Their responsibilities were increased when they performed well. Also, the standards these leaders were expected to achieve were raised constantly. Finally, potential leaders were selected based on a mix of business intelligence, emotional intelligence (i.e., self-awareness, motivation, empathy, social relationships) and judgment.

This succession management process was remarkably thorough. The same model could be easily applied in any organization that wants to diversify its leadership. More thinking and planning is needed to determine precisely which attributes leadership candidates should have and how to prevent biases from seeping into the process of identifying and selecting candidates. As board directors and senior executives are currently not well connected with potential leadership candidates who are Indigenous peoples, persons with disabilities, racialized minorities, or women, it will take more time and effort to include them in the recruitment process. Search firms, current board directors, and senior executives need to involve themselves more heavily. Consultations with leaders of other industries, institutions, and sectors are also needed. More time for succession management allows board directors, CEOs, and executives to do a more comprehensive job.

Strengthen Leadership Accountability

Basically, leadership accountability for diversity means two things: a firm commitment to diversity among board directors and senior executives; and the monitoring, review, and enforcement of that commitment.

Regarding the first issue – firm commitment – it can be addressed by raising the consciousness and commitment of board directors and senior executives through diversity competency education and training and by formalizing a corporate policy and strategy of diversity at the board and executive levels. Competency development takes time, and it should start with the board of directors and senior executives. At the start, professional expertise could be brought in to help jump-start the commitment. This commitment is best written down as a corporate policy statement signed by the board chair and/or the CEO, and it should be followed by an action plan and an allocation of human and financial resources to put the commitment into action.

The second issue – monitoring, review, and enforcement – can be addressed by placing diversity and inclusiveness as an agenda item on every board and executive meeting, complete with updates, reports, and decision items. Also, monitoring mechanisms should be established such as workforce data tabulation at the leadership level and progress updates on barrier-elimination measures and supportive mechanisms. Enforcement should be associated with the performance reviews of the CEO and senior executives quarterly and annually. Any regressions and deviations from the action plan are to be explained in an accountable manner. Awards/rewards are to be given to senior executives if progress is made, and penalties are to be imposed when regressions are noted with inadequate justifications.

The Canadian Imperial Bank of Canada (CIBC), one of the top 100 Best Diversity Employers in 2016, has developed many award programs intended to encourage employees to promote diversity. The bank's Diversity Champion Award and Team Impact Award and its Inclusive and Consultative Leader Award programs (which are not restricted to managers and executives) reward employees for developing trusting work environments. The Community Impact Award program was created to encourage individuals to take positive actions to promote diversity and inclusiveness outside the bank (MediaCorp Canada 2016a).

Lefarge Canada is a medium-sized concrete manufacturing company with more than 3,000 full-time employees. It was named one of Canada's Top 100

Best Diversity Employers in 2016. The company has a diversity and inclusion committee that reviews progress toward its diversity and inclusiveness goals on a regular basis. The company target is for women to constitute 35% of senior managers by 2020, and it employs people from diverse backgrounds. Lefarge Canada stands out for its performance evaluation of senior executives. Diversity and inclusiveness objectives are incorporated into their annual performance goals, and they are apprised of their progress during their annual performance evaluations (MediaCorp Canada 2016a).

Several Canadian companies were named among Canada's Best Diversity Employers in 2016 in part because they had set up accountability frameworks in the course of their diversity work. Loblaw Companies Limited is a supermarket and grocery chain with more than 28,000 full-time employees across Canada. It has established an inclusion council and an inclusion strategy. Monsanto Canada is a research and development company in life sciences. It has fewer than 400 full-time employees. In 2013, it established a diversity subcommittee at the leadership level, and it has recently established an Employee Diversity and Inclusion Council responsible for addressing diversity issues and making the company more inclusive. Procter & Gamble is a consumer product manufacturer with more than 1,700 full-time employees in Canada. Leadership accountability is integral to its diversity work; senior executives' performance results on diversity and inclusiveness are tied to their stock options (MediaCorp Canada 2016a).

Toronto Dominion (TD) Bank has more than 45,000 full-time employees. It has established a formal diversity leadership council responsible for diversity matters in Canada, the United Kingdom, and the United States. It maintains additional subcommittees focusing on leadership opportunities for women and racialized minorities, and it has developed agendas for Indigenous peoples, LGBTQs, and persons with disabilities.

Telus Corporation is a telecommunications firm with more than 24,000 full-time employees across Canada. The company has a diversity and inclusiveness office that maintains oversight of the corporate strategy on diversity, as well as a diversity and inclusiveness council, and that produces an annual report on diversity and inclusiveness outlining corporate progress (MediaCorp Canada 2016a).

PricewaterhouseCoopers (PwC) is a global consulting firm with more than 200,000 employees worldwide. Its leaders are committed to diversity and inclusiveness and strongly support workplace diversity. The company emphasizes diversity in its succession management, with oversight by its chief diversity officer (DiversityInc. 2016a).

Make Succession Management Policies and Procedures Transparent

Many organizations still hide their succession management policies and procedures. Yet transparency would take a lot of guesswork away from employees, especially middle managers who aspire to be executives. Increasing transparency mainly involves communicating clearly how middle managers are identified and selected as potential leaders, how many categories of "potentiality" there are for candidates (such as Procter & Gamble's categories of CEOs: "obvious CEO," "frontrunners," "rising contenders," and "future prospects"), what leadership developmental opportunities are available and how to access to them, how executive vacancies are formally communicated, and what it takes to be updated on succession management.

Transparency in succession management could also be enhanced by having written documents on the corporate strategy for succession management, with a special focus on diversity, fairness, and equal opportunity. Also, the CEO and senior executives could arrange regular briefing sessions on succession for middle managers.

Shell Canada is a petroleum and natural gas extraction company with more than 9,000 full-time employees. It was named one of Canada's Best Diversity Employers in 2016. It has established a career development program to help female employees reach their professional goals, as well as a leadership program for senior-level women (Senior Women Connect). And it has launched an annual cross-regional diversity and inclusion week across Canada, Brazil, and the United States that includes senior leadership engagement sessions (MediaCorp Canada 2016a).

Eliminate Identification and Selection Biases

As noted in chapter 5, efforts are needed to ensure as much objectivity, impartiality, and fairness as possible when identifying and selecting leadership candidates. These include the development of a board policy on diversity and an action plan with goals and timetables, outreach to diverse groups, the launching of educational sessions on stereotypes and prejudices, and reviews of emerging issues and how to address them.

Leighton (2010, 259–60) contended that until the selection criteria for board directors are made more objective and fair, having more qualified women at the board level is unlikely. Leadership profiles (such as "transparency" and "integrity") and attributes (such as "visionary" and "strategic") are culture- or gender-based and are difficult to measure. To address these issues, leadership profiles and attributes need to be made more specific and concrete through the use of objective indicators and measuring tools agreed upon by selection panelists prior to selection. The goal is to eliminate as much as possible the personal discretion and subjectivity of the selection panelists and decision-makers and avoid changing the weight of selection criteria during the decision-making process. Some selection criteria tend to be skewed against diverse groups. Criteria such as competitiveness, decisiveness, and strength align well with contemporary mainstream concepts of leadership and are likely to elicit images of masculinity that may put women at a disadvantage when they compete for leadership positions (Brady and McLean 2002, 7).

Selection criteria may have an adverse impact on Indigenous peoples, persons with disabilities, racialized minorities, and women. Given that these diverse groups seldom have an opportunity to rise to executive positions, an insistence on "five years of corporate executive experiences in pharmaceutical or similar industrial sectors" as a criterion virtually excludes these diverse groups and pretty much guarantees that they will never be promoted to board directorships or executive positions. To open door for diverse groups, a mandatory requirement of "five years of executive experiences" could be changed to "proven management experience," and these experiences could be indicated by a work history in any sector, including the public and not-for-profit sectors. When this flexibility is allowed, the selection criteria become more inclusive.

There is a tendency to inflate the value of interviews. When candidates do not have much of a record in executive accomplishments (because they have never been given the chance to acquire them), behaviourally based interviews favour those with executive experience – that is, white, able-bodied, non-Indigenous men. This bias points to the need to go beyond the model of behviourally based interviews. Personal interviews tend to be too subjective. An alternative is to utilize experiential opportunities (such as assignments, bridging positions, or acting positions) as a means to "test" how candidates handle real-life business situations. Or, personal interviews could supplement experiential opportunities.

In Canada, private-sector companies that fall under the Employment Equity Act and companies with federal contracts have a legal obligation to review and eliminate identification and selection biases in their employment policies and practices. These companies face program reviews or audits by the federal government (either the Canadian Human Rights Commission or Employment and Social Development Canada) on a regular basis to ensure that they are complying with legislative requirements. Even so, it is unclear how well these companies have succeeded in eliminating biases in their operations.

Optimize Flexibility and Accommodation

Women and some persons with disabilities find themselves confronted with exclusionary or inequitable policies and procedures (as well as negative stereotypes and prejudices) that limit flexibility and accommodation. It is time for leaders realize the disadvantages of being rigid in their expectations and requirements, and the advantages of being open to alternative approaches. This is both a leadership issue and a management one.

To address these barriers, job descriptions for leadership positions need to be written in such a way as to include more candidates by recognizing their transferrable skills from other industries or occupations, by eliminating (often implicit) relocation or mobility requirements, and by providing supports and accommodations for women who have family obligations (such as childcare and eldercare) and for other diverse groups that have special needs (Nicola 2019). Supportive measures (such as mentoring) need to be established for new executives and middle managers. Work schedules can be made more flexible to allow emergency childcare and eldercare services; external supports for family obligations can be provided for women to source regularly or on an emergency basis; requests for accommodation measures can be made user-friendly; procurement measures can be sped up; and safeguards can be developed to protect corporate secrets and human resources privacy lest these hinder accommodations for persons with disabilities.

Accenture Canada, a management consulting firm, was one of Canada's Best Diversity Employers in 2016. It has more than 3,000 employees. It has a global "Persons with Disabilities Champions" program with a focus on helping persons with disabilities acquire accommodation measures such as assistive technology; other corporate initatives include mentoring for persons with disabilities. Home Depot Canada, another of Canada's Best Diversity Employers in 2016, takes particular care in accommodating persons with disabilities. It has installed adjustable work desks and elevators at its office sites across the country. It also has an action committee that implements needed measures to ensure compliance with the Accessibility for Ontarians with Disabilities. In 2010, Toronto Dominion Bank (TD) introduced a "FlexWorkPlace" pilot program to accommodate changing work patterns by making floor space use more flexible. This included creating a "collaborative café" where employees can meet and work in a comfortable environment. 3M Canada Company provides maternity leave top-up payments for female employees who are new mothers, to 100% of salary for up to seventeen weeks (MediaCorp Canada 2016b).

Make Mentorship a Formal Corporate Practice

Mentors can provide strategic and tactical advice to mentees, coach and develop them, and make connections for them. They can show mentees the ropes and pull strings (Saunders 2019). Studies suggest that mentors are more important than personal diligence and intelligence (Branson 2007, 83). The Centre of Excellence for Women's Advancement has reported that 70.6% of organizations in Canada have a formal or informal mentoring program and that 25% of executive women believe that "a lack of mentoring is one of the top three barriers to women's advancement to senior levels" (Orser 2000, 16; Brady and McLean 2002, 16). It seems that the success of diversity initiatives is also indicated by the proportion of managers engaged in mentoring other employees. In 2016, for example, 63.8% of the managers in DiversityInc's list of the Top 10 Diversity Employers were engaged in mentoring, whereas only 36.6% of the managers in its Top 50 Diversity Employers were so engaged (DiversityInc. 2016a).

Literature on mentoring has shown that mentorship has varying effects depending on how men and women are linked up in mentoring. Women mentoring other women produced the most rewarding experiences, but female mentees earned the least compensation relative to other mentoring relationships such as male mentor–male mentee, male mentor–female mentee, and female mentor–male mentee. Male mentors are more influential, for they are found in higher echelons and thus are able to help their mentees more (Fine and Pullins, 1998, 89; McCauley, Moxley, and Van Velsor, 1998; Brady and McLean, 2007, 17–18).

Mentorship can be formal or informal. Both types are necessary for the success of mentorship, assuming that both are done properly. For the sake of transparency and corporate commitment, the formal approach is advisable.

Some large organizations have formal mentorship programs in which only a limited number of employees can enrol, largely because senior management lacks the commitment to expand mentoring and mentors are unavailable. Mentees are limited to potential management or executive candidates officially designated by the CEO or senior executives. They are identified and selected on the basis of recommendations by middle managers or senior executives. There are different formal models of mentorship, of which this chapter will highlight two:

One is a rotational model: each candidate is assigned to a group of mentors (experienced managers or executives), usually from different lines of business or functions, and that person moves from one mentor to the next on a regular basis; in this way, candidates learn from various perspectives and experiences.

This exposes each candidate to multiple lines of business and a more comprehensive view of the organization.

The other is an internship model: each candidate selects a mentor from a list, which is usually posted on the company's intranet. The mentor and mentee discuss the scope and purposes of the mentorship beforehand, and the duration of the mentorship may be limited or extended depending on their agreement. With this model, the mentee can learn in depth a particular line of business or occupation and acquire a more comprehensive view of it.

Other organizations are more laissez-faire about mentoring: employees may choose their mentors, and vice versa. The organization takes a "hands-off" approach, allowing the mentor-mentee pair to determine their own process. The informal model works best when the organization provides some guidelines and training for managers and non-management employees who wish to establish mentoring relationships.

A number of factors make mentoring programs successful. Chief among them is a trusting relationship between mentor and mentee; without it, the mentor may not be able to offer frank advice. Assessment of the needs of both the mentor and the mentee is a two-way process, and those needs may be used later on to measure the mentee's progress. At the start of the relationship, the two parties discuss and clarify their goals and expected results; these form their terms of reference and later serve as the basis for program evaluation. The competencies the mentee wishes to learn or upgrade should be written down as part of the mentoring plan. A successful mentoring program needs to broaden the learning experiences of the mentees and to provide practical hands-on work opportunities for them (Brady and McLean 2002, 18).

Royal Bank of Canada (RBC) was one of the Canada's Best Diversity Employers in 2016. It has formal mentorship programs, such as Diversity Dialogues, in which more than 2,000 employees participated. Its "Pursue Your Potential" program provides coaching for Indigenous peoples and persons with disabilities who wish to be employed by RBC. Similarly, Toronto Dominion Bank (TD) partners with the University of Toronto's Rotman School of Management in developing and implementing a program to help women who have been out of the workforce for many years by updating their networks, skills, and knowledge. It also develops opportunities for women through twenty Women in Leadership chapters and maintains a formal corporate Women in Leadership group mentoring program. As for mentoring and developing racialized minorities, TD has established a leadership development program for them in partnership with the Humphrey Group. This program comes with a one-year group mentoring cohort (MediaCorp Canada 2016a).

Recognized as one of the Canada's Best Diversity Employers in 2016, Telus Corporation is a telecommunications company with more than 24,000 full-time employees across Canada. It has a pilot mentorship program for Indigenous employees. Similarly, Xerox Canada was one of Canada's Best Diversity Employers in 2016. It is a computer equipment manufacturing firm with more than 3,000 full-time employees. It has established a diversity council whose members participate in the Corporate Champion Program. That program pairs senior executives with representatives of one of Xerox's six employee caucus groups. The program enables council members to be educated on the employee groups' perspectives and career aspirations (Media-Corp Canada 2016a).

Procter & Gamble has a Mentoring Up program in which mid-level female managers mentor higher-level male executives. In this way, it is the reverse of traditional mentoring programs (in which more senior managers and executives mentor junior employees). This program exposes mid-level female managers to higher-level executives, as a means to create communication across gender and to reverse the trend of female managers departing from the organization. The program has reduced by 95% the "regretted loss" of female managers over two years (Zielinski 2000, 136–41) (Brady and McLean 2002, 17).

Ernst & Young (EY) is a global consulting firm with more than 200,000 employees. It is the third top diversity employer among DiversityInc.'s Top 50 Employers. It has programs such as "EY Unplugged," which provides mentorship to minorities in the United States by minority executives within their first four months at the company. The "Inclusiveness Leadership Program" matches high-potential partners and principals with an executive coach and members of the American executive. The latter are mentors.

PricewaterhouseCoopers (PwC), headquartered in New York City, is a global consulting firm with more than 200,000 employees worldwide. It has a comprehensive, formal, corporate-sponsored mentoring program that has extended its reach to multiple levels of management. All managers and senior partners are involved in formal mentoring. Bob Mortiz, chairman and senior partner, takes the lead in diversity efforts at PwC and credits the success of the company to its diversity efforts (DiversityInc. 2016a).

Some not-for-profit organizations sponsor mentoring programs for women. In the United States, as early as 1988, the Clairol Mentoring Program for Women had female executives from different industries mentoring aspiring women in their fields. The Women's Network for Entrepreneurial Training, established by the Small Business Administration, has a mandate to encourage mentoring for women (Northcraft and Gutek 1993, 225).

Make Sponsorship Formal

Sponsorship is a championing process: a senior, experienced executive gives a junior, less experienced manager an extra push to enable that person to rise to a higher position. This goes beyond mentorship. Sponsorship is usually informal. It is up to the employee to develop a relationship with the influential person. Middle managers may develop and deepen their relationships with some senior executives, who may then champion them for executive positions. Some CEOs and executives take on the task informally to help women secure directorships or executive positions (Kiladze 2019b).

However, sponsorship can also be formal, in which case it is linked to mentorship in succession management. Sponsorship is much more specific than mentorship: its sole aim is to champion for a middle manager so that he or she will be promoted to an executive position or even participate in succession management. To make sponsorship more formal, an organization may need to establish terms of reference for sponsors. These terms of reference provide directions and processes for sponsors to follow. These include consulting with individual diverse groups on their career advancement barriers and proposed remedies; identifying candidates from diverse backgrounds; developing working relationships; developing an in-depth understanding of the strengths and weaknesses of selected diverse group members for promotion and their areas for additional improvement; and preparing briefing notes on individual candidates to pitch to the senior executive team and the CEO. These sponsors (usually comprised of the CEO and senior executives) discuss or pitch the merits of each of the candidates they are sponsoring among themselves and determine the future routes of candidates in leadership development and likely executive positions.

Ernst & Young (EY; see above) has made a concerted effort to provide sponsorship to women and racialized minorities. Research has shown that these two diverse groups are at a disadvantage when it comes to sponsorship in the organization. EY has developed several formal programs to link professionals to leaders to assist their career advancement. Each business unit in the company has sponsorship initiatives that designate sponsors for high-potential women and racialized minorities (DiversityInc. 2016a).

Make Networks Effective

Networking is an effective way to increase upward mobility for diverse groups. It allows diverse groups to share information and get advice on career advancement; it creates opportunities to meet colleagues and share names for

additional contacts; and it builds alliances inside and outside their organizations. In 2017, Blake, Cassels & Graydon LLP conducted a series of workshops
for women in senior in-house legal roles to win board appointments in various types of organizations, including businesses. The idea behind these workshops was to enhance women's networking skills and make them effective in
the long term (Dobby 2019; Branson 2007, 80).

Employee affinity groups play a supportive role for employees from diverse
backgrounds (Holton 2010, 153). As Asplund (1988, 131–2) noted, "networking is an expression of the working woman's new identity, and a definite sign
of her future progress in working life. Women are beginning to understand
that they need to support one another if they are going to 'make it.'" While
networking has been identified as effective way to develop high-potential
leadership candidates, the Centre of Excellence for Women's Advancement's
survey noted that only 42% of them support women's councils or networks
(McCauley, Moxley, and Van Velsor, 1998; Brady and McLean 2002, 16).

These internal employee groups are places for members to share information and ideas, exchange their own experiences, find consistent common
themes about themselves, and express themselves in one voice to leaders of the
organization. The engagement of diverse group members in these associations
enables them to build confidence and strength in themselves, not just in work
performance, but also in finding ways to reach to the top. If diverse groups
have representatives at higher echelons, their involvement in these associations enables them to share some of their learnings and success stories, to act
as role models, and to provide guidance to those members working in the
organization.

Studies had found that the networks of diverse groups are not as effective
in advancing their members' careers as networks of white, able-bodied, non-
Indigenous men. Corporate efforts are needed to make them more effective.
Senior executives may need to reach out to diverse groups' networks and work
with them to identify areas for improvement. These groups may find it difficult to acquire pertinent information on career advancement, develop connections with senior executives, secure mentorships and sponsorships, access
leadership development sessions, and so on. Senior executives can help them
on these fronts by establishing more formal opportunities for them to connect and be informed. These opportunities can boost the profiles of these
diverse group members; they may also pick up a few words of wisdom from
the leaders.

Senior executives can help strengthen these networks by sponsoring their
activities, involving themselves directly in their networking activities, and
providing facilities and financial assistance for them to organize corporate

networking events. They can also facilitate the linkages of various diverse groups' networks both inside and outside the organization, so that their networks' members can become more informed and connected. These kinds of supports develop trust between the mentors and mentees as well as between diverse groups and non-diverse groups (Brady and McLean 2002, 18).

Organizations may also wish to utilize these employees' networks as sounding boards for new policies and initiatives as well as in an advisory capacity on diversity. These networks can provide a lot of insight regarding what works best for their members and what workplace barriers they face, which makes them a "win–win" arrangement both for leaders and for employees of diverse backgrounds.

The success of diversity initiatives is also indicated by the numbers of employees engaged in employee affinity organizations. In 2016, DiversityInc. reported that 40.2% of the employees it surveyed for its list of Top 10 Diversity Employers were engaged with these groups, and 26.7% of the employees in its Top 50 Diversity Employers (DiversityInc. 2016a & b). This suggests that employee affinity organizations can make a strong contribution in terms of sterngthening organizations' diversity and inclusiveness. A key function of affinity organizations is to provide networking opportunities for their members, who appreciate those opportunities.

Corus Entertainment, one Canada's Top 100 Best Diversity Employers in 2016, has a Women's Leadership Network that enables women to learn more about their potential to become leaders or succeed as professionals. The company's Director of Learning and Development confirms that "the program has been very helpful in enabling me to build a support network." Corus has also established a Chair of Women in Management at the Richard Ivey School of Business at Western University. This chair plays a role in research and teaching in the field; she also helps reach out to women in management and draws their attention to the opportunities for women at Corus and in other industries (MediaCorp Canada 2016a).

Similarly, Home Depot Canada is known for its Women in Leadership program. Since its inception in 2010, it has hosted more than eighty events whose aim is to improve career opportunities for women at the company, and to help them network and develop their leadership and communication skills. It has many employee affinity groups, including Orange Ability (persons with disabilities), Orange Mosaic (multicultural groups), Orange Pride (LGBTQ), and Orange Women's Network.

Monsanto Canada, a small life sciences R&D company, was named one of Canada's Best Diversity Employers in 2016. It focuses on providing developmental assignments to high-potential female employees. Its Women in

Breeding Network supports female employees' networking activities. Also found at Monsanto are Access Network (for employees with disabilities) and Encompass (for LGBTQ employees).

National Bank of Canada has more than 15,000 full-time employees. It contains a group dedicated to helping female employees develop their professional networks and advance their careers. It encourages them to join Catalyst and the Association of Quebec Women in Finance. The same bank has employee affinity groups for LGBTQ and young people and a Diversity Ambassadors group for members of cultural communities and immigrants (MediaCorp Canada 2016a).

Royal Bank of Canada (RBC) was one of the Canada's Best Diversity Employers in 2016. It has more than 50,000 full-time employees. It has several employee groups, not just corporate-wide, but also in-house within departments. Women in Leadership is an accelerated development program that organizes workshops as well as opportunities to network with executives. It other networks include an online Women@RBC network, Women's Peer Coaching Network, REACH (persons with disabilities), MOSAIC (racialized minorities and new Canadians), Royal Eagles (Indigenous peoples), and PRIDE (LGBTQ) (MediaCorp Canada 2016a).

Rogers Communications has the Rogers Women's Network to foster women's advancement through workshops and networking sessions. Shell Canada, a petroleum and natural gas extraction company with more than 9,000 full-time employees, has established internal employee affinity groups such as AbNet (Indigenous peoples), Women's Network, New Professionals Network, Hispanic Network, AfNet (African Canadians), Asia Network, LGBTQ Network, and enAble (persons with disabilities) (MediaCorp Canada 2016a).

Create Diverse Role Models

Naming diverse group members to boards of directors and senior executive positions makes an organization more diverse and inclusive at the leadership level, besides serving as a powerful signal to employees, clients, and the public that the organization is fair, non-discriminatory, and inclusive. It also sends a clear message to the public, middle managers, and other employees with diverse backgrounds that they too could become board directors or senior executives. This message is important, for it encourages diverse groups to strive for those positions. Also, once diverse groups achieve representation at the leadership level, those leaders can champion diversity and inclusiveness, serve as mentors or sponsors, and ease the anxieties of existing white, able-bodied, non-Indigenous male executives and board directors, who have long been leery of people who do not look like them.

So it is imperative for organizations to begin appointing diverse group members to leadership positions. To do that, they have to reach out to potential candidates within the organization. That means carefully reviewing the current feeder pool of middle managers and providing the diverse group members with higher potential with leadership development opportunities, as well as opportunities to meet senior executives, to better postion them for career advance. It does not mean appointing "token" leaders from diverse backgrounds. It does mean establishing workable pipelines for qualified candidates and erasing past blockages. Tokenism does not foster diversity. It is better to have no tokens than an unqualified token leader.

CEOs can play a crucial role by appointing woman to boards: "54% of women directors were recommended by the CEO of the company for their first appointment compared to 32% who were recommended by a board member or recruited by the nomination committee." Women who had sat on another corporate board noted that CEOs played a lesser role in recommending them to other boards (Mattis 2010, 50–1). This observation does not deny that CEOs have played a major role in putting them on the current boards.

Another way to create role models is for CEOs and senior executives to work closely with the human resources department to develop leadership potential among diverse groups. CEOs need to know the "pulse" of employees in their organization – how they perceive their business vision, management and operations, new policies, programs and initiatives, the corporate values, and their potential to grow along with the organization. When they work closely with the human resources department, CEOs can pinpoint who the high-potentials are and who are likely to be the future leaders (Bell 2013).

The human resources department is not the only source of information for CEOs and senior executives. Employee affinity groups are another. Executive teams that liaise with these groups can hear directly from their members and come to understand that diverse role models at the top are important to them. Diverse role models among the executive symbolize "hope" for employees of diverse backgrounds as well as "good corporate citizenship" for the public.

In the United States, Kaiser Permanente, a health care organization and #1 Diversity Employer among the Top 50 Diversity Employers in 2016, has made a concerted effort to place racialized minorities in leadership positions as role models. Black and Asian Americans are doing well there in senior leadership (DiversityInc. 2016a). This provides hope for diverse groups and heightens their motivation and engagement.

Figure 6.2. How best to remove barriers in performance evaluation, succession management, and supportive programs

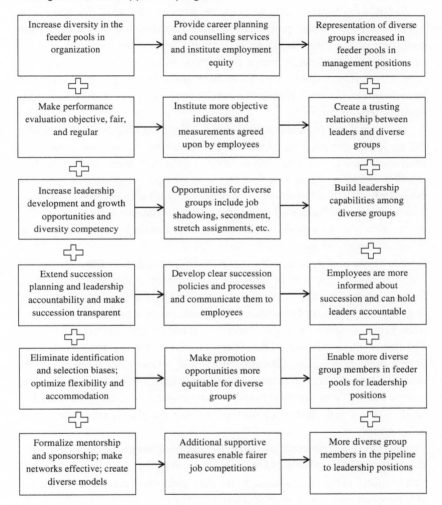

Conclusion

Statistics on diverse groups in Canada's federally regulated private sector indicate that they are underrepresented at senior executive levels. The data reflect a lack of sufficient critical mass for these groups to influence decision-making at the top. For Indigenous peoples and persons with disabilities, this lack is compounded by their underrepresentation in middle management and professional ranks, both of which are feeder pools for senior executive positions.

As noted in chapter 4, diverse group members are aware of this and blame negative stereotypes and prejudices for their situation, but they are not fully cognizant of the inner workings of human resources mechanisms when it comes to selection, performance evaluation, succession management, and supportive measures. A closer look at these mechanisms indicates that biases in promotion processes contribute heavily to the absence of diverse groups from leadership circles.

The formal and informal performance evaluations corporations currently use are laced with potential biases. Formal evaluation criteria and measuring tools are prone to bias, and when rating middle managers, evaluators may use their personal discretion, thus violating what is the essence of objective evaluation. Negative stereotypes and prejudices may also permeate decision-making processes. Some evidence suggests that the formal performance evaluation scores of diverse groups are lower than those of their white, able-bodied, non-Indigenous, or male counterparts. All of this dysfunctionality reduces the effectiveness of formal performance evaluation systems. Senior executives are increasingly resorting to informal performance evaluations even where formal systems are still in place. Informal evaluations are often tainted by negative stereotypes and prejudices, and this does not align well with contemporary mainstream concepts of leadership. It is difficult to detect subjectivity and ensure impartiality when these perceptions and feelings are embedded in formal evaluation systems. Because individual performance evaluation processes and results are confidential, employees find it even more difficult to compare notes. Thus, middle managers are unaware of the dysfunctionality and biases that make it difficult for them to pinpoint exactly why they are not being promoted.

Succession management as currently practised raises barriers to leadership positions. Those barriers are related current leaders' mindsets, skills, and governance. Leaders lack adequate diversity competency, tend toward cloning, are suspicious of outsiders and fearful of the risks associated with accommodation, and are weak in accountability and role-modelling. There are also barriers to management, related to how succession management is carried out in practice. Senior executives go about it in a non-transparent manner, communicate selectively about job vacancies, identify and select candidates without safeguards that would reduce or eliminate subjectivity and hidden biases, and limit diverse groups' access to leadership development opportunities. These psychological and administrative barriers are embedded in succession practices in various ways, only some of which are observable. Consequently, the barriers seem overwhelming to some diverse group members, who screen themselves out of the promotion process, further shrinking the supply lines.

As noted in the discussion of performance evaluation and succession management, biases can easily permeate supposedly impartial mechanisms. This is largely due to negative stereotypes and prejudices against diverse groups, "loopholes" that make mechanisms easier to end-run, the ways the mechanisms are applied, and the general lack of accountability (as in regular oversight, review, and enforcement by leaders). Failure in these factors suggests a lack of commitment to diversity and inclusiveness among leaders, who give these things a low priority.

Clearly, diverse groups do not enjoy a level playing field. They need supportive measures, which many organizations lack: mentorship and sponsorship are not formalized, and networks of diverse groups are largely ineffective. All of this makes succession management less proactive in addressing the hurdles facing diverse groups. Over the past decade, larger corporations have shown a surge of interest in building employees' supportive networks and formalizing mentorship and sponsorship programs, but these in themselves cannot transform the status quo, which tilts strongly toward homogeneity.

To raise organizations to a higher level of diversity and inclusiveness, the problem of dysfunctional and biased performance evaluations and succession mechanisms has to be addressed. Evaluations need to be made more objective, more regular, and more fair; senior executives and board directors need to raise their levels of diversity competency and accountability; succession time frames need to be extended; succession practices need to be made more transparent; identification and selection biases must be eliminated; flexibility and accommodation need to be optimized; mentoring and sponsorship must be more formalized; diverse groups' networks need to be made more effective; and diverse role models must be available. This chapter has offered many examples of best corporate practices in all of these regards.

chapter seven

Moving Out – Retention, Work Environment, and Corporate Cultures

As discussed in chapters 5 and 6, there are a number of reasons why diverse groups are underrepresented in leadership. They include employment barriers embedded in human resources policies as well as procedures and practices related to hiring and promotion. The impacts of these barriers are heightened by contemporary mainstream concepts of leadership (chapter 3), which serve as benchmarks for judging the candidates' potential and suitability. These concepts and human resources practices operate in a climate of negative stereotypes and prejudices toward diverse groups in the workplace and in the larger society (chapter 4). As a result, diverse group members who are qualified to be board directors or senior executives are overlooked or screened out systematically – and very likely unconsciously. Internally, middle managers and senior executives of diverse backgrounds may find themselves bypassed as potential candidates for board directorships or senior executive positions. All of this may explain why homogeneity persists in leadership.

To ensure the equitable representation of diverse groups in leadership positions, organizations have to establish pipelines that will enable qualified diverse employees to enter from outside and/or be promoted from within. But they also need to examine why these members, once in leadership positions or in the feeder pools for leadership, are discouraged from staying in their positions. To avoid a "revolving door" (i.e., the quick hiring and promotion – "in" – and quick termination or departure – "out" – of diverse groups) at the leadership level, it is not enough simply to hire and promote more diverse group members; it is equally important to ensure that they do not leave the organization once they are employed or have been promoted. Moran (2019) has noted that in the high-tech sector, women tend to leave in greater numbers than men, and this may also be happening in other sectors. Too much focus on external hires and internal promotions may distract leaders from issues related to the retention of diverse groups.

Retention is also an important issue in terms of feeder groups. The retention of diverse groups requires special attention *throughout* the workplace, especially in organizations where Indigenous peoples and persons with disabilities seem to be underrepresented at various occupational levels.

Canadian data indicate that since 2008 there has been an upward trend in voluntary turnover. In 2012–13 in Canada, it averaged 2.4% for senior executives; for executives, 3.3%; for lower management group, 4.5%; and for professionals, 5.8%. These seemingly low figures do not diminish the importance of leadership turnover. A variety of factors are associated with turnover rates, including economic upswings and downturns, geography, growth opportunities, compensation, engagement, performance, internal supports for leaders, and whether the sector is private or public. Every organization needs to examine its turnover data and identify the sources of turnover (Bernier 2013d, 1, 20).

Some organizations are most concerned about how retention and loyalty are intertwined. Recent studies suggest that most employees are prepared to leave their organizations at any time. It seems that organizational loyalty has been declining since the 1980s. Employees, even high performers, who are ready to walk away may feel uninspired by or bored with their work, or dissatisfied with their compensation or their advancement opportunities.

Employees' increased focus on their own careers has strengthened the trend toward shorter staying times. A 2014 report by Workopolis found that since 2002, 30% of Canadians have stayed at the same job, down from 55–60% between 1990 and 2002. Most people now seem to think in terms of a series of jobs at a series of organizations throughout their career rather than a single, lifelong career with one organization. "Job hopping" may be good for individual employees, but it is in companies' interest to retain those who can offer proven experience, immense industry knowledge, broad personal networks, demonstrated organizational contributions, and institutional memory. Given that two thirds or more of employees are prepared to leave when opportunities from competitors arise, it is important that the work environment and corporate culture not be part of what is driving out employees of diverse backgrounds. More and more studies are indicating that work environment (such as stress or workload) and corporate culture play an important role in retention (Eichler 2016).

In this chapter, we focus largely on workplace conditions and corporate cultural issues and how they may discourage or marginalize diverse groups to the point that they do not wish to stay in the organization.

Work Environment

"Work environment" covers a broad range of issues that impact diverse groups. This section highlights those issues that have implications for members of diverse groups who aspire to be leaders and those who are already in leadership positions. Work environment issues highlighted in this chapter may be divided into three areas:

- How the workplace is being managed
- How diverse employees are being treated in the workplace
- The lack of supportive measures for diverse groups

Management Issues

The lack of diverse role models and stressful work conditions impact not only diverse group members who are already on executive teams, but also those who aspire to join those teams. Limited promotion opportunities can be a major factor in motivating diverse group members to quit their jobs.

Lack of Diverse Role Models

As noted in the last chapter, a lack of diverse group members in leadership positions weakens their aspirations to become senior executives or board directors. They screen themselves out. When there are no diverse role models in leadership positions, diverse groups may come to believe that the organization does not value their contributions or see them as leadership material. When middle managers or senior executives of diverse backgrounds do not see any of their members or the board of directors or in senior executive positions, they may come to view themselves as tokens or as minor members of the leadership circle (Davidson and Cooper 1992, 87–8).

In this chapter, we examine the relative lack of role models in top positions from the perspective of new executives from diverse backgrounds. Because there are so few of these people, they have had to find their own paths to success. Navigating leadership circles for the first time is not risk-free, nor is it something one can learn from textbooks or the media. In particular, women who have risen to leadership find themselves surrounded by white, able-bodied, non-Indigenous men, so their advice on navigation may not be broadly applicable for other diverse groups. Executives from diverse group backgrounds have had their own experiences and can provide guidance to new appointees to leaderships circle simply by presenting living examples of how to conduct themselves in business.

Having role models with disabilities, visible or invisible, in leadership positions is especially important for executives with disabilities because, as Church and colleagues (2007) have noted, persons with disabilities have to map out their own courses of action, including how best to hide their disabilities for fear of stigmatization and labelling, how to develop strategies for getting work done, how to work around the constrained work structure and processes and the limitations of accommodation measures, how to balance their personal situations with their corporate responsibilities, and how to perform well in the eyes of their peers. They also have to estimate their physical and mental strengths and determine how best to use them. When role models with disabilities are available, junior executives can benefit greatly from them.

Studies on female executives have observed that for white, able-bodied, non-Indigenous men, it is long-standing practice to make decisions outside the boardroom or conference room, often at social gatherings or during informal conversations. Supposedly, decisions on agenda items tabled at formal executives' meetings are made at those meetings. In fact, they are often merely ratified there – the male executives have already decided what to do. New female members may not yet grasp this protocol.

Women, racialized minorities, and other diverse group members, being new to executive circles, may find this disheartening and frustrating because it marks them as outside the inner circle of senior executives, even when in theory they are a part of it (Israel, Banai, and Zeira 1980, 53–63; Davidson and Cooper 1992, 87–8). It would be easier for them to make inroads into the inner circles where business issues are discussed informally and confidentially prior to formal meetings if there were diverse role models for them to follow. Until current ways of doing things are changed – that is, until racialized minorities, women, and other diverse groups are fully brought into the inner circle – they will continue to find the C-suite culture exclusionary and at times secretive. Given that they lack role models to help them navigate the influencing and decision-making processes, it may take them some time to notice the informal aspects of business at the most senior levels.

Another reality is that white, able-bodied, non-Indigenous male leaders lack experience working with diverse groups and must somehow learn to do so. The entry onto boards and into executive ranks of people with diverse backgrounds generates new challenges and dynamics. For example, the existing leadership circle may feel anxious about the arrival of the first female executive, not knowing what to expect and how much she will deviate from (i.e., "disturb") the routine of executive meetings. They may feel threatened by her and feel that their "old boys' club" routines are at risk. The social distance is sure to be wide, and both sides have to learn how to work together.

Perhaps surprisingly, the presence of female role models may reduce the resistance of male executives. Male executives in the United Kingdom, the Netherlands, Belgium, France, and Germany have reported that they resist female executives largely because they have never worked with them before. Once these male gatekeepers become more comfortable with female role models in executive positions, their attitudes may change (Israel, Banai and Zeira 1980, 53–63; Davidson and Cooper 1992, 87–8).

Based on the above discussion, it is reasonable to conclude that the lack of role models places new executives and board directors from diverse backgrounds at a disadvantage, for they have to learn first-hand and on their own how to navigate the highest levels of the system. The men they encounter may have no experience interacting with peers from diverse groups and may well not make it easy for them. New junior leaders must find enough stamina to overcome this before they can excel in their new environment. Those who can't are less likely to stay.

Lack of Work/Life Balance

All of us have multiple roles to play (spouse, worker, parent, daughter, friend, and so on) at any given point in time. We also need to look out for our own physical and mental health. So we all have to find ways to juggle the demands of these conflicting roles when time is short (which it usually is).

The lack of work/life balance has been one of the main barriers for women in the workplace. Women in leadership positions face additional challenges, for today's mobile technology requires them to be "on duty" all the time. This was one finding of a survey of ten executives in six countries conducted by the Harvard Business School. One female executive at a German marketing firm noted: "If you have a position with a lot of responsibility … 24/7 availability is a given, has always been and will always be" (Tanner 2012). Similarly, employees with disabilities find it hard to balance work demands with their physical or mental health. The 24/7 workloads that executives face is often too much for them.

Balancing work and family is an important aspect of being a female executive. Women play a dual role – managing work and the family – and both roles are highly stressful. Executive work is demanding, and senior executives regularly take work home. It is especially stressful for female executives when they have young children or elderly parents. Female executives have reported that stress at work has damaged their home life, and most take work home to relieve some of the pressure at the office. Many female executives contend that they face more pressure than their male counterparts, largely because of the conflicting demands of home and work (Davidson and Cooper

1992, 132). This work/home imbalance often leads female executives to take time off from work.

Persons with more severe disabilities also take work home on evenings or weekends, and also make themselves available 24/7. However, their tolerance threshold for this is lower than for other employees. This is because they have to take care of their physical or mental health, and in some cases they have to coordinate with personal assistance services or make adjustments to their schedules.

In an organization in which work/life balance is lacking and that has made no concerted effort to help *all* of its employees achieve it, some female executives and executives with disabilities may eventually find the work conditions unbearable, to the point that they must think about quitting their jobs. When an organization provides no opportunities for female executives and executives with disabilities to balance their work and home lives, it does these people harm. Another aspect of this issue is that employees farther down the ladder may well choose not to apply for executive positions because they know what those more senior jobs would do to their home lives. This can only shrink the feeder pool.

Limited Promotion Opportunities

Diverse group members have far fewer chances to secure executive positions and board directorships than white, able-bodied, non-Indigenous men. This is demonstrated by the statistics on representation in leadership circles. From both observation and experience, members of diverse groups are well aware that few promotion opportunities are available to them.

Diverse groups find this frustrating. The author of this book reviewed the termination statistics at one corporation and found that Indigenous employees, across all occupational groups, quit their jobs at higher rates than non-Indigenous employees. Exit interviews revealed that one reason why was their dissatisfaction with their career growth. They felt they had reached a job plateau and would rise no more no matter how hard they worked or how qualified they were. This feeling of "career block" is quite common. The feeder pools for senior executives are usually smaller than they have to be because Indigenous employees "give up" before reaching the leadership positions. Some of them join another organization in the hope of better opportunities. Some employers expressed frustration about this and blamed other employers for being too generous with their financial or career offers.

Retention of existing diverse groups is as important as hiring and promoting them. Without a good supply of diverse group members in the occupational groups below middle management, the pipeline essentially dries up.

And when there are not enough middle managers of diverse backgrounds, the pipeline to executive positions dries up from within. The lack of promotion opportunities discourages diverse employees, who may opine that "the grass is greener over there" and leave the company. A company that prefers to hire from within but is perceived as not extending that practice to diverse groups may have problems retaining those groups.

Treatment of Diverse Groups

Diverse groups receive several types of treatment that make them ready to quit their jobs if they can. This section discusses social distancing, marginalizing, undermining, harassment, and discrimination. All of these, major or minor, can be viewed as forms of discrimination in that they erode the self-worth, dignity, and well-being of diverse groups, making them feel unwanted and "second-class" within the organization. However, there is value in discussing them separately. Although there are some variations, diverse groups are essentially in the same boat as far as treatment is concerned. It is no surprise that exit survey results for diverse groups (when they leave the organizations for good) tend to state "unfair treatment" as one reason why they are leaving. It is also a reason why they face problems getting promoted to management or leadership positions.

Social Distancing
Negative stereotyping and prejudices against diverse groups often result in social avoidance behaviours between white, able-bodied, non-Indigenous men (the in-group) and diverse groups (the out-group). They may minimize interactions with each other, pretending not to see each other, engaging only in superficial greetings, avoiding seeking help from each other, not supporting each other, and not inviting each other to social activities. These avoidance behaviours may deepen the divide between the in-group and out-groups, thus isolating the latter. Social distancing inhibits trusting and collaborative communications and working relationships. It also has a chilling effect on how diverse groups perceive their future in the organization. They find it uncomfortable to work there and see no point of being loyal; they may try their best to seek job opportunities elsewhere because going to work every day is uncomfortable for them (Bilimoria 2000, 25–40).

Many studies have found that white co-workers, supervisors, and managers exclude African American women and men from informal social networks and place unrealistic expectations on their performance. Experimental studies have found that white subjects make less eye contact with African Americans and have fewer verbal exchanges with them. This made African Americans feel isolated (Hughes and Dodge 1997, 581–99).

Studies on non-verbal behaviours have also found that people tend to establish greater interpersonal distance when interacting with persons with visible physical disabilities; they also spend less time with them. People displayed anxiety and discomfort in their interactions. Some tended to be "overly gracious and overly sympathetic or patronizing, and some tended to ignore them and treated them as non-persons." Persons with disabilities reported that people tend to "see through" them as if they do not exist even though they know each other. This is a form of social avoidance behaviour. As a result, persons with visible physical disabilities are deprived socially and gradually develop problems interacting with people in general (Bogdan and Biklen, 2013, 6). In other words, they lose their social interaction skills because they have less opportunity to practise them.

Due to social distancing, middle managers and senior executives with visible physical disabilities find it hard to bond with their colleagues and involve themselves in social networks with other employees. Discomfort and unease in the workplace makes leaders with disabilities believe they are unsuitable for leadership positions. Even when they do secure those positions, social distancing makes it harder for them to do their jobs well, for they are less involved in collaboration with their peers and in the inner circles of decision-making. Strong teamwork requires the ability to influence colleagues and establish a good rapport with them, so social distancing in any form jeopardizes the quality of their work, especially at the executive level. Church and colleagues (2007) studied disabilities at a large Canadian financial corporation and found that such people have to work harder or longer not only to minimize the negative impacts of their disability, but also to maintain their work performance. These daily stresses tax their physical and mental stamina, often grinding them down.

Social distancing is way for the in-group to tell out-groups they do not belong. It conveys a message of exclusion. Thus, while diverse group members may be their colleagues' equals in terms of job titles, in their daily work, they are not quite part of the leadership circle and come to grasp that their colleagues do not think they belong there. They do not gather this immediately; but as time passes, executives or board directors of diverse backgrounds begin to sense that they are not being informed about the latest developments within the organization, the coming agenda items for team meetings, the movement of people at the top, or pending restructuring plans. These are general signs of social distancing between the in-group and out-groups, and it takes a little time for new leaders from diverse groups to pick up on them.

Empirical studies have often noted the phenomenon of social distancing and how it affects various diverse groups, but comparison studies of its impact across different diverse groups are not readily available. That said, there have been a few corporate surveys in Canada that suggest it is employees with disabilities who feel social distancing the strongest, for it is they who feel a greater sense of social isolation in the workplace: they do not feel that they belong in their organization and are more dissatisfied with how they are being treated there. Racialized minorities and Indigenous peoples also sense that social distancing is at work and are dissatisfied with how they are being treated. They often interpret this behaviour as racially based. Of the four out-groups discussed in this book, it is probably women who are the most satisfied employees. Yet even female executives often report social distancing vis-à-vis their male counterparts; empirical studies have found that they too feel excluded from some social events (sports, social drinking) and decision-making processes. Although focus group discussions and interviews with employees in Canada have been small in scale, they confirm the general pattern of social distancing.

Marginalizing and Undermining

Diverse groups complain that their bosses and co-workers often undermine them. For example, racialized minorities are viewed as competent managers or leaders (Powell 1969, 209–25; Chung-Herrera and Laukau 2005) but are not perceived as trustworthy (Rana et al., 1998; Kulik and Bainbridge 2006, 34). This specific negative stereotype aimed at racialized minorities (one of several) has an adverse impact on their careers (Henry and Tator 2002). It also does nothing to raise the confidence levels of current leaders when it comes to evaluating candidates for promotion.

The author's own research in the private sector suggests that diverse groups are marginalized and undermined in various ways. For example, managers who are racialized minorities may find that their own superiors do not back them up when their subordinates have complaints about them. Executives may err on the side of accepting those subordinates' perspectives, with the result that racialized minority managers have to justify their own positions. For another example, executives may give a high degree of credibility to other executives' comments on racialized minority managers so that again, racialized minority managers have to justify what they have done. As noted earlier, social distancing fosters distrust between diverse groups and non-diverse groups and strengthens the likelihood of marginalization and undermining.

Women feel marginalized when they are not consulted on business or workplace issues and when their opinions are not sought. This applies to both managers and non-management employees. McGee and Sutton (2019) surveyed more than 2,000 employees and found that women were 1.2 times more likely than men to complain that their opinions were not being valued or sought in the workplace. Also, women with intersectional features (i.e., racialized minority women, LGBTQ women, women with disabilities) were up to 2.4 times more likely to complain of being marginalized or undermined. Chearly, this did them harm.

Persons with visible disabilities are perceived as less capable than those who are able-bodied (Shier, Graham and Jones 2008, 68). Managers are hesitant to give them a chance, even in job interviews (Raskin 1994, 82). When they are employees, managers may second-guess the quality of their work. The author's research in one corporation found that their colleagues often reviewed their work, and only after they endorsed it did managers gain more confidence in it. This tends to undermine the confidence of persons with disabilities once they notice it. This negative stereotype of persons with disabilities as poorer performers carries forward to the executive level, where high-profile assignments are sometimes allocated to able-bodied executives. Assigning a task force to co-chairs is another form of showing anxiety about the performance of executives with disabilities, for it signals that they are not trusted to bear the sole responsibility for chairing a task force. Joint responsibility is viewed as a way to ensure the quality of the work.

Female managers often complain that they feel undermined by the lack of clarity about their role and by their lack of clear authority. This often compromises the effectiveness of their actions. Often, because they lack backing and support from their bosses (senior executives), they constantly have to negotiate the boundaries of what they can do and cannot do. They find themselves walking a tightrope on a daily basis, knowing full well that their mistakes may bring down heavy penalties. Some studies have found that the quality of women's performance is compromised as a result of this poor role demarcation and status ambiguity. Women often feel that their work is undermined by such work arrangements, leaving them to deal with the fallout (Marshall 1995, 155–6). In this kind of work environment, it is difficult to see how women's performance can be viewed as high in quality or how they can possibly be promoted. Some women feel that their upward mobility in the organizations has been blocked as a result. Female middle managers are the most likely feeder pool for senior executive positions, so when they leave the organization as a result of frustration over promotion issues, the feeder pool diminishes.

The marginalizing of middle managers and the undermining of their performance and confidence pave the way to disenchantment with management positions and the organization itself. Studies of this issue as it relates to diverse groups at the senior executive and board directorship levels are not readily available, because so few of these people have risen that high, but one can expect that they feel disenchanted for one reason or another. Marginalization and undermining both signal that current leaders do not trust them and lead middle managers to doubt whether they have a future in the organization. One way for them to avoid career stagnation is to look for opportunities outside the organization.

Harassment

Female managers in the United Kingdom and the United States, though their status in the workplace has risen over the past few decades, continue to report being sexually harassed at work. In Canada, more than half of Canadian women reported that they knew women who had been sexually harassed. The Canadian Women's Foundation and Catalyst Canada have confirmed these findings (Patel 2019). Despite this, and despite the survey findings of many organizations (such as Statistics Canada, Insights West, and Abacus Data), 95% of 153 Canadian female executives in Canada denied that sexual harassment occurred in their own organizations, according to the Gandalf Group's quarterly C-Suite Survey (conducted on behalf of KPMG) in 2017. It seems that executives of larger corporations, especially in the financial sector, are more likely to report sexual harassment in the workplace. Some senior executives have acknowledged that corporate culture is the culprit in sexual harassment (O'Kane 2017).

Women tend to underreport sexual harassment, largely out of fear of reprisals, the seniority of the harassers, and worries about victim-blaming. This may explain why executives in general do not grasp how common workplace sexual harassment is. Female senior executives reported far fewer incidents of harassment. This is interpreted as less harassment, yet a general lack of reporting from female executives does not translate into that, because executives, whatever their gender, are responsible for overseeing their entire organizations. If they acknowledged harassment, they would be viewed as having failed to instil the values of respect and inclusiveness. Even the few reports of harassment acknowledged by female middle managers are troubling, for these people must be retained, given that they are the feeder pool for female senior executives (Davidson and Cooper 1992, 111–12).

The Canadian Human Rights Commission and other human rights commissions approach sexual harassment as a form of discrimination. In the workplace, it is defined as unwelcome conduct of a sexual nature that adversely affects the work environment. It also indicates a poisonous work environment in which women feel intimidated, threatened, and generally unsafe. Sexual harassment can be physical (hugging, grabbing, kissing), or it can be verbal (comments or insults about a person's appearance).

When the harassers go unexposed and unpunished, sexual harassment harms women's performance as well as their well-being more generally. When the harassers are male senior executives, female middle managers face a dilemma: Do they expose the incidents? Or do they keep silent because they want to stay on good terms with senior executives (by not exposing one of their colleagues)? It is not an easy situation for women to be in. Experiencing sexual harassment makes them think twice before applying for promotion to an executive position. When women complain about sexual harassment to higher levels (i.e., executives), they know they will never rise to executive ranks in that organization or any other. Leadership circles are small, and negative news travels fast.

Harassment seems to be especially common for women in non-traditional jobs (Schultz 1990, 1832–3). It is also found in workplaces where Indigenous peoples, persons with disabilities, and racialized minorities have long been absent. It seems to occur largely in workplaces heavily dominated by white, able-bodied, non-Indigenous men. The reasons why are unclear, but it has been hypothesized that these men feel threatened by the "intrusion" of women and other diverse groups. However, as empirical studies and human rights tribunals have shown, harassment is not found solely in these places. It arises in almost every type of workplace and in every industry. It is probable that in "traditional" workplaces where the corporate culture is more male-oriented or white-centred, harassment is more blatant and "unfiltered."

Harassment, whatever form it takes, has the effect of humiliating or offending racialized minorities, persons with disabilities, and Indigenous peoples. For racialized minorities, harassment can include racial jokes and derogatory remarks on their religion, food, or lifestyle. Many studies have found that white co-workers, supervisors, managers, and clients use discriminatory language in front of African-American women and men and assume they are incompetent (Hughes and Dodge 1997, 581–99). For persons with disabilities, it can be name-calling, personalized criticisms of their work, or simple bullying. For Indigenous peoples, it can be comments on their social status or stereotypical remarks and jokes. These harassment tactics violate the target's dignity and have negative job-related consequences for them (Siu, 2016, vol. 1, 1–1.2, 1–1.3).

Harassment ranges from small, incremental unwelcome acts repeated daily, to sporadic violence. Small, incremental acts include jokes, offensive comments, slurs, insults, innuendo, graffiti, and negative evaluations (Siu, 2016, vol. 1, 1–1.2, 1–1.3). When carried out repeatedly over then long term, these acts constitute discrimination and generate immense stress for individuals as well as tension in the workplace. The employees affected by them are likely to spend most of their working hours looking for new jobs.

In workplaces where the environment is hostile and alienating, harassment is usually the tip of the iceberg. It is a form of exclusionary conduct intended to block incursions by women and other minority groups, and it is usually part of a range of behaviours, such as personal interactions that signal to the targets they are different and out of place, as well as discriminatory performance appraisals and work assignments. Most studies of harassment have focused on women and found that it makes them feel belittled, ostracized, distressed, dismissed, marginalized, hurt, and discarded (Schultz 1990, 1938; Piotrkowski 1998, 33–43).

Harassment is sometimes a one-time event, but more often it is a daily occurrence. The targets of it are often silenced because there are no (or no effective) mechanisms for handling it. Few organizations have a fleshed-out policy on harassment, let alone written procedures for filing, investigating, and settling complaints, especially when the harassment occurs at the leadership level. And even when such procedures are in place, the resources to address it are usually inadequate. The usual result is a stressful work environment that damages the mental health of women and other diverse groups or drives them from the organization.

Discrimination

Some diverse group members perceive discrimination as the principal barrier to their promotion. They have applied to positions in management or executive positions and have not got an offer. When the representation of diverse groups is barely visible among middle managers and senior executives, and when almost all openings at that level are secured year after year by white, able-bodied, non-Indigenous men, diverse groups grow convinced that they are being discriminated against, especially when they perceive that the successful candidates are not as qualified as they are. This may well be a subjective interpretation, but the homogeneity of leaders, and the numerous biases noted in our early discussion, reinforce this interpretation.

Racialized minorities in Canada, being higher-educated than non-racialized minorities, have a strong sense of being discriminated against in their pursuit of middle-management and senior executive positions. Studies conducted in Chicago found that racial prejudice and discrimination account for job discrimination and job dissatisfaction among African-American women (Hughes and Dodge 1997, 581–99). Some allegations of racial discrimination can be proven, but most cannot be, because discrimination is very often subtle and can be masked by other rationales.

Racialized minorities are not the only out-group facing discrimination. Human rights cases that reach the Canadian Human Rights Tribunal have found that it also affects Indigenous peoples, persons with disabilities, and women at various occupational levels. Executives of diverse backgrounds have seldom brought their concerns to the attention of human rights commissions or tribunals. However, professionals who find it hard to secure middle-management positions are becoming more vocal in bringing their allegations to the attention of human rights commissions in Canada. Focus group discussions and interviews conducted with employees of several corporations in Canada by the author confirm the extent of perceptions of discrimination.

In addition to overt forms of discrimination supported by tangible evidence, there is another form of workplace discrimination, one that is harder to pinpoint and document. Deitch, Barksy, and Butz (2003, 1299–324) found that blatant racism is being replaced by more subtle forms such as social avoidance, unfriendly verbal and non-verbal communication, exclusion from group activities, and failure to provide help. These were described earlier in this chapter. Together, they delineate the "modern nature of racial prejudice," or, as Deitch and colleagues (2003, 1302) refer to it, "everyday discrimination" in the workplace. Small doses of subtle discriminatory acts can "get under your skin" and lead blacks to feel hopeless and resigned and women to feel angry, depressed, and low in self-esteem. These small actions or non-actions make women and racialized minorities feel stressed because they are ambiguous and hard to nail down. They are experienced daily but cannot be shown unequivocally to be the result of prejudice. Having to guess on an ongoing basis whether one has been mistreated based on a negative attitude has an adverse impact on one's job satisfaction and well-being.

Deitch and colleagues' (2003, 1308–9) study of blacks in the United States found that they have experienced more of these little things and noted that they enjoyed less job satisfaction and well-being than whites in the workplace. While this study did not discuss the implications of job dissatisfaction, other studies have pointed to the likelihood of absenteeism, role withdrawal, disengagement, high turnover, and poor performance as the results of job dissatisfaction. Clearly, the negative attitudes and discriminatory behaviours of managers and non-management employees do not help diverse groups rise to senior executive and leadership positions; they do, however, make the workplace more intolerable for diverse groups (Aguiar do Monte 2010; Clark 2001; Settles, Cortina, Buchanan, and Miner 2013; Green 2004; Lvy-Garboua,

Montmarquette, and Simonnnet 2007; Shields and Price 2002; Souza-Poza 2007; Wengryzn 2003–16)

Lack of Supportive Measures

To rise to leadership, diverse groups need supports of all kinds. This section highlights mentorship and networking. These two supportive measures enable diverse groups to better position themselves for promotion; they also help organizations retain diverse groups by "gluing" them to the organization. These two supportive measures were discussed in the previous chapter in relation to the promotion of diverse groups. In this section, they are discussed in relation to retaining these people at the executive level.

For new executives from diverse backgrounds (especially those from outside), surviving the first two years is important, and having one or more mentors will greatly enhance success in this. Supportive networks serve much the same functions as mentorships; they also provide a safe space as well as advice from multiple perspectives on an ad hoc basis. For diverse groups, these networks are likely to be external.

Lack of Mentoring

Having a mentor is important for new executives because they may not be familiar with the C-suite culture and the formal procedures and informal norms that govern executive activities. Without a mentor in the executive ranks, diverse group members are likely to find themselves at sea in their new positions. Negative perceptiosn, prejudices, and social distancing create barriers for diverse group members seeking mentors, even after they become executives.

Without mentors, diverse executives cannot acquire timely advice and may make mistakes at work as a result. This is especially the case for new executives from outside the organization. Given that the performance of diverse executives is likely to be under the microscope of other executives and employees, any mistakes they make as a result of lack of mentorship will likely be viewed as reflecting the performance quality of the entire diverse group. This places additional stress on new executives. When one adds other factors, such as isolation, social distancing, and lack of a sense of belonging, which do not favour diverse groups, it should be no surprise to anyone that they exhibit signs of stress, tension, and exhaustion.

It is hard for executives with disabilities to find mentors because of the negative stereotypes and prejudices they face. The result is an in-group/out-group dichotomy that increases the social distance they encounter. Other executives with diverse backgrounds may have similar problems finding mentors; this makes it more difficult for them to understand their roles, what they have to do to build influence, and how to conduct themselves in their daily activities. Mentors could provide them with this know-how. Having a mentor can be strategically important for female executives in the early stages of an executive career because mentors can help them navigate the C-suite. Without mentorship, female executives may be at a disadvantage at their jobs (Mack 2011).

Catalyst's study of racial minorities in corporate Canada found that among racialized minorities, women are more marginalized than their male counterparts. Racialized minority men have a better opportunities than their female counterparts to secure mentors for themselves. Men and women preferred different types of mentors to support various aspects of their careers. Racialized minority men were more strategic in getting advice from their mentors; racialized minority women were interested in having a positive relationship with their mentors and relied more on their managers for advice, support, developmental opportunities, and promotions. Because racialized minority women have problems gaining access to influential networks, they feel more isolated and less able to secure mentors for themselves (Silva, Dyer, and Whitham 2007, 14–16).

Lacking mentorship at the executive level may not make or break the career chances of diverse groups once they have risen that high, but it as important to their work satisfaction and to retaining them as potential executives.

Lack of Supportive Networks

In chapter 6 the networking opportunities of diverse groups were discussed with regard to promotion. It was noted that overall, their networks are not as effective as they need to be: they do not provide pertinent information or connections that could help diverse group members rise to leadership roles (Dobby 2019). That is why they tend to rely largely on their managers for support and feedback, but even then, they gain little managerial backing for their career development.

Persons with disabilities have reported that it is difficult for them to find supportive managers. A joint research project conducted by Ryerson University and the Royal Bank of Canada found that finding an understanding manager and developing webs of informal supports among co-workers were important for persons with disabilities (Church et al. 2007, 7–9).

Women and other diverse group members typically receive less than adequate support from their bosses and are not party to the informal and confidential communications their counterparts enjoy with *their* bosses (Asplund 1988, 27). Indigenous peoples feel alienated by their work environment with its embedded Western values and norms (individualism, self-promotion, competitiveness). They do not receive enough positive feedback on their performance from management, and this undermines their confidence (Dwyer 2003, 881–9). Without supportive networks within organizations, diverse groups have struggled to rise to leadership positions.

Another advantage that diverse groups find in developing their own effective networks is that they serve as "safe spaces" for drawing on peer support when difficulties arise at work (such as social distancing, marginalization, and undermining). These workplace difficulties could eventually destroy the self-confidence and self-esteem of diverse groups whether they are working as middle managers or senior executives. But given the high status of their positions and the inherent confidentiality of what they are discussing, middle managers and executives of diverse backgrounds may find their networks not "safe" enough for private conversations. They may be better off developing their own leadership networks. Given the limited number of diverse group members in top jobs, it is difficult for them to form their own effective support networks. As it happens, formal networks of diverse leaders barely exist in most organizations. However, there are networks of diverse groups – mainly women – external to organizations that offer supports and information pertinent to their survival in the C-suites.

Without effective networks to provide pertinent information, connections, and personal and career support, leaders from diverse backgrounds feel isolated. They have to figure out for themselves how to deal with work pressure (including work/family pressure). This does nothing to foster a satisfactory work environment that will make diverse group members want to stay. Many leaders believe, and sometime say it out loud, that it is lonely at the top. Leaders from diverse backgrounds find it even lonelier.

Corporate Culture

"Corporate culture" has a broad range of meanings. It permeates the organization and is embedded in its vision, mission, values, language, symbols, policies, procedures, strategies, norms, operations, and systems. Mayhew (2016) suggests that a given corporate culture is related to the size of the workforce, organizational structure (hierarchical or matrix), employee perceptions, workplace climate, and the actual location of the work. As a consequence, an organization's corporate culture is not homogeneous. Larger organizations will have different subcultures in various pockets, be they the C-suite, regional branches, management teams, occupational groups, or work units. International organizations may have different cultures in different jurisdictions. All of that said, there are several cultural *types* that are not conducive for diverse groups to become leaders or stay as leaders. This chapter highlights seven of them:

- tokenism
- individual competitiveness
- resistance to new ideas
- a culture built around white, able-bodied, non-Indigenous male leaders
- unwritten rules for diverse groups
- cultural dissonance
- toxic culture

Tokenism

Corporate culture is an important part of working life. The culture in the C-suite is often a subculture of the larger corporate culture. But some C-suite cultures are distinct from the larger organizational one. Suspicion of out-groups (and outsiders) and resistance to changing the status quo of an exclusive "old boys' club" are often part of the C-suite culture. Social pressure and, sometimes, government policies and regulations are bringing about changes in the composition of the boards of directors and senior executive teams. Tokenism is one way that has been adopted as a response to changing social mores.

Because Canada's Indigenous population is so small, and top executives are so few, it is very likely that just one Indigenous leader in an organization would amount to fair representation. In this sense, it is difficult to label the one or two Indigenous peoples in top jobs as "tokens." This cannot be said of persons with disabilities, racialized minorities, and women, for the pool of qualified candidates both inside and outside the organization may be large enough to warrant there being more than one or two of them at the leadership level.

The statistics for diverse groups provided in chapter 6 indicated that both racialized minorities (20.4%) and women (42.0%) are not underrepresented among middle managers. This suggests that there are plenty of them who could be promoted to senior executive levels. Currently, going by percentages, racialized minorities (8.7%) and women (24.8%) are underrepresented among senior executives in the private sector. In large corporations where the number of senior executives is in double digits, there is no reason why there should be only one or two racialized minorities and women are among them.

Persons with disabilities, racialized minorities, and women have observed that absent a trend line over years showing that their proportions are increasing at the leadership level, the current leaders are there only as tokens. When there is tokenism in leadership, diverse group members are few in number and find it hard to achieve critical mass among executives and board directors. Kanter (1977) suggested that when women comprise less than 15% of a category in an organization, they can be labelled as "tokens," that is, mere symbols of diversity. This does not constitute equitable representation (Davidson and Cooper 1992, 83).

Catalyst's 1993 survey of female board directors at *Fortune* 500/*Service* 500 companies found that among boards of directors that have only one female director, 37% of them do not see a need for more (Mattis 2010, 50–1; Burke 2010, 107). This suggests that in the eyes of some board directors, having one token woman on a board is enough. According to a Statistics Canada survey of 12,762 corporations with 44,658 directors, as recently as 2016, 56.8% of Canadian boards of directors were men-only, and 28.0% had only one woman on the board (Statistics Canada 2019). More than twenty years have passed since Catalyst's 1993 survey, and 84.8% of boards of directors in Canada still do not have more than one woman. This suggests that having women on boards could be merely a symbolic gesture, not a genuine attempt at gender equity.

Tokens serve symbolic purposes: having one female board director may be enough to polish the organization's reputation as a champion of diversity and inclusiveness. Organizations that are not truly committed to these may view appointing token persons with disabilities, racialized minority members, and women to leadership positions as all they need to do to make a public statement on diversity.

Tokenism has a psychological impact on diverse groups. Their members in leadership positions face strong pressure to perform well, for they recognize that they are stand-ins for the entire "universe" of Indigenous peoples, persons with disabilities, racial minorities, and women, and that they, as tokens, will be judged in that light.

Token women are highly conscious of how they present themselves and of the impact of their decisions, knowing they are carrying *all* women on their shoulders. They are test cases for future women's career opportunities, and they have to work harder, perform better, and to be seen to be doing both (Davidson and Cooper 1992, 84–6). They also face pressure be role models for other diverse groups. Because of all this, they may need to be more careful what they do or not do, and they have to work harder to earn recognition from CEOs and their own colleagues.

Yet token women executives cannot show off their accomplishments *too* much, or be *too* ambitious or aggressive, for their male peers may view them as a threat and start withholding their support and advice or even sabotaging their careers. Australians call this the "tall poppy syndrome" – those who rise up too soon and too visibly are cut down to size (Branson 2007, 113–15). Or as the Japanese say when women speak out or voice their concerns: "Nails that stick out get hammered in." The "self-promotion" advocated in literature about career advancement is a double-edged sword that may undercut women when the dominant culture is largely shaped by men.

Because they lack critical mass at the executive level, token executives from diverse backgrounds tend to be marginalized and isolated (Nilimoria 2010, 30–1). Studies have found that token women experience a particular kind of stress that men in the same occupations do not feel (Davidson and Cooper 1992, 83). This is not automatically the case, for it depends largely on the C-suite culture. In some C-suite cultures, the problem of tokenism has to do with visibility: because they look different from the dominant group, women and other diverse groups are more stereotyped. This is the phenomenon of "boundary heightening" or "gender demarcation." By these processes, white, able-bodied, non-Indigenous men feel uncomfortable and take steps to accentuate their own male identity and sameness. An example is male executives going out to bars or football games – activities that bond them together more. Female executives may still be invited to these functions, but once they get there, they may sense they are not particularly welcome. Some men tend to remind the token woman about the gender difference in subtle ways. In situations where there is more than one token, the dominant group members may play the tokens against one another by setting up one of them as the better performer (Branson, 207, 5, 110–12, 117, 121).

Being a minority (perhaps of one) on the executive team, token executives find themselves unable to garner support from their non-diverse peers. At the executive level, the power to influence peers is important; without it, executives of diverse backgrounds find their fresh ideas rejected as other executives resist collaborating with them. When they are not welcomed onto the executive team in a substantive ways, they soon grasp that they are there only as tokens, which they find disheartening (Kanter 1977; Freeman, 1990; Davidson and Cooper 1992, 83–6). Without support and collaboration, token executives come to see themselves as ineffective, uninfluential, and marginalized (Asplund 1988, 27). Token-related stresses and isolation are also experienced by female board directors when they are the only women on a board (Balimoria 2010, 27).

Being tokens, they may find it hard to locate tokens of other diverse backgrounds to act as their mentors, except perhaps outside their own organization. Also, negative stereotypes and prejudices and the associated social distancing make it hard for them to find white, able-bodied, non-Indigenous men to serve as their mentors. They are likely to find themselves on their own, without much advice, mentoring, coaching, counselling or supports from their colleagues.

This social isolation at the top, their ongoing failure to influence peers, and their marginalization in policy-making or strategy formulation, compounded by ongoing demands to excel and to serve as role models, is frustrating and unrewarding to say the least. Tokenism is a discouraging if not devastating experience for those with disabilities. Besides having to take care of their physical and mental health, they are pressured to perform at a high level. All of this can zap their energy on a daily basis and may ultimately cause them to resign, look for other opportunities outside of their organization, or accept an earlier retirement.

Individual Competitiveness

Many workplaces are fiercely competitive from top to bottom. The climate is often "confrontational and divisive," and as McLoughlin (1992, 111) noted, some women find it "destructive and wasteful," patriarchal, and dominated by a male ethos. As one female employee noted, "every step upward and onward [is] seemingly made over the bodies of defeated career-dead." Efforts to get a promotion or even just to survive resemble "a jousting match for the corporate king's favour." Those few women who climb the ladder to the executive level find that the higher they go, the more they must compete on men's confrontational terms.

Men tend to see competition as a fight *against* competitors, whereas women see it as a fight *with* competitors (McLouglin 1992, 114). Women may feel alienated by the rules of this cultural milieu. Some are reluctant to promote themselves and do it half-heartedly. Few women are as relentlessly competitive as men.

Members of other diverse groups view individual competitiveness as a cultural trait in the workplace, though this may not trouble them much in their early career stages. They perceive it as constant pressure to keep their jobs, maintain their performance, gain more face time with superiors, take on increased responsibilities, and position themselves for advancement. For Indigenous peoples, who have been socialized by their own communities to cherish collaboration and teamwork, individual competitiveness, as a cultural trait, is always in psychological conflict with their communal spirit.

Individual competitiveness, as a cultural value, is based on the assumption that employees who demonstrate their merit relative to others will succeed. To be successful can mean many things. It can mean keeping their own jobs; getting promotions, awards, or bonuses; being invited to join a high-profile task force; being approved for training courses; and other tangible rewards. When few promotion opportunites are made available to diverse group members, they begin to perceive that success may be based not on merit but on "who you know" or "who knows you," and that their efforts to advance can only be quixotic. Some of them look twice at the competitive culture and the mythical concept of "merit" and wonder whether the effort is worth it. When occupational mobility is blocked, frustration blooms. Individual competitiveness ceases to be a motivating cultural trait, and it may even demoralize diverse groups to the extent that some of them start looking elsewhere or abandon their aspirations to lead.

Resistance to New Ideas

In organizations that are open to only a narrow range of perspectives, it is likely that board directors and senior executives prefer to do things in a particular way. This sort of organizational culture is not receptive to new ideas, innovative approaches to problem-solving, or transformative strategies.

This type of traditionalist culture is usually fostered by board directors or senior executives who share one background and orientation and have been in their positions for a long time. As chapter 1 discussed, they may cling to the ways things have always been done and be oblivious to the changing world. Selby (2010, 248–9) described her experiences of boardroom culture as stifling because the other directors were so homogeneous in their specialized expertise and education that they viewed issues through blinkers. When questions were raised from different perspectives, they found it difficult to understand them or appreciate their importance and, in the end, usually just dismissed them. This sort of culture cannot not see the importance of diverse ideas or of having diverse groups on boards and senior executive teams.

This sort of culture shuts down new ideas about how to do business, be it strategic planning, product design, marketing, selling, customer service, or administration. As this lack of receptivity continues, it discourages diverse groups, who can often offer new perspectives based on their own upbringing and their cultural milieu. As noted in chapter 3 on concepts of leadership, diverse groups may have fresh ways to lead and manage an organization, and the existing directors and senior executives may feel threatened by those fresh ideas. Their ongoing disregard of new and challenging ideas may discourage diverse groups from staying in the organization.

Culture Built around White, Non-Indigenous, Able-Bodied Male Leadership

The cultural milieu of directors and senior executives may be isolated from and thus different from that of the organization as a whole. Yet given that the leadership that steers the corporation has long been and largely still is male-dominated, non-Indigenous, ability-focused, and race-based, the broader organizational culture is likely to reflect that C-suite subculture. Diverse group members may find that organizational culture foreign to them, with the result that at the top echelons, new leaders from diverse backgrounds may feel excluded, marginalized, and isolated.

Consistent with other studies, Marshall (1995, 301–3, 309) found that women cited organizational policies, the male-dominated corporate culture, and the lack of promotion opportunities as reasons why they left their organizations. Female managers even at senior levels have noted that a male-dominated culture makes interpersonal relations at that level "very aggressive, rude, territorial, status-conscious and hostile, with conflict, power struggles and politicking as common features." Some female executives felt as if they were interrupting the "normal life" of the boys' club and that they were not being allowed to "establish operating membership of the management groups to which they had been appointed." Some felt that "most senior men kept communication with them at a relatively superficial level, that very few reached out to form relationships or to support initiatives when requested." Some felt that hostility was being directed at them "because they had stood out as different in the culture."

In a male-centric culture, family duties are viewed as a distraction from work. The cultural features that infest such organizations favour people with few family obligations, which makes it difficult to attract and retain women (Marshall 1995, 310). At the top level, assessments of candidates' suitability (i.e., "corporate fit") for leadership based on these traits are biased in favour of the homogenous male group (Selby 2010, 249). Maddox and Parkin (1993, 3) referred to such cultures as "gender cultures." Gender-based cultures seem culturally neutral but still position men and women differently at work and tend to work against women (Marshall 1995, 310). Men and women see this issue differently. A study by the Young Women's Trust in the United States found that 63% of human resources directors and decision-makers believed that sexism still exists in most workplaces and that 76% of female employees had the same opinion. Only one quarter of male employees held the same opinion (Topping 2017). This suggests that male-oriented culture traits are harder for men than for women to recognize.

Policies, procedures, and practices that are inequitable and exclusive are markers of cultural traits that work against diverse groups. Aggressive hard-sell approaches, long or unscheduled working hours, intense competitiveness, expectations to relocate geographically, short notice for meetings or weekend work, putting organizational needs before life interests, and celebrations of physical and psychological endurance are all masculine traits. And these masculine traits have become the cultural traits of the organization, for men have historically dominated boards of directors and senior executive positions. They have built a corporate culture that is moulded in their own image and have established policies and procedures accordingly (Collinson and Hearn, 1994).

Other corporate cultural traits may be at odds with the cultures in which other diverse groups have been raised, and these people may have difficulty adjusting to them. For Indigenous peoples, a top-down culture in which employees are rarely consulted is incompatible with their own, much more collaborative culture. For some racial minorities, a male culture that sees social drinking, golfing, and attending sport events as a way of bonding – and perhaps bouncing off business ideas – may be at odds with their religious and social beliefs or lifeways. Given that Indigenous peoples and most racial minorities have been socialized in collective or communal cultures (which emphasize collective responsibilities and mutual support) and that most Western corporate cultures are individualistic (emphasizing individual responsibility), a corporate policy on career development based on individual responsibility ("you are on your own" in career growth) as opposed to collaboration and managerial support ("I can help you grow") does not benefit them much. In fact, they find such policies alienating and unsupportive.

Persons with disabilities seek a caring and nurturing culture that treats employees as human beings, not as transactional entities that can be swapped out as circumstances change. A corporate culture that overemphasizes productivity, quick performance, and quick results is likely to devalue human beings. These cultural traits are evident in the wording of some job descriptions: "a successful candidate must be made available 24/7," "the organization is a multi-tasking and deadline-driven work environment with short deadlines on tasks," "this workplace is a high pressure work environment." Persons with disabilities may find this kind of work culture demanding to the point of devaluing their well-being. One executive at a large Canadian corporation noted the fast-paced competitiveness of the C-suite and remarked, "We tend to forget that we are all human beings too."

A white, able-bodied, non-Indigenous male leadership with minimal diverse group participation fosters a corporate culture that values the standardized treatment of employees. All work arrangements, schedules, equipment, and facilities are standardized, with no deviations. Worksite designs, office arrangements, speed of delivery, working hours, and tools and equipment are rigidly planned according to occupational statuses and compensation, with no consideration given to the special needs of diverse groups. Some women may need more work/life balance to accommodate their family obligations; some persons with disabilities may need additional supports to help them do what able-bodied persons can do without those supports; some Indigenous peoples may need special consideration regarding their community obligations; and some racialized minorities may erquire religious accommodation (Asplund 1988, 53).

Some current leaders may find accommodation too demanding, though they know the law requires them to provide it. They often see it as something they *have* to do, not something they see any value in doing. But without special accommodation measures, diverse group members may be at a disadvantage as they try to rise in the organization.

When a corporate culture is built around the values, cultural norms, and operational modes of a homogeneous group, any accommodation measures and adjustments based on race, indigeneity, ability, or gender may be viewed as a disruption of "normal" ways of working, as a deviation from standardized treatments, or as a form of "favouritism." Such a culture tends to view flexibility in work arrangements, schedules, and equipment and facilities as opening the floodgates to demands which might threaten the organization's normal functioning. Some leaders may even fear the financial costs of accommodation measures (such as assistive devices for persons with disabilities and prayer rooms for racial minorities). This rigidity in upholding corporate cultural traits centred on the values, norms, and operational modes of a homogeneous cadre of leaders may undermine employee morale and productivity and result in higher turnover at all occupational levels. It may also reduce the number of diverse group members entering the leadership pipeline.

Unwritten Rules for Diverse Groups

When an organization has one set of unwritten rules for diverse groups and another for other people, diverse group members are perceptive enough to see through them. Wyche (2008) observed that for diverse groups to break through the glass ceiling to middle management or senior executive circles, being good is not good enough. The unwritten rules for them are: "you have to be competitive," "you have to work harder than others," "you have to be more prepared than others," "you have to continue to learn and pick up new skills," "you have to know and accept when changes are needed," "you have to make yourself visible," "you have to recognize the skills leaders need and keep them current," "you have seek out mentors and supports," and "you have to have a strong dedication not to give up" (Wilson 2014, 83–9). These rules are part of the organizational culture, and women and other diverse groups are expected to follow them if they hope to advance.

Some executive women have complained about the reasons men offer them for why can't be CEOs. Those reasons include: "women are not aggressive or assertive enough" and "women may not have enough evidence to show that they can excel in matters on the bottom line." This suggests that women have to do more. But what the *more* is that women must do is often unclear. A former executive at KPMG Canada, who applied unsuccessfully for the CEO position there, wrote to her female colleagues before she left KPMG: "I reached for the top rung and failed … I had a lot of boxes 'checked' on the competency and experience checklist and I still didn't make it – that is all the more reason why you should push, and push hard." These are words of frustration from a former female executive, who later landed on a CEO position at Dentons, a global corporate law firm, a few months after she left KPMG (Kiladze 2019a).

Then there are the promises that women have been hearing since the 1980s: "It is a matter of time to see progress in gender parity," "the executive ranks will have more women as time progresses" (Kiladze 2019a). It seems that these promises are merely stringing women along and delaying progress toward treating them with equality and respect. Other diverse groups hear the same sorts of promises and become fed up with them. One may wonder why the time for promotion has had to be postponed for diverse groups but not for white non-Indigenous, able-bodied men and why diverse groups seem to face different rules for promotion, and what those rules are.

These unwritten rules need to be placed in the context of the formal corporate culture. "Merit," as epitomized by qualifications and experiences, is a key principle in human resources development. The formal culture casts career advancement solely as a function of merit. The unwritten rules require diverse group members to make an extra effort to get a promotion, and those same rules provide "explanations" if they fail to advance. A survey by Monster.ca found that women still feel they have to work harder than men to get a promotion. More women (44%) than men (28%) believe that this has not changed in the last twenty-five years. Most women (74%) contend that while more women are in leadership positions, they still need to work harder to get there. Most women (72%) also believe that men are still the dominant force in the workplace (Dobson 2014, 9).

As employees of diverse backgrounds see it, the contrast between the "merit" principle and the unwritten rules is that the rules require them to do more than just acquire merit. They are still not being rewarded with the career development they seek. They also perceive, correctly or not, that those who have been promoted didn't deserve it. The common feedback on diverse group members whose efforts to be promoted fail is that other people had more merit and they can try again. This feedback is strongly grounded in the principle of merit but does not convince some diverse group members, who have heard it many times before. The unwritten rules, by implication, merely point out some of the "reasons" why diverse group members often come up short in competitions for advancement.

Unwritten rules are at odds with the principle of merit because diverse groups always have one more rule they must follow – that is, "learn more and work harder." Yet following the unwritten rules does not mean that the promotion outcomes for diverse groups are any better than for non-diverse groups.

Cultural Dissonance

Ideally, a variety of cultures are able to coexist in the workplace, and management and non-management employees are tolerant of that variety. When any arising issues are discussed, understood, and resolved by all involved, balance in the workplace is maintained. When it is not maintained, tensions simmer that if not addressed may lead to upsetting and abusive behaviours.

Whites and racialized minorities often have different perspectives on inclusion. Catalyst studied racialized minorities in forty-three Canadian corporations, conducting a series of focus groups to gauge the perspectives of white employees and managers regarding diversity and inclusiveness. It found that there are perception gaps between whites and racialized minorities. White executives, managers, and professionals tend to believe they are more inclusive than racialized minorities think they are, and that there are limits to what can be accommodated (in terms of, say, religious leaves and punctuality). White employees experience discomfort and distrust of their racial minority colleagues when their language, dress, or behaviour do not fit well with "Canadian" culture. They also expect their racialized minority colleagues to be more articulate in expressing themselves, for they are highly educated (Giscombe 2008, 27–33). White colleagues often perceive racialized minorities as not answering their questions directly and clearly, with the result that their ideas seem "fizzy" despite their high level of professional knowledge. These conflicting perspectives point to cultural tensions in the workplace along racial lines and underscore the importance of cross-cultural communication.

The Giscombe study also found that white employees tend to feel that "political correctness" tends to prevent sensitive multicultural issues from being discussed in the open. As a result, some white employees believe that their cultural norms or expectations are being challenged and are not being addressed openly and directly. Because these issues are often "glossed over," racialized minorities may be unaware of unresolved issues. Overall, white employees tend to work with racialized minorities in a polite but superficial way. They try not to come across as biased, but simultaneously, they are unable to understand why they behave the ways they do (Giscombe 2008, 27–33).

As noted in chapter 4, some negative stereotypes and prejudices are based on the behaviourial patterns of diverse groups, whose early socialization was different. Some racialized minorities in Canada feel they have to "Canadian-ize" themselves in order to fit more precisely the organizational culture and the image of a "leader." But they are also torn, because they are uncomfortable about giving up some of their own cultural attributes, which they have embraced since childhood. The resulting tensions can find their way into workplaces, where they become one more element of work-related stress that racialized minorities experience (Giscombe 2008, 2–5; Giscombe and Jenner 2009, 2–8).

Racialized minorities' attempts to "Canadianize" themselves so as to better fit the current image of a leader are especially difficult because that image is not well-defined, at least openly. Indeed, the image of a leader sometimes changes at the top. As discussed earlier, racialized minorities (and the other three diverse groups) are only weakly connected with the inner circles of leadership, are unlikely to have mentors in the executive ranks or to be part of effective networks, and lack diverse role models to emulate. So they are hard-pressed to know exactly what the organization's leadership values actually *are* and how they can be translated in behavourial terms. Knowing so little, and unsure about how to navigate the cultural waters without guidance, they are left wondering what their best moves should be.

Conflict between the bottom line (profits) and diversity policy can also create cultural tensions in the workplace. This can happen in private sector organizations where diversity has been formalized as official policy. Business growth depends on productivity, among other factors. When the accommodation measures for persons with disabilities and other diverse groups have not been carefully executed, these people's performance may lag behind that of able-bodied persons. When this happens, organizations often shift their priority more toward the bottom line, without thinking this out carefully.

A research project on employees with disabilities at the Royal Bank of Canada found that there is a sense that diversity policy and the drive for profits often conflict. That is, the imperative to boost productivity and revenues often clashes with the provisions extended to persons with disabilities. There is little real conflict here, but some leaders perceive there is. According to some persons with disabilities, the "bottom line" seems to have taken priority over "diversity" (Church et al. 2007, 7). Able-bodied co-workers and managers may be concerned about the apparently "slower" work pace of persons with disabilities because they feel liable for their work teams' lower productivity levels when persons with disabilities are present. They are also afraid to discuss issues related to disabilities with their disabled co-workers for fear of breaching their privacy or making both sides uncomfortable (Church et al. 2007, 8–9). Similarly, when women ask for additional flexibility in working hours or when Indigenous peoples or racialized minorities seek time off for community or religious events, issues of organizational performance and productivity often crowd the centre of managers' considerations. The tension between "diversity" and "profits" has seldom been discussed openly, and diverse employees are rarely consulted about solutions. As long as it is there – often hidden under the rug of "political correctness" – this issue is not going to resolve itself.

All of this suggests that diversity is linked to cultural tensions, which need to be resolved so that they do not erode the motivation and morale of employees of diverse backgrounds as well as other employees.

Toxic Culture

Values, beliefs, and attitudes are often woven into organizational norms and behaviours. They also permeate organization's culture, which includes its policies, procedures, programs, and practices. Cultural traits are usually invisible and intangible, yet they influence who gets hired, promoted, and terminated as well as how things are done and business is run. Some of those traits may be poisonous, but what makes them so is subject to interpretation. The consensus seems to be that a corporate culture becomes poisonous when it disrespects people, when its members behave in ways that others neither welcome nor solicit (e.g., harassment), when it generates and spreads harmful information and is rife with gossip and rumour, when it makes people suspicious of one another, when senior people practise management by fear, intimation, and bullying, when demanding and controlling behaviours have become stand practice, when corporate communication is inconsistent, when different standards are applied to leaders and the led – and, finally, when leaders view such things as acceptable (Moran, 2019). Leaders may be silent about this toxicity or do little too late to address it. When this poison persists and spreads through the workplace, it is culturally toxic. Fear, insecurity, secrecy, stress, aloofness, and factionalism among employees are signs of a toxic corporate culture (Ryan 2015; Siu 2016, vol. 1, 1–93).

We must distinguish between an organization's official culture and its informal cultural practices. "Official culture" represents the formal "party line" espoused by leaders and managers and is usually written down in policy statements, declarations of values, press releases, annual reports, and other official documents. "Informal cultural practices" refer to how leaders and employees actually conduct themselves in the organization. In other words, the official corporate culture is "on paper," and cultural practices are "in action." It is the latter that inform us of the corporate culture.

The following toxic cultural traits are discussed below: command and control, selective communication, workplace rumours, and corporate hypocrisy.

A "command and control" corporate culture is "top down" and requires employees to follow orders and directions from above. Its leaders are adamant that *they* make all corporate decisions and need not consult with employees. To ensure tight control, its leaders seldom provide more information than the employees need, which renders them subservient and fosters a climate of secrecy, suspicion, and fear. The leaders are opaque in their decision-making, and employees tend to work in silos without much communication. Little flexibility is allowed for fresh approaches, problem-solving, innovative ideas, or human resources development. Speaking out is discouraged, and employees' needs and interests are seldom prioritized. The contributions of employees are seldom recognized or rewarded; typically, it is leaders and managers who get all the "glory." New ideas from the various perspectives of diverse groups are seldom listened to, let alone adopted. When this "command and control" culture dominates, employees – including those of diverse backgrounds – often consider finding other jobs. Women and minority group members in leadership positions may be treated as "second class," especially if they are tokens.

As discussed earlier with regard to promotions, selective communication results in some employees having more information than others. Asplund (1988, 8) writes that those without information are "internal exiles," "excluded and invisible." This approach usually works against diverse groups, who are far from the leaders who hold the information. Because they do not have the latest news about the organization in terms of its direction (restructuring, human resources development, outsourcing, downsizing, business mergers or acquisitions), diverse group members may be at a disadvantage when competing for promotions or even performing their daily tasks.

When communication is less open to some than to others, rumours and gossip abound. This cannot make for a healthy work culture, for employees at the "closed" end of the communication spectrum often spend a lot of time trying to pry information from those who might know what is happening, besides discussing among themselves what might be going on. This leaves less time for them to do their jobs. And they are constantly on edge, especially when it is rumoured that major changes are coming (such as a restructuring or downsizing). They are also more receptive to gossip and sometimes create rumours just to keep people curious. In this type of culture, it is difficult for a man to promote a woman to management or a leadership position. People may spread rumours around promotions or job transfers of this nature by posing questions such as, "Is there something between them?" Questions like these can lead men to think twice about promoting women when there are equally qualified male candidates (Asplund 1988, 10).

Another problem with selective communication is that employees who are left out of the channels (including those from diverse backgrounds) feel marginalized or abandoned. Employees end up falling into two classes: a small number who are informed owing to their proximity to the sources of accurate information, and a (usually much) larger number who are out of the loop. When employees feel marginalized and abandoned by their leaders, they perceive they have no future in the organization, so how long are they likely to last there?

Another mark of a toxic culture is a disconnect between formal policy and actual practice. Organizational values and norms can be explicit or implicit. In an open and transparent culture, there is little or no discrepancy between policy and practice. In a non-transparent culture (i.e., top-down, authoritarian), explicit policies and practices may be in conflict with implicit ones. For example, the organization may make a formal statement valuing diversity and inclusiveness, but the leaders and managers practise something else – in other words, they do not "walk the talk." In focus group discussions with employees from diverse backgrounds conducted by the author, as examples of the discrepancy between policy and practice, the participants often pointed to diverse groups' lack of representation at the leadership and even management levels, the lack of diversity knowledge and skills among managers and supervisors, the half-hearted manner in which accommodation measures were provided to persons with disabilities, and the lack of leadership development (and promotions) for diverse groups.

Toxic workplace culture can also involve undermining or ostracizing high achievers from diverse groups. Leaders and managers often talk of the value of raising the productivity and performance quality of employees and the importance of employees putting in their best efforts. Some even bray about how they are helping employees succeed. But their actions speak louder than their words. Billan and Humber (2018), with partnership with Thomson Reuters, *Canadian HR Reporter*, Viewpoint Leadership, and Women of Influence, released a report titled *The Tallest Poppy* that documented how high-achieving women at work were being penalized by their supervisors, managers, and colleagues through undermining and ostracizing. These harmful behaviours damage women's self-esteem and self-confidence and deepen their isolation. They also make women more distrustful and disengaged and increase their absenteeism. These disconnect with their co-workers and start looking for new jobs.

Billian and Humber also found that these same behaviours fostered a corporate culture marked by fear, distrust, and hypercompetitiveness. Among those they interviewed, 44.2% noted a culture of fear, 78.7% noted a culture

Figure 7.1. Retention problems related to work environment and corporate culture

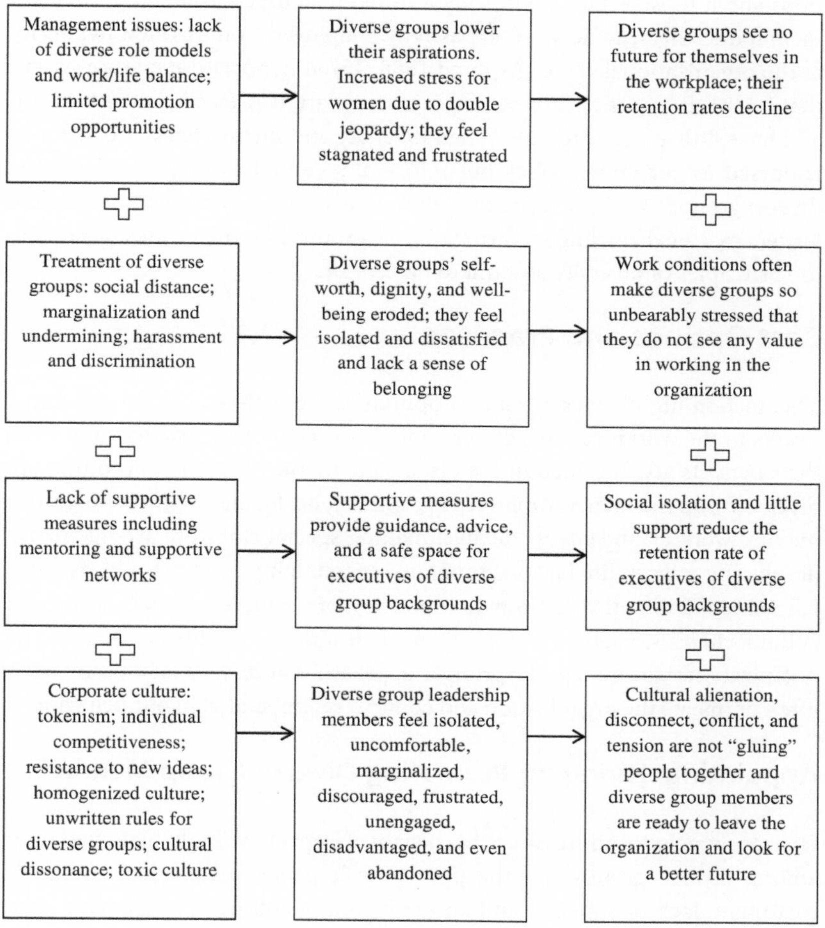

Management issues: lack of diverse role models and work/life balance; limited promotion opportunities	Diverse groups lower their aspirations. Increased stress for women due to double jeopardy; they feel stagnated and frustrated	Diverse groups see no future for themselves in the workplace; their retention rates decline
Treatment of diverse groups: social distance; marginalization and undermining; harassment and discrimination	Diverse groups' self-worth, dignity, and well-being eroded; they feel isolated and dissatisfied and lack a sense of belonging	Work conditions often make diverse groups so unbearably stressed that they do not see any value in working in the organization
Lack of supportive measures including mentoring and supportive networks	Supportive measures provide guidance, advice, and a safe space for executives of diverse group backgrounds	Social isolation and little support reduce the retention rate of executives of diverse group backgrounds
Corporate culture: tokenism; individual competitiveness; resistance to new ideas; homogenized culture; unwritten rules for diverse groups; cultural dissonance; toxic culture	Diverse group leadership members feel isolated, uncomfortable, marginalized, discouraged, frustrated, unengaged, disadvantaged, and even abandoned	Cultural alienation, disconnect, conflict, and tension are not "gluing" people together and diverse group members are ready to leave the organization and look for a better future

of distrust, and 50.4% noted a culture of hypercompetitiveness. While this study focused on professional women, it has great relevance for other diverse groups. This author has conducted many focus groups and interviews with Indigenous peoples, persons with disabilities, and racialized minorities in large corporations. The consensus of a segment of these diverse employees is that they feel discouraged by the lack of support from their peers and managers; they perceive that their real performance achievements seldom lead to promotions. They also feel badly undermined by their peers. This kind of culture makes employees feel insecure, unwanted, and ready to quit their jobs.

Moreover, this kind of culture sends employees contradictory messages. They observe that the official values are not being honoured and that any questions about those values are quickly muffled or shunted aside. This environment induces fear, cynicism, and passivity. Employees come to view hypocrisy as the organizational value (Asplund 1988, 45). A hypocritical culture signals that board directors and/or senior executives are two-faced, untrustworthy, and have little or no integrity. When diversity and inclusiveness are formally endorsed as corporate policy but informally denied as corporate practice, diverse groups may have difficulty joining the leadership circles, and existing leaders may be disinclined to bring diverse groups into their ranks, given that the principles of diversity amount to lip service.

Best Options and Practices

This section highlights several best options and practices with demonstrated results in the workplace. We discuss how to develop these practices and what their benefits are. Included in the discussion are the hiring and promoting of diverse group members; employee engagement; health and wellness programs; making work arrangements flexible; making special childcare arrangements; developing a work/life balance program; encouraging innovative ideas; anti-harassment and anti-discrimination policies, procedures, and education; and cultural changes. This discussion will make clear that to modify or transform an organization's culture, a multi-pronged approach is necessary, for cultural traits often permeate the organization and come to be embedded in our behaviours.

Appointing, Hiring, or Promoting Diverse Group Members

One approach to addressing the negative impact of high turnover rates among diverse groups and the poor morale generated by discriminatory treatment, lack of support, and an exclusionary culture is to hire and promote more members of diverse groups. There is nothing more concrete than actually seeing more diverse employees in the organization, especially among its leaders.

Tokenism, lack of role models, and limited promotion opportunities are marks of a workplace that is not retaining and advancing diverse groups. To address this problem, organizations must start appointing them to directorships and promoting them to executive positions. This is the most effective way to show diverse groups that the organization is committed to diversity and inclusiveness at the leadership level. When more diverse group members are appointed to that level, tokenism begins to vanish and diverse group members begin to reach a critical mass. Diverse groups begin to assume that they will be able to achieve their aspirations, having been inspired by seeing their representatives as leaders (who will serve as role models for them).

But hiring more diverse group members and promoting them to leadership positions is easier said than done, because there are so many factors to consider. These key steps must be taken:

- First, develop a solid database of board directors and senior executives, with diversity as one of the variables. This database will serve as a baseline and a monitoring device.
- Second, ascertain what the barriers are by having honest conversations among leaders and by reviewing the procedures for recruitment, selection, promotion, leadership development, and succession management.
- Third, develop an action plan for increasing the representation in leadership of Indigenous peoples, persons with disabilities, racialized minorities, and women. The action plan should include the prospective job vacancies most likely to arise in leadership positions over the next few years. This can help establish goals for directorship appointments and the hiring or promoting of executives.
- Fourth, as much as possible, remove the identified barriers to hiring, promotion, and board appointments in a timely manner in accordance to the action plan.
- Finally, keep an eye on the progress of all the tasks mentioned in the first four steps, modifying the approaches and operational details if progress is slow. All these steps have been outlined throughout this book in different chapters as best practices.

Examples of these best practices are found in the following companies:

Accenture PLC is a computer programming and consulting company with more than 3,000 full-time employees. It was one of the Canada's Best Diversity Employers in 2013. It established a Women's Initiative strategy for the advancement of women. Bombardier is an aircraft manufacturing company with more than 24,000 full-time employees in Canada. Its aerospace division developed a two-year plan to develop women for leadership positions. The National Bank of Canada has developed a succession pool for senior managers, and half the candidates are women (*Globe and Mail* 2013).

OceanRock Investments is working with the Shareholder Association for Research and Education on gender-gap issues. It is urging other firms to review their hiring and promotion policies and practices to uncover any systemic barriers (Pinto and Chapman 2016). In the United States, Novartis

Pharmaceuticals Corporation has been making a concerted effort in promoting women into management (DiversityInc. 2016a).

Employee Engagement

Marginalizing and undermining employees amounts to the opposite of employee engagement. Employee engagement is a management strategy that aims to mobilize employees to subscribe to the vision, values, and strategic direction of the organization and to translate those things into practice. This strategy is grounded in a trusting relationship between management and employees. Without that trust, employees will not put in their best efforts. Employees have to believe that they are integral and important to the organization and that the organization genuinely cares about them.

Employee engagement often begins by ascertaining employees' opinions on various aspects of the workplace and of themselves, usually through surveys. These survey results provide profiles of employees as well as a baseline for employee engagement. Ideally, these surveys will be conducted annually as a means to measure and monitor the organization's pulse.

Leaders can do a number of things to engage employees more: communicate clearly the vision, mission, values, and strategic direction of the organization; empower employees through training and delegation; be visible, and connect to employees; train leaders and managers to engage employees; engage employees by giving them a voice and lending them an ear; create an employee-based system of work activities (as opposed to top-down procedures); and foster regular communication between management and non-management staff. These are some of the ways in which an atmosphere of employee engagement could be developed.

Examples of best practices can be found in a number of organizations. Air Canada has regional diversity committees in Montreal, Toronto, and Vancouver as well as various committees comprised of diverse group representatives. These committees hold events where work experiences are shared and solutions for addressing workplace issues are identified. Lefarge Canada is a cement manufacturing firm with more than 3,000 full-time employees. To engage women who feel isolated in high-echelon positions, it has hosted several focus groups with the goal of attempting to understand how female employees view the firm's diversity messages. A number of high-potential millennial employees have been sent to participate in the NextGen Women Leaders Program. 3M Canada was one of the Canada's Top 100 Employers in 2017. The firm is keenly interested in ascertaining the level of employee satisfaction and engagement and arranges annual in-house surveys and employee surveys every three years, conducted by external consultants. Toronto Dominion Bank (TD) has more than 43,000 full-time employees across Canada. It values employees' perspectives and conducts in-house and external consultants' surveys every year to get the pulse of employee engagement (MediaCorp Canada 2016b).

Health and Wellness Programs

Work/life balance is an issue for many employees, including leaders from diverse backgrounds. An organization can provide them a valuable service by establishing a health and wellness program. These programs can benefit organizations by boosting productivity, employee morale, job satisfaction, employee commitment, engagement, and employee health. They can also reduce absenteeism, turnover, and idle time. At the individual level, they can help employees reduce their stress, exercise more, control their weight, and stop smoking, and perhaps address mental health issues. While the success and cost-effectiveness of these programs are still being assessed in both Canada and the United States, it is clear that more employers now recognize that employee health has a direct impact on organizational performance and that more organizations are getting behind these programs idea. According to Towers Watson's *Staying@Work* survey of 114 Canadian companies, 76% of them are planning to increase their support for workplace health initiatives (2013a, 1, 16; Bernier 2013e, 1–2).

Workplace health and wellness programs are established in part to comply with government OHS legislation and in part to enrich the mental and physical health and well-being of employees. Leaders have to make health and wellness a top priority. David Agus, Professor of Medicine and Engineering at the University of Southern California, has proposed that every company have a chief health officer (CHO). That person's task would be to jump-start the corporate agenda on health and wellness (Johne 2016). Given that employees' participation rates in these wellness programs are unlikely to be at the optimal point, and that other human factors are involved in participation (such as busy work schedules), the "one size fits all" approach to wellness may not work well (Bernier 2013c, 1, 16). So program planning might begin by establishing a working committee of various internal (and external) stakeholders (including labour and management, if the workplace is unionized), along with an employee advisory committee. These committees could help establish clear purposes, structures, processes, and deliverables as well as a schedule. Organizations need to work on a strategy for employee health and wellness (Sorenson 2013; Woodhouse and LaRue n.d.; Gamlem 2013).

A lawyer specializing in OHS law can identify all legally required areas for implementation, and employee advisers can identify additional health and wellness issues for action. Commitment from leaders and employee ownership of the program are of utmost importance. An employee advisory committee can identify employees' needs through surveys and/or focus groups. After gathering ideas from employees and other stakeholders, the working committee can then develop an action plan that sets priorities, goals, and timetables. Once the action plan has been approved by the leaders and resources to carry it out have been secured, the plan can then be implemented with regular monitoring, reviews, and adjustments.

A wellness program may cover both physical and mental health issues. Program initiatives might include health and nutrition education, employee kitchens, access to healthy food, meditation rooms, rest rooms, physical exercise classes, fitness facilities, mental health classes, personal growth seminars, and ergonomic equipment and furniture. The program may also alter policies and procedures regarding health insurance benefits or health club membership fees; and it may provide health information on diet, exercise, and work/life balance, as well as health counselling and workshops on managing stress. Wellness programs may also be linked with employee assistance programs as they relate to flexible work hours, telecommuting, flexible leaves, family support, childcare and eldercare supports, and work/life balance management.

3M Canada, a technology manufacturing firm, has a formal health and wellness program at its headquarters that features a fully equipped fitness facility with free memberships. 3M employees at the London manufacturing facility can book events at a park that offers baseball diamonds, a soccer field, a tennis court, shower rooms, a children's playground, and a clubhouse with kitchen and outdoor barbecues. The head office of 3M Canada has a kitchenette on every floor (with coffee makers) and an onsite cafeteria with healthy menus and special diet menus. It also has a religious observance room and an employee lounge with amenities such as television, a foosball table, table tennis, and magazines and newspapers. There is also an onsite fitness facility for employees only (free membership) with treadmills, stationary bikes, stairmasters, instructor-led classes, rowing machines, weights, shower rooms, and personal trainers. In addition, 3M offers multiple health plans for employees with adjustable premiums and coverage levels. The health plans cover employee assistance, physiotherapy, medical travel insurance, medical equipment and supplies, massage therapy, chiropracty, and alternative coverage (such as acupuncture) (MediaCorp Canada 2016b).

Toronto Dominion Bank (TD) has flexible health and wellness accounts to cover expenses that fall outside basic coverage, from buying home fitness equipment to fitness club memberships to health-focused counselling and support services; it also provides an online educational wellness video library. Commercial Real Estate Services Canada (CBRE), a global company, has a workplace transformation program. Several of its offices have been designed and launched in accordance with the WELL Building Standards, which focus on enhancing the health and wellness of employees. Those standards cover access to natural light and good air quality, temperature control, acoustic comfort, sit-stand workstations, accommodation devices for a variety of working styles, collaborative meeting spaces, and mobility-enhanced technology. This a multiyear program focusing on enhancing employee engagement through health and wellness (O'Neill 2016; CBRE 2016).

All of the health and wellness-centred programs described above have benefited all employees and signify that their employers care about them. These programs may not be specifically established for diverse employees, but they have benefited from them as well. Programs like these often demonstrate to employees their importance to the firm and its commitment to retaining them.

Flexible Work Arrangements

Flexible work arrangements can address work/life balance issues for diverse groups. They may take the form of (a) "flextime," in which employees tailor their work hours so that they can take their children to school and pick them up later; (b) "part-time work arrangements," as in adjusting the number of work hours per week or per day (Northcraft and Gutek 1993, 223); (c) "flexible working years," to enable employees to set annual quotas of hours worked and schedule them according to different months of the calendar year (a practice noted in Germany) (Davidson and Cooper 1992, 157–8); or (d) "work from home" and "flex hours" policies, which may reduce the rigidity of the traditional "9 to 5" workday or the rigidity of coming to work even when a child is sick at home. Some companies may even include "unlimited sick days" (including mental health days) (Midanik and Roy-Boulet 2019).

Other possible arrangements include flexible career adaptation schemes such as the following:

- "Voluntary reduced time," in which full-time employees reduce working hours for a specific period of time on a temporary basis, with reduction in salary. This can be reversed back to full-time status.
- "Career break schemes," in which employees take longer time off to accommodate their special circumstances (such as infant care) for a number of years. They can resume their employment status later with no loss of seniority.

- "Sabbaticals," in which employees take up to a year off after a certain number of years' work. This latter arrangement is found in the United Kingdom and Sweden in many occupations: employees older than fifty and with at least twenty-five years of service may take six-month sabbaticals (Davidson and Cooper 1992, 158–60).
- "Telecommuting," another flexible arrangement for balancing work and life demands. In the United States, the number of employees working at home and connecting with the office by telephone tripled from 20,000 to 60,000 between 1982 and 1987. By the 1990s, the number of professionals working at home was expected to reach 13 million – that is more than 11% of the US workforce (Castro 1987; Northcraft and Gutek 1993, 223). The Gallup State of the American Workplace's data of 2016 showed that 43% of employees work remotely with some frequency. Although most of these statistics are not comparable longitudinally due to the researchers' multiple definitions of remote working and the use of different methodologies, it is evident that there is a strong trendline: a increased proportion of people are working at home due to economic, business, technological, and health factors (Global Workplace Analytics n.d.).
- "Job sharing," which allows (usually) two employees to share one position. This arrangement works well for employees with more or less the same knowledge, skill sets, and work experiences when both require flexible work arrangements at a particular stage of life (Gupta-Sunderji 2018).

As flexible work arrangements are becoming more popular, companies would be well-advised to start preparing strategies for them, beginning with a pilot project to ascertain what might work and what would not. The strategy should outline clearly the objectives of flexible work arrangements, which types of work and which employees are eligible, what options are available, and the decision-making process in the organization. Arrangements of this nature are usually unique and depend on individual cases, so it is essential that the processes of communication and teamwork be mapped upfront and monitored regularly. There may be a need to focus on work results and deliverables and on whether they are available within the agreed-upon time frame (Gupta-Sunderji 2018).

Toronto Dominion Bank (TD) has extended its parental leave provisions and now also offers unpaid leave, emergency short-term daycare, flexible work hours, a shortened workweek, a compressed workweek, and telecommuting. In addition, it offers unique "mix and match" alternative work options (designed by the employees themselves) and has a Back to Business program to help women reintegrate into the workforce after being away for more than two years. It also has unpaid leaves of absence with the duration based on individual circumstances, along with other options for leaves of absence. Recognized as one of the Canada's Top 100 Employers, 3M Canada has flexible work hours, a shortened workweek, a compressed workweek, and telecommuting (MediaCorp Canada 2016b).

These examples suggest how flexible some companies have become for employees. There is evidence that when an organization offers alternative work arrangements, it reduces facility costs and, more importantly, increases employee productivity and engagement. In the long run, this improves employee retention, including the retention of diverse group members (Gupta-Sunderji 2018).

The above programs have the potential to benefit all employees, but they are especially attractive for diverse employees, especially those who face childcare or eldercare obligations or who have difficulty arranging transportation or attending medical appointments due to an impairment. Flexible working arrangements do not greatly impact the conduct of business, and employers can easily offer them as an option to make their employees' work lives easier, especially for some diverse employees. These programs make it more likely that employees will be retained.

Making Special Childcare Arrangements

In the past, many women had to extend their maternity leave or stop working entirely when they could not arrange childcare. In Europe, more and more organizations are arranging childcare centres for their employees – unfortunately, not enough of them to meet the demand (Davidson and Cooper 1992, 160–2).

Other childcare options include the following:

- On-site nurseries where employees drop off their children before starting work. Johnson & Johnson and Campbell Soup Company's operate daycare centres on-site.
- Childcare consortia, where a group of companies share childcare facilities for their employees.
- Childcare partnerships or joint ventures with local governments and the private sector.
- Care for sick children in prearranged sites. These might include in-home sick childcare services, special rooms in the workplace, special locations inside a hospital, and sick childcare facilities next to a childcare centre.

- After-school childcare programs, where transportation is arranged to move children from childcare centres to their parents' workplaces or after-school programs (Davidson and Cooper 1992, 160–2).
- Financial assistance for daycare referral services or summer camps (Northcraft and Gutek 1993, 224).

In Canada, childcare spaces are expensive and hard to find, and the competition for them is severe. There are simply not enough services available. As a result, many mothers of young children have decided to stay at home to take care of their children instead of going back to work. On-site childcare for employees is ideal for many parents, but for many reasons, including financial and regulatory ones, not enough of it is available. In Canada, there has been more noise than progress in this area.

To ease childcare requirements, Toronto Dominion Bank offers corporate membership rates with Kids and Company, which provides emergency childcare services (MediaCorp Canada 2016b). This has been a welcome initiative for many parents, especially for women with childcare responsibilities.

Work/Life Balance Programs

There are several ways that a work/life balance program, especially for women, can be developed (Brady & McLean 2002, 11–12). A good start is to convene, on a regular basis, focus groups of women who either are participating in leadership development opportunities or are already in leadership positions. These focus groups can identify work/life issues. The human resources department should arrange these sessions and conduct follow-up afterwards. Some of the participants may have special needs arising from individual circumstances; these women would benefit from one-on-one conversations.

After identifying women's work/life balance needs, the organization can develop special measures or accommodations specifically for women and/or customize packages for individual women. Before this is done, the organization should consult with these women about the specifics of the measures.

Female participants who are new to leadership development programs need to be informed clearly about the goals, focus, and priorities of their development assignments. Clarity in direction will maximize program effectiveness within working hours and ensure that the program activities do not eat up personal time.

For female participants in leadership development programs, the organization may delegate some of their regular responsibilities to junior members. The junior employees will benefit from hands-on work experiences and acquire new knowledge and skills. In this way, the senior and junior members will be developing at the same time.

The organization should provide training and support to male employees on how to support women undergoing leadership development as well as those already in executive positions. This training would raise male employees' awareness of and empathy for the challenges women face. This is an important first step toward addressing the work/life balance issues confronting women. Supports could be in the form of advice customized to individual cases, or in the form of programs such as parental leave or issue-based counselling.

As discussed earlier, the organization could provide supports for childcare, eldercare, spouse care, or household tasks, as well as flexible work hours or work-at-home options for times when family-related demands are especially high.

Air Canada, one of Canada's Best Diversity Employers in 2016, hosted Women in Aviation events where women were able to interface with internal senior-level women as well as female executives from across the aerospace industry. These events led to discussion groups about career development, work/life balance, and other topics relevant to women (MediaCorp Canada 2016a).

TD bank offers a maternity top-up to 100% of salary for mothers for six weeks, and parental top-up to 100% of salary for fathers for six weeks (Media-Corp Canada 2016b).

Encouragement of Innovative Ideas

Strongly traditional organizations feel threatened by innovative ideas and new concepts instead of welcoming and encouraging them. These corporate cultures are stagnant and resist change. By contrast, organizations that are open to new ideas are viewed by their employees as forward-looking, flexible, and adaptive. They are cognizant of the changing world and business environment and are willing to be part of it. Organizations that are innovative eventually replace the ones that are not. Innovative ideas, if encouraged, bring business advantages and foster competitiveness (Drucker 2002).

But generating innovative ideas is easier said than done. To open itself to fresh ideas, an organization has to create an innovation-receptive corporate culture. Some corporations wonder out loud how Google and Facebook can be so innovative when they themselves are always playing catch-up. Tellis, Prabhu, and Chandy (2009) studied 759 corporations in 17 societies regarding their records for innovation and found that corporate culture is what drives radical innovation. Creating a forward-looking corporate culture is largely a function of values, behaviours, workplace climate, success, resources, and processes. These are all related to one another. Most companies focus on "hard" components – on allocating resources, on development processes, and on the quantification of success – and tend to ignore the "soft" components – embracing values, modifying human behaviours, and developing a workplace climate (Rao and Weintraub 2013).

Building an innovative workplace culture requires a commitment from the top, which must then be cascaded down to all employees. Also, leaders have to convince their employees that the organization is serious about its commitment. Then, after consulting with the employees, they develop a strategy that prioritizes innovation. This means developing a consensus on what "innovation" means, making the workplace more conducive to new ideas, developing employees' knowledge and skills, establishing innovation as a performance evaluation measure, creating awards and rewards for innovation, and acting on innovations that arise from all this (Emmons, Hanna, and Thompson 2012).

This strategy includes mechanisms for motivating and encouraging employees at all levels to put forward their new ideas and for ensuring that their voices are heard. Also, they must *know* that their voices are being heard. These mechanisms may include collaboration among employees across lines of business within an organization; including innovation as a key ingredient in all job descriptions; conducting focus groups and surveys on new options; documenting and prioritizing all new ideas; analysing and assessing those ideas in depth; and then implementing some of them, with clear responsibility centres (Emmons, Hanna, and Thompson 2012).

There are many available examples of innovative corporate culture. IDEO, a global design consulting company based in California, places high value on creativity. It emulates the playful, exploratory behaviour of children. It encourages new ideas, defers judgment, builds on other ideas, and stays focused. IDEO has developed hundreds of products, ranging from a computer mouse to medical equipment, that have optimal functionality. W.L. Gore, a chemical products company in Delaware, is known for its high-performance products. This company accepts mistakes as part of the innovation process and evaluates the success or failure of ideas and products based on a desire to learn and improve, not to punish the innovators. Rite-Solutions, a systems and software development company in Rhode Island, harnesses the collective creativity of its employees, encouraging them to work on projects they favour and to make project decisions according to their own judgment. Whirlpool, the world's largest appliance maker, began prioritizing innovation in 1999. It trains all its salaried employees in innovation and develops special employees ("I-mentors") to facilitate innovation projects and help employees develop their ideas. It also provides an intranet portal for collective learning and for tracking progress as ideas evolve into products (Rao and Weintraub 2013).

These real-world examples illustrate the benefits of innovation, which also increases employee engagement, which is key to retaining employees. An organization that encourages innovative ideas is signalling that it is committed to diverse perspectives. Diverse employees may find this sort of work culture more open to their contributions than a "command and control" culture.

Anti-harassment and Anti-discrimination Policy and Procedure

More and more organizations are crafting diversity and inclusiveness policies that set down the principles of human dignity, respect, fairness, and inclusiveness in the workplace. However, these policies seldom include explicit statements about harassment and discrimination. Because both are so common, organization leaders need to declare a zero-tolerance position on these matters (Moran 2019). There are benefits to establishing clearly written anti-harassment and anti-discrimination policies and procedures: everyone will know what the rules are; employees will know what both terms mean and how they will be handled; and the organization will be seen as embracing equity, human rights, and equal opportunity.

Establishing anti-harassment and anti-discrimination policies and procedures requires a commitment from the top, consultation with various stakeholders (including lawyers, government human rights departments, management staff, minority groups, labour unions, and human rights practitioners), and communication of a document that outlines the following:

- The organization's human rights principles.
- Management's commitment to those principles.
- The corporate policy on anti-harassment and anti-discrimination.
- The roles and responsibilities of executives, managers, supervisors, and employees.
- Employee options for addressing an incident of harassment or discrimination.
- The procedures for filing a complaint.
- The procedures for mediation, investigation, and corrective action.
- The appeal procedure.
- Issues of confidentiality and privacy.
- Monitoring, review, revision, and evaluation of the policy. (Siu 2016, vol. 1, 13–73–80).

Many organizations in Canada have anti-harassment and anti-discrimination policies and procedures. The following are just a few examples. CIBC, one of Canada's largest chartered banks, has a Respect in the Workplace Anti-Discrimination and Anti-harassment Policy, a Violence in the Workplace Policy, an Employment Equity Policy, and a Workplace Accommodation Policy and Program. All of these aim at protecting and promoting human rights (CIBC 2012). Scotiabank does not have specific anti-harassment and anti-discrimination policies, but it does have an employment equity program and as well as a diversity and inclusiveness program; both address harassment and discrimination. Scotiabank also has a Vendor Code of Conduct that specifies that "harassment, discrimination, and violence and other disrespectful and/or inappropriate behaviour must not be tolerated by Service Provider/Vendors." Those vendors must also adhere to non-discrimination and human rights legislation (Scotiabank n.d.). The City of Toronto has an anti-discrimination and anti-harassment strategy for advancing equity in employment and service delivery. The strategy calls for allegations of harassment and discrimination made by employees and service recipients to be investigated, as well as for the provision of advice and resources on implementing accessibility standards required under provincial legislation on disabilities (City of Toronto n.d.).

Anti-harassment and anti-discrimination policies and procedures serve as declarations that organization leaders are committed to addressing allegations of this nature. For employees who experience or observe incidents, paths are available for them to be heard and to seek an investigation. And these internal policies and procedures are not the only alternative for diverse groups. The federal government and all provincial governments have human rights laws that amount to double protection for their human rights.

Anti-harassment and Anti-discrimination Education

Anti-harassment and anti-discrimination education (as distinct from diversity training) focuses on human rights laws that prohibit harassment and discrimination. In Canada, those grounds include race, national or ethnic origin, colour, religion, age, sex, sexual orientation, marital status, family status, disability, and a conviction for which a pardon has been granted or a record suspended (Canadian Human Rights Commission 2013). Education of this type boosts employees' awareness and knowledge of corporate policies and procedures as they relate to harassment and discrimination. It also enhances relations among co-workers and between management and non-management staff, besides raising workplace morale and productivity.

An anti-harassment and anti-discrimination educational program might start with consultations with management and non-management employees. This can help clarify the purposes, scope, contents, resources, and delivery modes. It is best to begin these activities with leaders and middle managers and then roll down the delivery to various occupational groups and lines of business. The objective is to ensure that everyone has a comprehensive understanding of harassment and discrimination and how not to let them happen.

Anti-harassment and anti-discrimination education was more common in Canada in the 1980s and 1990s than it is now. Back then, these sessions were conducted largely for management by federal or provincial officials, whose mandate was to educate the public on workplace harassment and discrimination. When federal employment equity legislation was enacted in the mid-1980s, there some education sessions were held during which private sector managers were briefed on the human rights components of employment equity. Again, this activity was rather limited in terms of the number of people who attended these sessions and the comprehensiveness of the topics.

It seems that when more companies embraced diversity management at the turn of this century, the anti-harassment and anti-discrimination elements were subsumed under diversity education. Anti-harassment and anti-discrimination represented only a small segment of this education, or none at all, when diversity education was launched. Overall, while it is useful for leaders and non-management employees to have a comprehensive education on anti-harassment and anti-discrimination, this has not been thoroughly conducted in workplaces. Most organizations that provide this education do so online for employees to study and review on their own time. As a result, irrespective of how these topics are mentioned on the intranet (which is how most companies inform and educate their employees), the knowledge and skills related to anti-harassment and anti-discrimination have not been instilled broadly or comprehensively among leaders and employees. That is why this education needs to be given a higher priority in the workplace.

Cultural Changes

"Corporate culture" is a configuration of formal and informal corporate symbols, values, policies, strategies, rules, and norms as well as the attitudes and behaviour of leaders and employees. All of these components are interlocked, mutually reinforcing, and geared to resist change. That is why it is extremely difficult to change corporate culture (Denning 2011). Rola Dagher, president of Cisco Canada, believes that diversity is vital to building a strong, adaptable workforce. It is important to establish "a corporate culture built on respect, enablement and trust," and leaders play a crucial role in fostering that cultural change (Dagher 2018).

Cultural change is hard, but there are a few ways to begin it. Larry Hrebiniak, of the Wharton School of Management at the University of Pennsylvania, writes that cultural change can take place in organizational structures or processes such span of control, decision-making, and rewards systems (Wharton@Work 2011). Those changes have to be balanced with work on the cognition and motivation of the leaders, managers, and non-management employees. They have to be convinced that cultural change is needed, and they have to be motivated to strive for it (Murray n.d.). Lapid-Bogda (1998) has suggested that diversity should be made part of the structural and attitudinal changes mentioned above and that for changes to be effective, leaders have to "walk the talk." Cultural change cannot come about through speeches, presentations, or formal statements. Employees look for their leaders to lead cultural change, and their daily conduct has to reflect that change.

Rodgers (2017) writes that "cultural management" is a more holistic approach to removing barriers and making workplaces more diverse and inclusive. The Coca-Cola Company has conducted a cultural overhaul that has focused its core values on leadership, passion, integrity, collaboration, diversity, quality, and accountability. These corporate values are vital to reshaping corporate policies, procedures, practices, and human attitudes and behaviours (Coca-Cola Co. n.d.).

The problematic corporate cultural traits identified earlier in this chapter were tokenism; competitiveness; resistance to new ideas; work policies, procedures, and approaches built around the dominant group's particular culture; unwritten rules for diverse groups; cultural dissonance; and cultural toxicity. Removing these cultural traits and replacing them with more inclusive ones requires a multifacted approach that starts at the leadership level.

Leaders can foster a culture that "supports learning and development for all employees" and that "welcomes the diverse perspectives and contributions that talented women can bring." In addition, achieving cultural change requires leaders to confirm their commitment to creating "an environment that is positive towards women's career advancement," to training employees "to recognize and leverage the diverse strengths of individuals," and to "ensur[ing the] workplace is harassment free" (Brady and McLean 2002, 10). When the values of diversity and inclusiveness are introduced and fostered, it instils a corporate climate in which problematic cultural traits such as tokenism, competitiveness, innovation-resistance, skewed cultural dominance, cultural dissonance, double standards, and toxic elements can be questioned and assessed in light of those values. The crucial issue is whether the current leaders are committed to taking that path. Once they make it their will that diversity and inclusiveness be core corporate policies, they will mobilize the organizational resources to follow that direction.

In addition to leadership commitment and the mobilization of resources, close collaboration between leadership and management is vital to success. With the help of human resources departments and line businesses, CEOs can change the corporate culture (Bell 2011). Abiding by the values of transparency and continuous improvement, leaders must take the lead, using their competencies in visioning, influence, negotiation, strategic planning, communicating, and role modelling to effect change.

Meanwhile, executives and managers have to translate the strategic plan for cultural change into actions by consulting with stakeholders, enabling self-organizing teams, creating new incentive systems, introducing new or improved human resources mechanisms (in hiring, promotion, training, development, and termination), crafting new roles and responsibilities, creating new systems and processes that support the organization's vision, and implementing new measurement tools for performance, monitoring, and enforcement. In this way, a new corporate culture may gradually take shape. Some elements of the above components and processes have helped transform the culture of the World Bank since 1968, although that success has not been linear or automatic (Denning 2011).

Cultural changes are holistic and are usually slow and incremental. After all, the interlocking of organizational components and their resistance to change are part of what constitutes "corporate culture," and a change in any one component will have multiple ramifications and some unanticipated consequences. Jon Katzenbach, Rutger von Post, and James Thomas, using Hewlett Packard and Southwest Airlines as examples, illustrated the glacial process of change and how the following three success factors can speed up the process slightly. First, the adoption of a few "critical behaviours" – that is, actions (such as good customer service) that can make a real impact on business and are easily adopted by different lines of business or work sites. Second, the adoption of a few existing "cultural traits" that have an emotional influence on people, traits that make people proud. Third, the mobilization of "informal leaders" who are credible, trustworthy, and effective at influencing other employees (Schachter 2014).

These same success factors can speed up progress toward diversity and inclusiveness by making some early wins as impactful as possible (as in appointing an Indigenous board director or department head); by helping the organization improve its reputation in the community and in the industry (as in adopting best practices in hiring or promotion); and by developing internal employees who can motivate other employees and galvanize their passions as they relate to diversity and inclusiveness.

By applying Denning's mix of leadership and management tools and Katzenbach, von Post, and Thomas's success factors, an organization can systematically reduce and remove the problematic cultural traits identified in this chapter. This may be time-consuming, and progress may be non-linear, but the effort will be worthwhile.

The challenges of bringing about cultural change are many, but when it succeeds, the benefits are immense. Those benefits include the development of new organizational structures, processes, human relations, and personal development, as well as a shift in people's perceptions and attitudes throughout the organization. These benefits are accompanied by many others, such as improvements in innovation, collaboration, engagement, morale, retention, and productivity.

In 1998, Deloitte & Touche introduced the Advancement and Retention of Talented People (ART) initiative with the goal of reforming its organizational culture. The program had five priorities: "ensuring opportunity for everyone to succeed, integrating work-life harmony into the culture, developing leaders who can support the new culture, leveraging the initiative's success for advantages in recruiting top talent, and supporting the change through measurements and a clear accountability framework" (Brady & McLean 2002, 11). This example highlights the importance of having leaders taking a public stand on changing the organizational culture as it relates to talent management.

Aimia, a Montreal-based global loyalty company, designed its Toronto office with the objective of fostering a corporate culture of collaboration and inspiration. It enlisted employees from different departments to help design and communicate key messages. Its offices are open-plan and have ample natural light. Aimia also chose the artwork from Canadian galleries. Its employees are proud of their workplace and have a sense of ownership, belonging, commitment, and empowerment. Furthermore, their involvement in building this corporate culture has created "an atmosphere of inquisitiveness, promotes dialogue and encourages progress." Its success is echoed in the new Montreal office as well as in its offices in London and Minneapolis (Burton 2016, 16).

Illustrating how changes in CEOs' leadership styles can impact corporate culture, DiversityInc Staff (2012) noted that Kraft Foods, Kellogg, Ernst & Young, Novartis Pharmaceuticals Corporation, Wells Fargo, Eli Lilly and Company, Marriott International, and Dell have developed management approaches that have impacted their corporate cultures in human resources development (hiring and motiving people), community development, multicultural team-building, flexible work programs, stakeholder care, employees'

Figure 7.2. How best to build an equitable work environment and corporate culture

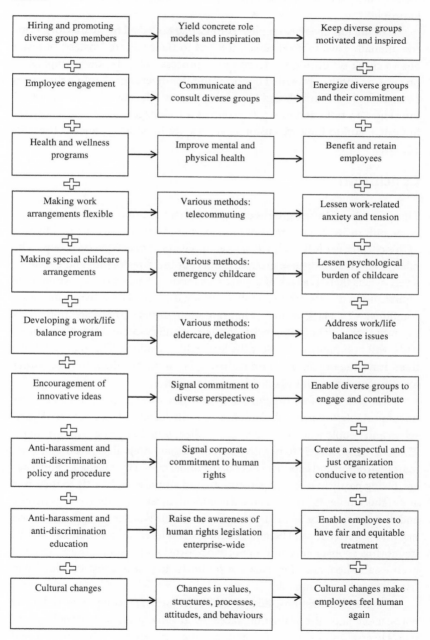

growth, and consumer service. All of these companies value diversity and inclusiveness as a new cultural approach to business growth and connection to people.

All of the top diversity employers in Canada selected by MediaCorp Canada annually have made diversity integral to their culture "instead of just a box to check off during the recruitment process." In 2014, these employers, one way or another, provided opportunities for diverse groups to network, to be mentored or coached, and to educate and be educated in diversity (as in Enbridge), to train and provide resources for managers to "do" diversity (as in CIBC), and to improve customer service (as in Sodexo Canada) (Bernier 2014a).

Conclusion

The retention of diverse groups depends on many factors in the work environment and corporate culture. A number of those factors have been highlighted in this chapter to illustrate how they can negatively impact diverse groups. The relative absence of diverse group members at the directorship and executive levels means there is a lack of diverse role models. This can easily weaken the aspirations of diverse group members. When the lack of diverse role models is combined with a lack of success in promotion, diverse groups are more likely to intuit that a glass ceiling exists in their organization and that their career paths will eventually stall below the leadership positions. This may not make them leave the organization immediately, but it pushes them to look harder for stronger opportunities outside the organization.

Other features of an organization can make diverse group members feel uncomfortable and isolated. One of these is the social distance between themselves and people who are white, able-bodied, non-Indigenous, and/or male. This is ascribed largely to negative stereotypes and prejudice. Another is their marginalization and experiences of being undermined by colleagues and leaders, owing partly to negative perceptions and attitudes and partly to their role and status ambiguity. In such an environment, diverse groups feel unwelcome and disrespected. For women, the lack of work/life balance compounded their negative experiences and heightened their stress levels. In some organizations, mentoring, sponsorship, and supportive networks for diverse groups have not been established, and they lack the supports they need most in a less than friendly work environment.

In some organizations, all the above features are compounded by the harassment and discrimination faced by diverse groups, be it alleged or real. Diverse groups observe – and, at times, experience – harassment and discrimination in their workplaces. Either of these can be blatant or (more often) subtle – either way, they signal to employees that they do not belong in the organization.

Corporate culture is another overarching factor that impacts employees, though it is a difficult one to measure. Several cultural features highlighted in this chapter are detrimental to diverse groups and drive them to consider leaving the organization. One such feature is tokenism at leadership levels. Tokenism discourages ambitious diverse group members and marginalizes the existing token diverse group members, who find themselves being treated more as symbols of inclusiveness than as peers with equal status. In organizations where cultural features exist such as competitiveness, resistance to new ideas, exclusionary culture (built around white, able-bodied, non-Indigenous male leadership), unwritten rules for diverse groups, cultural dissonance, and toxicity, diverse groups may find the work environment disrespectful, stressful, frustrating, intimating, or hypocritical.

These cultural features make it harder for diverse groups to survive, let alone grow in numbers. These features make it impossible for many employees, including those from diverse backgrounds, to perform effectively or efficiently in their jobs and to work in sync with the organization's vision. As a result, they have fewer opportunities to be recognized as "leadership material" and to be promoted to senior executive positions or appointed as board directors. Indeed, these cultural barriers discourage diverse group members from applying for promotions at all or staying with the organization. They are more likely to leave it before rising to management or leadership positions.

An emerging theme that expresses the feelings of diverse groups working in organizations with the above work environment and culture is their lack of a sense of belonging. They feel that they are not full members of the organization, though they are, officially, employees. This has been confirmed by various studies on minority and female executives, which show that they lack a sense of belonging (Burke 2010, 97). They perceive that their ideas are being rejected or undermined more often than those of others. They sense that their ideas are being marginalized or glossed over and that they do not command the attention of the CEO and other executives. The lone diverse executive may feel that he or she does not belong to the same "club" as the rest. That person finds it hard to build relationships with executive colleagues and to develop loyalty or commitment toward the organization. Again, this feeling is common among racialized minority groups and women (Burke 2010, 97) and may contribute to their turnover (Bilimoria 2000, 25–40).

Token executive women often complain about their isolation and lack of peer support. They feel awkward in social gatherings with their male peers from work, for their conversational styles and topics are subtly different. They often force themselves to attend these social functions, knowing full well that these are places where they make contacts and connections, build relationships, and, in some cases, make decisions. In some traditional male institutions, exclusive male customs and norms have been developed that reinforce the "old boys' club," safeguarding it from female intrusion (Davidson and Cooper 1992, 87–8).

These women may not be acknowledged by their peers for their contributions or receive positive feedback. Or they find themselves left out of communication networks they should expect to be in, and thus do not benefit from the information they would receive in a more inclusive work environment. This ongoing marginalization demoralizes women and, over time, shatters their sense of belonging and leaves them feeling isolated and vulnerable. They struggle to work productively in an environment in which their male peers do not accept their presence.

Negative stereotypes harm persons with disabilities when they apply for jobs. Some employers view some disabilities as posing safety issues for co-workers or customers (Shier, Graham, and Jones 2008, 68). Even when they are hired, employers tend to be cautious about assigning them responsibilities. Persons with visible disabilities are often assigned jobs (e.g., inside work) that hide them from clients or customers, or jobs (e.g., data entry) that are solitary so that they needn't interact much with co-workers. Those without visible disabilities put great effort into ensuring that their disabilities do not become evident. Once they reach executive or directorship ranks, they continue these efforts in order to avoid social labelling and stigmatization. They know their own limits in terms of career growth in the organization, which perhaps is why they do not feel they belong, whether they are board directors, executives, middle managers, or non-management employees.

In most organizations, it is very rare for Indigenous peoples and racialized minorities to get promoted to leadership levels. As noted in earlier chapters, there are a number of reasons for this: the impact of mainstream concepts of leadership, negative perceptions and attitudes, and human resources policies that work against their promotion. Another reason is a corporate culture that heightens their feelings of marginalization even when they do become leaders (often token leaders), at which point they often find themselves outside the inner circles. They find that other executives do not share deep business or human resources information with them, that new strategic or operational ideas are not discussed with them informally, that responsibilities are unfairly assigned, and that colleagues do not endorse or support their ideas. Because they do not form a critical mass at leadership levels, their influence is limited, and they sense that they have been marginalized even though they are in leadership positions.

Environments and cultures like these make diverse groups in the organization's feeder pools think twice before applying for promotion. If they are already in leadership positions, their marginalization and their sense that they do not belong may spur them to look outside the organization for more promising career paths. To address these problematic cultural traits and work environments, it is vital for an organization's leaders to make their workplace more diversity-inclusive. Until they make this happen, all talk about diversity and inclusiveness can only be just lip service. This chapter has suggested a number of practices that businesses could adopt, most of them already being used by various companies. Others promise to be effective but have yet to be tried. All of them, however, require leadership in order to succeed.

chapter eight

Diversity, Business, and Government

This book began with an overview of the changing world and why diversity in leadership is so important.

Globalization, demographic change, and economic development are reshaping business and the workplace. These macroscopic social changes, which are intensifying global competition, require innovation and increased productivity, and are changing the marketplace, provide a solid business case for diversity in leadership. From the organizational and business perspectives, diversity strengthens business competitiveness, introduces multiple perspectives and innovative ideas, increases productivity, grows the market share for companies, and boosts a firm's performance and profitability. In sum, diversity makes sense for the business world, and it is hard to imagine that diverse leadership is not part of the package, especially when the world is undergoing major economic and demographic shifts.

Throughout this book, we have pointed to the relative absence of diverse groups in leadership positions and the psychological, organizational, and cultural reasons for it. In this final chapter, we again ask the following question in order to illuminate the relationship between diversity and business: What is "diversity"?

Vafa Akhavan (2016), senior adviser at NueBridge and former co–Executive Sponsor of Diversity and Inclusion at McGraw Hill's Information and Media Segment, observed that

> diversity is not, in the end, about the colour of skin, one's religious faith, gender or sexual orientation. Diversity is what these categories signify – and can deliver – in terms of a unique set of experiences, beliefs, life lessons, knowledge, insight, and critical thinking. It's like being able to speak multiple languages that enable you to better understand and interact with employees, customers, suppliers, competitors, markets and the world at large.

Given this understanding, it is jarring that diverse groups are disproportionately absent among Canada's business leaders. All four groups discussed in this book are underrepresented on boards of directors and in senior executive ranks. That underrepresentation is indicated by "diversity gaps" – the differences between the current diverse groups' representation in the private sector and the representation one would anticipate based on their numbers in the broader society. Canadian data suggest that these differences are huge, especially for Indigenous peoples and persons with disabilities.

To understand why these diversity gaps exist at the leadership level, this book approached the issue from three perspectives – psychological, organizational, and cultural:

- At the psychological level, we examined and critiqued how current leaders define leadership. We looked at their mindsets, perceptions, and attitudes, focusing on how current leaders and diverse groups view leadership differently, and what the stereotypes of diverse groups are, as well as the prejudices that go with those stereotypes.
- At the organizational level, we examined the mechanisms used in current human resources management as they relate to recruitment, selection, performance evaluation, succession management, and supportive measures. Essentially, we wanted to uncover why and how diverse groups are disadvantaged by these mechanisms.
- At the cultural level, we analysed the work environment and corporate culture. Specifically, we discussed how diverse groups are treated as well as how corporate cultural traits in the workplace might be connected to employee retention.

The discussion of these psychological, organizational, and cultural factors brought to the surface a number of themes related to the current homogeneity of leadership and how it might be addressed. Key to this problem was how three factors interlock in ways that result in homogeneous leadership and how they need to be modified if lasting changes are to be made in the representation of diverse groups in leadership.

In this chapter, we discuss a number of core messages and strategies for change, all of which are drawn from our findings and analyses.

Core Messages

There are several core messages in this book, all of them are relevant to the issue of diverse groups' underrepresentation in leadership:

Shared Experiences of Diverse Groups

The experiences of the four diverse groups being examined here differ in some ways. But their experiences are also amazingly similar in terms of the adverse impacts of today's mainstream concepts of leadership – concepts that show themselves when we assess the prevalence and persistence of negative stereotypes of and prejudices toward diverse groups and the inherent biases in current human resources mechanisms and workplace cultures.

It is clear that all four diverse groups are underrepresented in leadership positions. This calls for a more holistic approach to effecting change than is currently found among various stakeholder groups, including the business sector. Finding ways to address the disadvantaged situations of only one group would not be impactful enough, or cost-effective.

Psychological Changes

Psychology is foundational to all three factors. Until we reduce or expunge negative stereotypes and prejudices ("unconscious biases," in contemporary management terms) and change the mindsets that are part and parcel of today's mainstream concepts of leadership, it will be difficult to effect meaningful changes at the leadership level and in the systems and cultures today's leaders have created and now maintain.

Organizational Changes

Biases have been built into current human resources mechanisms, which need to be revamped to ensure that they do not perpetuate the status quo when hiring, promoting, and/or retaining diverse groups. Human resources mechanisms can serve as a starting point for change; those changes may then spill over to other business functions and strategies.

Cultural Changes

Changes in the corporate culture are vital. The first target of these changes would need to be the present leaders' values and norms and resulting behaviours. This change might then be cascaded down throughout the organization, by means of effective strategies with observable and measurable outcomes. Cultural change could then be linked to the organization's business strategy and direction.

The rest of this chapter elaborates on these points and their implications.

Shared Experiences of Diverse Groups

This book highlighted the realities facing diverse groups in the private sector regarding leadership positions:

- First, they have for years been disproportionately excluded from board directorships and senior executive positions (chapter 2).
- Second, contemporary mainstream concepts of leadership used by some current leaders do not align well with those expressed by diverse groups or how people view them as leaders (chapter 3).
- Third, all diverse groups face some subtle or blatant forms of negative stereotyping, prejudice, social distance, marginalization, harassment, and discrimination. These have adverse impacts on their opportunities in terms of hiring, retention, and promotion (chapter 4).
- Fourth, present-day human resources mechanisms are largely biased, with adverse impacts on diverse groups when it comes to recruitment, selection, performance evaluation, succession management, and supportive measures (chapters 5 and 6).
- Fifth, negative features in the work environment and corporate culture work against retaining diverse groups in the workplace (chapter 7).

The common themes regarding how systems have a negative impact on diverse groups speak volumes for these groups' shared fate. Community organizations, associations, and agencies are being short-sighted when they focus their campaigns for social equity on a single diverse group and are unwilling to partner with other groups for the same cause. Their reluctance to share political platforms and resources to advocate for a common cause is bewildering.

Social justice is not a zero sum game. When one group is marginalized, all of them are, for the mindsets and systems created and maintained to exclude one group can easily expand to others. One may argue that the finite number of board seats and senior executive positions is a factor in battles to attain a piece of the leadership pie that end up excluding disadvantaged groups. This narrow interpretation of "inclusiveness" (i.e., the inclusion of one) and the resultant strategy of fighting for the "inclusion of one" is short-sighted because in the long term, the beneficiaries of inclusion are not limited to individuals of one social identity; as noted in chapter 1, the greater beneficiary is the business sector as a whole and the well-being of society at large.

Instead of limiting itself to women, the recently amended Canada Business Corporations Act, which received Royal Assent on 1 May 2018, recognizes the shared experiences of Indigenous peoples, persons with disabilities, and racialized minorities in addition to women. This is a positive development, for it expands equity and fairness to more people, thus broadening the social, business, and economic benefits. This book has focused on only four diverse groups in highlighting the importance of diversity and inclusiveness, but there are others – such as LGBTQs, older and younger age groups, and religious minorities – who deserve the same attention. The above-mentioned federal legislation will be discussed in more depth later in this chapter.

In the following sections, we address the critical issue of how the business sector can effect changes. Given that diversity in leadership is a long-standing issue with interlocking psychological, organizational, and cultural components, where should businesses start when setting out to reduce or remove the barriers that have hindered progress in diversity? The short answer is to approach the diversity gap problem in an integrated manner, focusing first on the psychological factors (concepts of leadership, stereotyping, and prejudice) and mixing these with organizational and cultural solutions.

An Integrated Psychological, Organizational, and Cultural Approach

This book has analysed diversity in leadership from the psychological, organizational, and cultural perspectives. We have to understand how these perspectives are related. Human actions express the interplay among human cognition and emotions (how people see and feel about other people), human resources mechanisms (how systems and tools are developed and used), and cultural features (how people justify and sustain their actions in social contexts through abstract ideas and formal/informal norms). The decisions leaders make when hiring, assessing, developing, and promoting leadership candidates are rooted in the cognitive and emotional filters they apply to them. These filters are values, world views, theories, and ideas they have learned throughout their lives, all of which are mixed in with their own interpretations and feelings. Some of these filters amount to stereotypes and prejudices against diverse groups, which may be conscious or unconscious.

But human actions are not derived solely from people's perceptions and attitudes; those actions are also constrained by various other factors, including structures and processes, available systems and tools, and the cultural environment. That environment is, in turn, developed, fostered, approved, and sustained by leaders, who essentially give permission (often symbolic) to create, adopt, continue, or halt certain types of actions. When the systems, policies, procedures, and operational tools are developed with built-in biases (perhaps without the awareness of those who have developed them), they will produce biased results, which are often invisible until they are tracked and analysed through the lens of diversity and inclusiveness, equity and equality. At times, those systems, policies, procedures, and operational tools may be misused to suit the wishes of those who turn to them.

Similarly, when corporate cultures are not conducive to diversity and inclusiveness, people may engage in biased actions, with adverse results for diverse groups. Those adverse results may well end up doing long-term harm to individual businesses and the economy as a whole. When a corporate culture emphasizes positive values (such as transparency, fairness, and integrity), people may still harbour negative stereotypes and prejudices, but these are likely be hidden and may not surface at all, except as behaviours (e.g., harassment and discrimination), which may go detected, or in data about the representation of diverse groups in leadership positions. The symbiotic relations among human cognition and emotion, systems, policies, procedures, tools, and cultural artefacts and ideas can intertwine to the point that they reinforce one another and perpetuate themselves in the workplace. This helps explain why leadership has been homogeneous for so long.

The intertwining of psychological, organizational, and cultural factors helps explain why changes to human resources policies at the leadership level are glacially slow in coming and why they do not yield a more diverse leadership in the ways they are meant to. The leadership status quo is the result of many years, even decades, of embedded factors. A comprehensive review of how these three factors coexist and interact with one another may provide insights as to which factors are more critical than others and how the adverse impacts on diverse groups might be reduced or removed. Usually, genuine consultations with diverse groups will yield some actionable items for change. In any case, the required changes may need to be carried out systematically and in one piece; otherwise, the missing or weak links may cause failure in efforts to make psychological, organizational, and cultural changes.

The Foundational Nature of Psychological Changes

To demonstrate how the above interplay of factors works, one might start by noting the built-in biases of current recruitment and selection mechanisms (as exemplified by the exclusive use of word-of-mouth and the quite subjective "corporate fit" criterion). These biases can be reduced or eliminated through outreach to diverse groups or by making selection criteria more measurable and free from discretion.

At each stage of recruitment and selection, some people will have blind spots or harbour unconscious biases, which affect how they perform their tasks. Only after their negative stereotypes and prejudices have been identified, neutralized, and removed can they make impartial decisions. Therefore, the crafting of systems, policies, procedures, and tools to make them as neutral and bias-free as possible is only one part of the battle against inequity, exclusiveness, and unfairness.

Biases are often built into human resources functions at their developmental and implementation stages by managers who are unwilling to remove their own biases even after they have been identified, because they can be justified in strictly business terms. As a consequence, they remain, on the basis of seemingly impartial justifications that bear no relation to fairness or equity. One example is the tendency among some leaders to recruit board directors or senior executives with long years of executive experience in a particular industry. This focus may be justifiable in strictly business terms. But when it is applied persistently, it eliminates a large segment of diverse group members, thus limiting the pool of potential candidates even further. This example illustrates the interplay between some current leaders' mindsets and the selection criteria for potential leaders.

Similarly, when the corporate culture emphasizes tokenism or resists innovative ideas, diverse groups are reluctant to bring forward new ideas or to aspire for greater organizational excellence. Such a culture is reluctant to listen to them, let alone try out their ideas, and this discourages them from striving for leadership positions, out of worry that their fresh perspectives may harm the organization. This suggests that when addressing the issue of underrepresentation in leadership, the relationship between the psychological, organizational, and cultural factors cannot be ignored. Any changes to rectify the current homogenized status of leadership must address this relationship.

The intertwining of psychological, organizational, and cultural factors has implications. To increase the representation of diverse groups in leadership, it is crucial to approach and address all three factors simultaneously. One cannot simply educate leaders and employees on diversity and inclusiveness in the hope that negative stereotypes and prejudices will automatically end or be reduced. Educational efforts need to be carried out in tandem with changes in human resources mechanisms (such as selection criteria, performance evaluation methods, succession management tools, and supportive measures) so that diverse groups do not simply get invited to apply for jobs (at the recruitment stage), only to be screened out by biased selection criteria (at the selection stage). This happens when the level of diversity awareness and knowledge has (supposedly) been raised but biases remain embedded in the selection tools. Sometimes, even when the biases in human resources systems, policies, procedures, and tools have been neutralized, decision-makers' judgments on candidates will still be biased, with results that are just as adverse for diverse groups as they were before.

Another implication is that psychological factors are supremely important. Take the contemporary mainstream concepts of leadership as an example. Pre-existing notions about which qualities a leader should have ("dynamic," "visionary"), which experiences he or she should have ("proven," "established" executive experience), how he or she should relate to people ("diplomatic," "inspirational"), or how he or she should conduct business ("aggressive," "collaborative") will have an impact on recruitment efforts (where to look for leadership candidates) as well as on the selection criteria (which attributes are considered significant, or not).

If the current leaders hold biased leadership concepts (while being unaware of them), the systems, policies, procedures, and tools for choosing leadership candidates may also be biased, for their design or implementation may follow these concepts (as found in the appointment of the interview panelists, the use of performance evaluation results, and the interview questions themselves, which may be skewed as to the types of information solicited from the leadership candidates). Even when the interviewees' answers are "scored," the results can still be biased, except they are now quantified, which gives the impression that they are "scientific." This approach tends to screen out diverse group members during hiring, promotion, leadership development, and/or succession planning.

Another example relates to leaders' perceptions of and attitudes toward people. These may affect how the behaviours of diverse group members are interpreted ("Are they trustworthy?") as well as assessments of their performance ("Are they high performers?"). Leaders' mindsets regarding what leadership *means*, and their perceptions and attitudes, remain pivotal even when human resources systems, policies, procedures, and tools have been made more impartial and objective than before. This is because, in the final analysis, it is human beings, not the systems, policies, procedures, and tools, who make decisions about leadership candidates, and it is they who interpret the results and make judgments.

All three factors – psychological, organizational, and cultural – are interrelated. In the final analysis, it is psychological factors that are foundational and will play a pivotal role in making leadership more diverse. Until mindsets change regarding what constitutes leadership, and until negative stereotypes and prejudices are eliminated, the leadership circle will likely remain an "old boys' club" dominated by white, able-bodied, non-Indigenous men.

Changes in Human Resources Mechanisms

The book has examined recruitment, selection, performance evaluation, succession management, and other human resources mechanisms, all through the diversity and equity lens. Some people view these mechanisms as impartial and as adhering to the principle of merit. This is debatable. Three key factors determine whether these mechanisms are indeed impartial: their intrinsic nature, the mindsets of the leaders who create and use them, and how they are utilized. Only after these three factors have been analysed and modified can human resources mechanisms become effective at opening doors for diverse groups at the leadership level. Otherwise, the mechanisms will continue to act as barriers for them.

As noted in chapter 5, word-of-mouth recruitment makes it much harder for diverse group members to be identified as leadership candidates as long as the current leaders are white, non-Indigenous, able-bodied men. Because they are all those identities, they do little to spread the word to diverse groups. This usually happens when there is a complete absence or no critical mass of diverse groups in the leadership circle. Furthermore, the formal selection criteria (which reflect contemporary mainstream concepts of leadership) and the informal ones ("corporate fit," "one of us") screen diverse group members out even when they do manage to reach the selection stage. Similarly, the performance management and succession management systems currently in use are prone to personal discretion, subjectivity, and manipulation with the consequence that diverse groups are too easily be screened out of leadership development or succession. When current leaders use negative stereotypes and prejudices as psychological filters, however impartial they might seem, this too screens out diverse groups.

Human resources mechanisms are created by an organization's leaders and managers. When they are biased, consciously or not, they develop systems, policies, procedures, and tools in alignment with their mindsets. So changing these mechanisms requires a thorough review on two fronts: how these mechanisms have failed to recruit, select, develop, and promote diverse group members in the past, and what values and assumptions these leaders and managers embrace when they develop and apply these mechanisms. Given that human beings are behind these mechanisms, there must a change of mindsets from exclusion to inclusion before or simultaneously with changes in human resources systems, policies, procedures, and tools.

Another key point is that human resources mechanisms consist of a series of interlocking components and processes and that any weak links in these will jeopardize the effectiveness of the human resources system as a whole.

One cannot simply remove barriers in one part of the process while leaving others barriers untouched. For example, one cannot simply change the selection criteria without retraining HR managers, changing the criteria and how they are weighted, revising interview questions and rating methods, and so on, and expect the results to be impartial. Changing mechanisms requires a full-scale renovation, not just patching up a few spots. Piecemeal modifications usually do not yield positive results. Therefore, human resources mechanisms must be looked in their totality, and changes to them must be holistic.

Changes in Corporate Culture

Corporate culture is one pillar in our model for change, along with psychological and organizational changes. This book has discussed a number of cultural traits and how they adversely impact diverse groups as they strive to join leadership circles. These cultural traits include tokenism, competitiveness, conformity, unwritten rules, exclusive norms, intolerance, cultural dissonance, and toxicity.

These cultural traits reflect traditional values and norms that seem to have lingered on from earlier times. They went unchallenged in the past, when leaders and their workforces were relatively homogeneous and stable. These traits have become problematic now that workforces and society as a whole are changing at a much faster pace than before. More members of diverse groups have joined the workforce, and some of them are pounding on the gates of leadership echelons. Various population segments have been raised and socialized into different social environments, and they have internalized different values, norms, and world views. The perspectives and experiences of diverse groups are different from those held by most white, able-bodied, non-Indigenous male leaders. Recognizing these changing realities is the first step in bringing about sustainable cultural changes in the workplace. Diverse groups may have different expectations and preferences regarding how people behave in the workplace and how things get done, and their relationships there may be guided by different values. This salient aspect of diversity becomes more noticeable when the organization expands to multiple workplaces in more than one country (Meyer 2015).

Corporate cultural change involves much more than formal announcements and official policy statements. These changes are slow to come and are shaped by many factors, the key ones being leadership and strategy (Katzenbach, Oelschlegal, and Thomas 2016). It is leaders who have to drive the new cultural direction. If tokenism is a part of the current corporate culture, they need to commit themselves to hiring and developing diverse group members and raising them to leadership positions; only in this way will the organization bring an end to tokenism. Leaders need to "walk the talk" about diversity and inclusiveness and set norms for managers and other employees to emulate.

"Walk the talk" leadership is vital, because employees will disengage quickly once they intuit that their leaders lack personal commitment to the organization's values and norms and that the official policy on diversity and inclusiveness is an empty gesture. Leaders have to hold one another accountable to their own policies and cultivate a corporate culture that is consistent with them.

Clarity in corporate strategy is also important. That strategy needs to include changing human behaviour. Bringing an end to negative stereotyping and prejudices against diverse groups will have long-lasting benefits for workplaces by improving work performance, human interactions, and decision-making. The necessary psychological changes can be observed and measured only in terms of behavioural changes, which should be rewarded when found.

Behavourial modification is a good place to begin making cultural changes. For example, the values of collaboration and inclusive teamwork are observable and measurable through outcomes such as productivity and employee satisfaction. Accordingly, these behaviours could be evaluated through performance management and rewarded by monetary and non-monetary means. Prejudice against women and racialized minorities is not observable unless it manifests itself as observable activities such as uttering racial slurs and making unwelcome sexual advances. Such harassing behaviours can be penalized. The focus, then, should be on observable human behaviours (actions) to detect whether there has been a change in mindsets, and those changes should be rewarded if they align well with the principles of diversity and inclusiveness, and penalized if they are at odds with those principles.

One hindrance to genuine cultural change in business is the perceived disconnect between the culture of diversity and inclusiveness on the one hand, and business direction and performance in real terms on the other. Leaders who find it hard to internalize that connection will also find it hard to communicate to employees the business advantages of diversity and inclusiveness. Moreover, when the claimed connection is not visible in terms of outcomes and impacts, employees and even leaders quickly become disengaged from the cultural ideal the organization has been promoting. Thus, successful cultural changes need early wins with tangible results. Those wins can then lead to further changes.

When the direction of cultural change is clear to everyone, when leaders are committed to it, when strategies for it are effective, when outcomes and impacts are observable, and when there is behavioural reinforcement (both positive and negative), employees will gradually be motivated to come on board and the corporate cultural traits of diversity and inclusiveness will slowly embed themselves in the organization. This will take time, but with regular monitoring and adjustment, it will happen.

Two Necessary Conditions for the Business Sector

This book has focused on the homogeneity of leadership and what can be done about it. The private sector can use the findings here to craft an integrated approach to making psychological, organizational, and cultural changes to their organizations. That will entail a wide range of actions, which include engaging and motivating employees and mid-level managers, establishing a management system to oversee and enforce the new policies and procedures, and allocating adequate financial and human resources to launch the action plan. Two internal factors stand out as the most crucial to all this: corporate commitment, and leadership accountability. These are the preconditions for the diversification of leadership.

Corporate Commitment

Corporate commitment is vital to integrated approaches to effecting psychological, organizational, and cultural change. That commitment should begin at the board level, and it needs to be formalized and communicated broadly both internally and externally. If backed by resources, monitoring, and reinforcement, that commitment will have a positive impact on the CEO, the senior executive team, mid-level management, and the rest of the organization.

Boards of directors are meant to provide policy and strategic direction to senior executives. They can play an important role in diversity efforts at the senior executive level by developing written formal policies on diversity and inclusiveness. When a board commits itself to this effort, it is likely to become more diverse, and the senior executive team is likely to follow suit.

The relationship between a board's diversity profile and that of the senior executive team has yet to be studied in depth. However, the limited research findings suggest that a symbiotic relationship exists. Female representation on a board tends to be mirrored in the senior executive. In Canada, boards with at least one female board member have an average of 18% female executives, and those with at least two female board directors have an average of 20% female executives. The Conference Board of Canada found that "organizations with women on their boards in 1995 had 30 percent more women executives in

2001 than organizations that began with all-male boards in 1995" (Brown, Brown, and Anastasopoulos 2002, 8).

While the reasons for this symbiotic relationship have yet to be researched systematically, there are several possible explanations. When a board of directors is determined to increase its own female representation, this signals to the CEO and executives that it is serious about having more women engaged in business discussions, strategy formulation, policy development, and decision-making, and about recruiting them for senior executive positions. Having more women on a board also puts pressure on the CEO to bring more women onto the executive team, for it signals that the organization aspires to gender parity.

In addition, having more women may slowly break down the stereotypes women face and increase the comfort level of their male colleagues on boards and executive teams. It also provides an opportunity for CEOs to see the value of having women in leadership circles. Another benefit is that board members are usually former or current corporate executives. The lack of female executives makes it difficult for the current board to recruit female members, in that the current board directors seem to demand they have an established track record in executive ranks. When more and more women join executive teams, it expands the feeder pool of women with executive qualifications and thus improves their chances of being appointed to boards later on. Overall, the benefits for boards and for senior executive teams reinforce each other.

Unfortunately, there are no available studies on other diverse groups regarding this issue. That said, the preceding discussion on the symbiotic relationship between board directors and senior executives may well be applicable to other diverse groups. A word of caution is warranted here. The statistics for diverse groups at senior executive levels in Canada indicate that this symbiotic relationship is not automatic. There is no guaranteed migration of senior executives of diverse backgrounds to boards of directors. In fact, as noted in chapter 2, except for Indigenous peoples (whose representation rate is higher on boards than among senior executives), the representation rates of diverse groups in senior executive ranks are higher than on boards in Canada. Even when there is a good supply of qualified executives from diverse groups, there is no guarantee they will rise to board directorships.

For an organization to become more diverse and inclusive at the board and senior executive levels, there must be a clear corporate commitment to diversification at those levels. That commitment is the most important driver of change (Brown, Brown, and Anastasopoulos 2002, 11). It is usually accompanied by a written corporate policy on diversity and inclusiveness and by a further commitment to implement that policy with adequate resources (financial and human), as well as to put in motion bias reduction efforts, mentorships, wellness programs, anti-harassment and anti-discrimination education, and leadership development programs (Brady and McLean 2002, 1). These initiatives and programs can expand feeder pools and ensure that more diverse group members are hired, retained, and promoted.

The amendments to the Canada Business Corporations Act that require boards of directors and senior executives of federally regulated companies to be diverse and include Indigenous peoples, persons with disabilities, racialized minorities, and women require a firmer corporate commitment from these companies so as to yield positive results. The amendments came into effect on 1 January 2020. This commitment is best communicated in a clearly written diversity and inclusiveness policy statement to the shareholders, management and non-management employees, external stakeholder groups, and the public.

Leadership Accountability

Even when all human resources mechanisms have been changed so as become inclusive, current leaders are still accountable for their actions (or lack thereof) in opening leadership positions to diverse groups. They must ensure that the diversity and inclusiveness policy become a concrete reality; they also need to keep an eye on the actual operations of human resources mechanisms and enforce all management and administrative policies and procedures related to them. This will ensure that the psychological, organizational, and cultural changes will have their intended impact and be sustained. Shareholders hold the board of directors accountable, the board holds the CEO and senior executives accountable, and they in turn hold the middle managers and employees accountable.

A policy statement on diversity and inclusiveness posted on office walls and on the corporation's website, followed by a half-hearted implementation of bias elimination, will do little good for diverse groups. Official statements can easily amount to lip service unless the board and the senior executives (including the CEO) are held accountable for translating corporate policies into programs that make real progress toward diversity representation.

This book has discussed a number of approaches to addressing barriers to leadership. These include systematic workforce data collection and analysis; review of the current concepts of leadership; implementation of diversity education for leaders and employees; development of a formal diversity and inclusiveness policy and bias-neutral systems in the areas of recruitment and selection, performance evaluation, and succession management; development of supportive measures (e.g., formal mentorship programs); creation of health and wellness programs; establishment of anti-harassment and anti-discrimination policies and procedures; and transformation of the workplace environment and culture. Leaders must take ownership of these actions and be answerable to the shareholders, the board, and the employees.

All of the above depends on proper program measurement and on regular monitoring and review. It also requires that diversity and inclusiveness be made integral to the performance evaluations of senior executives, including the CEO. Once some or all of the above approaches are adopted, leaders (i.e., directors, the CEO, senior executives) must oversee their progress by measuring outcomes and impacts, quantifying them if feasible. They can also require regular progress reports, asking tough questions if progress is slow. The impacts of these programs can be measured in terms of changes in the workforce profile and how well diverse groups are represented on the board and in senior executive ranks. Those impacts should also be evident in the human resources mechanisms and changes in corporate culture. Benchmarks based on industrial averages or demographic or labour force statistics can be used to determine the degree of representation and any diversity gaps. In addition, research (through interviews, focus groups, or surveys of leaders, middle managers, and non-management employees) can be utilized to ascertain and interpret longitudinal patterns and trends, perceptions of progress, and program outcomes.

But what would strengthen leadership accountability most is regular performance evaluations for leaders. They must be held accountable for any progress or regression in the representation of diverse groups among board directors and senior executives, just as they are when it comes to sales, market share, customer relations, product quality, productivity, or business development. Their performance could be monitored and reviewed on a quarterly basis, with rewards and penalties attached. Also, the performance of the board directors should be monitored regularly to determine whether progress is being made.

It is important that the business sector understand the value of diversity and inclusiveness and recognize the psychological, organizational, and cultural factors that result in the lack of representation of diverse groups. It is equally important that, having learned about best practices and various options, the business sector put its best efforts into making diversity in leadership happen. Corporate commitment and leadership accountability are not the only ingredients for success, but they are the most important ones.

Lessons from the Past from Business Voluntarism

Clearly, the business sector has a lot on its plate when it comes to enriching leadership with more diversity. Some businesses have greatly increased diversity rather quickly; others still have a long way to go. As noted, businesses have much more to think about than diversity and inclusiveness. These play supportive roles, but a given business's strategic requirements may induce it give them a higher priority. The question is: Can we rely solely on the business sector to bring about the necessary psychological, organizational, and cultural changes to ensure diversity in leadership? Answers to this question yield insights into government's role (if any) in diversity in leadership.

Historically, the core principle for the private sector has been the bottom line. Businesses are founded to make money and then make more money; any additional activities are conducted to support that endeavour. Equality, equity, fairness, human rights, and other social justice issues that do not generate profits are perceived as secondary. Only when they enhance the core principle or are legally required is the private sector prepared to support or tolerate them. It follows that the business sector will be more active or even proactive in opening up leadership circles to diverse groups when (a) it is legally required, and (b) it motivates employees, increases productivity, and raises reputation, thereby enhancing the bottom line. Unfortunately, diversifying leadership is a rather lengthy process, especially when the business organization is not ready, lacks the infrastructure or processes to speed up the process, or is too preoccupied with the core business.

Given that all activities not central to the core business are secondary, a heavy reliance on the private sector to carry out diversity and inclusiveness activities on a voluntary basis would be problematic. There are many historical examples of wholesale reliance on business voluntarism yielding little in tangible results. These examples can be found in areas such as occupational health and safety, equal pay for work of equal value, fair wages for workers, pollution abatement, food security, and information privacy, and many others. This does not mean that the private sector is blind to these matters. Often it merely means that they are viewed as secondary and that businesses have not integrated them into their core functions and accountability framework. When the sector is left alone to act voluntarily, these issues may take much longer to address, if they ever are.

So the government may have to play a more proactive role in intervening on diversity and inclusiveness, just as it had done often in the past regarding non-business matters. The government has many policy instruments at its disposal to speed up the process of making leadership more diverse; those instruments include taxation, public education, legislation, and coercive actions (Siu, 2020). Businesses tend not to like it when these policy instruments are applied to human resources management. They would rather that the government allowed them to self-regulate. But does self-regulation based on a voluntarism model yield positive results when it comes to diversity in leadership? The short answer is "unreliably likely," especially in the social justice area.

One lesson we have learned in the area of workforce equity is that past voluntary efforts on the part of the private sector have been largely ineffective, unreliable, unsustainable, or simply too slow. Examples may be found in the development of employment equity and gender parity on Canadian boards since the 1980s.

Lessons Learned from Employment Equity

Prior to the enactment of the federal Employment Equity Act (1986), Ottawa had made it known to the private sector that Indigenous peoples, persons with disabilities, racialized minorities, and women were underrepresented in many occupational groups, had high unemployment rates, and faced employment discrimination. Its message to the private sector was that businesses needed to make their workplaces more reflective of Canada's changing demographic composition. With this objective, in 1978 it launched a voluntary Affirmative Action Program focusing on the private sector. At that time, businesses had contended that they could make their organizations more representative on a voluntary basis without federal intervention.

Five years later, this voluntary approach had brought little tangible progress. In 1983, to set an example, the federal government introduced the Federal Affirmative Action Program in the Federal Public Sector, which aimed to increase the representation of four diverse groups: Indigenous peoples, persons with disabilities, racialized minorities, and women. At that point, the government also launched the Royal Commission on Equality in Employment, chaired by Rosalie Silberman Abella, with the mandate to find ways to promote equality for diverse groups. In 1984, the Royal Commission's report (the *Abella Report*) was released, which documented employment discrimination of diverse groups in Canada and set out the policy framework for the Employment Equity Act. Steps to speed up passage of the legislation began soon after.

Fast-forward to 1986. That year, the federal employment equity legislation received the Royal Assent. The law requires the federally regulated private sector and the non-federally regulated businesses with federal contracts in Canada to remove employment barriers and make their workplaces representative for the four diverse groups. This legislation reflected Section 15 of the Charter of Rights and Freedoms, enacted in 1982. Ten years later, in 1995, this legislation was amended to include the federal public service.

Over the eighteen years between 1978 and 1995, the federal government learned that the private sector's voluntarism on social justice issues had its limitations; also, that to become more effective the federal public service would have to be brought under a legislative framework for employment equity on par with that of the private sector. The strict legal requirements for both sectors to collect and analyse workforce data to identify underrepresentations, review their employment systems to identify employment barriers, and develop and implement employment equity plans with goals and timetables to rectify the underrepresentation of diverse groups should have been able to move the needle on workplace equity. As we will see later, it did not work the way the federal government expected it to work.

Lessons Learned from Gender Parity on Boards

Similarly, in light of the lack of gender parity on boards of directors and in executive ranks, the federal government began developing a "comply or explain" model (a regulatory instrument borrowed from Europe and this country's provincial governments) to increase female representation in leadership positions in the 2010s. The data so far indicate that about half the boards of directors of larger corporations still lack female representation. Data on Canada cited in chapter 2 of this book paint a picture of homogeneous boards on which diverse groups are inequitably represented.

Provinces with "comply or explain" models requiring the private sector to report the representation of women on boards and in senior executive ranks have found that the results have not been very satisfactory and that more progress is needed at least regarding the actual numbers and percentages of women in these positions. Regarding the proportion of women on boards, some progress was made between 2014 (when the regulations took effect) and 2018 (when a review was conducted), according to a Toronto-Dominion Bank study. That review was based on the 243 companies in the S&P/TSX Composite Index. However, a provincial securities commissions' report in 2018 found only modest progress in terms of the proportion of women holding boards seats at 648 companies in Canada (from 11% in 2015 to 15% in 2018) (McFarland 2019).

If 30% female board directors is the objective (as per the 30% Club's goal), at this rate it will take fifteen more years to reach it. If 50% (women's share of the population) is the goal, it will take 35 years. If historical data on employment equity is any guide, these percentages may go up and down, much like the stock market, and it will likely take even longer to reach the benchmark. Overall, voluntarism under the provincial "comply or explain" model had not moved the needle on gender parity as much as expected, though modest progress has been made (based on a smaller sample of companies). The search (or demand) for gender parity in leadership has been in motion for several decades, and it is not clear whether we will still be talking about it a generation from now, even though we have evidence that we are going in the right direction.

Catalyst Canada's 2016 report found little national progress under the voluntary "comply or explain" model. Accordingly, the Canadian Securities Administrators (CSA) have continued to monitor progress regarding female representation while seeking ways to accelerate it. After years of monitoring, they have not seen satisfactory progress in the private sector. The federal government has since amended Canada's Business Corporations Act, but those amendments, which took effect on 1 January 2020, remain aligned with the provinces' "comply or explain" model. With this legislative change, will parity of the four diverse groups – Indigenous peoples, persons with disabilities, racialized minorities and women – be reached within a reasonable time frame? Only time will tell. But based on the federal experience with business voluntarism in the 1970s and 1980s and that of provincial gender parity regulations between 2014 to 2018, progress under these amendments may not be fast enough for diverse groups and the federal government.

Limitations of Employment Equity Legislation and Law Enforcement

However much we may hope that recent federal legislation will work, the history of employment equity and gender parity on boards in Canada since 1986 has not been encouraging. Even with mandatory compliance, employment equity legislation has been slow to bring about equitable representation of the four designated groups.

The Senate Standing Committee on Human Rights reviewed the status of employment equity in the federal public service and released two reports, in 2007 and 2010. Both concluded that there had been only very slow progress. The statistics compiled by the federal government showed glacial progression toward equity, more for women than for other diverse groups. They also showed that Indigenous peoples and persons with disabilities were persistently underrepresented in most occupational groups and that little progress had been made (Canada 2015; 2016c).

More importantly, the pattern of progress in employment equity was uneven. It indicated ups and downs in representation – "two steps forward, and one step backward," or in a few cases, "one step forward, and two steps backward." In many organizations, underrepresentation of diverse groups was still widespread and severe. Agnocs (2014) reviewed the legislation's accomplishments and found that diverse groups still had a long way to go. The year 2016 marked the thirtieth year of employment equity in Canada. The statistics cited in this book's chapter 2 on diversity gaps illustrated that progress has been limited and that more work is needed to close the diversity gaps. Over the more than thirty-three years since legislation was passed, only tepid progress has been made in terms of equity for the four designated groups in various occupations, including in senior and mid-level management.

The legislation does not address parity at the directorship level. The regulatory efforts of the Canadian Securities Administrators (CSA) and the Ontario Securities Commission before 2020 have yielded little progress in gender parity on boards. The employment equity legislation's "goals and timetables" model is viewed as more demanding than the "comply or explain" model followed by the provinces, yet its effectiveness is still questionable.

The question is, why is progress on diversity so slow and uneven despite the more stringent requirements of Ottawa's "goals and timetables" approach and the provinces' recent "comply or explain" model of gender parity? Three factors are offered here to explain the slow progress:

- The modest and unfocused corporate implementation of employment equity.
- The lack of rigorous enforcement efforts for employment equity.
- The leniency of gender parity legislation.

Modest and Unfocused Efforts

Since the enactment of employment equity legislation in 1986, some businesses have viewed it as "unnecessary" government intervention in their human resources activities. For them, "employment equity" amounts to outright intrusion. They have implemented it only reluctantly, contending that it does not benefit their businesses, demands too much paperwork, and crowds out other more essential business functions.

Consequently, with the exception of a few large corporations (primarily in the finance and telecommunication sectors), some businesses have been reluctant to put sufficient effort or resources into employment equity. Some assign clerical staff to do most of the legally required work, with executives or managers barely involved, so that the results typically do not meet the legislative standards regarding reasonable efforts and progress (see ss. 11 and 12 of the act). Often, because of the shoddy results, some companies have to redo their paperwork – workforce data collection and analysis, employment systems reviews, and/or employment equity plans – after the federal compliance review. All of this delays progress for the four diverse groups, including in their efforts to rise toward senior management and beyond. Also, some companies make slight progress in representation, but that progress stalls between compliance reviews. This pattern may be contributing to the slow progress.

A key reason for slow progress in employment equity is that some businesses develop action plans to rectify underrepresentation without a focused effort to review their human resources systems to pinpoint the sources of diversity gaps; they take remedial action on problems before they are clear what their sources are. The result is misplaced and unfocused effort. By the time the employers realize their "solutions" are not removing employment barriers for diverse groups, a few years have usually gone by. Resources have been wasted, and time has been lost, but the problems of underrepresentation remain.

In the United States, diversity management began gaining momentum – and popularity – in the 1990s, soon after employment equity was implemented. In Canada since the turn of this century, it has gradually grown more popular, for some diversity management activities are compatible with employment equity laws. Some large corporations are now *glad* they have carried out the workforce data collection and analysis required under employment equity legislation, for they now have a platform on which to build their diversity and inclusiveness efforts. But despite this new momentum, most businesses are still lukewarm about diversity. They are generally receptive to the notion of it but still are not prepared to put much effort into it as part of their business strategy. Progress, then, has been made, but mainly in larger corporations, not so much in medium-sized or smaller ones.

Negotiable Enforcement

The federal government has been lenient in its enforcement efforts. Its employment equity legislation sets fairly high standards for how employers should collect and analyse workforce data; review their employment systems (such as recruitment, selection, hiring, promotion, training, and retention); and develop and implement employment equity plans. There are other legal requirements besides, related to communication, consultation, collaboration, and accountability. All of this is detailed in the legislation and regulations. To boost the quality of these activities, Ottawa has developed data compilation and analysis software, templates for statistical tables, educational and training sessions, resource materials, policies and guidelines, and many other tools and resources. The slow progress is not for the lack of federal resources to help the private sector implement employment equity; rather, it is for the lack of strong federal enforcement.

On the surface, the federal program is rigorous when it comes to monitoring, review, and enforcement. Businesses must submit annual workforce data, and the legislation requires them to develop short-term and longer-term plans for every major occupational group (including the "senior managers" group) with the goal of making their workforces more representative. The standards for measuring employment equity are "reasonable progress" (s. 11 of the act) and "all reasonable efforts" (s. 12). In simple terms, these two standards mean that businesses must show progress in employment equity on paper (as in their workforce data reports and employment equity plans) and put sufficient effort and resources into making it happen (as in plan implementation). Both must be "reasonable." However, that term is quite vague and at times ambiguous.

In this regard, the Canadian Human Rights Commission (which conducts compliance audits of federally regulated employers) and Employment, Workforce Development, and Labour Canada (which reviews the performance of federal contractors) both allow businesses to explain away their lack of reasonable progress and reasonable efforts, lack of focus in employment system reviews, lack of clarity on measures, lack of measurement and monitoring of program implementation, and issues related to goals and timetables. They also allow businesses plenty of time to redo their work and address their slow progress. Quite often, businesses are found to be making little progress for one or two designated groups in some occupational groups for many years, or regressing in some areas after minimal progress. In fairness, some businesses encounter circumstances (such as economic downturns or staff turnover) they cannot directly control that affect their program results.

The guiding principles for audits are collaboration and flexibility; non-compliance is to be addressed through persuasion and negotiation. Even when federally regulated employers are found to be in non-compliance, there are restrictions on what the Canadian Human Rights Commission can require and on orders the Canadian Employment Equity Review Tribunal can issue. Employers that have committed a violation face a penalty of no more than $10,000 for the first violation and no more than $50,000 for repeated or continued violations. Federal contractors that violate or do not comply with orders can find themselves "de-contracted," or ineligible for future contracts (Siu,2016, vol. 2, 15-1–15.87). These penalties are relatively mild, considering the wealth of the companies and the principle that is being compromised.

Compliance assessments, audits, and enforcement are all time-consuming, and at many points in these processes, the federal government is willing to be flexible. This may explain why, despite the legislation's intentions, progress has been elusive.

Legislative Leniency

Let us now fast-forward to 31 December 2014, when the provincial government of Ontario, and those of Saskatchewan, Manitoba, Quebec, Newfoundland and Labrador, New Brunswick, and Nova Scotia, as well as the territorial governments of the Northwest Territories and Nunavut, adopted the "comply or explain" model, which required private sector firms to disclose their reasons for non-compliance with gender parity poliicies. These governments now required businesses to disclose their diversity policies and plans as well as the representation of women on their boards of directors and in their executive ranks (Devereux and Linett 2013). This model is similar to the Australian and British ones (Lu 2016). After the first, failed legislative attempt to address employment equity in Ontario in the early 1990s, this model may be viewed as a re-emergent attempt on the equity front. Compared to the federal Employment Equity Act, the regulations of the Ontario Securities Commission (OSC) and in other jurisdictions are a much tamer and narrower; they have fewer "teeth" and are limited to women's parity on boards and in senior executive positions.

One year after "comply or explain" was enacted (i.e., thirty years after the federal Employment Equity Act, and twenty years after the repeal of employment equity legislation in Ontario) through the Canadian Securities Administrators – an umbrella group of provincial regulators – the Ontario Securities Commission (OSC) found that the representation of women had notched up only one percentage point, from 11% to 12%, among corporate board directors at the 677 companies listed on the Toronto Stock Exchange (TSX). Fifty-five per cent of these companies had at least one woman on their board – in other words, 45% of them did not. The rate of new female appointments was also slow: only 76 women (or 14.6%) had secured the 521 seat vacancies that year. Also, the percentage of companies with female senior executives remained roughly the same. Disclosure reports submitted to the OSC in 2016 revealed that only 21% of companies had adopted policies to identify and nominate women, a further 16% had general diversity policies, and 59% had no written policies at all. Larger corporations appeared to be showing slightly more progress (McFarland 2016; Lu 2016; McNelly and Batcho-Lino 2016; Pinto and Chapman 2016). Five years after the launch of "comply or explain" regulations in 2014, most publicly traded companies in Ontario still had not reached the minimum 30% threshold that would constitute a critical mass for women. A staff writer at *Advisor's Edge* gathered that "there is still a long way to go at further improving gender representation" (Advisor's Edge 2019).

The OSC and the Institute for Gender and the Economy at the Rotman School of Management (University of Toronto) consider this performance dismal and discouraging. The idea of setting quotas for companies and imposing penalties for non-compliance is becoming more and more appealing, even among those who once rejected these steps.

Looking Forward

Legislative leniency has been largely ineffective, and Ontario provides one more example of that. Lessons learned from Ontario, Canada as a whole, and other countries suggest that a voluntary approach to fairer female representation, weak efforts by the private sector, and lenient enforcement are unlikely to lead to more equitable representation of women (and, indeed, other diverse groups designated in the federal employment equity legislation).

True, some progress on employment equity has been made over the past thirty years, but the pace of that progress remains underwhelming. Past history in employment equity tells us that a legislative approach is effective when private sector employers (and public sector ones) are committed to and accountable for diversity and inclusiveness, when the enforcement framework has "teeth," and when the law enforcers have strong drive and sufficient resources to do their work.

In September 2016, the federal government introduced Bill C-25, which has a framework for board directorships and senior executive positions similar to those of the provincial and territorial governments. The bill contains amendments to the Canada Business Corporations Act that will affect all federally incorporated companies, including those listed on the smaller TSX Venture Exchange. Overall, then, it impacts 40% of publicly listed companies in Canada (McNelly and Batcho-Lino 2016; Canadian Board Diversity Council 2016; Milstead 2019). The amendments to the Canada Business Corporations Act were passed in 2018, and the amended legislation became effective on 1 January 2020. The amendments have extended gender parity to additional diverse groups, including Indigenous peoples, persons with disabilities, and racialized minorities with regard to directorships and senior management positions for companies falling under the legislation. However, it still holds to the "comply or explain" model as a compliance instrument (Milstead 2019; Bradshaw 2019). We must wait to see whether this legislative framework will address the issues identified earlier and is strong enough to have its intended impact.

Two Necessary Government Policies

The lessons we have learned from federal employment equity laws and provincial gender parity laws are clear: business voluntarism may not be enough to bring about diversity in leadership, and "goals and timetables" (as in employment equity) and "comply or explain" (as in gender parity) may be too weak to wrestle down the historically embedded and systemic biases in the private sector and the inertia displayed by leaders (and shareholders, and the public in general). Some small progress might be made if the private sector were left alone on this front, but full equity and parity could well be a long time coming.

This book has examined the mindsets, mechanisms, and cultures of private sector organizations. Given the evident slow progress the sector has made so far, it seems clear that stronger government policies are needed to augment the private sector's efforts to make diversity in leadership happen. Below I single out two necessary government policies for pushing the agenda further: legislative diversity quotas, and public education.

Legislative Diversity Quotas

Several European countries have adopted legislative quota systems to mandate diversity in leadership. Those systems are making a difference.

After several previous attempts to address gender parity, in 2011, France mandated that companies have at least 40% female board directors by the end of 2017. In 2018, European Women on Boards reported that among the 200 largest European listed companies in nine European countries, France had the highest share of women on company boards at 44.2%, followed by Italy (36.5%), Germany (33.7%), Finland (33.3%), Belgium (32.7%), the Netherlands (31.7%), the United Kingdom (29.9%), Spain (24.6%), and the Czech Republic (19.0%). The top three countries – France, Italy, and Germany – have all legislated gender parity quotas for directorships. Three other European countries (Iceland, Norway, Spain) have also mandated quotas for female directors (Zillman 2018). All of these countries with mandated quotas have made more progress toward female parity than the United Kingdom, Australia, and the United States, which have adopted laissez-faire approaches (Lu 2016). Sanctions need to be placed on companies that do not comply. Among the European countries, only Spain has a gender quota *without* sanctions for non-compliance. Incidentally, it is also the country where relatively little progress has been made in gender parity on boards (Comi et al. 2016). This suggests the importance of government monitoring and enforcement.

Quota systems remain controversial, yet there is evidence that they have succeeded in Europe. According to Rajeev Vasudeva, the CEO of Egon Zhender, one of Europe's largest executive search firms, "I'm not a great supporter of quotas but in this case it's making [a] difference … It has changed the conversation – it clearly has been put on the agenda of companies" (Staley 2016).

The legislative quota approach has been adopted by the State of California, which enacted a board diversity mandate in 2018. By 2019, every public company headquartered in the state had to have at least one woman on its board. By 2021, the law will require 40% women on five-person boards and 60% women on six-person boards (Coren 2018).

In Canada, there are still opponents of the legislative quota model for employment equity and diversity parity. Usually, the reasons for opposing quotas are: "the less intervention from the government, the better" and "quotas violate the merit principle."

The "government intervention" argument maintains that businesses should be allowed to set their own implementation processes as well as their own goals and timetables based on the circumstances at hand. Any mandatory process, like a quota system, may jeopardize business growth, create a backlash from stakeholders, and be counterproductive to a smooth transition. As noted in the history of employment equity, gender parity, and other public policy issues discussed earlier in this chapter, the facts are clear: voluntarism has not worked in the private sector and has been amazingly slow to yield results.

The "merit principle" assumes there are not enough qualified people in diverse groups. A yearly quota forces the private sector to hire or promote diverse group members of poorer quality to boards and senior executive ranks. This violates the merit principle in human resources management and may well result in a cohort of board directors or senior executives with weaker credentials, thus jeopardizing business growth. This assumption is faulty, as was shown in chapter 2. There is abundant data from Statistics Canada as well as real-world evidence that there are many qualified and available diverse group members capable of high-level board and executive work.

Canada has tried various ways to address inequality, beginning with the equal opportunity and human rights laws after the Second World War. These have had little impact, so it is high time that European-style diversity quota systems were adopted.

Public Education

The law has the potential to build a more equal society, but it needs the help of public education. For the law to have a real impact on society, people's mindsets and behaviours have to change. Without that, a piece of legislation can only do so much. Behind every rule, action, mechanism, and institution, there are human beings. History is full of examples of laws (such as apartheid, residential schools for Indigenous peoples, women as "non-persons," affirmative action) that were viewed as illegitimate and contemptible by many people but remained in force because those in power and their followers remained convinced that they were the right laws. Without public education, more people are likely to take the side of those in power who enforce unfairness and inequality.

To be achieve its goals, a law requires public buy-in. Gender parity, employment equity, pay equity, and human rights are all social justice issues. Those issues are not the cornerstone of the business sector – profit is. Due to this intrinsic nature of business, social justice does not have much traction in the private sector, absent a business case for corporate responsibility. When a government has a progressive agenda to promote diversity and has passed legislation in support of that agenda, the public needs to be educated to support the law.

The history of employment equity reminds us that lack of public education can weaken legislation's impact, sometimes greatly (as with Ontario's repeal of employment equity legislation in 1996). Legislative change is not in itself a remedy for social injustice. Unless it has public support, a new law can easily be repealed by a new government or resisted by (part of) the public. Legislation that has been entrenched for a number of years is more difficult to repeal, but even then, public education is still key to consolidating that legislation.

When developing employment equity legislation, the federal government made a strong effort to consult with employers, labour unions, community groups, service agencies, diverse groups, college and universities, government departments and agencies, non-federal jurisdictions, foreign governments, and many other groups. The consultations focused on informing the public about the government's agenda and how employment equity could be carried out in Canada. Educating the public and stakeholder groups regarding the value of employment equity was not a priority.

Furthermore, the government did not allocate enough human and financial resources for education or even communication on the issue. As a result, the question of *why* businesses and the public sector should embrace employment equity and how it could benefit them, the economy, and the country's well-being was largely never addressed. Some academics, unions, service agencies, and diverse group members might understand the benefits; but overall, employers, employees, the mass media, and the broader public were not "sold" on employment equity at the time the federal government was drafting the legislation (1980s).

In the years following the enactment of employment equity legislation, resistance from employers and segments of the population (as well as the media) surfaced occasionally. The *Globe and Mail* provided a forum for anti-equity forces that viewed the legislation as weakening the merit principle and threatening white men's jobs. Employers also complained that the government was interfering in businesses' hiring and promotion practices, and some of them intended to take the government to court over it.

When the Ontario government began preparing similar legislation in the early 1990s, it consulted extensively with various stakeholder groups, including employers, employees, unions, and community groups. Those consultations focused largely on what an employment equity program should look like, how employers could implement it, and how the government could roll it out. But again, not enough human and financial resources were allocated to public education work promoting the value of employment equity.

At the time Ontario (under Premier Bob Rae of the New Democratic Party) was preparing the legislation, most if not all of the media coverage was negative. The *Globe and Mail* ran many editorials and columns criticizing employment equity. As a result, most of the public either viewed it negatively or did not know or care what it was. What people did know they had learned from the negative media coverage. Employers were largely unconvinced of the business and economic benefits of employment equity that the government claimed. Their concerns revolved around government interference in their businesses, the amount of data gathering and administration the program would require, the amount of paperwork they would have to submit to the province, the erosion of management's authority (which would have to be shared with unions), and the prohibitive financial costs for businesses.

Stakeholder groups and the general public did not understand the concept of employment equity, or its benefits. Their mindset was that individualism (not state intervention) and the merit principle (not social identities of diverse groups) ruled supreme in the workplace – those with the best qualifications should be hired or promoted whatever their social or cultural identity. That was the prevalent ideology at that time, and the same ideology still holds. People do not believe the state has the right to require businesses to do what individuals should be doing for themselves, namely, acquiring sufficient merit to find work and grow their own careers.

In this cultural context, as soon as the new Conservative government came into power in 1996, it repealed the NDP's employment equity legislation. It was less than a year old. The new government felt certain the repealed legislation has little support among the public. Most people did not know enough to care, and some, especially some white, able-bodied, non-Indigenous men, viewed the legislation as an existential threat. They saw it as undermining their futures and their sons' futures, all for no benefit to businesses or the economy.

After the repeal, the concept of employment equity crumbled in Ontario. Later, though, the OSC would resurrect a small part of the old concept of employment equity and position it within a slightly different framework.

The lessons learned from the preceding account should not be forgotten. When employers, employees, shareholders, other stakeholders, the media, and the public at large are not knowledgeable about the value of gender parity (and of equitable representation of other diverse groups on boards and in senior executive positions), and when they are not supportive enough, a law can only do so much. Legality does not equate with legitimacy. The latter cannot be coerced, it can only be earned or learned. As the history of employment equity legislation in Canada suggests, passing a piece of legislation is only half the battle. Public education belongs to the other half, along with other factors.

In light of all this, the current movement in Canada for diversity parity in leadership positions may confront resistance in various forms – white nationalism, race hatred, religious bigotry, and anti-feminism – when its objectives and values are not well publicized and thoroughly explained. Counteracting this resistance to diversity parity, especially gender parity, is today's "Me Too movement"; the emergence of new ideas about corporate social responsibility, diversity, and inclusion and transparency; the prominence of systemic discrimination and Indigenous peoples and Black Lives Matter issues; and, finally, the new generation of millennials, who are developing their own mindset. These social currents make clear that public education in social justice is important, especially when governments in different jurisdictions are pushing the agenda for diversity in leadership.

Final Remarks

This book has discussed diversity in leadership in the context of global, demographic, and economic changes around the world and shown why it is a business advantage. Using statistics, it has shown that business leadership in Canada has long been homogeneous, with little participation from diverse groups. It has also examined concepts of leadership, perceptions and attitudes toward diverse groups, and human resources mechanisms related to recruitment, selection, performance evaluation, succession management, special programs, retention, work environment, and corporate culture.

This book has suggested a number of options and practices that would help address today's lack of diversity in business leadership. Businesses that have not adopted any of them would find it worthwhile to consult board directors, executives, managers, and employees of various backgrounds to see whether any of the solutions broached in this book are adoptable or adaptable for their organizations. As the effectiveness of solutions is based on an interaction of psychological, organizational, and cultural factors, a holistic (as opposed to piecemeal) approach is advisable.

Many organizations have put in practice policies, programs, and initiatives to make workplaces more diverse and inclusive. They have had various degrees of success in diversifying leadership, but more concerted efforts are needed. As with many organizational changes, the impacts are not immediately apparent. This book has identified leadership accountability and corporate commitment as necessary for organizational success. It also holds that business voluntarism in opening doors to diversity in leadership may not be enough and that the government sector may need to take stronger action by enacting a quota system for diversity parity, augmented by broad public education. A change in business mindset, organization, and culture, bolder legislation, and a concerted public education effort may be the way to go. After all, diversity in leadership benefits not only businesses but also people and the economy at large.

References

Aboud, Frances, Morton Mendelson, and Kelly Purdy. 2003. "Cross-Race Peer Relations and Friendship Quality." *International Journal of Behavioral Development* 27(2): 165–73. https://doi.org/10.1080/01650250244000164.

Adams, Amy. 2015. "How Group Dynamics Affect Decisions." *Stanford News*, 16 October. http://news.stanford.edu/features/2015/decisions/group-dynamics.html.

Adams, Renée B., and Daniel Ferreira. 2009. "Women in the Boardroom and Their Impact on Governance and Performance." *Journal of Financial Economics* 94(2): 291–309. https://doi.org/10.1016/j.jfineco.2008.10.007.

Adib, Amei, and Yvonne Guerrier. 2003. "The Interlocking of Gender with Nationality, Race, Ethnicity, and Class: The Narratives of Women in Hotel Work." *Gender, Work, and Organization* 10(4): 413–32. https://doi.org/10.1111/1468-0432.00204.

Advisor's Edge. 2019. "Report Finds Canada Lags in Board Diversity but Encourages Patience." 27 March. Transcontinental Media. https://www.advisor.ca/news/industry-news/report-finds-canada-lags-in-board-diversity-but-encourages-patience.

Agnocs, Carol. 2014. *Employment Equity in Canada: The Legacy of the Abella Report.* Toronto: University of Toronto Press.

Aguiar do Monte, Paulo. 2010. "Job Dissatisfaction and Labour Turnover: Evidence from Brazil." ANPEC. http://www.anpec.org.br/encontro2010/inscricao/arquivos/245-2ba4b8c7262a6e55eda59928ff66d1cc_.pdf.

Aguirre, Adalberto, Jr. 2000. *Women and Minority Faculty in the Academic Workplace: Recruitment, Retention, and Academic Culture.* ASHE-ERIC Higher Education Report 27(27). Josey-Bass Higher and Adult Education Series. San Francisco: Jossey-Bass.

Ahn, Tae, 2009. "An Exploratory Study in Leadership Styles of Asian-American Corporate Managers." PhD thesis, Pepperdine University, Malibu.

Aiden, Hardeep, and Andrea McCarthy. 2014. *Current Attitudes towards Disabled People.* London: Scope.

Akhavan, Vafa. 2016. "Smart Leaders See Diversity as an Immense Opportunity." *Globe and Mail*, 25 November.

Almandrez, Mary Grace A. 2010. "History in the Making: Narratives of Selected Asian Pacific American Leadership." PhD diss., University of San Francisco.

Almond, Steve. 2013. "Gender Diversity in Leadership Is Key to Business Success." *The Guardian*, 2 October. https://www.theguardian.com/sustainable-business /gender-diversity-leadership-business-success.

Angus Reid Group. 1991. *Multiculturalism and Canadians: Attitudinal Study 1991 National Survey Report*. Ottawa: Multiculturalism and Citizenship Canada.

Antal, A.B. and D.N. Izraeli. 1993. "A Global Comparison of Women in Management: Women Managers in Their Homelands and as Expatriates." In *Women in Management: Trends, Issues, and Challenges in Managerial Diversity*, edited by Ellen A. Fagenson, 52–96. Newbury Park, Sage.

Antoun, Ayman. 2019. "Minding the Gender Gap Isn't Enough: It's Time to Close It." *Globe and Mail*, 13 March.

Antunes, Pedro. 2004. *Making a Visible Difference: The Contribution of Visible Minorities to Canadian Economic Growth*. Ottawa: Conference Board of Canada.

APTN National News. 2016. "Negative Attitudes toward Indigenous Peoples Highest in the Prairie Provinces, National Poll," 8 June. http://aptnnews.ca/2016/06/08 /negative-attitudes-toward-indigenous-peoples-highest-in-prairie-provinces -national-poll-2.

Archard, Nicole. 2013. "Women's Participation as Leaders in Society: An Adolescent Girls' Perspective." *Journal of Youth Studies* 16(6): 759–75. https://doi.org/10.1080 /13676261.2012.756974.

Archer, Emerald M. 2013. "The Power of Gendered Stereotypes in the US Marine Corps." *Armed Forces and Society* 39(2): 359–91. https://doi.org/10.1177 /0095327x12446924.

Aronson, Joshua, and Michael Inzlicht. 2004. "The Ups and Downs and Attributional Ambiguity: Stereotype Vulnerability and the Academic Self-Knowledge of African American College Students. *Psychological Science* 15(12): 829–36. https://doi .org/10.1111/j.0956-7976.2004.00763.x. Medline:15563328.

Askarinam, Leah. 2016. "Asian Americans Feel Held Back at Work by Stereotypes." *The Atlantic*, 26 January. http://www.theatlantic.com/politics/archive/2016/01 /asianamericans-feel-held-back-at-work-by-stereotypes/458874/.

Asplund, G. 1988. *Women Managers: Changing Organizational Cultures*. Toronto: John Wiley and Sons.

Avolio, B.J., and W.L. Gardner. 2005. "Authentic Leadership Development: Getting to the Root of Positive Forms of Leadership." *Leadership Quarterly* 16(3): 315–38. https://doi.org/10.1016/j.leaqua.2005.03.001.

Ayman, Roya, and Karen Korabik. 2010. "Leadership: Why Gender and Culture Matter." *American Psychologist* 65(3): 157–70. https://doi.org/10.1037/a0018806. Medline:20350015.

Baklid, Bente, et al. 2005. *Business Critical: Maximizing the Talents of Visible Minorities – An Employer's Guide.* Ottawa: Conference Board of Canada.

Banerjee, Rupa. 2008. "An Examination of Factors Affecting Perception of Workplace Discrimination." *Journal of Labour Research* 29: 380–401. https://doi.org/10.1007/s12122-008-9047-0.

Barg, Carolyn J., Brittany Armstrong, Samuel Hertz, and Amy Latimer. 2010. "Physical Disabilities, Stigma, and Physical Activity in Children." *Journal of Disability, Development, and Education* 57(4): 371–82. https://doi.org/10.1080/1034912x.2010.524417.

Barrington, Linda, and Kenneth Troske. 2001. "Workforce Diversity and Productivity: An Analysis of Employer-Employee Matched Data." https://www.researchgate.net/publication/4825660_Workforce_Diversity_and_Productivity_An_Analysis_of_Employer-Employee_Match_Data.

Barta, Thomas, Markus Kleiner, and Tilo Neumann. 2012. "Is There a Payoff from Top-Team Diversity?" McKinsey. http://www.mckinsey.com/business-functions/organization/our-insights/is-there-a-payoff-from-top-team-diversity.

Basow, Susan A. 1992. *Gender: Stereotypes and Roles.* Pacific Grove: Brooks/Cole.

Bass, Bernard M. 1985. *Leadership and Performance beyond Expectations.* New York: Free Press.

– 1996. "Is There Universality in the Full Range Model of Leadership?" *International Journal of Public Administration* 19(6): 731–61. https://doi.org/10.1080/01900699608525119.

Beach, Charles M. 2008. "Canada's Aging Workforce: Participation, Productivity, and Living Standards." In *A Festschrift in Honour of David Dodge*, 197–218. Ottawa: Bank of Canada.

Becher, Jonathan. 2012. "Diversity Drives Innovation." *Forbes*, 10 October. http://www.forbes.com/sites/sap/2012/10/10/diversity-drives-innovation/#1d8ef77f6f90.

Belasen, Alan T. 2012. *Developing Women Leaders in Corporate America: Balancing Competing Demands, Transcending Traditional Boundaries.* Santa Barbara: Praeger/ABC-CLIO.

Bell, David W., and Victoria Esses. 1997. "Ambivalence and Response Amplification toward Native Peoples." *Journal of Applied Social Psychology* 27(12): 1063–84. https://doi.org/10.1111/j.1559-1816.1997.tb00287.x.

Bell, J. 2011. "Why CEOs and HR Should Be Joined at the Hip." SHRM Blog, 6 September. https://blog.shrm.org/blog/why-hr-and-the-ceo-should-be-joined-at-the-hip.

Beltrame, Julian. 2014 (May 21). "Aging Workforce Affecting Canada's Labour Market: RBC." Originally published in the Canadian Press. *The Telegraph*, 2016 (February 9). http://www.thetelegram.com/Business/2014-05-21/article-3733569/Aging-workforce-affecting-Canada%26rsquo%3Bs-labour-market%3A-RBC/1.

Benham, Maenette K.P. 1997. "Silences and Serenades: The Journeys of Three Ethnic Minority Women School Leaders." *Anthropology and Education Quarterly*, 28(2): 280–307. https://doi.org/10.1525/aeq.1997.28.2.280.

Benimadhu, P., and J. Gilson. 2001. *Leadership for Tomorrow: Playing Catch-p with Change*. Ottawa: Conference Board of Canada.

Bennis. W.G. 1959. "Leadership Theory and Administrative Behavior: The Problem of Authority." *Administrative Science Quarterly* 4(2): 259–69. https://doi.org/10.2307/2390911.

Bennis, Warren. 1984. "Transformative Power and Leadership." In *Leadership and Organizational Culture: New Perspectives on Administrative Theory and Practice*, edited by Thomas J. Sergiovanni and Bennis, W., and P.W. Biederman. 1997. *Organizing Genius. Reading*: Addison-Wesley.

Berdahl, Jennifer, and Ji-A Min. 2012. "Prescriptive Stereotypes and Workplace Consequences for East Asians in North America." *Cultural Diversity and Ethnic Minority Psychology* 18(2): 141–52. https://doi.org/10.1037/a0027692. Medline:22506817.

Bernier, Liz. 2013a. "Effective Performance Management Daunting Task for Employers." *Canadian HR Reporter*, 21 October.

– 2013b. "'Identity Conflicts' Holding Women Back." *Canadian HR Reporter*, 21 October.

– 2013c. "Low Participation Plagues Wellness." *Canadian HR Reporter*, 16 December.

– 2013d. "Rising Turnover Cause for Concern." *Canadian HR Reporter*, 18 November.

– 2013e. "Sedentary Lifestyle Rising Concern: Survey." *Canadian HR Reporter*, 2 December.

– 2014a. <WAS 2014> "Diversity Not Just about Compliance." *Canadian HR Reporter*, 10 March.

– 2014b. <WAS 2014> "Leader Isn't a Title." *Canadian HR Reporter*, 24 February.

Berry, John, Rudolf Kalin, and Donald Taylor. 1976. *Multiculturalism and Ethnic Attiudes in Canada*. Ottawa: Supply and Services Canada.

Bhardwaj, Rahul K. 2016. "Boardroom Innovation All Comes Down to Diversity." *Globe and Mail*, 28 November.

Biggles, Michael Dewayne. 2007. "Transformational Leadership Characteristics among Minority Federal Government Managers in California." EdD diss., Pepperdine University, Malibu.

Bilimoria, Diana. 2000. "Building the Business Case for Women Corporate Directors." In *Women on Corporate Boards of Directors: International Challenges and Opportunities*, edited by Ronald J. Burke and Mary C. Mattis, 25–40. Dordrecht: Kluwer Academic.

– 2010. "Building the Business Case for Women Corporate Directors." In *Women on Corporate Boards of Directors: International Challenges and Opportunities*, edited by Ronald J. Burke and Mary C. Mattis, 25–40. Dordrecht: Kluwer Academic.

Billan, Rumeet, and Todd Humber. 2018. *The Tallest Poppy: Successful Women Pay a High Price for Success*. Toronto: *Canadian HR Reporter*. Viewpoint Leadership, and Women of Influence.

Bixby, Irene, 2008. "An Exploration of a Church/Community Partnership for the Provision of After-School Programs for Children with Low-Incidence Disabilities and Their Families." EdD diss., Acadia University, Wolfville.

Bobbitt-Zeher, Donna. 2011. "Gender Discrimination at Work: Connecting Gender Stereotypes, Institutional Policies, and Gender Composition of Workplace." *Gender and Society* 25(6): 764–86.

Bogdan, Robert, and Douglas Biklen. 2013. "Handicapism." In Foundations of Disability Studies, edited by Matthew Wappett and Katrina Arndt, 1–16. New York: Palgrave Macmillan.

Boldry, J., W. Wood, and D.A. Kashy. 2001. Gender Stereotypes and the Evaluation of Men and Women in Military Training. *Journal of Social Issues* 57(4): 689–705.

Boon, Mary van der. 2003. "Women in International Management: An International Perspective on Women's Ways of Leadership." *Gender in Management* 18(3): 132–46. https://doi.org/10.1108/09649420310471091.

Bosak, Janine, and Sabine Sczesny. 2011. "Gender Bias in Leadership Selection? Evidence from a Hiring Simulation." *Sex Roles* 65(3–4): 234–42. https://doi.org /10.1007/s11199-011-0012-7.

Bosner, Kevin. 2008. "Gender Stereotypes and Self-Perceptions among College Students." *Journal of Diversity Management* 3(3): 41–52. https://doi.org/10.19030 /jdm.v3i3.4995.

Bouw, Brenda. 2019. "Canadian Public Firms Score Poorly against Global Peers on Gender Equality, Study Finds." *Globe and Mail*, 8 March.

Boyce, Lisa A., and Ann M. Herd. 2003. "The Relationship between Gender Role Stereotypes and Requisite Military Leadership Characteristics." *Sex Roles: A Journal of Research* 49(7–8): 365–78. https://doi.org/10.1023/a:1025164221364.

Bradshaw, James. 2019. "Banks Will Have to Disclose Diversity Plans as Liberals Point to Need for More Women on Boards." *Globe and Mail*, 20 March.

Bradshaw, P., and D. Wicks. 2010. "The Experiences of White Women on Corporate Boards in Canada: Compliance and Non-Compliance to Hegemonic Masculinity." In *Women on Corporate Boards of Directors: International Challenges and Opportunities*, edited by Ronald J. Burke and Mary C. Mattis, 197–212. Dordrecht: Kluwer Academic.

Brady, Penny, and Denis McLean. 2002. *In the Pipeline or on the Sidelines: Is Your Leadership Development Working for Women?* Ottawa: Conference Board of Canada.

Branson, Douglas M. 2007. *No Seat at the Table: How Corporate Governance and Law Keep Women out of the Boardroom.* New York: NYU Press.

Bratton, Kathleen A. 2005. "Critical Mass Theory Revisited: The Behaviour and Success of Token Women in State Legislatures." *Politics and Gender* 1(1): 97–125. https://doi.org/10.1017/s1743923x0505004x.

Breaugh, James. 2000. "Research on Employee Recruitment: So Many Studies, So Many Remaining Questions." *Journal of Management* 26(3): 405–34. https://doi .org/10.1177/014920630002600303.

–   2008. "Employee Recruitment: Current Knowledge and Important Areas for Future Research." *Human Resource Management Review* 18(3): 103–18. https://doi.org/10.1016/j.hrmr.2008.07.003.

Bright, Debra Antoninette. 2010. "Pioneering Women: Black Women as Senior Leaders in Traditionally White Community Colleges." EdD diss., George Washington University, Washington, DC.

Brinson, Henrietta. 2007. "The Effect of Race and Gender in Organizational Leadership Success: A Study of African American Women and Their Challenges to Become Leaders in Corporate America." PhD diss., Capella University, Minneapolis, MN.

Brizendine, Louann. 2008. "One Reason Women Don't Make It to the C-Suite." *Harvard Business Review*. June. https://hbr.org/2008/06/one-reason-women-dont-make-it-to-the-c-suite.

Brooks, Chad. 2011. "Diverse Staffs Are Happier, More Productive." *Business News Daily*, 14 December. businessnewsdaily.com/1787-staff-hiring-diversity.html.

Brown, David A.H., Debra L. Brown, and Vanessa Anastasopoulos. 2002. *Women on Boards: Not Just the Right Thing … But the "Bright" Thing*. Ottawa: Conference Board of Canada.

Brown, M. 2001. "The Best for Execs." *Canadian Business* 74(21): 105.

Brown, Stephen M. 1979. "Male versus Female Leaders: A Comparison of Empirical Studies." *Sex Roles* 5(5): 595–611. https://doi.org/10.1007/bf00287663.

Burgess, Zena M., and Phyllis Tharenou. 2010. "What Distinguishes Women Nonexecutive Directors form Executive Directors?" In *Women on Corporate Boards of Directors: International Challenges and Opportunities*, edited by Ronald J. Burke and Mary C. Mattis, 111–27. Dordrecht: Kluwer Academic.

Burke, R.J. 1993. "Women on Corporate Boards of Directors." *Equal Opportunities International* 12(6): 5–13. https://doi.org/10.1108/eb010613.

Burke, R.J. 1994. "Women on Corporate Boards of Directors: Views of Canadian Chief Executive Officers." *Women in Management Review* 9(5): 3–10. https://doi.org/10.1108/09649429410066974

Burke, Ronald J. 2010a. "Women on Canadian Corporate Boards of Directors: Still a Long Way to Go." In *Women on Corporate Boards of Directors: International Challenges and Opportunities*, edited by Ronald J. Burke and Mary C. Mattis, 97–109. Dordrecht: Kluwer Academic.

–   2010b."Women on Corporate Boards of Directors: Understanding the Context." In *Women on Corporate Boards of Directors: International Challenges and Opportunities*, edited by Ronald J. Burke and Mary C. Mattis, 170–96. Dordrecht: Kluwer Academic.

Burke, Ronald J., and Mary C. Mattis. 2010. *Women on Corporate Boards of Directors: International Challenges and Opportunities*. Dordrecht: Kluwer Academic.

Burton, Philippe. 2016. "The Art of Corporate Culture: Artwork Spruces Up Walls, Sets Tone for 'Inspirational' Office." *Canadian HR Reporter*, 24 February.

Busine, Mark, Tacy M. Byham, and Stephanie Neal. 2018. *Unleash Hidden Potential: Build Your Competitive Edge through Diversity and Inclusion*. Bridgeville: Development Dimensions International.

Business Week. 1992. "Corporate Women: How Much Progress?" 8 June, 74–83.

Cadsby, C. Bram, Marcos Servatka, and Fei Song. 2012. "How Competitive Are Female Professionals? A Tale of Identity Conflict." http://www.cireqmontreal .com/wp-content/uploads/2012/12/cadsby.pdf.

Campbell, K., and A. Minguez-Vera. 2008. "Gender Diversity in the Boardroom and Firm Financial Performance." *Journal of Business Ethics* 83(3): 435–51. https://doi .org/10.1007/s10551-007-9630-y.

Canada. 2009. *2006 Employment Equity Data Report*. http://www.labour.gc.ca/eng /standards_equity/eq/pubs_eq/eedr/2006/profiles/page16.shtml#disabilities.

– 2014a. *Employment Equity Act: Annual Report 2013*. http://www.labour.gc.ca/eng /standards_equity/eq/pubs_eq/annual_reports/2013/index.shtml.

– 2014b. *2011 Employment Equity Data Report*. Ottawa: Employment and Social Development Canada.

– 2015. *Employment Equity Act: Annual Report, 2014*. http://www.esdc.gc.ca/en /reports/labour_standards/employment_equity_2014.page#h2.2-h3.1.

– 2016a. *Employment Equity Act: Annual Report 2015. Appendix A, Table B*. http:// www.esdc.gc.ca/en/reports/labour_standards/employment _equity_2015.page.

– 2016b. *Federally Regulated Private-Sector Employers and Crown Corporations*. http://www.esdc.gc.ca/en/jobs/workplace/human_rights/employment_equity /crown_corporations.page.

– 2016c. *Work: Unemployment Rates*. http://well-being.esdc.gc.ca/misme-iowb/.3ndic .1t.4r@-eng.jsp?iid=16.

CanadaVisa. 2012. "Citizenship and Immigration Canada Announces New Immigration targets." *Canadian Immigration News*, 27 March.

Canadian Board Diversity Council. 2013. *2013 Annual Report Card*. Toronto.

– 2014. *2014 Annual Report Card*. Toronto. https://www.boarddiversity.ca/sites /default/files/ARC-2014-Final-ENG.pdf.

– 2015. *2015 Annual Report Card*. Toronto. http://boarddiversity.ca/sites/default /files/2015-Annual-Report-Card.pdf.

– 2016. *2016 Annual Report Card*. Toronto. http://www.boarddiversity.ca/sites /default/files/CBDC-Annual-Report-Card-2016.pdf.

– 2018. *Annual Report Card 2018*. Toronto. https://phasenyne.com/wp-content /uploads/2019/03/ARC-Annual-Report-Card-2018.pdf.

– n.d. "Diversity 50." https://www.boarddiversity.ca/diversity-50.

Canadian HR Reporter. 2014a. "More Women in Workforce Boosts Economy." 24 March.

– 2014b. "Women at Work." 24 March.

Canadian Human Rights Commission. 2013a. "What Is Discrimination?" http:// www.chrc-ccdp.gc.ca/eng/content/what-discrimination.

– 2013b. "What Is Harassment?" https://www.chrc-ccdp.gc.ca/eng/content/what -harassment-1.

Canadian Labour Congress. 2008. "Toward Inclusion of People with Disabilities in the Workplace." http://www.canadianlabour.ca/sites/default/files/pdfs/Toward -Inclusion-of-People-with-Disabilities-EN.pdf.

Canadian Press. 2019. "Few Young Canadians Picture a Woman When They Think of a CEO, Survey Finds." *Globe and Mail*, 11 October.

Cann, Arnie, and William D. Siegfried. 1990. "Gender Stereotypes and Dimensions of Effective Leadership Behavior." *Sex Roles: A Journal of Research* 23(7–8): 413–19. https://doi.org/10.1007/bf00289229.

Carless, Sally A. 1998. "Assessing the Discriminant Validity of Transformational Leader Behaviour as Measured by the MLQ (Mulitfactor Leadership Questionnaire)." *Journal of Occupational and Organizational Psychology* 71(4): 353–8.

Carter, David, Frank P. D'Souza, Betty J. Simkins, and W. Gary Simpson. 2007. "The Diversity of Corporate Board Committees and Firm Financial Performance." Working paper. Stillwater: Department of Finance, Oklahoma State University.

Carter, Kathryn, and Carol Spitzack. 1989. *Doing Research on Women's Communication: Perspectives on Theory and Method.* Norwood: Ablex.

Castro, J. 1987. "Staying Home Is Paying Off." *Time*, 26 October.

Catalyst. 1993. *Women on Corporate Boards: The Challenge of Change.* New York.

– 2013. "Why Diversity Matters." New York.http://www.catalyst.org/system/files /why_diversity_matters_catalyst_0.pdf.

– 2014. "Women in Management, Global Comparison." New York. http://www .catalyst.org/knowledge/women-management-global-comparison.

– 2015. "2014 Catalyst Census: Women Board Directors." New York. http://www .catalyst.org/knowledge/2014-catalyst-census-women-board-directors.

Catalyst and the Diversity Institute in Management and Technology, 2007. *Career Advancement in Corporate Canada: A Focus on Visible Minorities ~ Survey Findings.* Toronto.

Catling, Tina. 2013. "Are Men More Innovative Than Women? Does This Have an Effect on Abilities to Run Your Own Innovation Management Consultancy Business?" Think Global Innovation Management. http://www.thethinkteam .com/blog/are-men-more-innovative-than-women-does-this-have-an-effect -on-abilities-to-run-your-own-innovation-management-consultancy-business -from-h.

CBC News. 2014a. *CBC News Poll on Discrimination*, November. https://www .documentcloud.org/documents/1362391-cbc-discrimination-poll-november -2014.html.

– 2014b. "Women on Boards: 7 Provinces Sign On for New OSC Disclosure Rules," 15 October. http://www.cbc.ca/news/business/women-on-boards-7-provinces -sign-on-for-new-osc-disclosure-rules-1.2799604.

CBRE. 2016. "CBRE's New Toronto West Office Is a 'Workplace of the Future.'" 19 July. http://www.cbre.ca/EN/mediacentre/Pages/CBREs-New-Toronto-West -Office-is-a-Workplace-of-the-Future.aspx.

Center for American Progress. n.d. "Discrimination and Dollars." https://cdn
.americanprogress.org/wp-content/uploads/issues/2012/03/pdf/lgbt_biz
_discrimination_infographic.pdf.

Centre for Social Justice. n.d. "Aboriginal Issues." http://www.socialjustice.org/index
.php?page=aboriginal-issues.

Chamorro-Premuzic, Tomas. 2013. "Why Do So Many Incompetent Men Become
Leaders?" *Harvard Business Review*, 22 August. https://hbr.org/2013/08/why-do
-so-many-incompetent-men.

Chaney, Paul. 2012. "Critical Actors vs Critical Mass: The Substantive Representation
of Women in the Scottish Parliament." *British Journal of Politics and International
Relations* 14(3): 441–57. https://doi.org/10.1111/j.1467-856x.2011.00467.x.

Charles, Nickie, and Charlotte Aull Davies. 2000. "Cultural Stereotypes and the
Gendering of Senior Management." *Sociological Review* 48(4): 544–67. https://doi
.org/10.1111/1467-954x.00232.

Cheung, Fanny, and Diane Halpern. 2010. "Women at the Top: Powerful Leaders
Define Success as Work + Family in a Culture of Gender." *American Psychologist*
65(3): 182–93. https://doi.org/10.1037/a0017309.

Childs, Sarah, and Mona Lena Krook. 2006. "Should Feminists Give Up on Critical
Mass? A Contingent Yes." Politics and Gender 2(4): 522–30. https://doi.org/10
.1017/s1743923x06251146.

–   2008. "Critical Mass Theory and Women's Political Representation." Political
Studies 56(3): 725–36. https://doi.org/10.1111/j.1467-9248.2007.00712.x.

Chui, Tina, and Helene Maheux. 2011. *Visible Minority Women*. Statistics Canada
Cat. no. 89-503-X: *Women in Canada: A Gender-Based Statistical Report*. Ottawa:
Minister of Industry.

Chung-Herrera, Beth G., and Melenie Lankau. 2005. "Are We There Yet? An
Assessment of Fit between Stereotypes of Minority Managers and the Successful
Manager Prototype." *Journal of Applied Social Psychology* 35: 2029–56. https://doi
.org/10.1111/j.1559-1816.2005.tb02208.x.

Church, Elizabeth. 2009. "Who's in the Know: Women Surge, Men Sink in
Education's Gender Gap." *Globe and Mail*, 7 December.

Church, Kathryn, et al. 2007. *Doing Disability at the Bank: Discovering the Work of
Learning/Teaching Done by Disabled Bank Employee*. Toronto: Ryerson University
and Royal Bank of Canada.

Cianni, M., and B. Romberger. 1995. "Perceived Racial, Ethnic, and Gender
Differences in Access to Developmental Experiences." *Group and Organizational
Management* 20(4): 440–59. https://doi.org/10.1177/1059601195204004.

CIBC. 2012. "Corporate Responsibility Report and Public Accountability Statement."
https://www.cibc.com/content/dam/about_cibc/corporate_responsibility/pdfs
/cibc-2012-cr-report-full.pdf.

City of Toronto. 2000. "Employment Equity Policy." https://wx.toronto.ca/intra/hr
/policies.nsf/9fff29b7237299b385256729004b844b/755a03e5d9c008fd8525692700
4b786c?OpenDocument.

– 2014. "Talent Blueprint 2014–2018 (Toronto Public Service Workforce Plan)."
25 March. http://www.toronto.ca/legdocs/mmis/2014/ex/bgrd/backgroundfile
-68293.pdf.

City of Toronto, City Manager's Office. n.d. *Corproate Strategic Plan*. Toronto. https://
www.toronto.ca/wp-content/uploads/2019/10/9886-DS-19-0438-Corporate
-Strategic-Plan-V4-MG1.pdf

– n.d. *2015–2016 Strategic Plan*. Toronto: City of Toronto, City Manager's Office,
Equity, Diversity, and Human Rights Division: 15. http://www1.toronto.ca
/City%20Of%20Toronto/Equity,%20Diversity%20and%20Human%20Rights
/Divisional%20Profile/Policies%20-%20Reports/A1503399_Strat_Plan_web.pdf
Accessed on November 29, 2016.

Clark, A.E. 2001. "What Really Matters in a Job? Hedonic Measurement Using Quit
Data." *Labour Economics* 8: 223–42. https://doi.org/10.1016/s0927-5371(01)
00031-8.

Coca Cola. n.d. "Our Company: Workplace Culture." http://www.coca-colacompany
.com/our-company/diversity.

Codjoe, Henry. 2001. "Fighting a 'Public Enemy' of Black Academic Achievement:
The Persistence of Racism and the School Experiences of Black Students in
Canada." *Race, Ethnicity and Education* 4(4): 343–75. https://doi.org/10.1080
/13613320120096652.

Coenders, Marcel, Marcel Lubbers, and Peer Scheepers. 2003. *Majorities' Attitudes
towards Minorities in European Union Member States: Results from the Standard
Eurobarometers 1997–2000–2003*. Vienna: European Monitoring Centre on
Racism and Xenophobia.

Coleman, Baokim N. 2010. "A Study of Success Characteristics of East Asian
American Executives in Corporate America." EdD diss., Pepperdine University,
Malibu.

Collard, John. 2009. "Constructing Theory for Leadership in Intercultural Contexts."
In *Leadership and Intercultural Dynamics*, edited by John Collard and Anthony H.
Normore, 3–22. Charlotte: Information Age.

Collard, John, and Anthony H. Normore, eds. 2009. *Leadership and Intercultural
Dynamics*. Charlotte: Information Age.

Collins, Michael. 2011. "Innovation Driven by Diversity Is the Cornerstone of
Globalization." Diversity Best Practices. http://www.diversitybestpractices.com
/news-articles/innovation-driven-diversity-cornerstone-globalization.

Collinson, D., and J. Hearn. 1994. "Naming Men as Men: Implications for Work,
Organization, and Management," *Gender, Work, and Organization* 1(1): 2–22.

Comi, Simona, Mara Grasseni, Federica Origo, and Laura Pagani. 2016. "Quotas
Have Led to More Women on Corporate Boards in Europe." LSE, 30 September.
https://blogs.lse.ac.uk/businessreview/2016/09/30/quotas-have-led-to-more
-women-on-corporate-boards-in-europe/.

Conference Board of Canada. 2013. "He Says, She Says: Gender Gap Persists in
Attitudes toward Women's Advancement in the Workplace." 15 May. https://www

.newswire.ca/news-releases/he-says-she-says-gender-gap-persists-in-attitudes
-toward-womens-advancement-in-the-workplace-512416061.html.

Conger, J.A., D. Finegold, and E.E. Lawler III. (1998). "CEO Appraisals: Holding
Corporate Leadership Accountable." *Organizational Dynamics*, Summer, 7–20.
https://doi.org/10.1016/s0090-2616(98)90037-7.

Coren, Michael J. 2018. "California Is the First State to Require a Woman on
Company Boards." *Quartz at Work*, 1 October. https://qz.com/work/1408819
/california-is-the-first-us-state-to-mandate-a-board-quota-for-women.

– 2012b. "Visible Minority and Aboriginal Representation on Canadian Boards."
20 November. http://corporateknights.com/report/2012-diversity-index/visible
-minority-aboriginal-representation-canadian-boards.

Coyhis, Don. 1995. *Wisdom of the People*. Colorado Springs: White Bison.

Cranwell-Ward, Jane, Patricia Bossons, and Sue Gover. 2004. *Mentoring: A Henley
Review of Best Practice*. London: Palgrave Macmillan.

Creedon, Pamela, and Judith Carmer, eds. 2007. *Women in Mass Communication*.
Thousand Oaks: Sage.

Crisp, Dave. 2014. "How Do Top-Notch Leaders Develop?" *Canadian HR Reporter*,
24 February.

Cukier, Wendy. 2007. *Diversity – The Competitive Edge: Implications for the
ICT Labour Market – A Report Submitted to the Information and
Communications Technology Council (ICTC)*. Toronto: Diversity Institute,
Ryerson University.

Curry, Bill, and Teremy Torobin. 2011. "Canada Shrinking, Aging Work Force Poses
Economic Problems: Statscan." *Globe and Mail*, 17 August. http://www
.theglobeandmail.com/report-on-business/economy/jobs/canadas-shrinking
-aging-work-force-poses-economic-problems-statscan/article590840.

Dagher, Rola. 2018. "Diversity Is Integral to Building a Strong, Adaptable Work
Force." *Globe and Mail*, 29 October.

Dahlerup, Drude, 1988. "From a Small to a Large Minority: Women in Scandinavian
Politics." *Scandinavian Political Studies* 11(4): 275–98. https://doi.org/10.1111
/j.1467-9477.1988.tb00372.x.

– 2006. "The Story of the Theory of Critical Mass." *Politics and Gender* 2(4): 511–22.
https://doi.org/10.1017/s1743923x0624114x.

Daily, Catherine M., S. Trevos Certo, and Dan R. Dalton. 2010. "The Future of
Corporate Women: Progress towards the Executive Suite and the Boardroom?"
In *Women on Corporate Boards of Directors: International Challenges and
Opportunities*, edited by Ronald J. Burke and Mary C. Mattis, 000–000.
Dordrecht,: Kluwer Academic.

Dalton, D.R., J.W. Hill, and R.R. Ramsey. 1997. "Women as Managers and Partners:
Context Specific Predictors of Turnover in International Public Accounting
Firms." *Auditing Practice and Theory*, 16: 29–50.

Daniels, Sally, Bradford Fay, and Nicholas Tortorello. 1998. *Public Perspective*
(December–January): 47–9.

Darden, Derrick. 2012. "The Impact of Transformational Leadership Styles among Minority Leaders in the Federal Government." PhD diss., Capella University, Minneapolis.

D'Aveni, R.A. 1990. "Top Managerial Prestige and Occupational Bankruptcy." *Organization Science* 1: 121–42.

Davidson, Marilyn, and Cary L. Cooper. 1992. *Shattering the Glass Ceiling: The Woman Manager*. London: Paul Chapman.

Davies, Carole Boyce. 2011. "'She Wants the Black Man Post': Construction of Race, Sexuality, and Political Leadership in Popular Culture." *Agenda* 25(4): 121–33. https://doi.org/10.1080/10130950.2011.633371.

Davies, Paul, Steven Spencer, and Claude Steele. 2005. "Clearing the Air: Identity Safety Moderates the Effects of Stereotypes Threat on Women's Leadership Aspiration." *Journal of Personality and Social Psychology* 88(2): 276–87. https://doi.org/10.1037/0022-3514.88.2.276. Medline:15841859.

Deitch, Elizabeth, Adam Barsky, Rebecca M. Butz, Suzanne Chan, and Arthur P. Brief. 2003. "Subtle Yet Significant: The Existence and Impact of Everyday Racial Discrimination in the Workplace." *Human Relations* 56(11): 1299–1324. https://doi.org/10.1177/00187267035611002.

Denning, Steve. 2011. "How Do You Change an Organizational Culture?" *Forbes*, 23 July. http://www.forbes.com/sites/stevedenning/2011/07/23/how-do-you-change-an-organizational-culture/#3ef00b0b3baa.

Dennis, Jeffrey. 2012. "Men, Masculinities, and the Cave Man." In *The Handbook of Gender, Sex, and Media*, edited by Karen Ross, 105–17. Toronto: John Wiley and Sons.

Devarachetty, Shilpika. 2013. "Women as Charismatic Leaders." PhD diss., University of Akron.

Devereux, Mike, and Amanda Linett. 2013. "Striving for Greater Gender Diversity on Boards." Strikeman Elliott, 1 November. https://www.stikeman.com/en-ca/kh/canadian-securities-law/striving-for-greater-gender-diversity-on-boards.

Dion K.L. 1989. "Ethnicity and Perceived Discrimination: A Comparative Survey of Six Ethnic Groups in Toronto." Paper presented at the 10th Biennial Conference of the Canadian Ethnic Studies Association, Calgary, 18–21 October.

Dion, K.L., and K. Kawakami. 1996. "Ethnicity and Perceived Discrimination in Toronto: Another Look at the Personal/Group Discrimination Discrepancy." *Canadian Journal of Behavioural Science* 28: 203–13.

DiversityInc Staff. 2012. "8 CEOs Whose Inclusive Styles Change Corporate Culture." DiversityInc, 1 November. http://www.diversityinc.com/diversity-management/8-ceos-whose-inclusive-styles-change-corporate-cultures.

– 2016a. "The 2016 DiversityInc. Top 50 Companies for Diversity." DiversityInc, 20 April. https://www.diversityinc.com/2016-diversityinc-top-50-companies-diversity.

– 2016b. "2016 Top 50 Facts and Figures. DiversityInc, 20 April. https://www.diversityinc.com/2016-top-50-facts-figures-2.

Diversity Institute, 2020. "DiversityLeads 2020 – Diverse Representation in Leadership: A Review of Eight Canadian Cities." Ted Rogers School of Management, Ryerson University.

Dixon, Jeffrey, and Michael Rosenbaum. 2004. "Nice to Know You? Test Contact, Cultural, and Group Threat Theories of Anti-Black and Anti-Hispanic Stereotypes." *Social Science Quarterly* 85(2): 257–80. https://doi.org/10.1111/j.0038-4941.2004.08502003.x.

Dizikes, Peter. 2014. "Study: Workplace Diversity Can Help the Bottom Line." *MIT News*, 7 October. http://news.mit.edu/2014/workplace-diversity-can-help-bottom-line-1007.

Dobby, Christine. 2019. "Women in Senior Legal Roles Make Gains on Public Boards." *Globe and Mail*, 18 November.

Dobson, Sarah. 2014. "Female MBAs Seeing Less Pay, Lower Job Levels, and Fewer Key Career Opportunities: Survey." *Canadian HR Reporter*, 27 January. https://www.hrreporter.com/news/hr-news/female-mbas-seeing-less-pay-lower-job-levels-and-fewer-key-career-opportunities-survey/315198.

Dodd, F. 2012. "Women Leaders in the Creative Industries: A Baseline Study." *International Journal of Gender and Entrepreneurship* 4(2): 153–78.

Dovidio, John, John C. Brigham, Blair T. Johnson, and Samuel L. Gaertner, 1996. "Stereotyping, Prejudice, and Discrimination: Another Look." In *Stereotypes and Stereotyping*, edited by Neil Macrae, Charles Stangor, and Miles Howstone, 276–319. New York: Guilford Press.

Drucker, Peter F. 2002. "The Discipline of Innovation." *Harvard Business Review*, August. https://hbr.org/2002/08/the-discipline-of-innovation.

Dujon, Genither. 2010. "Women and Leadership: Towards a Gender, Race, and Class Analysis." MA thesis, Ontario Institute for Studies in Education, University of Toronto.

Dunk, Thomas. 1991. *It's a Working Man's Town: Male Working-Class Culture in Northwestern Ontario*. Montreal and Kingston: McGill–Queen's University Press.

Dwyer, Rocky. 2003. "Career Progression Factors of Aboriginal Executives in the Canadian Federal Public Service." *Journal of Management Development* 22(10): 881–9. https://doi.org/10.1108/02621710310505476.

Eades, Diana. 1994. "A Case of Communicative Clash: Aboriginal English and the Legal System." In *Language and the Law*, edited by John Gibbons, 234–64. London: Routledge.

Eagly, Alice H., and Mary C. Johannesen-Schmidt, 2001. "The Leadership Styles of Women and Men." *Journal of Social Issues* 57(4): 781–97.

Eagly, Alice H., and Steven Karau. 2002. "Role Congruity Theory of Prejudice toward Female Leaders. *Psychological Review* 109(3): 573–98. https://doi.org/10.1037/0033-295x.109.3.573. Medline:12088246.

Eagly, Alice H., Steven Karau, and Mona Makhijani. 1995. "Gender and the Effectiveness of Leaders: A Meta-Analysis." *Psychological Bulletin* 117(1): 125–45. https://doi.org/10.1037/0033-2909.117.1.125. Medline:7870858

Ecklund, Elaine H. 2006. "Organizational Culture and Women's Leadership: A Study of Six Catholic Parishes." *Sociology of Religion* 67(1): 81–98. https://doi.org /10.1093/socrel/67.1.81.

Edlund, Carol J. 1992. "Humanizing Organizational Systems: Learning from Women's Leadership Styles." Conference Papers and Proceedings, Society for the Study of Social Problems.

Eichler, Leah. 2016. "Two-Thirds of Employees Are Ready to Jump." *Globe and Mail*, 1 October.

Eisenhart, Joann M. 2006. "The Meaning and Use of Power among Female Corporate Leaders." PhD diss., Fielding Graduate University, Santa Barbara.

Ekos Politics. 2013. *Attitudes to Immigration and Visible Minorities: A Historical Perspective.* http://www.ekospolitics.com/wp-content/uploads/full_report _immigration_february_26_2013.pdf.

Elliott, James R., and Ryan A. Smith. 2004. "Race, Gender, and Workplace Power." *American Sociological Review* 69(3): 365–86. https://doi.org/10.1177 /000312240406900303.

Emmons, Garry, Julia Hanna, and Roger Thompson. 2012. "Five Ways to Make Your Company More Innovative." *Working Knowledge*, 23 May. http://hbswk.hbs.edu /item/five-ways-to-make-your-company-more-innovative.

Eng, Phoebe. 2009. "The Era of the Bridge Builder: Identifying the Qualities of 'Fluent Leaders.'" *National Civic Review* 98(3): 34–9. https://doi.org/10.1002/ncr.263.

Environics Institute for Survey Research. 2016. *Canadian Public Opinion on Aboriginal Peoples: Final Report.* Toronto.

Erhardt, Nicolas L., James D. Werbel, and Charles B. Shrader. 2003. "Board of Director Diversity and Firm Financial Performance." *Corporate Governance: An International Review* 19 March, 102–11. https://doi.org/10.1111/1467-8683.00011.

Ernst and Young. n.d.a. "Redrawing the Map: Globalization and the Changing World. The New Global Reality." http://www.ey.com/GL/en/Issues/Business-environment /Redrawing-the-map--globalization-and-the-changing-world-of-business---The -new-global-reality.

– n.d.b. "Redrawing the Map: Globalization and the Changing World of Business." http://www.iberglobal.com/Archivos/globalization_changing_world_business_ey.pdf.

Estler, Suzanne E. 1975. "Women as Leaders in Public Education." *Signs* 1(2): 363–86. https://doi.org/10.1086/493227.

European Monitoring Centre on Racism and Xenophobia (EUMC). 2005. *Majorities' Attitudes towards Minorities: Key Findings from the Eurobarometer and the European Social Survey: Summary.* Vienna.

Ewing, Doris W. 2002. "Disability and Feminism: Goffman Revisited." *Journal of Social Work in Disability and Rehabilitation* 1(2): 73–82. https://doi.org/10.1300 /j198v01n02_05.

Fairholm, M. 2004. "Different Perspectives on the Practice of Leadership." *Public Administration Review* 64(5): 577–90. https://doi.org/10.1111/j.1540-6210 .2004.00405.x.

Fine, L., and E.B. Pullins. 1998. "Peer Mentoring in the Industrial Sales Force: An Exploratory Investigation of Men and Women in Developmental Relationships." *Journal of Personal Selling and Sales Management* 18(4): 89.

Fishbein, Cheryl, 1979. "An Investigation of Sex-Role Stereotypes and Assertive Behaviour in Men and Women." PhD diss., State University of New York – Stony Brook.

Flores, Ernest Yutze. 1981. *The Nature of Leadership for Hispanics and Other Minorities*. Saratoga: Century Twenty One.

Flores, Kevin. 2012. "'Leadership Is Behaving and Acting Like a Leader': A Narrative Exploration in the Life Stories of Three Latino Leaders in Healthcare." PhD diss., University of Nebraska, Lincoln.

Foley, Dennis, 2010. "Can We Educate and Train Aboriginal Leaders within Our Tertiary Education Systems?" *Australian Journal of Indigenous Education* 39: 138–50. https://doi.org/10.1375/s1326011100000995.

Foley, Dermot. 2019 (Winter). "Investing in Gender Diversity: Companies Make Better Decisions with Diverse Boards." *Your Guide to Responsible Investing*, 5.

Fondas, Nanette. 2010. "Women on Boards of Directors: Gender Bias or Power Threat?" In *Women on Corporate Boards of Directors: International Challenges and Opportunities*, edited by Ronald J. Burke and Mary C. Mattis, 171–7. Dordrecht: Kluwer Academic.

Ford, J. 2010. "Studying Leadership Critically: A Psychosocial Lens on Leadership Identities." *Leadership* 6: 47–65. https://doi.org/10.1177/1742715009354235.

Foster-Fishman, Pennie, Tiffeny Jimenez, Maria Valenti, and Tasha Kelley. 2007. "Building the Next Generation of Leaders in the Disabilities Movement." *Disability and Society* 22(4): 341–56. https://doi.org/10.1080/09687590701337488.

Freeman, S.J.M. 1990. *Managing Lives – Corporate Women and Social Change*. Amherst: University of Massachusetts Press.

Fuegen, Kathleen. 2007. "The Effects of Gender Stereotypes on Judgments and Decisions in Organizations." *Advances in Group Processes* 24: 79–98. https://doi.org/10.1016/s0882-6145(07)24004-4.

Galabuzi, Grace-Edward, and Sheila Block. 2013. "Whatever You Call It, Discrimination Is Alive and Well in the Workplace." *Globe and Mail*, 14 June. http://www.theglobeandmail.com/opinion/whatever-you-call-it-discrimination-is-alive-and-well-in-the-work-place/article12513864.

Galle, Omer, Candace Wiswell, and Jeffrey Burr. 1985. "Racial Mix and Industrial Productivity." *American Sociological Review* 50: 20–33. https://doi.org/10.2307/2095337.

Gamlem, Cornelia. 2013. "Trend: Wellness Programs Enhance Employee Engagement." *Triple Pundit*, 19 March. http://www.triplepundit.com/2013/03/trend-wellness-programs-enhance-employee-engagement.

Garcia, L.J., J. Barette, and C. Laroche. 1999. "Toward a Social Model on the Integration of Persons with Human Communication Disorders into the Workplace." *International Journal of Practical Approaches to Disability* 23(3): 14–23.

Garcia-Retamero, Rocio, and Esther Lopez-Zafra. 2009. "Causal Attributions about Feminine and Leadership Roles: A Cross-Cultural Comparison." *Journal of Cross-Cultural Psychology* 40(3): 492–509. https://doi.org/10.1177/0022022108330991.

Gardenswartz, Lee, and Anita Rowe. 1998. *Managing Diversity: A Complete Desk Reference and Planning Guide.* New York: McGraw-Hill.

Garnero, Andrea, and Francois Rycx. 2013. "The Heterogeneous Effects of Workforce Diversity on Productivity, Wages, and Profits." Institute for the Study of Labour (IZA). Discussion Paper no. 7350 (April). Bonn: University of Bonn.

George, W. 2003. *Authentic Leadership: Rediscovering the Secrets to Creating Lasting Value.* San Francisco: Jossey-Bass.

Gibbins, Roger, and Rick Ponting. 1986. "Historical Overview and Background." In *Arduous Journey: Canadian Indians and Decolonization*, edited by Rick Ponting, 000–000. Toronto: McClelland and Stewart.

Gionet, Linda. 2009. "First Nations People: Selected Findings of the 2006 Census." *Canadian Social Trends* 11-008-X (no. 87). Statistics Canada (May).

Giscombe, Katherine. 2008. "Career Advancement in Corporate Canada: A Focus on Visible Minorities ~ Workplace Fit and Stereotyping." *Catalyst.* http://www.rbc.com/diversity/research.html.

Giscombe, Katherine, and Laura Jenner. 2009. "Career Advancement in Corporate Canada: A Focus on Visible Minorities ~ Diversity and Inclusive Practices." *Catalyst.* http://www.rbc.com/diversity/docs/diversity_and_inclusion_practices.pdf.

Gitek, Barbara A., and Laurie Larwood, eds. 1987. *Women's Career Development.* Newbury Park: Sage.

Globe and Mail. 2013. "Canada's Best Diversity Employers for 2013," 19 February. http://www.theglobeandmail.com/report-on-business/careers/top-employers/canadas-best-diversity-employers-for-2013/article8678159.

Global Workplace Analytics. n.d. "Latest Work-At-Home/Telecommuting/Mobile Work/Remote Work Statistics." https://globalworkplaceanalytics.com/telecommuting-statistics

Goff, Phillip Atiba, Claude Steele, and Paul Davies. 2008. "The Space between Us: Stereotype Threat and Distance in Interracial Contexts." *Journal of Personality and Social Psychology* 94(1): 91–107. https://doi.org/10.1037/0022-3514.94.1.91. Medline:18179320.

Goleman, D. 1998. "What Makes a Leader?" *Harvard Business Review*, January, 82–91.

Grahn, J., D. Swenson, and R. O'Leary. 2001. "A Comparative Analysis between American Indian and Anglo American Leadership." *Cross Cultural Management* 8: 3–20. https://doi.org/10.1108/13527600110797164.

Grant, Tavia. 2019. "All Industries Lack Gender Diversity on Boards: Data." *Globe and Mail*, 8 May.

Green, M.E. 2002. "Ensuring the Organization's Future: A Leadership Development Case Study." *Public Personnel Management* 31(4): 431–9. https://doi.org/10.1177/009102600203100401.

Green, F. 2004. "Work Intensification, Discretion, and the Decline in Well-Being at Work." *Eastern Economic Journal* 30: 615–25.

Greenfield, Rebecca. 2016. "So What Kind of Performance Review Do You Want, Anyway?" *Bloomberg*, 15 December. https://www.bloomberg.com/news /articles/2016-12-15/so-what-kind-of-performance-review-do-you-want-anyway.

Greenhaus, J., S. Parasuraman, and W. Wormley. 1990. "Effects of Race on Organizational Experiences, Job Performance Evaluations, and Career Outcomes." *Academy of Management Journal* 33(1): 64–86. https://doi.org/10.5465/256352.

Grey, Sandra. 2006. "Numbers and Beyond: The Relevance of Critical Mass in Gender Research." *Politics and Gender* 2(4): 492–502. https://doi.org/10.1017 /s1743923x06221147.

Griffith, P., J. McBride-King, and B. Townsend. 1998. *Closing the Gap: Women's Advancement in Corporate and Professional Canada*. Ottawa: Conference Board of Canada and Catalyst.

Griffiths, Vivienne. 2012. "Women Leaders in Higher Education: Organizational Cultures and Personal Resilience." *GENEROS: Multidisciplinary Journal of Gender Studies* 1(1): 70–94.

Grillo, Gina. 2014. "Diverse Workforces Are More Innovative." *The Guardian*, 27 March. http://www.theguardian.com/media-network/media-network-blog/2014 /mar/27/diversity-innovation-startups-fortune-500-companies.

Gupta-Sunderji, Merge. 2018. "Five Ways to Make 'Flexible Work' Actually Work." *Globe and Mail*, 29 October.

Haddock, G., M.P. Zanna, and V.M. Esses. 1994. "The (Limited) Role of Trait-Laden Stereotypes in Predicting Attitudes toward Native Peoples." *British Journal of Social Psychology* 33(1): 83–106. https://doi.org/10.1111/j.2044-8309.1994.tb01012.x.

Hamilton, Barton, Jack Nickerson, and Hideo Owan. 2004. "Diversity and Productivity in Production Team." http://apps.olin.wustl.edu/workingpapers /pdf/2004-05-001.pdf.

Hamilton, Cheresa Y. 2010. "The Perceptions of African American Administrators Regarding Their Work Experiences at Predominantly White Institutions of Higher Education." Dissertation Abstracts International, A: The Humanities and Social Sciences. Ann Arbor: ProQuest.

Hannawa, Annegret F., and Brian H. Spitzberg, eds. 2015. *Communication Competence*. Berlin: Deutsche Nationalbibliothek.

Hannon, Frances. n.d. *Literature Review of Attitudes towards Disability*. Dublin: National Disability Authority. http://www.ucd.ie/issda/static/documentation/nda /nda-literature-review.pdf.

Hannon, Kerry. 2014. "Are Women Too Timid When They Job Search?" *Forbes*, 11 September. http://www.forbes.com/sites/nextavenue/2014/09/11/are-women -too-timid-when-they-job-search/#46b49e992f83.

Harding, Robert, 2006. "Historical Representations of Aboriginal People in the Canadian News Media." *Diversity and Society* 17(2): 205–35. https://doi .org/10.1177/0957926506058059.

Hartman, Mary S., ed. 1999. *Talking Leadership: Conversations with Powerful Women*. New Brunswick: Rutgers University Press.

Harvey, Michael, and Ronald Riggio, eds. 2011. *Leadership Studies: The Dialogue of Disciplines*. Cheltenham: Edward Elgar.

Hawkins, Naoko. 2013. *Overcoming Barriers to Leadership for Young Women*. Ottawa: Conference Board of Canada.

Hay Group. 2014. "Best Companies for Leadership 2014." http://www.haygroup.com /bestcompaniesforleadership/downloads/Best_Companies_for_Leadership _2014_Executive_summary.pdf.

Heilman, Madeline E. 1995. "Sex Stereotypes and Their Effects in the Workplace: What We Know and What We Don't Know." *Journal of Social Behaviour and Personality* 10(4): 3–26.

Heilman, Madeline E., and Elizabeth Parks-Stanton, 2007. "Gender Stereotypes in the Workplace: Obstacles to Women's Career Progress." *Advances in Group Processes* 24: 47–77.

Helgesen, S. 1990. *The Female Advantage: Women's Ways of Leadership*. New York: Doubleday.

Heller, Trudy. 1982. *Women and Men as Leaders: In Business, Educational, and Social Service Organizations*. South Hadley: J.F. Bergin.

Hellerstein, J.K., D. Neumark, and K.R. Troske. 1999. "Wages, Productivity, and Worker Characteristics: Evidence from Planet-Level Production Functions and Wage Equations." *Journal of Labour Economics* 17(3): 409–46. https://doi.org/10.1086/209926.

Henry, Frances, and Carol Tator. 2002. *Discourses of Domination: Racial Bias in the Canadian English-Language Press*. Toronto: University of Toronto Press.

Herring, Cedric. 2009. "Does Diversity Pay?: Race, Gender, and the Business Case for Diversity." *American Sociological Review* 74(2): 208–24. https://doi.org/10.1177 /000312240907400203.

Hertz, Barry. 2020. "Diversity Database Aims to Quash Exclusionary Hiring in Canadian Film and TV Once and for All." *Globe and Mail*, 9 January.

Hill, Antoinette. 2013. "Are There Differences in Leadership Styles at Local, State, and National/Federal Levels among Advocates for People with Disabilities?" PhD diss., Our Lady of the Lake University, San Antonio.

Hill, S. 1995. "The Social Organization of Boards of Directors." *British Journal of Sociology* 46(2): 245–78. https://doi.org/10.2307/591788.

– 2014. "When I Learned the Value of Diversity for Innovation." *Scientific American*, 1 October. http://www.scientificamerican.com/article/when-i-learned-the-value -of-diversity-for-innovation.

Holton, V.M. 2010. "Taking a Seat on the Board: Women Directors in Britain." In *Women on Corporate Boards of Directors: International Challenges and Opportunities*, edited by Ronald J. Burke and Mary C. Mattis, 000–000. Dordrecht: Kluwer Academic.

HR Council. n.d. "Diversity at Work: Why a Diverse Workplace Matters." http:// hrcouncil.ca/hr-toolkit/diversity-workforce-matters.cfm.

Huddy, Leonie, and Nayda Terkildsen. 1993. "Gender Stereotypes and the Perception of Male and Female Candidates." *American Journal of Political Science* 37(1): 119–47. https://doi.org/10.2307/2111526.

Hughes, Diane, and Mark Dodge. 1997. "African American Women in the Workplace: Relationships between Job Conditions, Racial Bias at Work, and Perceived Job Quality." *American Journal of Community Psychology* 25(5): 581–99. https://doi.org/10.1023/a:1024630816168.

Hughes, Michael, and Steven A. Tuch. 2003. "Gender Differences in Whites' Racial Attitudes: Are Women's Attitudes Really More Favourable?" *Social Psychology Quarterly* 66(4): 384–401. https://doi.org/10.2307/1519836.

Human Rights Tribunal of Ontario. 2017. Baljiwan Singh Sandhu vs Regional Municipality of Peel Police Services Board's Decision (Citation: 2017 HRTO 445).

Humber, Todd. 2014. "Pace Accelerates in Era of Change: Roundtable." *Canadian HR Reporter*, 10 March, 7–8.

Hunt, J.G. 1999. "Transformational/Charismatic Leadership's Transformation of the Field: An Historical Essay." *Leadership Quarterly* 10: 129–44. https://doi .org/10.1016/s1048-9843(99)00015-6.

Huynh, Kenneth, and Benjamin Woo. 2015. "'Asian Fail': Chinese Canadian Men Talk about Race Masculinity, and the Nerd Stereotype." *Social Identities: Journal for the Study of Race, Nation, and Culture* 20(4–5): 1–16. https://doi.org/10.1080 /13504630.2014.1003205.

IAT Corp. n.d. "Implicit Association Test." https://implicit.harvard.edu/implicit /canada/takeatest.html.

Ibarra, Herminia. 1993. "Personal Networks of Women and Minorities in Management: A Conceptual Framework." *Academy of Management Review* 18(1): 56–87. https://doi.org/10.5465/amr.1993.3997507.

Ibarra, Herminia, 1995. "Race, Opportunity, and Diversity of Social Circles in Managerial Networks."*Academy of Management Journal* 38(3): 673–703.

Indira, Doreen. 1979. "South Asian Stereotypes in the Vancouver Press." *Ethnic and Racial Studies* 2(2): 166–89. https://doi.org/10.1080/01419870.1979.9993261.

International Organization for Standardization. n.d. "ISO/TC 260: Human Resource Management." https://committee.iso.org/home/tc260.

Irizarry, Amber H. 2012. "Understanding Diversity: Top Executives' Perceptions of Racial and Ethnic Diversity in Public Relations." MA thesis, Georgia State University, Atlanta. http://scholarworks.gsu.edu/cgi/viewcontent.cgi?article=1092 &context=communication_theses.

Islam, M.R., and M. Jahjah. 2001. "Predictors of Young Australians' Attitudes toward Aboriginals, Asians and Arabs." *Social Behaviour and Personality* 29(6): 569–79. https://doi.org/10.2224/sbp.2001.29.6.569.

Jain, Harish, Parbudyal Singh, and Carol Agocs. 2000. "Recruitment, Selection, and Promotion of Visible Minority and Aboriginal Police Officers in Selected Police Services." *Canadian Public Administration* 43(1): 46–74. https://doi.org/10.1111 /j.1754-7121.2000.tb01560.x.

James, Carl. n.d. "Stereotyping and Its Consequence for Racial Minority Youth." Race Policy Dialogue Papers, Ontario Human Rights Commission. http://www.ohrc .on.ca/en/race-policy-dialogue-papers/stereotyping-and-its-consequence-racial -minority-youth.

Jedwab, Jack. 2008. "Visible Minorities and Education in Canada." https://acs-aec.ca /pdf/polls/12118157146168.pdf.

Johne, Marjo. 2016. "C-Suite Executives Urged to Make Health of Employees a Priority." *Globe and Mail*, 2 November.

Jollevet, Felix. 2008. "African American Police Executive Careers: Influences of Human Capital, Social Capital, and Racial Discrimination." *Police Practice and Research* 9(1): 17–30. https://doi.org/10.1080/15614260801969904.

Joseph, Bob. 2013. "8 Basic Barriers to Aboriginal Employment." http://www.ictinc .ca/8-basic-barriers-to-aboriginal-employment.

Joy, Lois, Nancy Carter, Harvey Wagner, and Sriram Narayanan. 2007. *The Bottom Line: Corporate Performance and Women's Representation on Boards*. New York: Catalyst.

Juniper, Paul. 2014. "Can Your Workforce Thrive in a Global Economy?" *Canadian HR Reporter*, 27 January, 18.

Kadeřabková, A., M. Beneš, M. Rojíček, J. Kahoun, K. Müller, M. Pazour, J. Basl, and J. Pour. 2007. "Innovation and Competitiveness." Working Paper no. V, Centre for Economic Studies. http://www.matematikavsem.cz/data/data/ces-soubory /working-paper/gf_WPV07.pdf.

Kanter, R.M. 1977. *Men and Women of the Corporation*. New York: Basic Books.

Karakowsky, L., and I. Kotlyar. 2012. "Do 'High-Potential' Leadership Programs Really Work?" *Globe and Mail*, 2 January.

Katzenbach, Jon, Caroline Oelschlegal, and James Thomas. 2016. "10 Principles of Organizational Culture." *strategy+business* 82. http://www.strategy-business.com /article/10-Principles-of-Organizational-Culture.

Kendall, Shari, and Deborah Tannen. 1997. "Gender and Language in the Workplace." In *Gender and Discourse*, edited by Ruth Wodak, 81–105. London: Sage.

Kerby, Sophia, and Crosby Burns. 2012. "The Top 10 Economic Facts of Diversity in the Workplace." Center for American Progress, 12 July. https://www .americanprogress.org/issues/labor/news/2012/07/12/11900/the-top-10-economic -facts-of-diversity-in-the-workplace.

Kiladze, Tim. 2019a. "Corporate Star Honoured for His Supporting Role for Women." *Globe and Mail*, 29 April.

– 2019b. "Female Executives Are Still Scarce in Corporate Canada: The Few Who Made It Are Fed Up." *Globe and Mail*, 8 April.

King, P., and W. Zhang. 2010. "Chinese and Western Leadership Models: A Literature Review." *Journal of Management Research* 6(2): 1–21. https://doi.org/10.5296/jmr .v6i2.4927.

Kirkbride, P. 2006. "Developing Transformational Leaders: The Full Range Leadership Model in Action." *Industrial and Commercial Training* 38(1): 23–32. https://doi.org/10.1108/00197850610646016.

Kirkpatrick, S.A., and E.A. Locke. 1991. "Leadership: Do Traits Matter?" *Academy of Management Executive* 5(2): 48–60. https://doi.org/10.5465/ame.1991.4274679.

Kleinsorge, R. 2010. "Expanding the Role of Succession Planning." *T+D*(American Society for Training and Development) (April): 66–69.

Knightbridge, Clarkson Centre for Board Effectiveness, and Institute of Corporate Directors. 2011. *Beyond the CEO: The Role of the Board in Ensuring the Organizations Have the Talent to Thrive.* Research Report. Toronto: Rotman School of Management, University of Toronto.

Kochman, T. 1981. *Black and White Styles in Conflict.* Chicago: University of Chicago Press.

Kopecki, D., 2010. "Women on Wall Street Fall Further Behind." *Bloomberg News,* 7 October.

Kovitz, Jodi. 2019. "In 2019, Your Company's Gender-Diversity Strategy Shouldn't Be a Secondary Focus." *Globe and Mail,* 8 March.

Kramer, Lisa. 2019. "Economics Needs to Acknowledge Its Diversity Problems." *Globe and Mail,* 15 January.

Krumm, Bernita L. 1998. "Leadership Reflections." *Tribal College Journal* 9(3): 24–7.

Kulik, Carol, and Hugh Bainbridge. 2006. "Psychological Perspectives on Workplace Diversity." In *Handbook of Workplace Diversity,* edited by Alison Konrad, Pushkala Prasad, and Judith Pringle, 25–52. London: Sage.

Lafley, A.G. 2011. "The Art and Science of Finding the Right CEO." *Harvard Business Review,* October, 67–74.

Langford, Tom, and Rick Ponting. 1992. "Canadians' Responses to Aboriginal Issues: The Roles of Prejudice, Perceived Group Conflict, and Economic Conservatism." *Canadian Review of Sociology and Anthropology* 29(2): 140–66. https://doi.org/10.1111/j.1755-618x.1992.tb02433.x.

Lapid-Bogda, Ginger. 1998. "Diversity and Organizational Change." http://bogda.com/articles/DiversityandOrgChange.pdf.

Larew, Deborah Kamm. 2011. "Visions: Accounts from Deaf Women in Leadership." PhD diss., University of North Florida, Jacksonville.

Lee, B.A. 1993. "The Legal and Political Realities for Women Managers: The Barriers, the Opportunities, and the Horizon Ahead." In *Women in Management: Trends, Issues, and Challenges in Managerial Diversity,* edited by Ellen A. Fagenson, 246–73. Newbury Park: Sage.

Legace, Martha. 2004. "Racial Diversity Pays Off." *Working Knowledge,* Harvard Business School, 21 June. http://hbswk.hbs.edu/item/racial-diversity-pays-off.

Leighton, David S.R. 1993. "How Can Women Access Boards?" *Women in Management* 4(2): 1, 7.

– 2010. "Making Boards Work." In *Women on Corporate Boards of Directors: International Challenges and Opportunities,* edited by Ronald J. Burke and Mary C. Mattis, 253–61. Dordrecht: Kluwer Academic.

Leitch, Jessica, David Lancefield, and Mark Dawson. 2016. "10 Principles of Strategic Leadership." *strategy+business* 84. http://www.strategy-business.com

/article/10-Principles-of-Strategic-Leadership?gko=25cec&utm_source=itw&utm
_medium=20161208&utm_campaign=resp.

Li, Peter. 2008. "The Market Value and Social Value of Race." In *Daily Struggles: The Deepening Racialization and Feminization of Poverty in Canada*, edited by Maria Wallis and Siu-ming Kwok, 21–33. Toronto: Canadian Scholars Press, 2008.

Lillevik, W. 2007. "Cultural Diversity, Competencies and Behaviour: Workforce Adaptation of Minorities." *Managing Global Transitions* 5(1): 85–102.

Lindstädt, Hagen, Michael Wolff, and Kerstin Fehre. 2011. *Frauen in Führungspositionen: Auswirkungen auf den Unternehmenserfolg*. Institut für Unternehmensführung, Karlsruher Institut für Technologie.

Littrell, Romie F., and Stella M. Nkomo. 2005. "Gender and Race Differences in Leader Behaviour Preferences in South Africa." *Gender in Management* 20(8): 562–80. https://doi.org/10.1108/09649420510635204.

Long, Tom. 2016. "So You Want to Be a Director? Be Warned, It's Not for Everyone." *Globe and Mail*, 22 October.

Lowe, Frank, 2013. "Keeping Leaders White: Invisible Blocks to Black Leadership and Its Denial in White Organizations." *Journal of Social Work Practices* 27(2): 149–62.

Lowell, Anne. 2001. "Communication in Aboriginal Health Care: An Overview." In *Communication and Cultural Knowledge in Aboriginal Health Care*, 3–18. Casuarina: Cooperative Research Centre for Aboriginal and Tropical Health.

Lu, Vanessa. 2016. "Virtually No Change in Getting Woman on Boards in Canada, Stats Show." *Toronto Star*, 28 September. https://www.thestar.com/business /2016/09/28/virtually-no-change-in-getting-woman-on-boards-in-canada-stats -show.html.

Lvy-Garboua, L., C. Montmarquette, and V. Simonnnet. 2007. "Job Satisfaction and Quits." *Labour Economics* 14: 251–68. https://doi.org/10.1016/j.labeco.2005.08.003.

MacDougall, Andrew, et al. 2019. *2019 Diversity Disclosure Practices: Women in Leadership Roles at TSX-Listed Companies*. Toronto: Osler, Hoskin and Harcourt LLP. https://www.osler.com/osler/media/Osler/reports/corporate-governance /2019-Diversity-Disclosure-Practices-Women-in-leadership-roles-at-TSX-listed -companies.pdf.

Mack, Yvette E. 2011. "Women in the C-Suite: A Study of How Succession Planning May Best Be Utilized for Career Advancement of Medical College Executives." PhD diss., Capella University.

Maddox, S., and D. Parkin. 1993. "Gender Cultures: Women's Choices and Strategies at Work." *Women in Management Review* 8(2): 3–9.

Maher, Karen. 1997. "Gender-Related Stereotypes of Transformational and Transactional Leadership." *Sex Roles* 37(3–4): 209–25. https://doi.org/10.1023 /a:1025647811219.

Maher, Mary Lou, and Elio Luongo. 2019. "Integrating More Immigrant Women into Canada's Work Force Is Vital." *Globe and Mail*, 8 March.

Mahtani, Minelle. 2004. "Mapping Race and Gender in the Academy: The Experiences of Women of Colour Faculty and Graduate Students in Britain, the

US, and Canada. *Journal of Geography in Higher Education* 28(1): 91–9. https://doi.org/10.1080/0309826042000198666.

Malenfant, Caron, Andre Lebel, and Laurent Martel. 2010. "Projections of the Diversity of Canadian Population, 2006 to 2031." Ottawa: Statistics Canada. http://www.statcan.gc.ca/pub/91-551-x/91-551-x2010001-eng.htm.

March, James G. 1984. "How We Talk and How We Act: Administrative Theory and Administrative Life." In *Leadership and Organizational Culture: New Perspectives on Administrative Theory and Practice*, edited by Thomas J. Sergiovanni and John E. Corbally, 18–35. Champaign: University of Illinois Press, 1984.

Marshall, J. 1984. *Women Managers: Travellers in a Male World.* Chichester: John Wiley and Sons.

– 1995. *Women Managers Moving On: Exploring Career and Life Choices.* New York: Routledge.

Martin, P.Y. 1993. "Feminist Practice in Organizations: Implications for Management." In *Women in Management: Trends, Issues, and Challenges in Managerial Diversity*, edited by Ellen A. Fagenson, 274–96. Newbury Park: Sage.

Mattis, Mary. 2010. "Women Corporate Directors in the United States." In *Women on Corporate Boards of Directors: International Challenges and Opportunities*, edited by Ronald J. Burke and Mary C. Mattis, 43–56. Dordrecht: Kluwer Academic.

Mayhew, Ruth. 2016. "How Does Culture Impact HR Policies?" *Chron.* http://smallbusiness.chron.com/culture-impact-hr-policies-61558.html.

Mayovich, Minako Kurokawa. 1972. "Stereotypes and Racial Images: White, Black, and Yellow." *International Journal of Social Psychiatry* 18(4): 239–53. https://doi.org/10.1177/002076407201800402.

McAdams, D. Claire. 1991. "Environmental Activism and the Intersection of Race, Class, and Gender: Patterns in Central Texas." Conference Papers and Proceedings, American Sociological Association.

McCauley, C., R. Moxley, and E. Van Velsor, 1998. *Handbook of Leadership Development.* Greensboro: Centre for Creative Leadership.

McGee, Laura, and Camilla Sutton. 2019. "Culture, influence, and measurement are the secret to accelerating diversity." *Globe and Mail.* https://www.theglobeandmail.com/business/commentary/article-culture-influence-and-measurement-are-the-secret-sauce-to

McDaniel, Catherine M. 2007. "Leadership Styles of Female Educational Leaders and Female Police Leaders: A Comparative Study." EdD. diss., Northern Arizona University.

McDiarmid, Jessica. 2016. "Canada's Best MBAs I 2016." *Canadian Business*, 23 June. http://www.canadianbusiness.com/lists-and-rankings/best-mba-programs/why-arent-women-enrolling-in-canadas-mba-schools.

McFarland, J. 2012. <WAS 2012a> "Women's Work." *Globe and Mail*, 26 November.

– 2015. "Women, Minorities Making Gains on Corporate Boards, Report Says." *Globe and Mail*, 19 November.

– 2016. "Companies Drag Feet on Board." *Globe and Mail*, 29 September. http://globe2go.newspaperdirect.com/epaper/viewer.aspx.

– 2019. "TD Study Calls for Regulators to Stay the Course on Gender Disclosure Policies." *Globe and Mail*, 27 March.

McGee, Mickey Patrick. 2003. "An Examination of the Impact of the Americans with Disabilities Act on Monterey-Salinas Transit: Implementation of an Unfunded Public Policy." *Dissertation Abstracts International, A: The Humanities and Social Sciences*, 64(5) (November).

McKinsey & Company. 2013. *Women Matter: A Latin American Perspective. Unlocking Women's Potential to Enhance Corporate Performance*. New York.

– 2015. *The Power of Parity: How Advancing Women's Equality Can Add $12 Trillion to Global Growth*. New York.

McLeod, Martha. 2002. "Keeping the Circle Strong: Learning about Native American Leadership." *Tribal College Journal* 13(4): 10.

McLeod, Saul. 2008. "Social Identity Theory." *Simply Psychology*. http://www.simplypsychology.org/social-identity-theory.html.

McLoughlin, J. 1992. *Up and Running: Women in Business*. London: Virago Press.

McLure, Beverley, and Tony Stanco. 1996. "The Peloton: Riding the Winds of Change." *Leadership Abstracts* 9(12): 1–8.

McNelly, Allison, and Stefanie Batcho-Lino. 2016. "Gender Disparity: Quotas May Be Only Way." *Globe and Mail*, 17 November.

MediaCorp Canada. 2016a. "Canada's Top 100 Employers (2016). http://www.canadastop100.com/diversity.

– 2016b. Canada's Top 100 Employers (2017). http://www.canadastop100.com/national.

Menendez, Robert. 2010. *Corporate Diversity Report*. http://www.menendez.senate.gov/imo/media/doc/CorporateDiversityReport2.pdf.

Mercer. 2013. *2013 Global Management Performance Survey Report: Executive Summary*. https://www.mercer.com/content/dam/mercer/attachments/global/Talent/Assess-BrochurePerfMgmt.pdf.

Merton, Ennette Y. 2014. "Leadership Traits and Characteristics of Elected California Women Political Leaders." EdD diss., Pepperdine University, Malibu.

Metoyer, Cheryl A. 2010. "Leadership in American Indian Communities: Winter Lessons." *American Indian Culture and Research Journal* 34(4): 1–12. https://doi.org/10.17953/aicr.34.4.m78g416545510r18.

Meyer, Erin. 2015. "When Culture Does Not Translate." *Harvard Business Review*, October, 66–72. https://hbr.org/2015/10/when-culture-doesnt-translate.

Midanik, Jonah, and Frederique Roy-Boulet. 2019. "Women Make Up More Than Half of Our Tech Team: Here's How We Did It." *Globe and Mail*, 1 April.

Miller, Dorothy L. 1978. "Native American Women: Leadership Images." *Integrated Education* 91: 37–9. https://doi.org/10.1080/0020486780160108.

Miller, Sandra, and James Tucker. 2013. "Diversity Trends, Practices, and Challenges in Financial Services Industry." *Journal of Financial Service Professionals*, November, 46–58.

Mills, D. Quinn. 2005. "Asian and American Leadership Styles: How Are They Unique?" *HBS Working Knowledge,* 27 June.

Milstead, David. 2019. "Board Appointments of Women Hit Five-Year Low." *Globe and Mail,* 27 February.

Mohr, Tara Sophia. 2014. "Why Women Don't Apply for Jobs Unless They're 100% Qualified." *Harvard Business Review,* 25 August. https://hbr.org/2014/08/why -women-dont-apply-for-jobs-unless-theyre-100-qualified.

Moran, Dave. 2019. "Tech Companies Can Boost Their Diversity with These Hiring Practices." *Globe and Mail,* 31 October.

Murray, Alan. n.d. "How to Change Your Organization's Culture." *Wall Street Journal.* http://guides.wsj.com/management/innovation/how-to-change-your -organizations-culture/.

Nadim, A., and P. Singh. 2008. "Do All Institutions Benefit from Leadership Training? A Systems Inquiry." *Journal of Leadership Studies* 1(4): 74–83. https:// doi.org/10.1002/jls.20034.

National Center for Public Policy and Higher Education. 2005. "Fact #1: The U.S. Workforce Is Becoming More Diverse." *Policy Alert,* November.

Nicholson, N., and M.A. West. 1988. *Managerial Job Change: Men and Women in Transition.* Cambridge: Cambridge University Press.

Nicola, Tea. 2019. "Universal Child Care Is Key to Seeing More Women in Executive Roles." *Globe and Mail,* 7 October.

Northcraft, G.B., and B. Gutek. 1993. "Point-Counterpoint: Discrimination against Women in Management – Going, Going, Gone, or Going But Never Gone?" In *Women in Management: Trends, Issues, and Challenges in Managerial Diversity,* edited by Ellen A. Fagenson, 219–45. Newbury Park: Sage.

O'Day, Bonnie, and Susan Foley. 2008. "What Do We Know and Not Know about Women with Disabilities in the Workplace?" *Impact* 21(1): 4–5, 35. https://ici .umn.edu/products/impact/211/211.pdf.

Ohlott, P.J., and M. Hughes-James. 1997. "Single Gender and Single Race Leadership Development Programs: Concerns and Benefits." *Leadership in Action* 17(4): 8–12.

Ohlott, P.J., M.N. Ruderman, and C.D. McCauley. 1994. "Gender Differences in Managers' Developmental Job Experiences." *Academy of Management Journal* 37(1): 46–67. https://doi.org/10.2307/256769.

O'Kane, Josh. 2017. "Canadian Executives Say Sexual Harassment Isn't an Issue at Their Companies: Report." *Report on Business, Globe and Mail,* 18 December. https://www.theglobeandmail.com/report-on-business/canadian-executives-say -sexual-harassment-isnt-an-issue-at-their-company-report/article37359943.

Olsen, Deborah, Sue Maple, and Frances Stage. 1995. "Women and Minority Faculty Job Satisfaction: Professional Role Interests, Professional Satisfactions, and Institutional Fit." *Journal of Higher Education* 66(3): 267–93. https://doi .org/10.2307/2943892.

Olsson, Cecillia, 2006. "The Kaleidoscope of Communication: Different Perspectives on Communication Involving Children with Severe Multiple Disabilities." EdD diss., Stockholm Institute of Education.

O'Neill, Ashley. 2016. "The New Frontier in Health and Wellness: The Office." *Globe and Mail*, 3 December.

Ontario Federal of Indian Friendship Centres. 2013. *Urban Aboriginal Labour Force and Training Strategic Framtionwork: Identifying Our Potential*. Toronto. http://www.ofifc.org/sites/default/files/docs/2013-04-17%20Labour%20Force%20and%20Training%20Strategy%20-%20FINAL.pdf.

Ontario Ministry of Finance. 2014. News release: "Increasing Gender Diversity in Corporate Leadership," 2 December. http://news.ontario.ca/mof/en/2014/12/increasing-gender-diversity-in-corporate-leadership.html.

Ontario Securities Commission. 2014. News release: "Canadian Securities Regulators Finalize Rule Amendments Regarding Disclosure of Women on Boards and in Senior Management," 15 October. https://www.osc.gov.on.ca/en/NewsEvents_nr_20141015_csa-regarding-disclosure-of-women.htm.

O'Reilly, Charles A. III, and Brian G.M. Main. 2012. "Women in the Boardroom: Symbols or Substance?" Stanford Graduate School of Business Research Paper 2098, Stanford.

Organ, D.W., 1988. Organizational Citizenship Behaviour: The Good Soldier Syndrome. Lexington: Lexington Books.

Organ, Dennis W., Philip M. Podsakoff, and Scott Bradley MacKenzie. 2006. *Organizational Citizenship Behaviour: Its Nature, Antecedents, and Consequences.* Newbury Park: Sage.

Orser, Barbara. 2000. *Creating High Performance Organizations: Leveraging Women's Leadership*. Ottawa: Centre of Excellence for Women's Advancement, Conference Board of Canada.

Ospina, S., and E. Foldy. 2009. "A Critical Review of Race and Ethnicity in the Leadership Literature: Surfacing Context, Power, and the Collective Dimensions of Leadership." *Leadership Quarterly* 20(6): 876–96. https://doi.org/10.1016/j.leaqua.2009.09.005.

Page, Steward, and Samantha Meretsky. 1998. "Gender Stereotypes and Perceptions of Men, Women, and 'Persons' in the Workforce." *Employee Assistance Quarterly* 14(1): 23–32. https://doi.org/10.1300/j022v14n01_02.

Park, Justin H., Jason Faulkner, and Mark Schaller. 2003. "Evolved Disease-Avoidance Processes and Contemporary Anti-Social Behaviour: Prejudicial Attitudes and Avoidance of People with Physical Disabilities." *Journal of Nonverbal Behaviour* 27(2): 65–87. https://doi.org/10.1177/1368430204046142.

Parker, Patricia S. 2005. *Race, Gender, and Leadership: Re-Envisioning Organizational Leadership from the Perspectives of African American Women Executives*. Mahwah: Lawrence Erlbaum Associates.

Patel, Arti. 2019. "Majority of Canadian Women Know Other Women Who Have Been Sexually Harassed: Report." Global News, 26 March. https://globalnews.ca/news/5097065/sexual-harassment-canada.

Patton, A., and J.C. Baker. 1987. "Why Directors Won't Rock the Boat." *Harvard Business Review* 65: 10–12, 16, 18.

Perez, Alycia L. 2013. "Gendered Expectations of Leaders and the Androgyny of Leadership." PhD diss., University of Akron.

Pernick, R. 2001. "Creating a Leadership Development Program: Nine Essential Tasks. *Public Personnel Management* 30(4): 429–44. https://doi.org/10.1177/009102600103000401.

Petersen, Lars-Eric, and Joerg Dietz. 2006. "Prejudice and Enforcement of Workforce Homogeneity as Explanations for Employment Discrimination." *Journal of Applied Social Psychology* 35(1): 144–59. https://doi.org/10.1111/j.1559-1816.2005.tb02097.x.

Pettigrew, A. 1992. "On Studying Managerial Elites." *Strategic Management Journal* 13(S2): 163–82. https://doi.org/10.1002/smj.4250130911.

Pfaff, Larry. n.d. "Women versus Men as Managers: Are They Different?" SELECTPro. http://www.selectpro.net/index.php/ScrArtWomenMen.html.

Picou-Broadnax, Amber. 2010. "African American College Women in the San Francisco Bay Area: Perceptions of Cross's Nigrescence Model and Potential Leadership Style." EdD diss., University of San Francisco.

Pinto, Fred, and Peter Chapman. 2016. "Investors Must Speak Up about Corporate Inequality." *Globe and Mail*, 28 November.

Piotrkowski, Chaya S.,1998. Gender Harassment, Job Satisfction, and Distress among Employed White and Minority Women." *Journal of Occupational Health Psychology*,3(1): 33–43.

Pointer, M.P., 2001. "The Relationship between Transformational Leadership, Self-Reported Knowledge, Education, Educational Relevancy, and Experience among State Vocational Rehabilitation Directors and Rehabilitation Rate." Ed.D. diss., George Washington University.

Pollak, Merle. 2010. "Catalyst Corporate Board Placement: New Seats at the Table." In *Women on Corporate Boards of Directors: International Challenges and Opportunities*, edited by Ronald J. Burke and Mary C. Mattis, 263–9. Dordrecht: Kluwer Academic.

Pollard, Diane S. 1997. "Race, Gender, and Educational Leadership: Perspectives from African American Principals." *Educational Policy* 11(3): 353–74. https://doi.org/10.1177/0895904897011003005.

Powell, R.M. 1969. *Race, Religion, and the Promotion of the American Executive.* Columbus: Ohio State University Press.

PricewaterhouseCooper. 2015–16. "Where Are Future Leaders Hidden?" http://www.pwc.co.uk/services/human-resource-services/human-resource-consulting/where-are-future-leaders-hidden.html.

Ramirez, A. 2005–6. "Hispanic Leadership Development and Its Policy Impact." *Harvard Journal of Hispanic Policy* 18: 85–9.

Ramsundar, Susan. 2006. "The Leadership Styles of Female African American Administrators at the Deans Level and Higher." PhD diss., Morgan State University, Baltimore.

Rana, Kaur B., C. Kaghan, S. Lewis, and U. Rout, 1998. "British South Asian Women Managers and Professionals: Experiences of Work and Family." *Women in Management Review* 13(6): 221–32.

Rao, Jay, and Joseph Weintraub. 2013. "How Innovative Is Your Company's Culture?" MIT Sloan Management Review, Spring. http://sloanreview.mit.edu/article/how -innovative-is-your-companys-culture/.

Raskin, Carl, 1994. "Employment Equity for the Disabled in Canada." *International Labour Review* 133(1): 75–88.

Reitz, Jeffrey G., and Rupa Banerjee. 2007. "Racial Inequality, Social Cohesion, and Policy Issues in Canada." In *The Art of the State, vol. 3: Belonging? Diversity, Recognition, and Shared Citizenship in Canada*, edited by Keith Banting, Thomas Courchene, and F. Leslie Seldie. Montreal: Institute for Research on Public Policy. https://irpp.org/wp-content/uploads/2014/08/reitz.pdf.

Reynolds, Jennifer. 2015. "Corporate Canada Needs a Plan for Diversity in the Boardroom." *Globe and Mail*, 22 October.

– 2016. "A Role for Men in Canada's Gender Diversity Challenge." *Globe and Mail*, 24 October.

RHR International. 2012. "Inside CEO Succession: First Steps." *Executive Insight* 28(2): 1–2.

Roberts, Lance W., et al. 2005. *Recent Social Trends in Canada, 1960–2000*. Montreal and Kingston: McGill–Queen's University Press.

Robinson, Marcus, Charles Pfeffer, and Joan Buccigrossi. 2003. *Business Case for Inclusion and Engagement*. Rochester: wetWare.

Roby, Pamela, 1998. "Gender, Emotions, and Leadership: Perspectives from Ten Trade Unions." Conference Paper and Proceedings, American Sociological Association Scales, 2011.

Rodgers, James. 2017. "Managing Culture and Diversity in the Modern Workplace." James Rodgers: The Diversity Coach. http://thediversitycoach.com/managing -culture-diversity-in-the-modern-workplace.

Rodler, Christa, Erich Kirchler, and Erik Hölzl. 2001. "Gender Stereotypes of Leaders: An Analysis of the Contents of Obituaries from 1978 to 1994." *Sex Roles* 45(11– 12): 827–43. https://doi.org/10.1023/a:1015644520770.

Rogers, Paul, and Todd Senturia. 2013. "How Group Dynamics Affect Decisions." Bain and Company, 3 December. http://www.bain.com/publications/articles/how -group-dynamics-affect-decisions.aspx.

Rost, Joseph. 1991. *Leadership for the Twenty-First Century*. New York: Praeger.

Roy-Cesar, Edison. 2011. *Canada's Aging Population and Public Policy: 2. The Effects on Economic Growth and Government Finances*. Publication 2011-121-E. Ottawa: Parliament Information and Research Service, Library of Parliament.

Ryan, Liz. 2015. "Six Signs Your Company's Culture Is Toxic." *Forbes*, 3 August. http://www.forbes.com/sites/lizryan/2015/08/03/six-signs-your-companys -culture-is-toxic/#3bb8e7083659.

Samuel, John, and Kogalur Basavarajappa. 2006. "The Visible Minority Population in Canada: A Review of Numbers, Growth, and Labour Force Issues." *Canadian Studies in Population* 33(2): 241–69. https://doi.org/10.25336/p6kk7s.

Sanchez-Hucles, Janis V., and Donald D. Davis. 2010. "Women and Women of Colour in Leadership: Complexity, Identity, and Intersectionality." *American Psychologist* 65(3): 171–81. https://doi.org/10.1037/a0017459. Medline:20350016.

Saunders, Mark. 2019. "How to Attract Top Talent in the Tech Sector." *Globe and Mail*, 8 February.

Saxena, Ankita. 2014. "Workforce Diversity: A Key to Improve Productivity." *Procedia Economics and Finance* 11: 76–85. https://doi.org/10.1016/s2212-5671(14)00178-6.

Scales, C. (2010). "The African American Women's Leadership Experience in Corporate America: The Influence of Race and Gender." UMI Dissertations Publishing: 3448387

Scarborough, Michelle. 2019. "How Management Teams Can Break the Deadlock on Gender Diversity." *Globe and Mail*, 26 October.

Schachter, H. 2012. "Piecing Together the Senior Leader Puzzle." *Globe and Mail*, 4 January.

– 2014. "Key Steps to Change Corporate Culture." *Globe and Mail*, 23 March. http://www.theglobeandmail.com/report-on-business/careers/management/key-steps-to-change-corporate-culture/article17557724.

Schachter, H., 2019. "France achieved gender balance on boards: Can Canada do the same?" *Globe and Mail*, 21 June, https://www.theglobeandmail.com/business/careers/management/article-france-achieved-gender-balance-on-boards-can-canada-do-the-same

Schon, Donald A., 1984. "Leadership as Reflection-in-Action." In *Leadership and Organizational Culture: New Perspectives on Administrative Theory and Practice*, ed. Thomas J. Sergiovanni and Edward Corbally, 36–63. Chicago: University of Illinois Press.

Schultz, Vicki, 1990 (June). "Telling Stories about Women and Work: Judicial Interpretations of Sex Segregation in the Workplace in Title VII Case Raising the Lack of Interest Argument." *Harvard Law Review* 103(8): 1749–843.

Scinto, Mary Elisa, 2006. "African American Women Leaders in Predominately Caucasian Schools." D.Ed. diss., Arizona State University.

Scotiabank. n.d. "Vendor Code of Conduct." http://www.scotiabank.com/ca/en/0,,8635,00.html.

Scotiabank. n.d. "Vendor Code of Conduct," http://www.scotiabank.com/ca/en/0,,8635,00.html

Scott, Kristyn A., and Douglas J. Brown, 2006. "Female First, Leader Second? Gender Bias in the Encoding of Leadership Behavior." *Organizational Behavior and Human Decision Processes* 101: 230–242.

Sczesny, Sabine, Janine Bosak, Daniel Neff, and Birgit Schyns. 2004. "Gender Stereotypes and the Attribution of Leadership Traits: A Cross-Cultural

Comparison." Sex Roles: A Journal of Research 51(11–12): 631–45. https://doi
.org/10.1007/s11199-004-0715-0.

Selby, Cecily Cannan. 2010. "From Male Locker Room to Co-ed Board Room: A
Twenty-Five Year Perspective." In *Women on Corporate Boards of Directors:
International Challenges and Opportunities*, edited by Ronald J. Burke and Mary
C. Mattis, 239–51. Dordrecht: Kluwer Academic.

Semple, John. 2015. "How Diversity Can Drive Innovation." *Globe and Mail*,
14 September. http://www.theglobeandmail.com/report-on-business/careers
/leadership-lab/how-diversity-can-drive-innovation/article26356524.

Sengupta, S.B. 2012. "An Overview of Succession Management: Contemporary
Policies and Practices." *Abhigyan* 30(1): 1.

Sergiovanni, Thomas J. 1984a. "Cultural and Competing Perspectives in Administrative
Theory and Practice." In *Leadership and Organizational Culture: New Perspectives
on Administrative Theory and Practice*, edited by Thomas J. Sergiovanni and John E.
Corbally, 1–11. Champaign: University of Illinois Press. 1984.

– 1984b. "Leadership as Cultural Expression." In *Leadership and Organizational
Culture: New Perspectives on Administrative Theory and Practice*, edited by
Thomas J. Sergiovanni and John E. Corbally, 105–14. Champaign: University of
Illinois Press.

Sergiovanni, Thomas J., and John E. Corbally, eds. 1984. *Leadership and
Organizational Culture: New Perspectives on Administrative Theory and Practice*.
Champaign: University of Illinois Press.

Settles, Isis, NiCole Buchanan, and Stevie Yap. 2010. "Race Discrimination in
the Workplace." In *Handbook on Understanding and Preventing Workplace
Discrimination*, edited by M.A. Paludi, C.A. Paludi Jr., and E. DeSouza, 000–000.
Westport: Praeger.

Settles, Isis H., Lilia M. Cortina, NiCole T. Buchanan, and Kathi N. Miner. 2013.
"Derogation, Discrimination, and (Dis)Satisfaction with Jobs in Science: A
Gendered Analysis." *Psychology of Women Quarterly* 37(2): 179–91. https://doi
.org/10.1177/0361684312468727.

Sheridan, Fiona. 2013. "Prejudice against Women Leaders: Sex of Voice." In
Handbook of Research on Promoting Women's Careers, edited by Susan
Vinnicombe et al., 269–88. Northampton: Edward Elgar.

Shields, M., and S. Price. 2002. "Racial Harassment, Job Satisfaction, and Intentions
to Quit: Evidence from the British Nursing Profession." *Economica* 69(274):
295–362. https://doi.org/10.1111/1468-0335.00284.

Shier, Michael, John Graham, and Marion Jones. 2008. "Barriers to Employment as
Experienced by Disabled People: A Qualitative Analysis in Calgary and Regina."
Canada in Disability and Society 24(1): 63–75. https://doi.org/10.1080
/09687590802535485.

Shih, Margaret, Todd Pittinsky, and Nalini Ambady. 1999. "Stereotype Susceptibility:
Identity Salience and Shifts and Quantitative Performance." *Psychological Science*
10(1): 80–3. https://doi.org/10.1111/1467-9280.00111.

Shively, Michael G., James R. Rudolph, and John P. De Cecco. 1978. "The Identification of the Social Sex-Role Stereotypes." *Journal of Homosexuality* 3(3): 225–34. https://doi.org/10.1300/j082v03n03_04. Medline:659844.

Shuey, Kim M., and Emily Jovic. 2013. "Disability Accommodation in Nonstandard and Precarious Employment Arrangements." *Work and Occupations* 40(2): 174–205. https://doi.org/10.1177/0730888413481030.

Silva, Christine, Monia Dyer, and Lilly Whitham. 2007. *Career Advancement in Corporate Canada: A Focus on Visible Minorities – Critical Relationships.* Toronto: Catalyst.

Siu, Bobby. 2011a. *HR Manager's Guide to Diversity and Inclusive Practices.* Toronto: Carswell.

– 2011b. *HR Manager's Guide to Managing Diversity and Employment Equity.* Toronto: Carswell.

– 2016a. *The Federal Equity Manual.* Toronto: Thomson Reuters Canada.

– 2016b. "Why Are Leaders So Homogenous?" *Journal of Promising Practices on Diversity and Equity:* 3–9.

– 2020. *Developing Public Policy: A Practical Guide.* 2nd ed. Toronto: Canadian Scholars Press.

Skills Research Initiative. 2008. *The Labour Market and Skills Implications of Population Aging in Canada: A Synthesis of Key Findings and Policy Implications.* Ottawa: Human Resources and Social Development Canada.

Slater, Stanley, Robert Welgand, and Thomas Zwirlein. 2008. "The Business Case for Commitment to Diversity." *Business Horizons* 51(3): 201–9. https://doi.org/10.1016/j.bushor.2008.01.003.

Smith, Ryan A. 2002. "Race, Gender, and Authority in the Workplace: Theory and Research." *American Review of Sociology* 28: 509–42.

Social Development Canada. 2004. *Advancing the Inclusion of Persons with Disabilities: A Government of Canada Report.* Ottawa: Government of Canada.

Somer, Marcia G. 2008. "The Experiences of Asian American Females Seeking Vice President and President Positions in Community Colleges: A View of the Barriers and Facilitators." PhD diss., Oregon State University, Corvallis.

Sorenson, Susan. 2013. "How Employee Engagement Drives Growth." *Business Journal,* 20 June. http://www.gallup.com/businessjournal/163130/employee-engagement-drives-growth.aspx.

Soroka, Stuart, and Sarah Robertson. 2010. *A Literature Review of Public Opinion Research on Canadian Attitudes towards Multiculturalism and Immigration, 2006–2009.* Ottawa: Immigration Canada.

Souza-Poza, A. 2007. "The Effect of Job Satisfaction on Labour Turnover by Gender: An Analysis for Switzerland." *Journal of Socio-Economics* 36(6): 895–913. https://doi.org/10.1016/j.socec.2007.01.022.

Spence, Betty. 2009. "Board of Directors Caucus: Establishing Board Leadership in Corporate Diversity and Inclusion." *Diversity Best Practices.* http://www

.diversitybestpractices.com/publications/board-directors-caucus-establishing
-board-leadership-corporate-diversity-inclusion.

Stainback, Kevin, and Soyoung Kwon. 2012. "Female Leaders, Organizational Power, and Sex Segregation." *Annals of the American Academy of Political and Social Science* 639(1): 217–35. https://doi.org/10.1177/0002716211421868.

Staley, Oliver. 2016. "You Know Those Quotas for Female Board Members in Europe? They're Working." Quartz, 3 May. https://qz.com/674276/you-know-those -quotas-for-female-board-members-in-europe-theyre-working/.

Statistics Canada. 2001. "Labour Force Activity (8), Indigenous Status (3), Age Groups (11A) and Sex (3) for Population 15 Years and Over, for Canada, Provinces, Territories, Census Metropolitan Areas and Census Agglomerations, 1996 and 2001 Censuses – 20% Sample Data." http://www12.statcan.gc.ca/english /census01/products/standard/themes/Rp-eng.cfm?TABID=1&LANG=E&APATH =3&DETAIL=1&DIM=0&FL=A&FREE=0&GC=0&GK=0&GRP=1&PID=79667 &PRID=0&PTYPE=55430,53293,55440,55496,71090&S=0&SHOWALL=0&SUB =0&Temporal=2001&THEME=46&VID=0&VNAMEE=&VNAMEF=.

– 2005a. Study: Canada's Visible Minority Population in 2017. *The Daily*, 22 March.

– 2005b. *Women in Canada 2005: A Gender-Based Statistical Report.* http:// publications.gc.ca/collections/Collection/SW21-78-12-2005E.pdf.

– 2006a. "Participation and Activity Limitation Survey of 2006: Labour Force Experience of People with Disabilities in Canada." http://www.statcan.gc.ca /pub/89-628-x/89-628-x2008007-eng.htm.

– 2006b. *Persons with Disabilities, by Age and Sex.* http://www.statcan.gc.ca/tables -tableaux/sum-som/l01/cst01/health71a-eng.htm.

– 2007a. "Study: Employment Trends in the Federal Public Service." *The Daily*, 5 March. http://www.statcan.gc.ca/daily-quotidien/070305/dq070305a-eng.htm.

– 2007b. "Study: Female Employment in the Core Public Administration." *The Daily*, 4 September. http://www.statcan.gc.ca/daily-quotidien/070904/dq070904a -eng.htm.

– 2008a. "Canada's Immigrant Labour Market." *The Daily*, 13 May. http://www .statcan.gc.ca/daily-quotidien/080513/dq080513a-eng.htm.

– 2008b. *Canadian Demographics at a Glance.* Ottawa: Ministry of Industry. http:// www.statcan.gc.ca/pub/91-003-x/91-003-x2007001-eng.pdf.

– 2008c. "Indigenous Peoples Living Off-Reserve and the Labour Market." *The Daily*, 15 December. http://www.statcan.gc.ca/daily-quotidien/081215 /dq081215a-eng.htm.

– 2008d. "Participation and Activity Limitation Survey: Employment." *The Daily*, 24 July. http://www.statcan.gc.ca/daily-quotidien/080724/dq080724a-eng.htm.

– 2008e. "Study: Immigrants' Education and Required Job Skills." *The Daily*, 22 December. http://www.statcan.gc.ca/daily-quotidien/081222/dq081222b-eng.htm.

– 2008f. "Study: The 2006 Canadian Immigrant Labour Market: Analysis by Region or Country of Birth." *The Daily*, 13 February. http://www.statcan.gc.ca /daily-quotidien/080213/dq080213b-eng.htm.

– 2008g. *The 2006 Participation and Activity Limitation Survey: Analytical Report – Growth in Disability Rates from 2001 to 2006.* http://www.statcan.gc.ca/pub/89 -628-x/2007002/4125018-eng.htm.
– 2010a. "Indigenous Statistics at a Glance." http://www.statcan.gc.ca/pub/89-645 -x/89-645-x2010001-eng.htm.
– 2010b. "Study: Indigenous Labour Market Update." *The Daily*, 13 May. http:// www.statcan.gc.ca/daily-quotidien/100513/dq100513b-eng.htm.
– 2010c. "Study: Projections of the Diversity of the Canadian Population." *The Daily*, 9 March. http://www.statcan.gc.ca/daily-quotidien/100309/dq100309a-eng .htm.
– 2010d. "Table 1: Adults with Disabilities That Need Help with Everyday Activities, by Sex and Age Groups, Canada, 2001 and 2006." http://www.statcan.gc.ca /pub/89-628-x/2010015/tbl/tbl1-eng.htm.
– 2010e. "Table 2: Adults with Disabilities That Need Help with Everyday Activities, by Age Groups and Types of Disability, Canada, 2001 and 2006." http://www .statcan.gc.ca/pub/89-628-x/2010015/tbl/tbl2-eng.htm.
– 2011a. "Indigenous Peoples." http://www.statcan.gc.ca/pub/11-402-x/2011000 /chap/ap-pa/ap-pa-eng.htm.
– 2011b. "Population Projections by Indigenous Identity in Canada." *The Daily*, 7 December. http://www.statcan.gc.ca/daily-quotidien/111207/dq111207a-eng .htm.
– 2011c. "Study: Aboriginal People and the Labour Market." *The Daily*, 23 November. http://www.statcan.gc.ca/daily-quotidien/111123/dq111123b -eng.htm.
– 2011d. *2006 Census of Canada: Topic-Based tabulations: Labour Force Activity (8), Indigenous Identity (8B), Age Groups (13A), Sex (3) and Area of Residence (6A) for the Population 15 Years and Over of Canada, Provinces and Territories, 2001 and 2006 Censuses – 20% Sample Data.* http://www12.statcan.gc.ca/census -recensement/2006/dp-pd/tbt/Rp-eng.cfm?TABID=1&LANG=E&APATH=3&D ETAIL=0&DIM=0&FL=A&FREE=0&GC=0&GK=0&GRP=1&PID=92101&PRI D=0&PTYPE=88971,97154&S=0&SHOWALL=0&SUB=0&Temporal=2006&TH EME=74&VID=0&VNAMEE=&VNAMEF=.
– 2011e. "2011 National Household Survey: Portrait of Canada's Labour Force." http://www.statcan.gc.ca/daily-quotidien/130626/dq130626b-eng.htm.
– 2011f. "Women in Canada: A Gender-Based Statistical Report." http://www .statcan.gc.ca/pub/89-503-x/2010001/article/11475-eng.htm.
– 2012a. "Canada's Population Estimates: Age and Sex, July 1, 2012." *The Daily*, 27 September. http://www.statcan.gc.ca/daily-quotidien/120927/dq120927b -eng.htm.
– 2012b. "Study: Canada's Immigrant Labour Market, 2008–2011." *The Daily*, 14 December. http://www.statcan.gc.ca/daily-quotidien/121214/dq121214b-eng.htm.
– 2013a. "Guide to the Labour Force Survey." http://www.statcan.gc.ca/pub/71 -543-g/2012001/part-partie3-eng.htm.

–   2013b. "Canada's Population Estimates: Age and Sex, 2013." *The Daily*,
    25 November. http://www.statcan.gc.ca/daily-quotidien/131125/dq131125a
    -eng.pdf.
–   2013c. "Immigration and Ethnocultural Diversity in Canada." http://www12
    .statcan.gc.ca/nhs-enm/2011/as-sa/99-010-x/99-010-x2011001-eng.cfm.
–   2013d. "Indigenous Peoples in Canada: First Nations People, Métis and Inuit."
    http://www12.statcan.gc.ca/nhs-enm/2011/as-sa/99-011-x/99-011-x2011001
    -eng.cfm.
–   2013e. "2011 National Household Survey: Data Tables." http://www12.statcan
    .gc.ca/nhs-enm/2011/dp-pd/dt-td/Rp-eng.cfm?LANG=E&APATH=3&DETAIL
    =0&DIM=0&FL=A&FREE=0&GC=0&GID=0&GK=0&GRP=1&PID=105611&P
    RID=0&PTYPE=105277&S=0&SHOWALL=0&SUB=0&Temporal=2013&THEM
    E=96&VID=0&VNAMEE=&VNAMEF=.
–   2013f. "2011 National Household Survey: Indigenous Peoples in Canada: First
    Nations People, Métis and Inuit." http://www.statcan.gc.ca/daily-quotidien
    /130508/dq130508a-eng.htm.
–   2015a. "Disability in Canada: Initial Findings from the Canadian Survey on
    Disability." http://www.statcan.gc.ca/pub/89-654-x/89-654-x2013002-eng.htm.
–   2015b. "Portrait of Canada's Labour Force." http://www12.statcan.gc.ca/nhs-enm
    /2011/as-sa/99-012-x/99-012-x2011002-eng.cfm#a6.
–   2015c. "A Profile of Persons with Disabilities among Canadians Aged 15 or Older,
    2012." http://www.statcan.gc.ca/pub/89-654-x/89-654-x2015001-eng.htm.
–   2015d. "Table 7: Educational Attainment of Population Age 15 and Over by
    Visible Minority Group, Canada, 2006." http://www.statcan.gc.ca/pub/89
    -503-x/2010001/article/11527/tbl/tbl007-eng.htm.
Statistics Canada. 2016a. "An Aging Population." *2012 Canada Year Book* (11-402-X),
    https://www150.statcan.gc.ca/n1/pub/11-402-x/2010000/chap/pop/pop02-eng.htm.
–   2016b. "Study: Women in Canada: First Nations, Métis and Inuit Women." *The
    Daily*, 23 February. http://www.statcan.gc.ca/daily-quotidien/160223/dq160223a
    -eng.htm?cmp=mstatcan.
–   2019. "Study: Representation of Women on Boards of Directors, 2016." *The Daily*,
    7 May. https://www150.statcan.gc.ca/n1/daily-quotidien/190507/dq190507a-eng
    .htm.
Status of Women Canada. 2015 (25 February). "Fact Sheet: Economic Security."
    http://www.swc-cfc.gc.ca/initiatives/wesp-sepf/fs-fi/es-se-eng.html.
Staw, Barry M. 1984. "Leadership and Persistence." In *Leadership and Organizational
    Culture: New Perspectives on Administrative Theory and Practice*, edited by Thomas
    J. Sergiovanni and John E. Corbally 72–84. Champaign: University of Illinois Press.
Stead, Valerie, and Carole Elliott. 2009. *Women's Leadership*. New York: Palgrave
    Macmillan.
Steffens, Melaine C., and Battina Mehl. 2003. "Do 'Career Women' Appear Less
    Socially Competent Than 'Career Men'? Gender Stereotypes and the Attribution

of Competence." *Zeitschrift für Sozial Psychologie* 34(3): 173–85. https://doi
.org/10.1024//0044-3514.34.3.173.

Stephan, Walter, and Cooke White Stephan. 2000. "An Integrated Threat Theory of
Prejudice." In *Reducing Prejudice and Discrimination*, edited by Stuart Oskamp,
23–46. Mahwah: Lawrence Erlbaum.

Stewart, Paulette M. 2010. "Themes of Racial Discrimination in the Experience
of Black Female Nurse Managers." PhD diss., Ontario Institute for Studies in
Education, Toronto.

Stogdill, Ralph M. 1974. *Handbook of Leadership: A Survey of Theory and Research.*
New York: Free Press.

Streifer, Mark. 2016. "Beyond the Board: Succession Risk Should Be All-Inclusive."
Workforce. http://www.workforce.com/2016/12/27/beyond-board-succession
-risk-inclusive.

Stuart, Sandra. 2019. "Enough Talk about Diversity: Corporate Canada Needs to Get
Acting." *Globe and Mail*, 6 November.

Stump, Jane Barr. 1985. *What's the Difference? How Men and Women Compare.* New
York: William Morrow.

Sullivan, P. 2006. "Diversity, Leadership, and the Community College: A Case Study."
CommunityCollege Journal of Research and Practice 30(5–6): 383–400. https://doi
.org/10.1080/10668920500208096.

Sullivan, Patricia Ann, and Lynn Hoar. 1996. *From the Margins to the Center:
Contemporary Women and Political Communication.* Westport: Praeger.

Sveiby, Karl-Erik. 2011. "Collective Leadership with Power Symmetry: Lessons from
Aboriginal Prehistory." *Leadership* 7(4): 385–414. https://doi.org/10.1177
/1742715011416892.

Sweetgrass, Shari Narine. 2016. "Attitudes about Aboriginal Women Focus of New
Research Project." *Alberta Sweetgrass* 23(3). http://www.ammsa.com/publications
/alberta-sweetgrass/attitudes-about-aboriginal-women-focus-new-research
-project.

Sweetman, K.J. 1996. "Women in Boardrooms: Increasing Numbers Qualify to
Serve." *Harvard Business Review*, January–February, 13.

Tajfel, H. 1982. *Social Identity and Intergroup Relations.* Cambridge: Cambridge
University Press.

Tajfel, Henri, A. Sheikh, and R.C. Gardner. 1964. "Content of Stereotypes and
the Inference of Similarity between Members of Stereotyped Groups." *Acta
Psychologica* 22: 191–201. https://doi.org/10.1016/0001-6918(64)90017-4.

Tajfel, H., and J.C. Turner. 1986. "The Social Identity Theory of Inter-Group
Behavior." In *Psychology of Intergroup Relations*, edited by S. Worchel and L.W.
Austin, 000–000. Chicago: Nelson-Hall.

Tannen, Deborah. 1994. *Gender and Discourse.* New York: Oxford University Press.

Tanner, A. 2012. "Executives see worsening work-life imbalance." www.hrreporter
.com/articleview/12604-executives-see-worsening-work-life-imbalnace.

Taub, Diane E., Pagtricia L. Fanflik, and Penelope A. McLorg. 2003. "Body Image among Women with Physical Disabilities: Internalization of Norms and Reactions to Nonconformity." *Sociological Focus* 36(2): 159–76. https://doi.org/10.1080/0038 0237.2003.10570722.

Tellis, G.J., J.C. Prabhu, and R.K. Chandy. 2009. "Radical Innovation across Nations: The Preeminence of Corporate Culture." *Journal of Marketing* 73(1): 3–23. https://doi.org/10.1509/jmkg.73.1.3.

Tencer, Daniel 2011. "Forbes Survey: Workplace Diversity Key to Innovation." *Huffington Post Canada*, 29 July.

Thomas, Philippe Dejarnac. 2012. "The Underrepresentation of Black Senior Executive Service Federal Government Employees: A Phenomenological Qualitative Study." PhD diss., University of Phoenix.

Thompson, Caroline Joan, 2008. "Inside School Administration in Nunavut: Four Women's Stories. PhD diss., University of Western Ontario, London.

Thompson, Doug Cooper. 1985. *As Boys Become Men: Learning New Male Roles: A Curriculum for Exploring Male Role Stereotyping*. New York: Irvington.

Thompson, Robert Alan. 2001. "Racial Integration in the Law Enforcement Leadership: A View from the Top." PhD diss.

Toller, Carol. 2015. "Why Addressing Race in the Workplace Makes Good Business Sense." *Profit Guide*, 13 May. https://www.canadianbusiness.com/leadership/why -addressing-race-in-the-workplace-makes-good-business-sense.

Topping, Alexandra. 2017. "Workplace Sexism Survey Shows 'Disturbing' Gap in Male and Female Perception." *The Guardian*, 4 September. https://www .theguardian.com/world/2017/sep/04/workplace-sexism-survey-shows -disturbing-gap-in-male-and-female-perception.

Torres, Helena. 2002. "Psycho-Social Indicators on Social Exclusion of Women with Disabilities." Conference Papers and Proceedings, International Sociological Association.

Tran, Kelly. 2004. "Visible Minorities in the Labour Force: 20 Years of Change." *Canadian Social Trends*. Cat. no. 11-008. Ottawa: Statistics Canada.

Tremblay, Louise. 2011. "Inclusion of Persons with Disabilities in the Workplace." MA thesis, Royal Roads University, Colwood.

Tremblay, Manon. 2006. "The Substantive Representation of Women and PR: Some Reflections on the Role of Surrogate Representation and Critical Mass." *Politics and Gender* 2(4): 502–11. https://doi.org/10.1017/s1743923x06231143.

Trimble, Joseph E. 1988. "Stereotypical Images, American Indians, and Prejudice." In Eliminating Racism, edited by P.A. Katz et al., 181–202. New York: Springer Science+Business Media.

Troffer, Beth S. 1975. "A Study of the Relationships between Sex-Role Stereotypes, Mental Health, and Attitudes towards Women's Roles." MA thesis, University of Regina.

Trottier, T., M. Van Wart, and X. Wang. 2008. "Examining the Nature and Significance of Leadership in Government Organizations." *Public Administration Review* 68(2): 319–33. https://doi.org/10.1111/j.1540-6210.2007.00865.x.

Turner, Travis N. 2013. "Qualities of Visionary Leaders." http://www.creativeleader
.com/qualties-of-visionary-leaders.

Turner, Travis N., 2014. "Creativity and Web Design: Designing and Producing a
Successful Site on Creativity and Leadership." International Centre for Studies in
Creativity, Buffalo State College, Department of Creative Studies, State University
of New York, MSc thesis, August 2014. https://digitalcommons.buffalostate.edu
/cgi/viewcontent.cgi?article=1219&context=creativeprojects.

Tyler, Anne Charette. 2013. "Perfecting Performance Management." Canadian HR
Reporter, 18 November.

Unger, Darlene D. 2002. "Employers' Attitudes toward Persons with Disabilities in
the Workforce: Myths or Realities? Focus on Autism and Other Developmental
Disabilities 17(1): 2–10. https://doi.org/10.1177/108835760201700101.

Unger, Rhoda K., ed. 1975. Sex-Role Stereotypes Revisited: Psychological Approaches to
Women's Studies. New York: Harper and Row.

United Nations. 2001. World Population Ageing: 1950–2050. New York: Population
Division, Department of Economic and Social Affairs.

– 2013. "The Number of International Migrants Worldwide Reaches 232 Million."
Population Facts, no. 2013/2. Department of Economic and Social Affairs,
Population Division.

– n.d. Declaration of the Rights of Indigenous Peoples. https://www.un.org
/development/desa/indigenouspeoples/wp-content/uploads/sites/19/2018/11
/UNDRIP_E_web.pdf.

Uppal, Sharanjit. 2005. "Disability, Workplace Characteristics, and Job Satisfaction."
International Journal of Manpower 26(4): 336–49. https://doi.org/10.1108
/01437720510609537.

Vaccaro, Alex. 2016. "4 Ways HR Can Better Align with the CEO." HR People +
Strategy, Society for Human Resource Management (SHRM), 7 December.
https://blog.hrps.org/blogpost/4-Ways-HR-Can-Better-Align-with-the-CEO.

Vaill, Peter. 1984. "The Purposing of High-Performing Systems." In Leadership and
Organizational Culture: New Perspectives on Administrative Theory and Practice,
edited by Thomas J. Sergiovanni and John E. Corbally, 85–104. Champaign:
University of Illinois Press.

Valentine, Carol Ann, and Nancy Hoar. 1988. Women and Communicative Power:
Theory, Research, and Practice. Annandale: Speech Communication Association.

Volker, Michael. 2008. "The Board of Directors." In Business Basics for Engineers.
http://www.sfu.ca/~mvolker/biz/bod.htm.

Wakshul, Barbara. 1997. "Training Leaders for the 21st Century." Winds of Change
(Spring): 24–8.

Walton, Gregory M., and Geoffrey Cohen 2007. "A Question of Belonging: Race,
Social Fit, and Achievement." Journal of Personality and Social Psychology 92(1):
82–96. https://doi.org/10.1037/0022-3514.92.1.82. Medline:17201544.

Wang, J., and S.J. Odell. 2002. "Mentored Learning to Teach According to Standards-
Based Reform: A Critical Review." Review of Educational Research 72(3): 481–546.
https://doi.org/10.3102/00346543072003481.

Ward, Dawn, and Jack Balswick. 1978. "Strong Men and Virtuous Women: A Content Analysis of Sex Roles Stereotypes." *Pacific Sociological Review* 21(1): 45–53. https://doi.org/10.2307/1388866.

Wattanasupachoke, Teerayout. 2006. "Managerial Styles of Asian Executives: The Case of Thailand." *International Journal of Social Sciences* 1(1): 7–13.

Weber, M. 1947. *The Theory of Social and Economic Organization*. London: Free Press.

Webster, Cynthia, Oscar Grusky, Deborah Podus, and Alexander Young. 1999. "Team Leadership: Network Differences in Women's and Men's Instrumental and Expressive Relations." *Administration and Policy in Mental Health* 26(3): 169–90. https://doi.org/10.1023/a:1021394113278.

Wengrzyn, Rob. 2003–16. "Job Dissatisfaction: Causes, Reasons, and Responses." http://study.com/academy/lesson/job-dissatisfaction-causes-reasons-and-employee-responses.html.

Werhun, Cherie D., and April Penner. 2010. "The Effects of Stereotyping and Implicit Theory on Benevolent Prejudice toward Aboriginal Canadians." *Journal of Applied Social Psychology* 40(4): 899–916. https://doi.org/10.1111/j.1559-1816.2010.00603.x.

Werner, Charlotte, Sandrine Devillard, and Sandra Sancier-Sultan. 2010. "Moving Women to the Top: McKinsey Global Survey Results." McKinsey & Company. http://www.mckinsey.com/business-functions/organization/our-insights/moving-women-to-the-top-mckinsey-global-survey-results.

Wharton@Work. 2011. "Culture as Culprit: Four Steps to Effective Change." Wharton Executive Education, University of Pennsylvania. http://executiveeducation.wharton.upenn.edu/thought-leadership/wharton-at-work/2011/09/four-steps-culture-change.

Willis, L., and J. Daisley. 1997. "Women's Reactions to Women-Only Training." *Women in Management Review* 12(2): 56–60. https://doi.org/10.1108/09649429710162811.

Willis Towers Watson. 2012. "2012 Global Workforce Study: Engagement at Risk – Driving Strong Performance in a Volatile Global Environment." https://www.towerswatson.com/Insights/IC-Types/Survey-Research-Results/2012/07/2012-Towers-Watson-Global-Workforce-Study.

Wilson, Eleanor. 2014. "Diversity, Culture, and the Glass Ceiling." *Journal of Cultural Diversity* 21(3): 83–9. https://doi.org/10.12987/yale/9780300223309.003.0005.

Wingfield, Adia Harvey. 2015. "Being Black – but Not too Black – in the Workplace." *The Atlantic*, 14 October. http://www.theatlantic.com/business/archive/2015/10/being-black-work/409990.

Wodak, Ruth, ed. 1997. *Gender and Discourse*. London: Sage.

Wong, Joel, Angela Horn, and Shitao Chen. 2013. "Perceived Masculinity: The Potential Influence of Race, Racial Essentialist Beliefs, and Stereotypes." *Psychology of Men and Masculinity* 14(4): 452–64.

Wood, Michael T. 1973. "Power Relationships and Group Decision Making in Organizations." *Psychological Bulletin* 79(5): 280–95. https://doi.org/10.1037/h0034618.

Woodhouse, Sheila E., and Stacey LaRue. n.d. "Employee Engagement: Working to Improve Productivity." *Corporate Wellness Magazine.com.* http://www .corporatewellnessmagazine.com/worksite-wellness/employee-engagement.

Wyche, K.R. 2008. *Good Is Not Good Enough and Other Unwritten Rules for Minority Professionals.* New York: Penguin.

Wyn, Johanna, Sandra Acker, and Elisabeth Richards. 2000. "Making a Difference: Women in Management in Australian and Canadian Faculties of Education." *Gender and Education* 12(4): 435–47.

Yarnall, J. 2011. "Maximizing the Effectiveness of Talent Pools: A Review of Case Study Literature." *Leadership and Organization Development Journal* 32(5): 510–26. https://doi.org/10.1108/01437731111146596.

Zajac, E., and J. Westphal. 1996. "Who Shall Succeed? How CEO Board Preferences and Power Affect the Choice of New CEOs." *Academy of Management Journal* 39(1): 64–90. https://doi.org/10.2307/256631.

Zaleznik, A. 2004 (January). "Managers and Leaders: Are They Different?" *Harvard Business Review*, no page number. .

Zielinski, D. 2000. "Mentoring Up." *Training* 37(10): 136–41.

Zillman, Claire. 2018. "Need Proof That Companies Can Have Gender Diverse Boards? Look to France." *Fortune*, 3 December. https://fortune.com/2018/12/03 /board-diversity-france.

Zulu, C.B. 2011. "Women Leaders' Construction of Leadership and Management of the Academic Department." *South African Journal of Higher Education* 25(4): 838–52.

Index

Lightning Source UK Ltd.
Milton Keynes UK
UKHW010216310321
381292UK00006B/148/J